The Appalachian Trail Reader

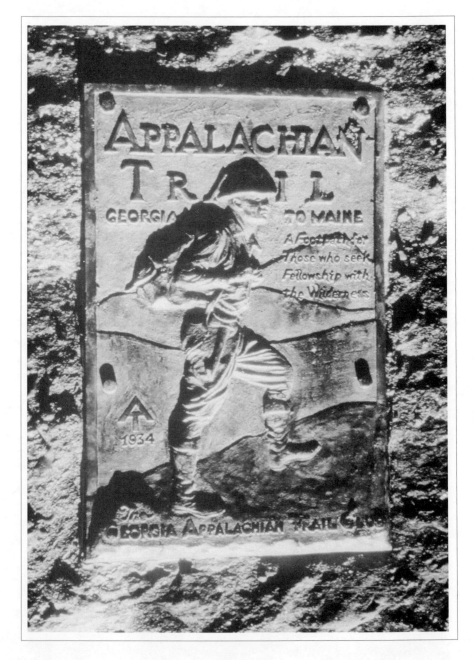

The Appalachian Trail Reader

EDITED BY

David Emblidge

OXFORD UNIVERSITY PRESS

NEW YORK   OXFORD

Oxford University Press

Oxford New York
Athens Auckland Bangkok Bogotá Bombay
Buenos Aires Calcutta Cape Town Dar es Salaam
Delhi Florence Hong Kong Istanbul Karachi
Kuala Lumpur Madras Madrid Melbourne
Mexico City Nairobi Paris Singapore
Taipei Tokyo Toronto Warsaw

and associated companies in
Berlin Ibadan

First published by Oxford University Press, Inc., 1996

First issued as an Oxford University Press paperback, 1997

Oxford is a registered trademark of Oxford University Press

Produced for Oxford University Press by
David Emblidge — Book Producer
Great Barrington, Massachusetts

Editor: David Emblidge
Design & Composition: Rodelinde Albrecht
Copy Editor: Katherine Ness
Maps: Bill Cooke + Company
Proofreader: Norma Frankel
Photographs: Michael Warren
Manuscript Scanning: Victoria Wright
Cover Art: Michael McCurdy

Frontispiece: Appalachian Trail terminus marker at Springer Mt., Georgia.

The text of this book was set in Palatino, using Aldus Pagemaker.
Map information was drawn from a National Park Service map of the Appalachian Trail;
map production via the Map Art Designer Series from Cartesia and Adobe Illustrator.

A portion of the royalties from this book will be donated by David Emblidge — Book Producer
to the Appalachian Mountain Club and the Appalachian Trail Conference
to help support the Appalachian Trail.

Library of Congress Cataloging-in-Publication Data
The Appalachian Trail reader / edited by David Emblidge
p. cm.
Includes bibliographical references
ISBN 0-19-510091-3—ISBN 0-19-510090-5 (Pbk.)
1. Appalachian Region—description and travel. 2. Appalachian
Trail—Description and travel. 3. Hiking—Appalachian Trail.
I. Emblidge, David.
F106.A63 1996 96-2121
917.404'43—dc20

3 5 7 9 10 8 6 4

Printed in the United States of America
on acid-free paper

Contents

PART TWO: VOICES ALONG THE TRAIL

THE SOUTH

For those who walked with me
on the Massachusetts Appalachian Trail—
Adam, Abigail, Sarah, and *Miriam*—
and those who taught me to walk in the first place—
Jeane and *Ralph,* and *Richard.*

Introduction

It took that pause to make him realize
The mountain he was climbing had the slant
As of a book held up before his eyes
(And was a text albeit done in plant).
—Robert Frost, from "Time Out"

APPALACHIA, THE APPALACHIANS, THE APPALACHIAN TRAIL

One of the most highly evolved of Appalachian crafts is quilting. Like so many other handicrafts, quilting's origins lie in the old habit of letting necessity be the mother of invention. A smart hill country homemaker, short on cash but rich in initiative, would save every scrap of cloth from no matter what project or worn piece of clothing. In due time, with a pattern in mind, perhaps a starburst, she would begin to stitch, and some weeks later, after an investment of love, skill and labor, a handsome, comforting quilt would emerge. Its colors would be highly varied, its textures happily inconsistent, but the bursting star pattern would shine through nonetheless.

This book is meant to be such a quilt, a quilt of words, stitched together by the themes of walking on the Appalachian Trail,* of appreciating the Appalachian wilderness. Follow the pattern, as you would the blaze on the trail, and be alert for surprise.

It takes a geologist's long view—of time and landforms—to grasp the fact that even if you're standing on a hillside in Maine, rather than on one in Georgia, you're still in the Appalachian Mountains.

And it takes an historian's equally long view—of social and economic developments—to recognize that despite the many colorful differences among specific groups of Appalachian peoples (Confederates and Yankees can still seem as different as oil and water), they have far more in common than not.

What unites all these Appalachian places (over 2,500 miles of more or less continuous mountain ridges and valleys)? And what unites all these Appalachian peoples (Native Americans, small-town merchants, hill country farmers, urban vacation homeowners, and countless hiking visitors)? The bonds lie in our common experience of what's underfoot; in our aes-

*The abbreviation "AT" is frequently used for "Appalachian Trail" throughout this book and in other writings about the trail.

thetic appreciation of what we see and hear and smell in the mountains; and in what our time in the forest or on the mountaintop, be it ever so brief, does to lift our spirits.

Underneath, in the Appalachian landform, is an undulating series of mountain ridges (with accompanying valleys), formed in various ways over a vast span of geologic time (mostly from the upwardly thrusting pressures caused by tectonic plates, entire continents advancing and retreating, abrading each other deep in the earth's crust, leaving mountains as their calling cards). Look at the topographic or relief maps of eastern North America: from Alabama to Nova Scotia (some would say extending under the north Atlantic to resurface even in Iceland), the sensuous curves of the Appalachians are easy to trace.

Strip away the buildup of contemporary civilization (the interstate highways and canals and the grids of high-voltage power lines or of airplane routes in the sky) and look at the shape of the land. Notice how the Appalachian Mountains formed a barrier against easy westward expansion by land-hungry colonists, how the west-to-east flow of most of the rivers shaped the development of manufacturing and commerce, how the placement of gaps and passes between the mountains determined travel and trading routes as well as the locations of major cities.

Whether a man or woman speaks with a North Carolina drawl or in the clipped tones of a Vermont Yankee, the Appalachian landform underfoot shaped and continues to shape economic, social and recreational life. Political lines on the map (state borders, the Mason-Dixon Line) and differences in climate and economy (maple syrup and dairy farms up in the chilly north, molasses and tobacco down in the steamy south) are all nonetheless part of a grand bioregional system, the greater Appalachians.

It's only a quirk of place-naming that one part of the Appalachian chain— the extreme southern and south-central end—came to be called "Appalachia." And it's only an ironic, sad fact that this beautiful area with its stalwart people came to be a poor and underdeveloped (though much exploited) socioeconomic territory. For our purposes in this book, we'll acknowledge the term "Appalachia" as belonging to specific places and people, and we won't expropriate it for use elsewhere.

That time spent in the woods and on the mountain ridges touches our sense of beauty and recharges our emotional and spiritual batteries is a theme as old as history itself. The remarkable thing is that even hikers whose blisters might otherwise have ruined the day seem to find the mental space to acknowledge the glorious view from the mountaintop; even the equipment-obsessed backpacker who fusses more with his gizmos than he listens to birdsong will write about the loveliness of the early morning chorus he hears each day as he awakens in his high-tech tent. The Appalachian Trail is far more than an experience of geology and social and natural history. It is a kind of linear cathedral, a linear museum where the spirit, the emotions and the senses all meet in equal opportunity for enjoyment and the possibility of insight. This collection of writings bears out this simple truth in a hundred ways.

The Appalachian Trail, the longest continuous recreational footpath in America, perhaps in the world, links together all the disparate but neighborly Appalachian mountains and peoples. It originates (if you're headed northward) at Springer Mt. in northern Georgia and terminates, if you walk all 2,150-some miles, atop mile-high Mt. Katahdin in northern Maine. Passing through fourteen states, it serves the recreational needs of the most intensely populated region of the United States. The result both of a grand vision of one bold land-use planner—Benton MacKaye, of Massachusetts and Washington, D.C.—and of endless hours of labor by thousands of volunteer and government workers, the Appalachian Trail is a national treasure. MacKaye's prophetic 1921 essay about why urban America needed "a linear park" with a mountain and valley footpath from Maine to Georgia has rarely been reprinted; the entire essay is included here, as are other comments MacKaye made in subsequent years as he promoted his grand idea to anyone who would listen.

Under the administrative supervision of the National Park Service (since passage of the National Trails System Act in 1968), the trail is maintained by a confederation of powerful private regional organizations. The two most prominent caretakers are the *Appalachian Trail Conference,* based in Harpers Ferry, West Virginia, right on the trail itself; and the *Appalachian Mountain Club,* with headquarters in Boston and chapters from Maine to the Mid-Atlantic area. Smaller local hiking clubs also share trail maintenance responsibilities. The overall project is surely one of the great success stories of the American way of blending public funds and skilled service people (foresters, land-use planners, and the like) with private dollars and a host of volunteer efforts, ranging from editing guidebooks and maps to carrying heavy supply packs to mountainside trail huts.

At this writing, access to the trail is free. However, federal funding for trail maintenance programs is under serious attack in Congress, as part of a budget balancing process, and should government support decline substantially, the need for private sector dollars will rise ever higher. A debate about access fees, sales taxes on outdoor recreation gear, and other ways of generating the money required to sustain the trail—which surveys show attracts over 4 million users per year—will no doubt run on for years to come. This book looks back in time to explain how the trail came to be, how the expertise and funding from various sources worked together to achieve a near miracle (there were many points when the goal of a continuous marked footpath seemed impossible). Yet there are no selections here offering pre-scriptions for the Appalachian Trail politics of the future, at least not on the micro-management level. Still, many would argue that the visionaries who inspired the building of the trail in the first place—be they activists like Benton MacKaye or philosopher-naturalists whose inspiring words predated the trail itself, like Henry David Thoreau—were right then and are just as right today. Their thesis was, and is, that wilderness is a necessary tonic for a competitive, fast-paced, increasingly urban civilization, and they argue, convincingly I think, that anything we do to diminish the remaining wilder-ness is not only an insult to ourselves but a disservice to our descendants. In this philosophical and literary sense—of seeing the inestimable value in wil-derness experience for all of us—the writings in this collection do indeed ponder a time-tested cluster of values that can serve as a basis for our "trail-building" work in the future.

Selections in *The Appalachian Trail Reader* come from Georgia to Maine and even farther afield, focusing sometimes on the Appalachian Trail itself and often on the trail's surrounding wilderness. Hikers' private journals stand next to scientists' close observations of the natural world, and these readings mingle with poets' evocations of the natural world and its spirit. Historians remind us of how Appalachian culture developed, and early ex-plorers report the thrill of seeing uncharted territory and wildlife for the first time. Some of the writings come from celebrated literary professionals; many come from enthused amateurs whose experience on the trail inspired them to capture what they could of it in words. Among the amateurs' work, we find both the surprisingly eloquent and the undeniably raw. Unlike many literary anthologies where only "the best of the best" in a given genre may appear, here we strive to cover the subject colorfully, as would the patch-work quilt the bed, without an insistent regard for literary merit alone as a ticket of admission. Many of the most appealing of the hikers' diaries, for instance, were never meant for publication, and the excerpts used here have not been corrected or polished. And why should they be? Hiking the trail has always been more a matter of gusto than of finesse, more a game of stamina than of precision. The meaning each hiker draws from the experi-ence will be his or her own. Listening closely to the differences in their sto-ries is part of the reward for having made the effort to make the climb.

ABOUT "TRAIL DIARIES," "2,000-MILER REPORTS" AND "TRAIL REGISTERS"

Travelers and pilgrims have always kept journals. Scratched in the rocks along the Oregon Trail are words of encouragement and warning left by pioneers for those coming after them. On the path from southern France through the Pyrenees and across the Spanish plains, religious pilgrims en route to Santiago de Compostella left similar messages for brethren coming behind them, whom they would never meet but with whom they shared a common experience, a common goal. Appalachian Trail hikers are no different. Most Appalachian Trail diaries remain private. Some are pushed forward into print by ambitious self-publishing hikers, by small presses whose niche is the outdoor recreation market, and occasionally, when the literary merits are high enough, by a major publisher who recognizes a genuinely important voice. We have some of all these types of reports in this anthology.

The Appalachian Trail Conference collects "2,000-Miler Reports" by AT hikers, written primarily by thru-hikers who make it from Georgia to Maine, or vice versa, either in one fell swoop or piecemeal over several years. What really is this literary genre? Pilgrimage tales? A subliterary genre, like pioneers' diaries from America's great westward expansion of the 19th century? The majority of thru-hiker reports are hand-written with no literary pretensions, but they do attest to the fact that a major effort yields major rewards, that this time apart from the ordinary cares of civilized life becomes a precious memory (people are both disappointed and relieved when it's over, and some have adjustment problems back in the thick of things). Increasingly, thru-hikers repeat the adventure, on the AT or on another long trail. Perhaps there's an addiction factor, both psychological and physical. Surely the endorphin-enriched aerobic blood flow combined with great views, the intoxicating thrill of potential danger, and the titillation of meeting new people make for a heady brew. Who wouldn't want more, compared to the predictability of normal life?

As of 1995, there were ten archival storage boxes in the Appalachian Trail Conference's Harpers Ferry headquarters devoted to "2,000-Miler Reports," and in each one are a hundred-plus reports, letters, newspaper articles, postcards, and other scraps attesting to the accomplishments and documenting the trials and tribulations of the inveterate thru-hikers. There's far too much in the archive to read in even a substantial amount of time, and no one has yet gone through it all with an eye toward culling the best of it. My reading in this AT mother lode was necessarily somewhat random. I scanned first pages, looking for colorful beginnings. I looked for people with addresses in far-away places for whom the Appalachians were new. I looked for evidence of humor, struggle or fresh insight. But I am sure that I overlooked many reports that really are worth reading. This is metal-detector-on-the-beach research. Another editor would find different gems.

The "AT Trail Registers" are still another category of writing, and this one has few if any parallels away from long-distance hiking footpaths. At each lean-to or shelter, at each official lodge and at some unofficial AT inns and B&Bs along the route, the hiker finds scrappy notebooks, often grimy from unwashed hands or weather-beaten by exposure to the elements. In these rough notebooks hikers write a few comments about the section they've just walked, about the weather they've suffered through or enjoyed, about God, politics, the economy, their new trail friends, or about boots, blisters and endless meals of beans. Anything goes. Occasionally a stunning haiku appears. Now and then a practical note ("Joe, you left your lights on in the Toyota at the trailhead. Couldn't get in to turn 'em off. Ya better head back to avoid dead battery tonight."). For this anthology I have selected a few trail register comments, from the two ends of the AT, Georgia and Maine, and from Massachusetts. Neither the Appalachian Trail Conference nor any-one else has as yet collected "the best of the trail registers," perhaps a daunt-ing but in the end no doubt a worthwhile task. The results would surely keep hikers remembering and laughing during the long winter wait for the trail to open again in the spring.

A NOTE TO THE READER

In a collection as diverse as this one, writing from many eras and many pens produces a wide variety of styles in grammar, spelling and punctua-tion. To preserve the authenticity of the material, some of which was not in-tended for publication, we have opted to use the texts as we found them rather than to edit them to conform to contemporary or professional standards.

ACKNOWLEDGMENTS

Like the "trail magic" AT thru-hikers enjoy along the way, help came from all quarters to create this book. Sincere thanks go to the following people and institutions.

For *inspiration, shelter or other assistance* — Timothy Evans, who first led me to Mt. Katahdin and who, with Laura Fillmore, offered hospitality dur-ing Boston visits. Miriam Jacobs and her children (Adam, Abigail, Sarah), who hiked the Massachusetts' AT with me (and Sarah, again, for a grand walk above tree line in New Hampshire). Bob Paviour and Peggy Brown, who led me into Virginia's Blue Ridge and provided hospitality in Charlottesville. Staff at Nantahala Outdoor Center, Wesser, North Carolina, who recommended hikes in the Smoky Mountains. David Scribner, Editor, *Berkshire Eagle*, for sponsoring my series of articles about the Massachusetts AT. Casey Sheehan, Marketing Director, Merrell Boot Co., for providing an indestructible pair of hiking boots. Rich Woller, President, Berkshire Hiking Holidays, for hiring me as tour leader and pointing me toward Vermont's Killington Peak. The Alsdorfs, innkeepers at Harpers Ferry Guest House, for hospitality and AT thru-hiker stories.

For *research assistance* and *information* — Librarians at Library of Congress; New York Public Library; Berkshire Athenaeum; Widener Library (Harvard); Sawyer Library (Williams College); Boston Public Library; Boston Athenaeum; Rare Books Division, Alderman Library (Univ. of Virginia); St. Petersburg Public Library; Simon's Rock College Library; and other university and public libraries near the AT. Archivists at Appalachian Trail Conference (Jean Cashin) and Appalachian Mountain Club (Jessica Gill). Publishing staff at ATC (Brian King) and AMC (Gordon Hardy and Cathi Buni) and at the regional offices of both organizations. Daniel Chazin, Editor, *AT Data Book*. Don King and other Information Specialists at the AT Project Office, National Park Service. *The Thru-Hiker's Handbook*, by Dan "Wingfoot" Bruce. Several contributors to this volume who kindly suggested still other writers whose work appears here.

For *sponsorship, publishing service*, and *steady encouragement* — Editor Ellen Chodosh and staff at Oxford University Press.

For *production assistance* — Rodelinde Albrecht, book designer; Michael McCurdy, cover art; Michael Warren, photographs (and to Larry Luxenberg for introducing me to Warren's work); Bill Cooke, maps; Katherine Ness, copy editing; Norma Frankel, proofreading; Eugene Bailey, cost estimating.

Each of these skilled people is a fine team player.

For *keeping the Appalachian Trail alive and well*: hundreds of anonymous trail maintenance volunteers.

To everyone mentioned here, and to any whom I have inadvertently overlooked: your kind help has been like a cool, refreshing drink in the midst of a long day's hike.

David Emblidge
Great Barrington, Massachusetts
January 1996

PART ONE

BACKGROUND

Elevation and Regions

Mt. Washington, 6,288 ft.

Mt. Katahdin, 5,267 ft.

Mt. Greylock
3,491 ft.

Bigelow Mt.
4,150 ft.

Clingmans Dome
6,643 ft.

Hudson River
124 ft.

Mt. Rogers
5,729 ft.

High Point
1,803 ft.

Springer Mt.
3,728 ft.

Northern
New England

Southern
New England

Mid-Atlantic
Lowlands

Virginia
Highlands

Southern
Mountains

Thousands of feet
above sea level

6
5
4
3
2
1
0

MAINE

VT.

N.H.

MASS.

CONN.

R.I.

NEW YORK

CANADA

PENNSYLVANIA

N.J.

OHIO

MD.

DE.

WEST
VIRGINIA

VIRGINIA

KY.

NORTH
CAROLINA

TENN.

SOUTH
CAROLINA

GEORGIA

9 White Moutain
National Forest

8 Green Mountain
National Forest

7 Shenandoah
National Park

6 George Washington
National Forest

5 Jefferson
National Forest

4 Pisgah National
Forest

3 Great Smoky Mts.
National Forest

2 Nantahala
National Forest

1 Chatahoochee
National Forest

N

|← 150 mi. →|

THE APPALACHIAN TRAIL: GEORGIA TO MAINE

Think of this section of the book as "packing your pack." A literary walk on the Appalachian Trail requires a certain amount of historical and even psychological preparation.

What does it mean "to walk"? The section "A Timeless Diversion" asks this question. Seems elementary, but in the hands of masters like Henry David Thoreau and others featured here, the ordinary becomes the extraordinary. From different angles the writers reflect on the ways that walking slows us down enough to see (and touch and smell and "hear") the landscape, and perhaps to see into ourselves, more clearly than we do when rushing through everyday life. Thru-hikers on the AT, feeling the pressure of the onrushing season, may find the advice to slow down hard to take, but there you are. It was AT founder Benton MacKaye, a devotee of Thoreau's writing, who said the purpose of walking on the trail was "to see, and to see what you see."

In the section "Appalachian Landscape," we range from broad social history, to geology, to nomenclature, to the ethics of wilderness preservation. Scholar Gerald Lowrey shows us that the very idea of "wilderness" has evolved in the national mind; Wallace Stegner and Aldo Leopold remind us that a well-informed sense of the landscape itself is the basis for any moral vision of how we might use it without destroying it.

Under "Appalachian Footpaths" are gathered writings specific to the Appalachian Trail. The 1921 essay by Benton MacKaye that started the ball rolling lays out themes still debated today as we struggle to manage our parks, forests, and networks of trails, while population growth and technology pose ever greater threats to the environment. MacKaye's visionary voice rings clearly over the decades. The history of building the AT is a mix of colorful leadership and selfless volunteerism. Selections here profile key figures who pushed the project forward, among them MacKaye, Arthur Perkins, and Myron Avery. Then there are the hikers themselves. A British walker, Miles Jebb, reflects on the psychology of today's backpackers, and a reporter for Backpacker *magazine, Michael Lanza, reviews statistics about who thru-hikes and why.*

Each walker and each walk taken is different, to be sure, but here we explore common themes and our collective background in building and maintaining the AT. These are the historical, psychological and ethical roots of the "linear community" along the trail that so many day-hikers and thru-hikers refer to as their home away from home.

A TIMELESS DIVERSION

HENRY DAVID THOREAU

"The walking of which I speak has nothing in it akin to taking exercise," says Thoreau. Indeed, in our aerobic exercise– and weight lifting–obsessed culture, Thoreau's attitude toward inner growth through exploration of the outer world may strike many as irrelevant. Inveterate long-distance hiker though he was, it's unlikely Thoreau would have joined the Appalachian Mountain Club to find companions. He eschewed crowds and loved a serendipitous saunter, hopping fences and fording streams as need be. Thoreau was faithful to his mentor Emerson's transcendentalist philosophy, which taught him to see not just botany in the elegant spine and ribs of the fallen leaf but a metaphor for divine order and process in the universe. Meet Thoreau on his own terms, and you're in for a stimulating journey.

Walking

I WISH TO SPEAK A WORD FOR NATURE, FOR ABSOLUTE FREEDOM AND WILD-ness, as contrasted with a freedom and culture merely civil, — to regard man as an inhabitant, or a part and parcel of Nature, rather than a member of society. I wish to make an extreme statement, if so I may make an emphatic one, for there are enough champions of civilization: the minister and the school committee and every one of you will take care of that.

I have met with but one or two persons in the course of my life who understood the art of Walking, that is, of taking walks, — who had a genius, so to speak, for *sauntering*, which word is beautifully derived "from idle people who roved about the country, in the Middle Ages, and asked charity, under pretense of going "*à la Sainte Terre*," to the Holy Land, till the children exclaimed, "There goes a *Sainte-Terrer*," a Saunterer, a Holy-Lander. They who never go to the Holy Land in their walks, as they pretend, are indeed mere idlers and vagabonds; but they who do go there are saunterers in the good sense, such as I mean. Some, however, would derive the word from *sans terre*, without land or a home, which, therefore, in the good sense, will mean, having no particular home, but equally at home everywhere. For this is the secret of successful sauntering. He who sits still in a house all the time may be the greatest vagrant of all; but the saunterer, in the good sense, is no more vagrant than the meandering river, which is all the while sedulously seeking the shortest course to the sea. But I prefer the first, which, indeed, is the most probable derivation. For every walk is a sort of crusade, preached by some Peter the Hermit in us, to go forth and reconquer this Holy Land from the hands of the Infidels.

It is true, we are but faint-hearted crusaders, even the walkers, nowadays, who undertake no persevering, never-ending enterprises. Our expeditions are but tours, and come round again at evening to the old hearthside from which we set out. Half the walk is but retracing our steps. We should go forth on the shortest walk, perchance, in the spirit of undying adventure, never to return, — prepared to send back our embalmed hearts only as relics to our desolate kingdoms. If you are ready to leave father and mother, and brother and sister, and wife and child and friends, and never see them again, if you have paid your debts, and made your will, and settled all your affairs, and are a free man, then you are ready for a walk.

To come down to my own experience, my companion and I, for I sometimes have a companion, take pleasure in fancying ourselves knights of a new, or rather an old, order, — not Equestrians or Chevaliers, not Ritters or Riders, but Walkers, a still more ancient and honorable class, I trust. The chivalric and heroic spirit which once belonged to the Rider seems now to reside in, or perchance to have subsided into, the Walker, — not the Knight, but Walker, Errant. He is a sort of fourth estate, outside of Church and State and People.

We have felt that we almost alone hereabouts practiced this noble art; though, to tell the truth, at least if their own assertions are to be received, most of my townsmen would fain walk sometimes, as I do, but they cannot. No wealth can buy the requisite leisure, freedom, and independence which are the capital in this profession. It comes only by the grace of God. It requires a direct dispensation from Heaven to become a walker. You must be born into the family of the Walkers. *Ambulator nascitur, non fit.* Some of my townsmen, it is true, can remember and have described to me some walks which they took ten years ago, in which they were so blessed as to lose themselves for half an hour in the woods; but I know very well that they have confined themselves to the highway ever since, whatever pretensions they may make to belong to this select class. No doubt they were elevated for a moment as by the reminiscence of a previous state of existence, when even they were foresters and outlaws.

> "When he came to grene wode,
>   In a mery mornynge,
> There he herde the notes small
>   Of byrdes mery syngynge.

"It is ferre gone, sayd Robyn,
    That I was last here;
Me lyste a lytell for to shote
    At the donne dere."

I think that I cannot preserve my health and spirits, unless I spend four hours a day at least — and it is commonly more than that — sauntering through the woods and over the hills and fields, absolutely free from all worldly engagements. You may safely say, A penny for your thoughts, or a thousand pounds. When sometimes I am reminded that the mechanics and shopkeepers stay in their shops not only all the forenoon, but all the afternoon too, sitting with crossed legs, so many of them, — as if the legs were made to sit upon, and not to stand or walk upon, — I think that they deserve some credit for not having all committed suicide long ago.

I, who cannot stay in my chamber for a single day without acquiring some rust, and when sometimes I have stolen forth for a walk at the eleventh hour, or four o'clock in the afternoon, too late to redeem the day, when the shades of night were already beginning to be mingled with the daylight, have felt as if I had committed some sin to be atoned for, — I confess that I am astonished at the power of endurance, to say nothing of the moral insensibility, of my neighbors who confine themselves to shops and offices the whole day for weeks and months, aye, and years almost together. I know not what manner of stuff they are of, — sitting there now at three o'clock in the afternoon, as if it were three o'clock in the morning. Bonaparte may talk of the three-o'clock-in-the-morning courage, but it is nothing to the courage which can sit down cheerfully at this hour in the afternoon over against one's self whom you have known all the morning, to starve out a garrison to whom you are bound by such strong ties of sympathy. I wonder that about this time, or say between four and five o'clock in the afternoon, too late for the morning papers and too early for the evening ones, there is not a general explosion heard up and down the street, scattering a legion of antiquated and house-bred notions and whims to the four winds for an airing, — and so the evil cure itself.

How womankind, who are confined to the house still more than men, stand it I do not know; but I have ground to suspect that most of them do not *stand* it at all. When, early in a summer afternoon, we have been shaking the dust of the village from the skirts of our garments, making haste past those houses with purely Doric or Gothic fronts, which have such an air of repose about them, my companion whispers that probably about these times their occupants are all gone to bed. Then it is that I appreciate the beauty and the glory of architecture, which itself never turns in, but forever stands out and erect, keeping watch over the slumberers.

No doubt temperament, and, above all, age, have a good deal to do with it. As a man grows older, his ability to sit still and follow indoor occupations increases. He grows vespertinal in his habits as the evening of life approaches, till at last he comes forth only just before sundown, and gets all the walk that he requires in half an hour.

But the walking of which I speak has nothing in it akin to taking exercise, as it is called, as the sick take medicine at stated hours, — as the swinging of dumbbells or chairs; but is itself the enterprise and adventure of the day. If you would get exercise, go in search of the springs of life. Think of a man's swinging dumbbells for his health, when those springs are bubbling up in far-off pastures unsought by him!

Moreover, you must walk like a camel, which is said to be the only beast which ruminates when walking. When a traveler asked Wordsworth's servant to show him her master's study, she answered, "Here is his library, but his study is out of doors."

From *Walking,* by Henry David Thoreau, *Atlantic Monthly,* June 1862.

DONALD CULROSS PEATTIE

1942. Wartime. Gasoline rationing. A sharp curtailment of mobility for recreation. What to do? Learn to walk, of course, though it's more easily said than done if habituated to riding about the countryside on four wheels. Peattie saw deprivation in one area as a gift in another, an attitude not inappropriate for hikers to take on the trail.

The Joy of Walking

A
MERICA, LAND OF THE MOTOR CAR, LAND OF THE RUBBER TIRE, IS GOING off wheels and learning to walk.
Of this I sing.
If ever you complained of a speed-mad America and extolled the charms of tile horse-and-buggy age, if ever you jeered that wheels had made us a nation of tenderfeet and groaned that our highways kill more than the bombing of London, your prayers are answered and your fears made groundless. For America is finding its feet again.

Yesterday I moved from a house eleven miles from my children's school to a new home, where, by walking three-quarters of a mile, they can board the school bus. So I save rubber. But this morning I discovered that to get the morning mail I must also go down to the highway, making a mile-and-a-half round trip during which I climb back up a 300-foot hill.

I set out, my mind full of the usual Monday morning humdrums and problems, complaining to myself that in this way I missed the morning news broadcast and consumed a valuable half-hour of my freshest energies, in order to get the post. I was even "noble" about it, assuring myself that it was just one of countless inconveniences that we were all facing.

But I came back to my desk with my blood tingling, with every stale and mundane concern washed out of my head and all self-pity jeered out of me by jays and crows, frisking, scolding squirrels and errant Spring winds.

I had heard the titmouse calling his merry song of peet-o, peet-o, and song sparrows tuning up on the alder bushes where the catkins were hanging out all pollen-dusty and fertile. I had heard the brook gurgling among its boulders, and smelled fresh loam, lichen wet with dew, spawn of toad-stool. I had seen the mountains in long shafts of early light and a flight of band-tailed pigeons flashing white wings as they crossed a little valley on important pigeon business. The oats were shooting, pale green and tender, out of the fine black earth in the fields, and I heard a plowman shout at his old white horse as he turned at the end of the velvety furrow and set the blade in the next row.

Had I taken my car to run down to the mailbox I should have had only a fleeting glimpse, or none, of all these fine sights. Of all these fragrances I should have caught not a whiff, but only gasoline fumes. Above the noise of the wheels how should I have heard the sea-dirge of the pines, or the chuckling of the linnets, or the jolly scampering of lizards on old leaves?

True, I should have "saved" about twenty-five minutes of my priceless time. For what? For the sake of a more sluggish digestion, of a wider girth beneath my belt, staler air in my lungs, duller thoughts in my head, a posture grown by that much older. I should have lopped off half an hour of fresh and living experience. For, after all, time is not money; time is an opportunity to live before you die. So a man who walks, and lives and sees and thinks as he walks, has lengthened his life.

It was Thoreau, himself one of the most inveterate of walkers, who insisted that if you took the train from Concord to Fitchburg, and he took shanks' mare, he would arrive first. For, he reasoned, you would have to stop and work till you had earned the price of a ticket. While you were doing that he would be in Scotland afore ye. And have seen enough sights and had enough encounters to write another immortal chapter.

All the great naturalists have been habitual walkers, for no laboratory, no book, car, train or plane takes the place of honest footwork for this calling, be it amateur's or professional's. Gilbert White and Izaak Walton were devotees of the art and tireless exponents of its charms. W. H. Hudson in England was practically a tramp, and so was John Muir in this country. John thought nothing of walking from one end of the Sierra to the other, just to see a tree or a flower; he once walked from Wisconsin to the Gulf of Mexico! Asked what preparations he made for these famous treks, he replied: "I throw a loaf of bread and a pound of tea in an old sack and jump over the back fence."

There spake the true walker, as contrasted with those persons with over-developed thyroids who walk to set records, who add stones to their packs when climbing mountains and count their steps to calculate how far they have come. Not thus did John Burroughs walk, or Richard Jefferies or Alexander Wilson. John James Audubon could and often did walk a hundred miles in two days. It sounds like a startling record, but on one of my own walks, along the old Roman Road from Canterbury to London, I was overtaken by a little Welsh soldier, though I was walking fast; he had come thirty-five miles that day, and hoped to make it fifty before he slept — in some hedge. He slowed to my pace for ten miles, while he told me his adventures in many parts of the world. Then he had to leave me because he could not wait.

He was quite a philosopher, that fellow, and indeed all walkers become philosophers. Didn't Plato and Socrates pace up and down in the stoas of the Acropolis while they pulled their beards and unriddled the universe? Robert Louis Stevenson and Ralph Waldo Emerson were Peripatetics too, as you can easily tell by the kind of philosophy they expounded, one peculiarly kindly, reasonable, hopeful, cheerful and refreshing.

Something happens to the walker who knows how to think and observe as he goes. In the first place he is physically prevented from wasting his time and cluttering his mind in a great many ways that, we get to imagining, are inevitable or even pleasant or important. While you are walking you cannot be reached by telephone or telegraph, and you cannot reach anybody in those ways. That in itself is a great blessing. You cannot put out a hand, as you do even in an automobile, and twiddle the radio and so let in the war and the stock market, a flood of soda-pop and chewing-gum spiels, and all the quizzes and jazzes that wrangle on the innocent airs. You cannot play bridge or consult an astrologer, bet on a horse or go to a movie. In the compensation for these keen deprivations, walking offers you health, happiness and an escape from civilization's many madnesses.

I have often started off on a walk in the state called mad — mad in the sense of sore-headed, or mad with tedium or confusion; I have set forth dull, null and even thoroughly discouraged. But I never came back in such a frame of mind, and I never met a human being whose humor was not the better for a walk. It is a sovereign remedy for the hot-tempered and the low-spirited.

From *The Joy of Walking,* by Donald Culross Peattie, *The New York Times Magazine,* April 5, 1942.

APPALACHIAN LANDSCAPE

European Discovery

THOMAS CONNELLEY

Like the explorers whose meanderings he documents here, historian Thomas Connelley travels widely in time from DeSoto's rapacious days in the southern Appalachians (1540) to the Crawfords of New Hampshire, who set the tourism trade going in northern New England (beginning in the 1790s). The history of the mountains through which the AT passes is laced with heroes and villains, both serious scientists with an eye toward preservation and self-aggrandizing developers with an eye toward an easy fortune. This overview may open doors for further exploration, through reading, of your own.

The Explorers: From DeSoto to Kephart

L ONG LINES OF CHAINED INDIAN SLAVES AND CONCUBINES STRUGGLED across the mountain trails. Behind them came more baggage carriers and a herd of squealing pigs. Ahead marched helmeted Spanish conquistadores with their leader, Hernando De Soto. De Soto might well have been the first white man to explore the Appalachians. During 1539 and early 1540, his column moved in a long, meandering line northward through Georgia and South Carolina.

De Soto's route through the Blue Ridge and Unaka country has been the subject of much disagreement, but many scholars believed his party reached the Blue Ridge in Pickens County, South Carolina (present-day North Carolina State Highway 107). The party then struggled through the Terrapin, Toxaway, and Whiteside Mountain area between present-day Cashiers and Highlands, North Carolina (U.S. Highway 64), then passed through Highlands (U.S. Highway 64), and followed Cullasaja Creek (now followed by State Highway 28) to the vicinity of Franklin, North Carolina. Near Franklin, they found the Little Tennessee River, probably the first tributary of the Mississippi River to be discovered by Europeans. Following the general course of present-day U.S. 64 westward from Franklin, De Soto crossed the

Nantahala Mountain range probably at Wallace Gap (3,640 ft.; 13 miles west of Franklin). The Spaniards then crossed Yellow Mountain Ridge at Black Gap (3,700 ft.; U.S. 64, 20 miles west of Franklin), and descended along Shooting Creek, on the route now followed by U.S. 64, to present-day Hayesville, North Carolina.

West of Hayesville, the party struck the Hiwassee River and there saw an opportunity to escape the encompassing mountain country. They followed the river along its course to present-day Murphy, North Carolina. West of Murphy, the party continued along the Hiwassee gorge through the main Unaka range, on a route now followed by North Carolina State Highway 294, and entered the Tennessee Valley at the Hiwassee River gap between Chestnut and Bean mountains, probably along the present-day Tennessee State Highway 30. The river gap itself may be seen from the Hiwassee River bridge on U.S. Highway 411 south of Wetmore, Tennessee. The Spaniards continued down the Hiwassee at least as far as the mouth of Conasauga Creek, which flows into the Hiwassee about a mile west of U.S. 411.

Here the Spanish travelers turned southwest along the Great Indian Warpath. Their entrance into the Chattanooga area was blocked by long White Oak Mountain. Historians believe they crossed this mountain at Ooltewah Gap (U.S. Highway 11, 17 miles east of Chattanooga) and then followed the Tennessee River through the narrow gorge below present-day Chattanooga, between Raccoon and Signal mountains. Near Guntersville, Alabama, the Spaniards marched south across Sand Mountain, possibly along present-day U.S. Highway 431 from Guntersville to Gadsden, Alabama. From here they crossed Lookout Mountain to the Coosa River valley, and left the southern Appalachians.

THE KNIGHTS OF THE GOLDEN HORSESHOE

The next significant exploration of the southern mountains occurred in 1716. On September 5, 1716, a gaily dressed band of Virginia gentlemen, scarcely costumed for mountain exploration, paused at Swift Run Gap to toast themselves. Governor Alexander Spotswood of Virginia had just led the first organized body of Englishmen across the Blue Ridge Mountains. Spotswood, long interested in discovering a good pass through the Blue Ridge, led his expedition from Williamsburg, across the Piedmont, and to the east side of the mountains near present-day Stanardsville, Virginia (U.S. Highway 33). From here, on a route approximating U.S. 33, the party approached the Blue Ridge via Swift Run Gap, and then followed the small Swift Run upstream. On September 5, they reached the mountain crest in the gap (2,400 ft.). The party paused to toast the King and the Governor, and then rode down into the Shenandoah Valley along the route now followed by U.S. Highway 33.

They encamped by the Shenandoah River near where the highway now crosses the river, some seven miles west of Swift Run Gap. They named the river Euphrates, and buried a bottle with a paper enclosed that claimed the territory for George I. They drank to the king's health with champagne, and fired a volley. They then drank to the remainder of the royal family, and fired more volleys. After several other toasts, they turned their horses east and recrossed the gap. Later, the Governor presented each member of the party with a jeweled miniature horseshoe, and the explorers became . . . known as the Knights of the Golden Horseshoe.

EXPLORATION ROUTES OF DANIEL BOONE

While Daniel Boone is often associated with Indian fighting, he actually ranks among the major early southern Appalachian explorers. Born in Pennsylvania in 1734, Boone migrated to North Carolina. The graves of his parents may be seen east of the Blue Ridge in the old Joppa Presbyterian Church cemetery (U.S. Highway 601, 1.5 miles from Mocksville).

Boone's mountain explorations may be divided into two phases and two decades. During the 1760's, his base of operations for hunting and exploring remained centered along the eastern slopes of the Blue Ridge. Between 1760 and 1769, the jumping off point for many of his expeditions was a cabin at present-day Boone, North Carolina (corner of Faculty and Newland streets). In the Yadkin River Valley near Lexington, North Carolina, the site of another cabin used by Boone has been marked in the Boone Memorial Park (on State Highway 150). Near this cabin site is Boone Cave, a small opening in a rock bluff overlooking the Yadkin River. Here Boone is said to have hidden once from pursuing Indians.

During the 1760's, as Boone ranged into the Tennessee Unakas on hunting expeditions, he used a trail across the Blue Ridge and Unakas which gradually became known as Boone's Trail. The route originated at his home (Boone, North Carolina, U.S. Highway 421), and crossed the Blue Ridge at Deep Gap (3,131 ft.; U.S. Highway 421). The trail crossed the Unaka range at Boone's Gap (3,159 ft.; U.S. 421 between Zionville, North Carolina, and Trade, Tennessee) and then led through east Tennessee's Watauga River Valley through present-day Elizabethton.

During the 1770's, Boone's explorations widened into the Cumberland Mountains of Kentucky. Boone had made several long hunting expeditions into Kentucky and in 1773 had attempted colonization unsuccessfully. In 1775, in the employ of Judge Richard Henderson of the Transylvania Land Company, Boone was placed in charge of building a road for settlers to follow through Cumberland Gap. This road, first called Boone's Trace and later the Wilderness Road, followed the route of present-day U.S. 25E through Cumberland Gap.

WASHINGTON AND THE CENTRAL APPALACHIANS

Strangely enough, George Washington's adventures as a mountain explorer have not been fully appreciated. In the light of his fame as a war chieftain and statesman, it is sometimes forgotten that Washington was also probably the greatest explorer of the central Appalachians. His expeditions encompassed a period of some fifty years, from his youthful surveys into western Virginia in the 1740's for Lord Fairfax, until his travels in the 1790's. During this period Washington's mountaineering feats were indeed impressive.

His first expedition was in 1748, when at the age of sixteen, he accompanied George William Fairfax on a surveying trip into the Shenandoah Valley and the Alleghenies. The two young men crossed the Blue Ridge at Ashbys Gap (1,150 ft.; U.S. Highway 50 near Upperville, Virginia). Following the Potomac River upstream through the Alleghenies, Washington reached the South Branch of the Potomac, on a route now followed by U.S. Highway 220. Near present-day Old Fields, West Virginia (U.S. 220), Washington visited the Trough. This narrow canyon between two mountain ledges formed an impassable barrier some eight miles long. Washington then returned to the Shenandoah Valley and recrossed the Blue Ridge at Snickers Gap. . . .

Gradually, Washington gained the admiration of grayer heads for his ability in surveying rough country. Between 1749 and 1752, he made several trips into the West Virginia Alleghenies to survey the South Branch and Cacapon rivers. In 1753, he was ready for more important explorations.

Governor Robert Dinwiddie of Virginia was disturbed by reports that the French were planning a chain of forts from Lake Erie to the present site of Pittsburgh in order to seal off the trans-Allegheny country from British expansion. Dinwiddie was particularly disturbed over reports that the French planned to build a fort at the forks of the Ohio River, where the Monongahela and Allegheny rivers join to form the Ohio at the site of present-day Pittsburgh. Since Virginia claimed this country, Dinwiddie dispatched Washington to observe the French activities, to win Pennsylvania Indians over to the British, and above all, to demand of the French that they retire from the upper Ohio. The same day that young Washington received his commission, he set out for the mountains. Crossing the Blue Ridge and the Shenandoah Valley, Washington traveled through the outlying Allegheny ridges up the Potomac River to Wills Creek (now Cumberland, Maryland; at the junction of U.S. 40 and 220). Here he obtained the services of the well-known western scout, Christopher Gist. Together, in November, 1753, the two explorers pushed nortbwestward through the Alleghenies.

The men struggled across Big Savage and Negro mountains, Keysers Ridge and Laurel Hill, along the route later followed by the National Road (now traversed by U.S. Highway 40). Four days out of Wills Creek, the party reached Gist's home at what is now Braddock, Pennsylvania. The site of

Gist's plantation may still be seen (U.S. 119, 6 miles south of Connellsville, Pennsylvania). Gist and Washington then continued toward the forks of the Ohio. Walking through ankle-deep snow, they crossed the Youghiogheny River just below present-day Connellsville (U.S. 119), perhaps at Broad Ford, which was known by the Indians as "the crossing place." Pausing at a small settlement on Jacobs Creek not far from present-day Mt. Pleasant, Pennsylvania (State Highway 31), they came to the Monongahela River almost at the spot where the highway bridge now crosses the river between Duquesne and McKeesport. The party crossed the river, and moved to a point slightly downstream from the confluence of the Allegheny and the Monongahela. There at McKees Rocks (Pennsylvania State Highway 51, 4 miles northwest of Pittsburgh), British landholders had planned to build a fort at the mouth of Chartier's Creek. Washington saw that the actual junction of the two rivers was a far better site for the proposed fort and so reported to the British. Later, from this recommendation came Fort Pitt, on the site of present-day Pittsburgh.

Pushing northward, Washington and Gist reached a French outpost at Venango (present-day Franklin, Pennsylvania; junction of U.S. Highways 62 and 322). Here, where French Creek empties into the Allegheny River, Washington was advised that he must carry warnings to the French high command at Fort Le Boeuf at the head of navigation on French Creek (remains of fort exist in present-day Waterford, Pennsylvania, U.S. 19). After delivering his message to the French commander, Washington recrossed the Alleghenies and Blue Ridge. On the return trip, Washington was almost drowned when his raft overturned as he was crossing the ice-swollen Allegheny River (at site of the present-day Butler-Pittsburgh highway bridge in Pittsburgh). By January of 1754, Washington had retraced his steps to Williamsburg after a 1,000-mile journey through the wilderness, much of which was mountain country.

EARLY NEW ENGLAND EXPLORERS

The New England Appalachians long mystified explorers. The identity of the first European to view the range is unknown. Possibly this honor belongs to the Florentine explorer and navigator, Verrazano. In 1524, while exploring the Rhode Island and New Hampshire coasts for the French king, Francis I, Verrazano sighted tall mountains to the west. In 1605, the founder of French Canada, Samuel de Champlain, sighted the Appalachians while skirting the Maine coast near present-day Portland. Three years later, while sailing the waters of Lake Champlain, the Frenchman spotted the snowcapped peaks of Mt. Mansfield, Vermont's highest summit (4,393 ft.). Champlain supposedly shouted "Voila! Les Verts Monts," and thus gave the Green Mountains their name. Later, in 1614, Captain John Smith of Jamestown fame evidently spied Mt. Washington while cruising along the New England coast. Smith dubbed the peak "the twinkling mountain." By 1529, the New England mountains were already being located on European charts, and by 1677, the White Mountains were being described on European maps as the "White Hills."

The first New England mountaineer was Darby Field. Once believed to have been an Irishman, Field was actually a native of Boston, England. In 1642, he pushed westward from his home at Exeter, New Hampshire, in search of the White Hills. Field halted at an Indian village in the Saco River valley, probably near present-day Glen, New Hampshire (U.S. 302), and persuaded several Indians to join his expedition.

It is not known exactly what route Field took to Mt. Washington on the first recorded climb of that peak by a European. He may have trudged the narrow valley of Rocky Branch, between the Montalban and Rocky Branch ridges in the White Mountain National Forest, along the route of the present-day Rocky Branch Trail. Some believe Field may have pushed up the Ellis River toward Pinkham Notch (State Highway 16). Regardless, he evidently reached Boott Spur, and continued to the crest of Mt. Washington.

When he neared the mountain top, his Indian friends wavered. The awesome mountain was alleged to be the home of the Great Spirit. Only two brave souls chose to accompany Field on this final stage of the climb. From the summit, Field evidently saw large clouds or fog banks which he mistook for a vast sea. While atop the mountain, the tiny band was lashed by a fierce storm. The Saco River Indians were sure that Field and his companions would never be seen again, and that they had been punished by the Great Spirit for trespassing. However, Field was seen again, and about a month later, he made a second climb up the mountain. He returned with some large stones, probably quartz crystals, which he mistook for diamonds.

In 1672, explorer-traveler John Josselyn published his famous work, *New England Rarities Discovered*. This contained the first appearance in print of the name "White Mountains." Josselyn recounted his own excursion to the mountains, probably made in 1663. He recorded having seen a pond of pure water atop Mt. Washington. Some believe this to have been a body of water which once existed on the mountain crest, but others think Josselyn was referring to the Lake of the Clouds southwest of the mountain summit at the head of the Ammonoosuc Ravine. Josselyn also mentioned a large mossy plain, which probably was Bigelow Lawn, lying between the summit of Mt. Washington and the Boott Spur. (Bigelow Lawn is crossed by the Camel and the Lawn cut-off trails of the Appalachian Mountain Club.)

Most of these early explorations were spurred by tales of wealth. Until he died, Darby Field spoke of the diamonds and emeralds that flashed on the White Mountain slopes. Many Indian legends of the mountains concern a huge garnet which was allegedly hidden in a cave by Indians, and was guarded by an evil spirit. This gem shone so brightly that those who viewed it became mad and were doomed to wander the mountains in search of the treasure. Early New England Indian sorcerers, hopeful of acquiring its powers, supposedly combed the mountains for this stone. One hapless witch doctor reportedly was swept away in an avalanche of fire which quenched itself in the Lake of the Clouds between Mt. Monroe and Mt. Washington (reached by foot trail from Marshfield Base Station of the White Mountain Cog Railway). Once when Nathaniel Hawthorne was a guest at a mountain hotel in Crawford Notch, he heard of these legends, and used them as a basis for his story, "The Great Carbuncle."

The most colorful early explorer of the New England mountains was Reverend Samuel Peters. This circuit-riding preacher toured the Killington Peak area (south of U.S. 5 near Sherburne) in 1763 on a preaching tour. The first Protestant clergyman to enter Vermont, and later the first Bishop of Vermont, the blustery Reverend Peters claimed that in 1763, while atop Killington Peak, he broke a bottle of whisky across a rock there and christened the state "Verd-Mont." Peters' claim has been challenged by some writers, who point out that he also claimed to have an L.L.B. degree from the non-existent University of Cortona in Tuscany.

THE DISCOVERY OF CRAWFORD NOTCH

For over fifty years, further exploration of the mountains was almost completely halted because of Indian wars in New England. Nevertheless, in 1777 a major breakthrough occurred. A pioneer hunter, Timothy Nash, was climbing Cherry Mountain (east side of State Highway 115, north of Carroll, New Hampshire) in search of a moose. Climbing a tree, he discovered the long-sought pass, Crawford Notch, between the seacoast and the Connecticut River Valley. Nash, probably the first white man to learn of the secret pass, excitedly followed the twisting course of the Saco River through the notch and made his way to Portsmouth, New Hampshire, to inform Governor Benning Wentworth of his find. The dubious governor told Nash that if he could bring a horse through the pass from Jefferson, New Hampshire, to Portsmouth, he would be rewarded by an ample land grant at the mouth of the pass. Aided by a fellow hunter, Benjamin Sawyer, Nash managed to lower his horse down the rocky gorge with the aid of a rope and tackle. According to tradition, Sawyer Rock (U.S. 302, 8.8 miles north of Glen, New Hampshire) was named during this expedition. When the two hunters lowered the horse over Sawyer Rock, the final obstacle, Sawyer drank the last of his ration of rum and broke the bottle on the rock.

SCIENTIFIC ASSAULT ON MT. WASHINGTON

In 1784, the first full-scale scientific assault was made on the New England mountains. Armed with muskets, pistols, barometers, thermometers, compasses, a sextant, and a telescope, a party of prominent scientists, historians, and others moved up the Ellis River along the route of present-day State Highway 16 and into Pinkham Notch. After camping near the beautiful Glen Ellis Falls (State Highway 16 in Pinkham Notch), the party decided to tackle Mt. Washington. Amidst heavy rain and fog, the tenacious band fought its way up the Cutler River through a forest of fir, spruce, pine, and hemlock. From Boott Spur they continued up the east slope of Mt. Washington. Heavy fog and clouds marred the view, and because of the dropping temperature, the party turned back down Tuckerman Ravine. The path was rough because of low-hanging clouds and the group had to spend a cold, damp night in the ravine. The following morning, they returned to their Pinkham Notch camp. Because Reverend Cutler mentioned the name Mt. Washington in a manuscript which he prepared in 1784, some believe this exploring group gave the mountain its name. . . .

THE HERITAGE OF ARNOLD GUYOT

Perhaps the greatest explorer of the Great Smokies was the Swiss geographer, Arnold Guyot. Guyot not only undertook the first exhaustive exploration of the Smokies, but also provided the first concerted naming of mountain peaks. Shortly after coming to America in 1854 as a professor of geology and physical geography at Princeton, Guyot became deeply interested in the Appalachians. Soon he was in the Great Smokies, where he methodically mapped the region and measured elevations. Some of the names Guyot gave to peaks have not survived. His Mt. Henry, named for Joseph Henry of the Smithsonian Institution. later became known as Old Black because of its dark foliage of black-green spruce (6,536 ft.; 17.5 miles northwest of Newfound Gap on the Appalachian Trail). Guyot named an outlying segment of Mt. Le Conte as Mt. Safford, for Vanderbilt University geologist James Safford. Later this name was changed to Myrtle Point because of the large quantities of Allegheny sand myrtle which once grew there. This area is reached by a trail from the crest of Le Conte. A curious summit on the southwest edge of the present national park is topped by a strange 200-acre grassy patch. This spot Guyot named the Central Peak of Great Bald. Later this peak (4,948 ft.) was named Gregory Bald, for an early settler in the region.

Still, many of Guyot's names have remained, and he is credited with the first scientific exploration of the Smokies. Armed with fragile barometers and other instruments, this intrepid scientist literally forced his way through thick patches of laurel and fallen timber to measure peaks. The junction of the main Great Smoky range with the outlying Balsam range Guyot named Tricorner Knob (15 miles northeast of Newfound Gap on the Appalachian Trail). This name has remained unchanged. Guyot also was responsible for the naming of Clingman's Dome and of Mt. Buckley (6,592 ft.; 7.96 miles southwest of Newfound Gap on the Appalachian Trail). Mt. Buckley was named for another explorer and naturalist, Samuel Buckley. He had roamed the Smokies as early as 1840 and had accompanied Guyot on some explorations in 1856. Guyot probably also first laid the basis for the name of Newfound Gap, where the heavily traveled U.S. 441 between Gatlinburg, Tennessee, and Cherokee, North Carolina, cuts across the main Great Smoky range in the national park. Guyot called this pass New Gap.

UNSUNG FEATS OF WINTER SURVIVAL

Perhaps the most exciting nineteenth-century New England explorations were two unsung scientific feats during the period from 1869 to 1871. In 1869, a New Hampshire geologist and a photographer volunteered to spend a winter on top of Mt. Moosilauke to gauge winter temperatures and wind conditions. The purpose of the trip was partially to demonstrate that humans could survive a winter on top of the range. In December, 1869, the two men began the climb of Mt. Moosilauke (4,810 ft.; east of the village of North Haverhill). A furious wind- and snowstorm drove them back down the trail, but they succeeded in reaching the crest on the following day, and established winter camp at the Tip Top House. This was a stone structure built in 1860 which was destroyed by fire in 1940. For over two months. the two weathermen braved 100-mile winds, fierce snowstorms, and biting cold. Finally, after running short of food, they descended the mountain on the last day of February, 1870.

Part of the purpose of this Mt. Moosilauke expedition was to experiment in techniques of winter survival to prepare for the Mt. Washington expedition during the winter of 1870-71. The state geological survey hoped to open a weather station on this mountain. . . . A telegraph cable was laid down the railway line to relay if possible weather information which might aid farmers and ships at sea. On November 13, 1870, the party started from the Marshfield Base Station of the cog railway during a heavy snow. By the time they arrived at the mountain's top, snowdrifts had completely covered several buildings there, including the Summit House. Several photographers, who ascended a few days later to join the party, almost perished in a fierce blizzard which wracked the mountain. By early February, wind speeds measured well over 100 miles per hour and the mercury fell to fifty-nine degrees below zero. In May, 1871, with snow still lingering on several peaks, the triumphant party returned to civilization.

THE LEGACY OF HORACE KEPHART

Recent years have seen few men who retain the exploring spirit of early mountain trail blazers. One such man was Horace Kephart. In 1904, Kephart alighted from a train at the little mountain depot in Sylva, North Carolina, to begin a new career. A former librarian and an ardent student of the West, Kephart had left his family to seek a new life here for two reasons: to regain his shattered health, and to witness firsthand a civilization he considered America's last frontier. Already a writer of some note on hunting and fishing, Kephart was to become the foremost writer of the Appalachian outdoors. His poignant book, *Our Southern Highlanders*, is reprinted periodically and remains the best chronicle of the Smoky Mountain people. His *Camping and Woodcraft*, also continually in reprint, remains the best source on the art of outdoor living in the southern mountains. Both books were based on Kephart's twenty-seven years of experience tramping the Smokies. He lived an idyllic life in these mountains. Supporting himself by writing stories for popular magazines, he became the friend of moonshiner and revenue agent alike. He usually camped and hunted alone, often with muzzle-loading rifles, with which he was an expert.

Kephart died in an automobile accident outside Bryson City in 1931. His last camping place (Bryson Place, 8 miles up Deep Creek from the present-day national park campground near Bryson City) has been marked by a Bryson City Boy Scout troop who placed a marker in an old gristmill stone on the site. Kephart was buried in a hillside cemetery overlooking Bryson City. When the national park was created, Horace Kephart was not forgotten. On the Appalachian Trail two miles northeast from U.S. Highwav 441 at Newfound Gap is the top of Mt. Kephart (6,200 ft.).

His superb books and many articles on mountain people were only part of Kephart's legacy to the southern mountains. He was an early advocate of forming a national park in the Great Smokies. Probably he was the first writer to bring the charm of this area to national attention.

From *Discovering the Appalachians*, by Thomas Connelley, Stackpole, 1968.

The Land Underfoot

FERDINAND LANE

Geologist Ferdinand Lane explores the geological history of the Appalachian mountain range in the next selection. Lane's review of the mountains' biography, from 1950, gives a (then) settled interpretation of their origins. In the 1980s, John McPhee reported on a new, unresolved argument about the role of tectonic plates as causal factors in the formation of the Appalachians. Thus even something as solid as the rocks underfoot turns out to be as debatable as the weather overhead. Perhaps, when in a heavy sweat while scaling the tallest peaks along the AT—Clingman's Dome, North Carolina; Mt. Washington, New Hampshire; and Mt. Katahdin, Maine—hikers can distract themselves from their arduous efforts by contemplating how long it took the gods to build these mountains in the first place.

The Appalachians: Their Rise and Fall

T HE SPANISH ADVENTURER DE SOTO . . . GAVE A NAME NOT ONLY TO ONE of the world's most interesting mountain systems but to a geological period as well, for these mountains were born in that era of turmoil and crustal readjustment called the Appalachian revolution.

If we could turn back the clock of time to the remote Proterozoic era, we would find the oceans covering far more of the global surface than they do today. Here and there, though widely scattered, areas of dry land were emerging, concentrated mainly in eastern Brazil, southern Africa, and western Australia, with notable sections in upper and lower Asia. But probably the largest and the most studied was that territory of vague boundaries stretching across northern and eastern North America, comprising some two million square miles, known as the great Canadian shield. All this occurred before the dawn of the Cambrian period, which ushered in the first forms of life, whose fossils have left a distinct impress upon the rocks.

Pre-Cambrian time, though much longer than the eras that succeeded, interposes a geological iron curtain beyond which science can make only feeble forays into the unknown. But the Cambrian period began the immensely long Paleozoic or era of Old Life which saw animal life develop from humble invertebrates through the fishes and the amphibians to the dawn of the Mesozoic era of mid-life with its swarming reptiles culminating in ponderous dinosaurs.

The Paleozoic era is thought to have lasted at least three hundred million years. Midway up its ascending ladder was the Carboniferous, which gave the world its coal fields. The oldest foldings of the Appalachians date back to this period, and a subdivision of geological time is known as the Pennsylvanian. But the great period of crustal warping and folding came later. This so-called Appalachian revolution had its counterpart in the Hercynian revolution in Europe, which produced the worn-down ranges of western Europe and the Ural Mountains, while in Asia it takes its name from the Altai Mountains, still rearing their crumbling stumps above the aboriginal rocks of the Angara shield.

The Appalachians are hoary with age. Foldings whose structure is still visible had their beginnings perhaps two hundred million years ago. Resultant peaks which once rivaled the Alps or Rockies in altitude were ground down through passing centuries only to experience a subsequent upheaval followed by prolonged erosion to their present smoothed and rounded contours.

The Appalachians comprise many parallel ridges or foldings of the global crust. These have received various names, while, for geographical simplicity, the entire system has been divided into three great sections. The first, beginning in Newfoundland, extends through Nova Scotia and embraces the rocky escarpment of the Gaspé Peninsula. The rim of this peninsula is outlined by the northern outpost of the Appalachians, known as the Shickshock Mountains, their chief peak named for Jacques Cartier, looming 4,350 feet above the St. Lawrence. Trending southwesterly, the Appalachians give Maine its rugged hinterland and in New Hampshire reach their apex in Mount Washington. The Green Mountains of Vermont and the Berkshires of Massachusetts are natural continuations, but the Adirondacks in New York have a somewhat different geological origin.

The Hudson River, as scenic as the Rhine, cuts through the main system to set apart the second section, the low mountains of New Jersey, the more precipitous ridges of Pennsylvania, and the Blue Ridge and other ranges extending farther south. The third section embraces the loftiest heights of all, the Great Smokies, although Mitchell, the highest peak, 6,711 feet, is on an offshoot known locally as the Black Mountains. These ranges subside in ever-lowering summits through Georgia until they terminate in Alabama.

The Appalachians comprise two great divisions of rock formation. First, and much the older, is the Pre-Cambrian, a tangled assortment of marble schists, gneisses, and granites much metamorphosed and dating back beyond the dawn of recognizable life. The second type is sedimentary, also much metamorphosed, laid down in mid or later Paleozoic times.

There is considerable mineral wealth. The marble quarries of Vermont are famous, as are the limestones of Pennsylvania. Outcroppings of iron occur in the Champlain region, and still more so in the mountains of ore which created the great steel center at Birmingham, Alabama. But more important is coal. Many ridges of the Appalachians, particularly in Pennsylvania and West Virginia, show extensive veins laid down in the Carboniferous era, forming with iron the basis of that Mechanical Age which has endowed America with its present wealth and prestige in world affairs. Pennsylvania also has the richest deposits of anthracite in the Western Hemisphere.

Forest resources have always been important. No summit rises above the snow line, and only a few emerge much above the tree line. For the most part their rounded slopes are clothed with dense timber, ranging from the spruce and pine and birch of Newfoundland to the hardwoods of the mid section and southern ranges.

Although the Appalachians are about fifteen hundred miles long, nowhere are they much over a hundred miles wide. Yet they have played an important role in the development of the United States. In colonial times English settlers were restricted to the coastal area. This gave the original thirteen colonies a solidarity and community of interest which explains their successful effort to achieve independence. The mountains, however, are crossed by several river systems which have gouged out notches or passes like the Delaware Water Gap and the Cumberland Gap. Through these gateways immigration penetrated westward, sweeping on until it presented a broad frontage on the Pacific coast.

Unlike the Andes and the Himalayas, the Appalachians are not lofty enough to control moisture distribution in the interior. But their chief peaks are weather breeders, and the southern section, comprising the Great Smokies, has the heaviest rainfall east of the Pacific coast.

From *The Story of Mountains*, by Dr. Ferdinand Lane, Doubleday, 1950.

Appalachian Names

ANN & MYRON SUTTON

Despite the homogenizing effects of jet travel and television, we are still a polyglot nation with delightfully different regional accents and a host of exotic place names. A hiking trip on the AT brings many aural nuances to the attentive ear, and not just from the birds' songs. "Appalachian" sounds different in the south (from about Pennsylvania onward) than it does in the north. Ann and Myron Sutton hiked the entire AT and noted the kaleidoscope of colorful place names Americans have invented, imported or expropriated in the Appalachian region. AT aficionado Robert Reddington wrote that "the name 'Appalachian' is apparently derived from the word 'Appalachee,' a tribe of the Muskhogean Indians who lived in northwest Florida. The tribe's name is said to mean 'people on the other side' (of a river, presumably) in the Choctaw language. . . . The famous Spanish explorer, Hernando de Soto and his party became the first known white men to see as well as to visit the Appalachian Mountains [1539], which were mainly those in North Carolina. He is said to have named these mountains after the Apalachee tribe."

A Special Dignity in Naming

PERHAPS THE BEST INDICATION OF THE CHARACTER OF A LAND AND ITS people is in the names applied to topographic and other physical features. There is a special dignity in naming. Whoever searches for something undiscovered and unnamed, and finds it, thinks first of what or whom he will immortalize by affixing the name of that person or thing to the enduring feature discovered. Names denote what is treasured in a culture, and have a peculiar way of bringing out the humor of the people.

So it is along The Appalachian Trail. The very names of side trails the hiker passes, or topographic features he strides on, or objects he sees in the course of 2,000 miles of trail are rooted in history and legend and folklore.

The A.T. is spiced with names as distinctive and homespun as Sassafras Gap, Panther Creek, Roaring Fork, Buzzards Rock, Dogtail Corners, Cranberry Pond, Music Mountain, Shady Valley, Buttermilk Falls, Devils Den, Breezy Point, and Podunk Brook. There is a point where the Blue Ridge joins the Chunky Gal Mountains. In Georgia, the Trail leads between Blood and Slaughter Mountains. Maine has Mooselookmeguntic Lake; New Jersey, a Wawayanda Mountain; and Tennessee, a Tuckaleechee Cove.

The Trail passes such places as Stink Creek, Gooch Gap, Ekaneetlee Gap, Humpback Rocks, Rocky Row, Run Road, Grout Job, and Lost Spectacles Gap. You can enjoy a side trip to Potato Top, Koiner's Deadening, and Cuckoo Lookout, or take off on the Raccoon Branch Trail, the Asquamchumauke Trail, or the Skookumchuck Trail.

There is a Black Brook and a White Brook; a Straight Mountain and a Bent Arm Ridge; an Angels Rest and a Devils Pulpit.

You can look out over such features as Spy Run Gap, Nesuntabunt Mountain, Umbagog Lake, Jobildunk Ravine, and Ottauguechee Valley. If you wish to cover part of your hike with maps of the United States Geological Survey, you might choose quadrangles by the names of Noontootla and Bashbish Falls.

Devils Fork Gap lies between Big Bald and Big Butt. There are enough unprintable names to fill a booklet, and puzzling ones such as Female Pond, Surplus Pond, Fishin' Jimmy Trail, and Six Husbands Trail.

These names add the final touch to a land that literally breathes with adventures of the past. If he has even half a historian's perception and an adventurer's mind, the hiker sees in the distant valleys those hallowed grounds where men fought against the land, and then for it, then conquered it in more ways than one, and finally submitted to be conquered by it.

Down there, Daniel Boone led his men on a trail to the west. Down there, Davy Crockett was born and Matthew Fontaine Maury played as a boy before going to sea. Morgan fought down there, and Stonewall Jackson led his Confederates into the Shenandoah. Farther north it was Ethan Allen and his band of raiders in Vermont, and the Crawfords who tried to settle in the wild and primitive mountains of New Hampshire. The lands of The Appalachian Trail are the lands of Robert Frost, of Walt Whitman, of Thomas Jefferson.

With memories of men like these the hiker is never alone. One hiker, in fact, spent months on the trail with a backpack of only the barest essentials — and one of these essentials was, to him, a book by Henry David Thoreau.

From *The Appalachian Trail: Wilderness on the Doorstep,* by Ann and Myron Sutton, Lippincott, 1967.

Preserving the Wilderness

GERALD LOWREY, JR.

It was the great British Victorian sociologist-economist Arnold Toynbee who advised that those who refuse to study history are condemned to repeat it. Gerald Lowrey, an admirer of the AT and its founders, took Toynbee to heart and wrote his doctoral dissertation in American Studies about the Appalachian Trail as a cultural symbol, with a careful examination of the history of American concepts of the wilderness as background. Lowrey's work situates AT visionary Benton MacKaye clearly among the romantics who feared that urbanization and secularization would eventually wreck the landscape and weaken the soul. From Lowrey's articulate overview we can also see our own generation as a participant in a continuing debate about the importance of wilderness to the national psyche.

American Ideas of Wilderness

THE CREATION OF THE APPALACHIAN TRAIL WAS STRONGLY INFLUENCED BY changing attitudes toward the idea of wilderness in America. When Benton MacKaye presented his idea for the Trail in 1921, Americans were very supportive of his suggestion to create and preserve a long distance hiking trail through the wild country along the crests of the Appalachian Mountains. By 1920, the preservation of wilderness was viewed by a great many Americans as worthwhile and desirable. However, this high valuation of wilderness has not always been the case. Early in American history, the wilderness was viewed as a hindrance to settlement, an inexhaustible storehouse for raw materials or a godless zone to be exorcised and civilized. The first Europeans to settle in America brought with them Old World views of wilderness. With a bias against the wilderness derived from Classicism, Judaism and Christianity, the early settlers fought against the savagery, godlessness and desolation of the wild American continent. Feeling that they had been given dominion over the earth as the Bible specified, the new inhabitants of America set about clearing the land and reaping the harvest. As early as 1831, Alexis de Tocqueville, who was traveling in the American frontier area of Michigan, observed in his journal that the American pioneer living in the wilderness "only prizes the works of man," while he, as a European, was attracted to the novelty of wild nature. He said that "in Europe people talk a great deal of the wilds of America, but the Americans themselves never think about them; they are insensible to the wonders of inanimate nature and they may be said not to perceive the mighty forests that surround them till they fall beneath the hatchet. Their eyes are fixed upon another sight . . . they . . . march across these wilds, draining swamps, turning the course of rivers, peopling solitudes, and subduing nature."

The American pioneers' bias against wilderness involved two main aspects. On the direct physical level, wilderness represented an obstacle and a threat to their survival. As the first European settlers arrived in America, they left behind the advances of western civilization and encountered an uncontrolled wilderness which was terrifying to them. It was as if the settlers had entered a time machine which stripped away centuries of western civilization and brought them to a land which was as wild and untamed as any that their primitive ancestors had encountered. Wave after wave of pioneers arrived in America and, in pushing the frontier farther westward, they were continually faced with the challenge of physical survival in what they saw as a savage land. Frederick Jackson Turner pointed out that "in this advance, the frontier is the outer edge of the wave — the meeting point between savagery and civilization." Wilderness had to be overcome in order to obtain food and shelter, safety and comfort. A large portion of the early settlers' time was spent in meeting the needs of personal survival in a hostile environment. To the settlers the primeval forests they entered were terrifying and filled with real or imagined dangers. "For the first Americans, as for medieval Europeans, the forest's darkness hid savage men, wild beasts, and still stranger creatures of the imagination. In addition civilized man faced the danger of succumbing to the wildness of his surroundings and reverting to savagery himself" (R. Nash, *Wilderness and the American Mind,* 1973). Consequently, the pioneers were living too close to the growing edge of civilization to appreciate the wilderness. Their approach to wildness was hostile and utilitarian. There was no shortage of wilderness from the settlers' perspective. What was in short supply were the amenities of civilization. The early settlers' goal was to conquer the wilderness and insure survival for family and community.

A second aspect of the American pioneers' bias involved their depiction of wilderness as a "dark and sinister symbol" (Nash 1973). The settlers arriving from Europe shared the idea that wilderness was a chaotic land inhabited by damned souls who lived in a moral vacuum. They accepted the traditional Western notion which equates wild land with moral and physical wasteland. Therefore, the Puritans and other religious frontiersmen saw their efforts at civilizing the land in the context of good versus evil, light versus darkness, order versus chaos. They sought to subdue wilderness not only for personal survival but also for God and nation. "In the morality play of westward expansion, wilderness was the villain, and the pioneer, as hero, relished its destruction" (Nash 1973). The Puritans placed little value on wilderness itself since they sought to carve a garden from the wilds and create a spiritual sanctuary in the savage land. The pioneers felt that they had been given a mandate to impose their will over nature. After all, didn't the Bible spell out in Genesis that God had given man dominion over the earth? . . .

Artists and writers, not pioneers, were the first to point out positive values associated with wilderness. . . . In America, one of the first individuals whose writing gives evidence of the new appreciation of nature was William Bartram. William was the son of John Bartram who had been appointed Royal Botanist to the King of England in 1765. From 1773 to 1777 William Bartram traveled throughout the American Southeast engaged in one of the first efforts to study the native plant and animal life of the region. He made detailed sketches, collected seeds and specimens, described the American Indians he encountered and kept a journal of his travels. After returning to Philadelphia, Bartram edited his journals and in 1791 published a book *Travels Through North and South Carolina, Georgia, East and West Florida, the Cherokee Country, the Extensive Territories of the Muscogulges, or Creek Confederacy, and the Country of the Choctaws*. William Bartram paid close attention to describing the wilderness landscapes he encountered. He valued the wild lands as majestic or awe inspiring, clearly indicating a more sympathetic or Romantic appreciation for the primitive. During one of his trips in the Southern Appalachians, he said: "I began again to ascend the Jore mountains, which I at length accomplished, and rested on the most elevated peak; from whence I beheld with rapture and astonishment, a sublimely awful scene of power and magnificence, a world of mountains piled upon mountains. Having contemplated this amazing prospect of grandeur, I descended the pinnacles" (Bartram 1791). Bartram's *Travels* had a significant impact on European readers. Within a few years of the first printing of the book, "nine European editions appeared in six different languages" (National Park Service). Coleridge, Wordsworth and other Romantic writers read *Travels* and used images, ideas and "echoes" of Bartram's prose in their works. "For the Romantics, Bartram's *Travels* stated all the principles of order — God, man and Imagination — that they also recognized as central. Bartram was an unconscious herald of the new ideas they were about to spread; throughout their careers they consciously echoed his single book." Bartram admired the scenic splendor of wilderness; and in this sense, he was far ahead of his age's standards. Other American writers began to praise the beauty of nature in the early years of the nineteenth century. William Cullen Bryant, for example, included wilderness themes in his poetry. As one of the first major American writers to celebrate wild nature, Bryant contributed to the growing Romantic interpretation of nature. The writings of William Bartram and the Romantic poets helped to idealize nature and to diffuse a more positive valuation of wilderness in America.

Contributing to this slowly spreading wilderness appreciation was the development of a distinctively American national identity centered on a celebration of wild nature. After the United States achieved independence from England, the new nation was faced with a painful realization that it could no longer point with pride to the achievements of Western civilization. Americans began to search for proof of their national greatness. Many citizens took pride in the inventiveness, resourcefulness and material progress of the new nation. Patriots tried to reassure themselves that the future of America would be glorious. However, doubts were bound to surface since the achievements of American writers and artists were negligible when compared to the cultural heritage of the Europeans. "Unlike established, European countries, which traced their origins far back into antiquity, the United States lacked a long artistic and literary heritage. The absence of reminders of the human past, including castles, ancient ruins, and cathedrals on the landscape, further alienated American intellectuals from a cultural identity" (A. Runte, *National Parks and the American Experience*, 1979). Since there were no ancient human accretions on the landscape, American intellectuals and artists turned to the wild landscape itself as the only viable alternative source of pride. One thing that Europe had very little of and America possessed in abundance was wilderness. Monumental wonders of nature such as Niagara Falls, Yosemite Valley, Yellowstone geysers and the giant California redwoods, were pointed to as evidence of America's antiquity and uniqueness. Americans began to feel that they had something valuable to contribute to the culture of the world. "Although Europe's castles, ruins, and abbeys would never be eclipsed, the United States had 'earth monuments' and giant redwoods that had stood long before the birth of Christ. Thus, the natural marvels . . . compensated for America's lack of old cities, aristocratic traditions, and similar reminders of Old World accomplishments" (Runte 1979).

With the rise of the Hudson River School of landscape painting, American nationalists, for the first time, were justified in their cultural chauvinism. This uniquely American genre of landscape painting broke with the traditional European approach and looked directly to nature for inspiration and guidance. Instead of focusing on Old World buildings or ruins, the American painters celebrated wild nature and often showed no trace of mankind on their canvases. Thomas Cole, who is recognized as the founder of the Hudson River School, said in 1836 that "though American scenery is destitute of many of those circumstances that give value to the European, still it has features, and glorious ones, unknown to Europe . . . the most distinctive, and perhaps the most impressive, characteristic of American scenery is its wilderness" (Nash 1973). The Hudson River School searched for meaning in the verities and realities of the natural world. Its artists were advised to give detailed attention to rendering with realism the wild landscapes they encountered. In this way, it was felt that the hidden but ever-present laws of nature found in the wilderness scenes could be best communicated. After Cole's death in 1848, Asher B. Durand, another pioneer in the Hudson River School, painted *Kindred Spirits* as a memorial to Cole. The painting showed Cole and William Cullen Bryant, one of the first American poets to treat wilderness sympathetically, admiring the rugged beauty of a wild mountain gorge. This painting, as well as many others produced by the new American landscape genre, achieved widespread popularity.

One of the first calls for the preservation of American natural areas came from George Catlin. Catlin, as a student and painter of the American Indian, was distressed at the rapid disappearance of the Indians and wildlife from the American plains. He became convinced that a portion of the primitive conditions, which existed prior to the incursions of American settlement, should be preserved. In 1832 he called upon the government to establish a park that would be "a beautiful and thrilling specimen for America to preserve and hold up to the view of her refined citizens and the world, in future ages! A *nation's Park*, containing man and beast, in all the wild[ness] and freshness of her nature's beauty!" (Nash 1973). He was the first American to call on the national government to preserve a portion of the wilderness. It is important to note that Catlin was a product of the settled Eastern cities where his early training was in law and art. He could appreciate the uniqueness of the Western wilderness in contrast to the bustling city life of the East. The Eastern artist, not the Western pioneer, was the first to call for wilderness preservation.

Of all the early American writers advocating wilderness preservation, Henry David Thoreau is perhaps the most important. He not only issued one of the most compelling early calls for preserving America's wild natural environment, but also penetrated the Romantic and nationalistic clichés about wilderness to offer a new philosophical rationale for valuing wilderness within the American cultural context. Thoreau maintained that "in wildness is the preservation of the world." In order to appreciate adequately this extreme statement, it is necessary to understand Thoreau's philosophical attitude toward the role and value of wilderness in America. As a Transcendentalist, he felt that there was a direct correspondence or parallelism between the realm of material objects and a higher realm of spiritual truth. The natural objects of this world were felt to reflect universal spiritual truths. Nature provided a mirror for the higher laws originating from God. By using intuition or imagination instead of rational understanding, an individual could penetrate the outward natural world and achieve insight into universal spiritual truths. Transcendentalism, as a way of viewing the man/ nature relationship, helped spread the idea in America that nature was the proper source of religion. Transcendentalism refuted the earlier notion of the amorality or wickedness of wild country. In fact, the wilderness was seen to be a purer source of universal spiritual truth than the city since wild nature had been less changed by the hand of mankind. Instead of the Puritan fear of the innate evil and sinfulness of human nature which might bring forth the beast in man when faced with the moral chaos of wilderness, the Transcendentalists felt that the human inner spark of divinity might best lead toward moral perfection in the wilderness environment.

Thoreau went beyond the spiritual argument for wilderness to maintain that wilderness was the source of vigor and strength within any human being or culture. He felt that any kind of human greatness was dependent upon the tapping of the primeval vitality of wild nature. He said that "the forest and wilderness" provide "the tonics and barks which brace mankind." It is the essential "raw-material of life" (Nash 1973). Thoreau believed that an individual or a culture became uninspiring, dull and weak to the extent that it lost contact with wilderness. Wilderness symbolized the unexplored and untapped capacities within an individual. The outer wilderness was conducive to the individual's inward journey toward heightened capabilities and achievements.

Thoreau felt that the ideal life drew from both the strength of wilderness and the refinements of civilization. Drawing in a balanced way from both the city and the wilderness brought forth the best in mankind. If it became necessary to choose one place for permanent residence, Thoreau advocated the rural environment. From the rural one could most easily maintain contact with both ends of the spectrum. Prior to Thoreau's arguments for wilderness, most Americans idealized the rural as an escape from both wild nature and over-civilization. Thoreau arrived at his appreciation for the rural by maintaining contact with both the wild and the civil. "The rural was the point of equilibrium between the poles. According to Thoreau, wildness and refinement were not fatal extremes but equally beneficial influences Americans would do well to blend. With this concept Thoreau led the intellectual revolution that was beginning to invest wilderness with attractive rather than repulsive qualities" (Nash 1973). Thoreau's ideas about the spectrum of environments ranging from the wild to the rural to the civilized greatly influenced Benton MacKaye's writings. . . .

Like George Catlin, Henry David Thoreau was concerned with the possible extinction of Indians and wild animals along with the threatened loss of wild natural environments. Thoreau asked: "why should not we . . . have our national preserves . . . in which the bear and panther, and some even of the hunter race, may still exist, and not be 'civilized off the face of the earth'

— our forests . . . not for idle sport or food, but for inspiration and our own true recreation?" (Nash 1973). In 1859, Thoreau advocated the establishment of wilderness areas as preserves or parks by the various townships in Massachusetts. He felt that every township should set aside a primitive forest area of five hundred to a thousand acres as a public preserve. These parks would help preserve a certain degree of primitiveness and wild nature in the towns thereby insuring that all of the forests would not be destroyed in the name of profit and progress. Thoreau broadened the rationale for wilderness protection to include more than the nationalistic and Romantic justifications. He enlisted spiritual, cultural, recreational and other arguments in the defense of wilderness preservation.

Another important person who contributed to the intellectual foundation underpinning the growing movement to preserve wild nature was George Perkins Marsh. His book, *Man and Nature: or, Physical Geography as Modified by Human Action*, was published in 1864 at the height of American optimism that the nation's resources were inexhaustible. He was the first person to challenge the myth of superabundance and call for reform. Marsh pointed out, in thorough detail, that man was involved in a destructive relationship with the land. He found that, contrary to popular belief, nature did not heal itself once it had been dominated and abandoned by mankind. Rather than returning to its primitive diversity and vigor, the land became impoverished, in some cases permanently. Harsh felt that man's actions upset the natural balance and harmony of the environment. The chief reason for this had to do with the mistaken idea that mankind enjoyed dominion over the earth. Marsh pointed out that man was only one link in the great chain of being. As he said, "man has too long forgotten that the earth was given to him for usufruct alone, not for consumption, still less for profligate waste" (G. P. Marsh, *Man and Nature*, 1864). The "chain of being" idea held that all the life-forms were created by God and any given species existed for the sake of the completeness of the whole. All living things had a right to exist. From this perspective, the belief that man had dominion over the earth was seen to be absurd. The proper role for mankind was stewardship of the earth rather than the single-minded pursuit of profit which left a ravaged environment and the possible extinction of species as its legacy to the next generation. Marsh's views were revolutionary at the time when they were first expressed; although, now many of his basic ideas are taken for granted. For many years, George Perkins Marsh was virtually alone among his contemporaries in recognizing the destructiveness of most man-land relationships. He was the first to attempt a scientific examination of man's effect on the environment and in many ways he anticipated the later ecological ideas of John Muir, Benton MacKaye and Aldo Leopold. Marsh's arguments were used to illustrate the economic advantages of wilderness preserves. According to Marsh, forest areas in their natural state, for example, not only served recreational, poetical and spiritual purposes but also helped to control erosion and to regulate stream flow. "Primarily because it made protecting wilderness compatible with progress and economic welfare, Marsh's arguments became a staple for preservationists. Even Romantics recognized their force" (Nash 1973). In addition to the impetus provided by Marsh's writing, the movement to preserve wilderness also drew support from the new landscape architecture profession in America.

A concern with the quality of the scenic environment on human behavior led Andrew Jackson Downing to publish in 1841 *A Treatise on the Theory and Practice of Landscape Gardening Adapted to North America*. The book, which was enormously popular both in America and abroad, stimulated interest in the improvement of the American countryside. It also awakened Americans to the need to improve the quality of their residential areas, and assured Downing of a permanent place as one of the founders of American landscape architecture. "Downing's place in the history of landscape architecture rests also upon two other significant acts of service. It was he who in 1850 found and brought to America the young English architect Calvert Vaux. Seven years later, Vaux asked Frederick Law Olmsted to join him in the competition for a plan for Central Park and the two won. . . .

Frederick Law Olmsted quickly established himself as the leading American landscape architect of his day and spread his views through his able apprentices — perhaps the most notable being Charles Eliot. Eliot, whose father was the President of Harvard, went on to play a key role in the creation of the Greater Boston park system. Meanwhile, Olmsted journeyed to California in 1863 after the first of his several resignations from the Central Park project. He accepted a position with the Mariposa Mining Company as superintendent of their gold-mining properties. While he was in California, he became interested in the Yosemite Valley and the grove of Redwoods near his Mariposa Mining headquarters in Bear Valley. "It was probably at this time that he began to meet men in San Francisco to whom he could talk about a public reservation for the Big Trees of Mariposa and the valley of the Yosemite. . . . He, probably among others, saw that a federal bill in the United States Congress would be the best method of preserving these areas" (E. Stevenson, *Park-Maker*, 1977). The lobbying work of Olmsted and his friends paid off when President Lincoln signed the bill on June 30, 1864, to set aside the Yosemite Valley and the adjoining Mariposa Grove for public use. This Congressional action, withdrawing land from the public domain and ceding it to California for a state park, established the first scenic area in the United States reserved explicitly for permanent public enjoyment. . . . "The writing of a preliminary report on behalf of the Commission logically fell to Olmsted, and in this remarkable paper, presented in 1865, he spelled out for the first time a clear and sensible pattern of sound thinking about the fundamental purposes, social values, and appropriate development of such great scenic areas, then unprecedented as a type of public reservation. His counsel had lasting influence; and the report, though some portions disappeared from sight until recovered in 1952, is one of the great basic documents in the story of American state and national parks" (N. Newton, *Design on the Land,* 1971). Olmsted felt that scenic beauty had a favorable influence on the physical, psychological and spiritual health of mankind; hence, the Yosemite Commission had a responsibility to preserve the natural scenery. He felt that Yosemite should provide a place where people could relax from the tensions of everyday life, enjoy the majesty of nature and return to their homes refreshed and renewed. "Olmsted's ambition was for a new kind of park, a 'wild park' for the people of the future" (Stevenson 1977). . . .

John Muir was another American who saw the value of wilderness. He was an outspoken advocate of wilderness preservation. In fact, as a publicizer of the need for wilderness protection, he was without equal in the late nineteenth and early twentieth century. Muir wrote that "thousands of tired, nerve-shaken, over-civilized people . . . are beginning to find out that going to the mountains is going home, that wildness is a necessity, and that mountain parks and reservations are useful not only as fountains of timber and irrigating rivers, but as fountains of life" (Runte 1979). Muir followed in the footsteps of the great American Transcendentalists, Emerson and Thoreau, with whom he became thoroughly acquainted through his readings as a student at the University of Wisconsin. Most of Muir's writing was done for a didactic purpose. He sought to sell the idea of wilderness and its preservation to the American people. He had about him a crusading air — Muir, the wilderness lobbyist. . . . Muir was one of the first individuals to recognize the ecological connectedness of nature. Like George Perkins Marsh, he felt that all living things were related and that toying with one affected all others to some degree. He said that "whenever we try to pick out anything by itself, we find it hitched to everything else in the universe." For John Muir, the mystery of nature lay in the marvelous order, design and life inherent in each part of the universe.

John Muir founded the Sierra Club in 1892 and served as its President for over twenty years. This club became one of the prime advocates of preserving not only the California Sierras but also wild lands in other parts of the United States. Muir's widely-read articles in *Century* magazine helped lead to the transfer of the Yosemite lands to the federal government for inclusion in a national park in 1890. In 1908 Muir's efforts to preserve the Grand Canyon met with success when President Roosevelt designated the area a national monument. At first Muir joined with Gifford Pinchot and other conservationist foresters in seeking to get new forest reserves (later to be called "national forests") set aside under the 1891 Forest Reserve Act. There was a need to unite to overcome the objections of the lumber, grazing and mining interests who sought to block the creation of protected forest areas. By 1900, Presidents Benjamin Harrison and Grover Cleveland had designated over 34,000,000 acres of forest reserves. But the efforts by Muir and others to establish national parks, national monuments and forest reserves did not guarantee that these areas would, in fact, be preserved and permanently protected. A rift soon developed between those individuals who became known as the "conservationists" led by Gifford Pinchot and Muir's "preservationists." . . .

Pinchot favored the wise use of parks and forest preserves to serve the utilitarian interests of the most people. Only a few hardy individuals would visit the Hetch Hetchy area each year if it remained part of the national park while over 500,000 people would benefit daily from the fresh water of the reservoir not to mention the hydro-electric power generated by the dam. John Muir gave his opinion of the utilitarian approach by using spiritual metaphors: "These temple destroyers, devotees of ravaging commercialism, seem to have a perfect contempt for Nature, and instead of lifting their eyes to the God of the Mountains, lift them to the Almighty Dollar" (Nash 1973). To Muir, wild country had an ability to renew and inspire toil-weary Americans. He felt that entering a national park such as Yosemite was akin to entering a temple where one's spirit, mind and body be refreshed.

The two men, Pinchot and Muir, were engaged in a new version of the old struggle between the pioneer and the Romanticist approaches to nature. Pinchot and those who believed as he did were like the American pioneers who saw the wilderness as a storehouse of raw materials and unused potential. To Pinchot the forest preserves and parks should be managed wisely to attain sustained yield from the resources they contained. If there was grass it should be grazed. If there was timber it should be cut. Muir and the preservationists were the direct descendants of the Romanticists. To them the wilderness was not a storehouse but a paradigm of the proper harmonious relationship between God, mankind and the natural world. The preservationists believed that if we could discover the universal laws inherent in scenes of wild nature and model ourselves after these precepts, then we would be able to contribute to the common good of all mankind. Consequently, preservationists equated wilderness with the spiritual, the aesthetic and the life-ordering. Pragmatic, utilitarian efforts to use the wilderness were equated with anti-religious commercialism.

The receptivity of the American public to the ideas of Muir and his colleagues and the unprecedented popularity of wilderness in the early twentieth century were rooted in significant changes taking place in American life and thought around the turn of the century. The settlement of the country was largely complete. Industries and labor-saving agricultural machines had brought many Americans from the farm to the city. Life in the city, not life on the frontier, became the essential experience of most people. The frontier had almost completely disappeared by 1890 and the remaining wilderness areas were being destroyed rapidly. With life in frontier America fast becoming a distant memory to the citizens of industrial cities, a new appreciation of wilderness developed. "From the perspective of city streets and comfortable homes, wild country inspired quite different attitudes than it had when observed from a frontiersman's clearing. . . . Specifically, the qualities of solitude and hardship that had intimidated many pioneers were likely to be magnetically attractive to their city-dwelling grandchildren" (Nash 1973).

When Frederick Jackson Turner wrote his historical essays in the 1890s on the value of the frontier in developing desirable American traits, the intellectual arguments for protecting wilderness became even more compelling. Although Turner's articles discussed the frontier, it was obvious that the wildness of the country was the essential ingredient in the frontier experience which helped shape our national character. In his article "The Frontier in American History," which first appeared in the September 1896 issue of *Atlantic Monthly*, Turner argued that the American was different and better than the European because "out of his wilderness experience, out of the freedom of his opportunities, he fashioned a formula for social regeneration — the freedom of the individual to seek his own." Turner felt that democracy was a product of the frontier. The rugged individualism, inventiveness, independence and confidence required for frontier living promoted self-government in the American people. He argued that the wild frontier presented the Americans with a clean slate on which to write new combinations of social organization to provide a better life for the nation's citizens. Turner gave the wilderness new value by associating the frontier with essential traits of the American character. He helped change the perception of wilderness "from that of an enemy which civilization had to conquer to a beneficent influence on man and institutions. His greatest service to wilderness consisted of linking it in the minds of his countrymen with sacred American virtues" (Nash 1973). Turner pointed out in the early 1900s that the 1890s were a watershed in the nation's history since it was the first decade in which there was no frontier.

When it became clear that the frontier had ended, many Americans searched for ways to preserve the wilderness influence in modern America. One approach was to set aside wilderness areas for preservation in national parks and forests. Belatedly, many Americans began to appreciate the wilderness values of areas such as Yellowstone National Park which had been established in 1872 to protect the monumental scenery not the wilderness that it contained. John Muir and other preservationists helped encourage this growing public concern for wilderness protection. Theodore Roosevelt took advantage of the popularity of protecting wild areas by designating millions of acres of new forest preserves and new national parks and monuments. "Wilderness camping and mountain climbing became an important part of the widespread 'outdoor movement.' These pursuits had a special appeal to city people, who found in them temporary relief from artificiality and confinement" (Nash 1973). A number of outdoor clubs were organized in the late nineteenth century, and the interest in outdoor recreation, primitive camping and nature study saw a tremendous growth in popularity. "As the antipode of civilization, of cities, and of machines, wilderness could be associated with the virtues these entities lacked. In the primitive, specifically, many Americans detected the qualities of innocence, purity, cleanliness, and morality which seemed on the verge of succumbing to utilitarianism and the surge of progress" (Nash 1973).

By the 1920s the growing public appreciation of the virtues associated with wilderness had helped to create a receptive context for Benton MacKaye's Appalachian Trail idea. MacKaye's suggestion for the creation of the Appalachian Trail both influenced and was influenced by the development of the wilderness idea in America. MacKaye's Trail idea and his related work and writings helped to further the preservation of wilderness—through his work with the Appalachian Trail Conference, his work with the Wilderness Society, his influence on the National Trails and Wilderness Acts and in other areas. Also, MacKaye's debt to earlier advocates of wilderness preservation become[s] readily apparent.

From *Benton MacKaye's Appalachian Trail as a Cultural Symbol*, by Gerald Lowrey, Jr., doctoral dissertation, Graduate Institute of the Liberal Arts, Emory University, 1981.

WALLACE STEGNER

Pulitzer Prize–winning novelist Wallace Stegner was a longtime member of the Wilderness Society. He wrote the following article as a letter to a federal recreation agency, and the piece made its way—on the basis, no doubt, of its beauty and moral fervor—to Secretary of the Interior Stewart Udall, who read it to the Society and shepherded its publication. For all those who would, if called upon, lie down in the path of the bulldozer about to rape the landscape or who would protest the politician's or corporation's funding the bulldozer's rapacious advance, Stegner stands as a quiet, unflappable hero. Unafraid to assert that the wilderness is suffused with mystical qualities, Stegner carries forward the spiritual bloodline of Thoreau and Whitman.

Wilderness and the Geography of Hope

S OMETHING WILL HAVE GONE OUT OF US AS A PEOPLE IF WE EVER LET THE remaining wilderness be destroyed; if we permit the last virgin forests to be turned into comic books and plastic cigarette cases; if we drive the few remaining members of the wild species into zoos or to extinction; if we pollute the last clear air and dirty the last clean streams and push our paved roads through the last of the silence, so that never again will Americans be free in their own country from the noise, the exhausts, the stinks of human and automotive waste. And so that never again can we have the chance to see ourselves single, separate, vertical and individual in the world, part of the environment of trees and rocks and soil, brother to the other animals, part of the natural world and competent to belong in it. Without any remaining wilderness we are committed wholly, without chance for even momentary reflection and rest, to a headlong drive into our technological termite-life, the Brave New World of a completely man-controlled environment. We need wilderness preserved — as much of it as is still left, and as many kinds — because it was the challenge against which our character as a people was formed. The remainder and the reassurance that it is still there is good for our spiritual health even if we never once in ten years set foot in it. It is good for us when we are young, because of the incomparable sanity it can bring briefly, as vacation and rest, into our insane lives. It is important to us when we are old simply because it is there — important, that is, simply as idea.

We are a wild species, as Darwin pointed out. Nobody ever tamed or domesticated or scientifically bred us. But for at least three millennia we have been engaged in a cumulative and ambitious race to modify and gain control of our environment, and in the process we have come close to domesticating ourselves. Not many people are likely, any more, to look upon what we call "progress" as an unmixed blessing. Just as surely as it has brought us increased comfort and more material goods, it has brought us spiritual losses, and it threatens now to become the Frankenstein that will destroy us. One means of sanity is to retain a hold on the natural world, to remain, insofar as we can, good animals. Americans still have that chance, more than many peoples; for while we were demonstrating ourselves the most efficient and ruthless environment-busters in history, and slashing and burning and cutting our way through a wilderness continent, the wilderness was working on us. It remains in us as surely as Indian names remain on the land. If the abstract dream of human liberty and human dignity became, in America, something more than an abstract dream, mark it down at least partially to the fact that we were in subtle ways subdued by what we conquered.

The Connecticut Yankee, sending likely candidates from King Arthur's unjust kingdom to his Man Factory for rehabilitation, was over-optimistic, as he later admitted. These things cannot be forced, they have to grow. To make such a man, such a democrat, such a believer in human individual dignity, as Mark Twain himself, the frontier was necessary, Hannibal and the Mississippi and Virginia City, and reaching out from those the wilderness, the wilderness as opportunity and as idea, the thing that has helped to make an American different from and, until we forget it in the roar of our industrial cities, more fortunate than other men. For an American, insofar as he is new and different at all, is a civilized man who has renewed himself in the wild. The American experience has been the confrontation by old peoples and cultures of a world as new as if it had just risen from the sea. That gave us our hope and our excitement, and the hope and excitement can be passed on to newer Americans, Americans who never saw any phase of the frontier. But only so long as we keep the remainder of our wild as a reserve and a promise — a sort of wilderness bank.

As a novelist, I may perhaps be forgiven for taking literature as a reflection, indirect but profoundly true, of our national consciousness. And our literature, as perhaps you are aware, is sick, embittered, losing its mind, losing its faith. Our novelists are the declared enemies of their society. There has hardly been a serious or important novel in this century that did not repudiate in part or in whole American technological culture for its commercialism, its vulgarity, and the way in which it has dirtied a clean continent and a clean dream. I do not expect that the preservation of our remaining wilderness is going to cure this condition. But the mere example that we can as a nation apply some other criteria than commercial and exploitative considerations would be heartening to many Americans, novelists or otherwise. We need to demonstrate our acceptance of the natural world, including ourselves; we need the spiritual refreshment that being natural can produce. And one of the best places for us to get that is in the wilderness where the fun houses, the bulldozers, and the pavements of our civilization are shut out.

Sherwood Anderson, in a letter to Waldo Frank in the 1920's, said it better than I can. "Is it not likely that when the country was new and men were often alone in the fields and the forest they got a sense of bigness outside themselves that has now in some way been lost. . . . Mystery whispered in the grass, played in the branches of trees overhead, was caught up and blown across the American line in clouds of dust at evening on the prairies. . . . I am old enough to remember tales that strengthen my belief in a deep semireligious influence that was formerly at work among our people. The flavor of it hangs over the best work of Mark Twain . . . I can remember old fellows in my home town speaking feelingly of an evening spent on the big empty plains. It had taken the shrillness out of them. They had learned the trick of quiet. . . ."

We could learn it too, even yet; even our children and grandchildren could learn it. But only if we save, for just such absolutely non-recreational, impractical, and mystical uses as this, all the wild that still remains to us.

It seems to me significant that the distinct downturn in our literature from hope to bitterness took place almost at the precise time when the frontier officially came to an end, in 1890, and when the American way of life had begun to turn strongly urban and industrial. The more urban it has become, and the more frantic with technological change, the sicker and more embittered our literature, and I believe our people, have become. For myself, I grew up on the empty plains of Saskatchewan and Montana and in the mountains of Utah, and I put a very high valuation on what those places gave me. And if I had not been able periodically to renew myself in the mountains and deserts of western America I would be very nearly bughouse. Even when I can't get to the back country, the thought of the colored deserts of southern Utah, or the reassurance that there are still stretches of prairie where the world can be instantaneously perceived as disk and bowl, and where the little but intensely important human being is exposed to the five directions and the thirty-six winds, is a positive consolation. The idea alone can sustain me. But as the wilderness areas are progressively exploited or "improved," as the jeeps and bulldozers of uranium prospectors scar up the deserts and the roads are cut into the alpine timberlands, and as the remnants of the unspoiled and natural world are progressively eroded, every such loss is a little death in me. In us.

I am not moved by the argument that those wilderness areas which have already been exposed to grazing or mining are already deflowered, and so might as well be "harvested." For mining I cannot say much good except that its operations are generally short-lived. The extractable wealth is taken and the shafts, the tailings, and the ruins left, and in a dry country such as the American West the wounds men make in the earth do not quickly heal. Still, they are only wounds; they aren't absolutely mortal. Better a wounded wilderness than none at all. And as for grazing, if it is strictly controlled so that it does not destroy the ground cover, damage the ecology, or compete with the wildlife it is in itself nothing that need conflict with the wilderness feeling or the validity of the wilderness experience. I have known enough range cattle to recognize them as wild animals; and the people who herd them have, in the wilderness context, the dignity of rareness; they belong on the frontier, moreover, and have a look of rightness. The invasion they make on the virgin country is a sort of invasion that is as old as Neolithic man, and they can, in moderation, even emphasize a man's feeling of belonging to the natural world. Under surveillance, they can belong; under control, they need not deface or mar. I do not believe that in wilderness areas where grazing has never been permitted, it should be permitted; but I do not believe either that an otherwise untouched wilderness should be eliminated from the preservation plan because of limited existing uses such as grazing which are in consonance with the frontier condition and image.

Let me say something on the subject of the kinds of wilderness worth preserving. Most of those areas contemplated are in the national forests and in high mountain country. For all the usual recreational purposes, the alpine and forest wildernesses are obviously the most important, both as genetic banks and as beauty spots. But for the spiritual renewal, the recognition of identity, the birth of awe, other kinds will serve every bit as well. Perhaps, because they are less friendly to life, more abstractly non-human, they will serve even better. . . .

These are some of the things wilderness can do for us. That is the reason we need to put into effect, for its preservation, some other principle than the principles of exploitation or "usefulness" or even recreation. We simply need that wild country available to us, even if we never do more than drive to its edge and look in. For it can be a means of reassuring ourselves of our sanity as creatures, a part of the geography of hope.

From "Wilderness and the Geography of Hope," by Wallace Stegner, as reprinted in *Voices for the Earth: A Treasury of the Sierra Club Bulletin,* Sierra Club Books, 1979.

ALDO LEOPOLD

It's a fair guess that in the 1920s, when AT visionary Benton MacKaye was promoting his Appalachian footpath idea, he was also reading the early work of a young, ambitious wildlife and forestry management visionary named Aldo Leopold (born in Iowa, 1887). It was the precious wildness of the Wisconsin and Minnesota north woods, and later the southwestern deserts, that first inspired Leopold to translate practical wildlife management techniques into a philosophical view of society's responsibility for wild places and creatures.

Leopold too, like MacKaye, had read Thoreau, had absorbed from President Theodore Roosevelt the energy of the incipient wildlife-preservation movement, and had committed himself to a career of speaking out for the beautiful and fragile wild world. In line with MacKaye, Leopold wrote, "Recreational development is a job not of building roads into lovely country, but of building receptivity into the still unlovely human mind."

The Ethical Sequence

T HIS EXTENSION OF ETHICS, SO FAR STUDIED ONLY BY PHILOSOPHERS, IS AC-
tually a process in ecological evolution. Its sequences may be described
in ecological as well as in philosophical terms. An ethic, ecologically,
is a limitation on freedom of action in the struggle for existence. An ethic,
philosophically, is a differentiation of social from anti-social conduct. These
are two definitions of one thing. The thing has its origin in the tendency of
interdependent individuals or groups to evolve modes of co-operation. The
ecologist calls these symbioses. Politics and economics are advanced symbioses in which the original free-for-all competition has been replaced, in
part, by co-operative mechanisms with an ethical content.

The complexity of co-operative mechanisms has increased with population density, and with the efficiency of tools. It was simpler, for example,
to define the anti-social uses of sticks and stones in the days of the mast-
odons than of bullets and billboards in the age of motors.

The first ethics dealt with the relation between individuals; the Mosaic
Decalogue is an example. Later accretions dealt with the relation between
the individual and society. The Golden Rule tries to integrate the individual
to society; democracy to integrate social organization to the individual.

There is as yet no ethic dealing with man's relation to land and to the
animals and plants which grow upon it. Land, like Odysseus' slave-girls, is
still property. The land-relation is still strictly economic, entailing privileges
but not obligations.

The extension of ethics to this third element in human environment is, if
I read the evidence correctly, an evolutionary possibility and an ecological
necessity. It is the third step in a sequence. The first two have already been
taken. Individual thinkers since the days of Ezekiel and Isaiah have asserted
that the despoliation of land is not only inexpedient but wrong. Society,
however, has not yet affirmed their belief. I regard the present conservation
movement as the embryo of such an affirmation.

An ethic may be regarded as a mode of guidance for meeting ecological
situations so new or intricate, or involving such deferred reactions, that the
path of social expediency is not discernible to the average individual. Animal instincts are modes of guidance for the individual in meeting such situations. Ethics are possibly a kind of community instinct in-the-making. . . .

In all of these cleavages, we see repeated the same basic paradoxes:
man the conqueror *versus* man the biotic citizen; science the sharpener of
his sword *versus* science the searchlight on his universe; land the slave
and servant *versus* land the collective organism. Robinson's injunction to
Tristram may well be applied, at this juncture, to *Homo sapiens* as a species in geological time:

Whether you will or not
You are a King, Tristram, for you are one
Of the time-tested few that leave the world,
When they are gone, not the same place it was.
Mark what you leave.

From *A Sand County Almanac and Sketches Here and There,* by Aldo Leopold, Oxford University Press, 1949.

APPALACHIAN FOOTPATHS

Dreamers and Doers

ANN & MYRON SUTTON

Appalachian Trail hikers often ask whether the footpath is actually an old Native American trail. In fact it's not, for the native peoples chose more efficient paths at lower elevations to move their warriors and nomadic populations through the wilderness. Nonetheless, the network of Native American wilderness paths was the forerunner of the first trails used by settlers, and those trails in some cases became the paths of roads and highways to follow. Ann and Myron Sutton describe here the ancient woodland paths of native peoples.

Who then were the early trail builders after the Native Americans were displaced? Anyone who has ever bushwhacked through the wilderness or, more likely these days, volunteered on a trail maintenance crew for the Appalachian Mountain Club or a similar organization, knows well that the trail-building pioneers did a mountain of work—and all without chain saws, backhoes or weed trimmers. What inspired the earliest builders of footpaths? Sometimes the love of the woods, sometimes the love of a dollar.

The Adventurers

THERE HAVE PROBABLY ALWAYS BEEN TRAILS OF SOME SORT ON THE LAND surface of what is now North America. Some made by prehistoric animals were probably followed by deer, buffalo, and other animals, and these in turn by the earliest Indians.

European explorers remained in debt to narrow Indian trails for dependable access to the wilderness. Rivers were sometimes unreliable — the water too high or too low, or the surface choked with ice or debris — and rivers did not always go where the explorers wanted to go. On the contrary, Indian trails, like buffalo trails, often existed in dry places where the walking was best.

Ridges, for example. If more rain fell there than in the valleys, it also ran off more quickly. Wind-blown mountain crests were often free of snow in winter, and of leaves and undergrowth at other times of the year. This meant less wear and tear on clothing. A warrior could walk silently on the ridges, and see more land around him, including the distant signs of enemies.

Indian trails were sometimes hardly trails at all. Some were narrow runways through the woods, and others less than that. The Indians shunned such things as blazes; that was a white man's innovation. Making them would have caused delay. The Indian relied upon more subtle guideposts: a broken branch, a scarcely visible footprint, a familiar grove of trees, even the stars.

If you were an Indian, you worried very little about trail maintenance. You built no bridges. You had no conveniently placed log lean-tos. You skirted obstructions, or crawled over them, or fought your way through. You simply left no sign of passage.

The Indian often traveled on hands and knees — out of sheer necessity. And woe unto him who knew not the weather, or sites of bogs and river crossings. These could mean delay, and delay could mean death.

The Indians had hunting paths that led from their own depleted environs to distant concentrations of animals. Their warrior paths connected them with enemies. Where portages and river paths were unavoidable, they grew into networks linking lakes and ponds. A few trails came to be deeply worn and rutted by the moccasins of many travelers. Trade trails, for example, followed routes of least resistance, and came to be lines of Indian commerce. Over them, naturally, rode the early scouts and traders from foreign lands: such trails led to water or salt licks, or to sources of food and materials for clothing.

Archeologists feel that North American Indians, in the days before the horse, traveled far more widely than is generally thought. There are authenticated cases of Indians traveling up to 2,000 miles and being gone for two months or more, on trips to visit friendly tribes. Some Plains Indians are known to have traveled equally far on warlike raids. Phenomenal speeds were not unheard of, either; the Tarahumare mail carrier from Chihuahua to Batopilas, Mexico, ran regularly more than 500 miles a week. *The Handbook of American Indians* tells of a Hopi messenger who had been known to run 120 miles in fifteen hours.

There was, in fact, a network of paths across the continent. One authority lists, for the southeastern United States alone, a total of 125 early Indian trails. The Iroquois of central New York went west to the Dakotas and south to Florida. The Great Warpath extended from the Creek country in what is now Alabama and Georgia to the Cherokee settlements of eastern Tennessee and then divided; a Chesapeake branch led off to Virginia and Pennsylvania and points north, while an Ohio branch led down the New and

Kanawha Rivers to Indian settlements in Ohio and western Pennsylvania. This was not only a path for warriors. It was a route of emigration for no telling how many generations of people.

Other trails utilized by early white emigrants — the Black Fox Trail, the Old Cherokee Path to Virginia, the Catawba Trail, the Tuckaleechee and Southeastern Trail, the Unicoi Turnpike, and Rutherford's War Trace — were likewise "borrowed" from the Indian and helped to determine the social geography of the region. The Warrior Path itself lured many an emigrant from Maryland and Pennsylvania into the newly opened Kentucky and Tennessee regions about 1780. The reason was simple: here was a route through the wilderness that nobody had to fight to open. The distance from Philadelphia to the interior of Kentucky was nearly 800 miles if you went through Cumberland Gap. After the Indians came Thomas Walker, who turned off on the old Shawnee Trail and thence made his way to "Kaintuckee." After him came Daniel Boone, and with that the way was open for "publick travel."

"We start Early & git to Foart Chissel," wrote one of the chroniclers of the time, "whear we git some good loaf bread & good Whiskey."

Settlers and emigrants improved the Indian trails and blazed new ones of their own, continually hacking, felling, clearing and widening the paths. "Come to a turabel mountain that tired us almost to death to git over it," was an understandable complaint.

The hard work wasn't all: "We all pack up & started across Cumberland Gap. About 1 o'clock this day we met a great many people turned back for fear of Indians but our company goes on still with good courage."

Ultimately the trails were widened into roads. The Common Road between Boston and Providence was opened in 1654; the Boston Post Road to New York (now U.S. 1), in 1672. Some were surfaced, a toll was charged, a pike was turned to let in traffic — and the turnpike came into being.

Braddock's Road, the Kentucky Road, the Cumberland Road, the Old Charleston Trail, the Natchez Trace, the Mohawk Trail, the Iroquois Trail, the Connecticut Path, the Kittanning Path, Nemacolin's Path — north and south, the great trails turned into major avenues of communication and access. Some were simply paths of renown or notoriety, as the Trail of Tears followed by the Cherokees upon their removal to Oklahoma in 1838. Some connected with western systems, as for example, the Oregon, California, and Lewis & Clark Trails.

So North America has long had a history of trails through the wild and savage frontier. But then came the change. Stagecoaches, wagons and the pony express called for the making of roads — and when a road was born, a wilderness trail was lost. Walking, what there was of it, was never the same again.

The trails fell into disuse. Now and then a civic organization decried the abandonment of all physical signs of our glorious heritage, but the cries were muffled by the noise of construction gangs obliterating the ruts, burning the old signs, and tearing down the toll cabins and gatekeepers' cottages. All this, of course, was to provide a better way of life, with everything easier and more comfortable than before.

The wonder is that any part of the original trails remain. There are a few — a segment of the Oregon Trail at Scottsbluff, Nebraska; a few yards of the Santa Fe Trail here and there; a scrap of the Wilderness Road through Cumberland Gap. There are attempts to commemorate with auto routes such famous trails as the Benedict Arnold Trail in Maine and the Anthony Wayne Trail in Ohio. But a superhighway, or even a parkway, seems considerably removed from the original sweat and grime and tears and death that were required to cut these paths through the wilderness. About the only remaining place to commemorate and recreate the toil of the pioneers as they slogged along is on the backcountry trails of today.

From *The Appalachian Trail: Wilderness on the Doorstep*, by Ann and Myron Sutton, Lippincott, 1967.

BENTON MacKAYE

Benton MacKaye, the person, is profiled later in this section. Here we have his seminal essay of 1921, published in the Journal of the American Institute of Architects, *proposing for the first time a footpath running the entire length of the Appalachian mountain chain, in itself an audacious idea. But MacKaye proposes even more: by this time, as a still young land-use planner and self-styled social philosopher, he recognized that not only was the western frontier closed, but also the agrarian and even the hands-on industrial life that had required of Americans hard physical labor for generations was fading, evolving into a more sedentary, decidedly urban and, he believed, crowded, uncomfortable and unhealthy way of living.*

The essay recommends a long, continuous footpath in the wilderness, convenient to city dwellers for short hiking trips. MacKaye never envisioned thru-hiking and would have scorned the hasty pace of AT thru-hikers who completely misconstrue his intentions, missing the point of his famous statement of purpose for hiking on the AT: "To walk, to see and to see what you see." He also proposed a series of recreational camps where outdoor play and work could combine in an atmosphere of robust good health. If you hear the echoes of Thoreau's mystic vision of nature and of Teddy Roosevelt's enthusiasm for the restorative qualities of wilderness in all this, you're right.

MacKaye wrote, "Wilderness is two things—fact and feeling. It is a fund of knowledge and a spring of influence. It is the ultimate source of health." If you see the outlines of today's wildlife and forestry management practices, at their best, here too, you're right again.

MacKaye campaigned tirelessly for the establishment of the Appalachian Trail, and though the project became in subsequent decades far bigger and more bureaucratically complex than he imagined it ever could, his guiding spirit and enthusiasm are still cited as the AT's wellsprings of foresight and commitment. The essay was widely quoted and reprinted, and MacKaye himself, a self-propelled whirlwind of public relations activity, sent copies to everyone he could think of who might join the effort to establish the Appalachian Trail. Like a huge oak growing from a tiny acorn, MacKaye's long-distance hiking trail took root, and it is still growing in public usage and national importance today. The following paragraphs are the acorn itself.

An Appalachian Trail: A Project in Regional Planning

SOMETHING HAS BEEN GOING ON IN THIS COUNTRY DURING THE PAST FEW strenuous years which, in the din of war and general upheaval, has been somewhat lost from the public mind. It is the slow, quiet development of a special type of community — the recreation camp. It is something neither urban nor rural. It escapes the hecticness of the one, the loneliness of the other. And it escapes also the common curse of both — the high powered tension of the economic scramble. All communities face an "economic" problem, but in different ways. The camp faces it through co-operation and initial helpfulness, the others through competition and mutual fleecing.

We civilized ones also, whether urban or rural, are potentially as helpless as canaries in a cage. The ability to cope with nature directly — unshielded by the weakening wall of civilization — is one of the admitted needs of modern times. It is the goal of the "scouting" movement. Not that we want to return to the plights of our Paleolithic ancestors. We want the strength of progress without its puniness. We want its conveniences without its fopperies. The ability to sleep and cook in the open is a good step forward. But "scouting" should not stop there. This is but a faint step from our canary bird existence. It should strike far deeper than this. We should seek the ability not only to cook food but to raise food with less aid — and less hindrance — from the complexities of commerce. And this is becoming daily of increasing practical importance. Scouting, then, has its vital connection with the problem of living.

The problem of living is at bottom an economic one. And this alone is bad enough, even in a period of so-called "normalcy." But living has been considerably complicated of late in various ways — by war, by questions of personal liberty, and by "menaces" of one kind or another. There have been created bitter antagonisms. We are undergoing also the bad combination of high prices and unemployment. This situation is world wide — the result of a world-wide war.

It is no purpose of this little article to indulge in coping with any of these big questions. The nearest we come to such effrontery is to suggest more comfortable seats and more fresh air for those who have to consider them. A great professor once said that "optimism is oxygen." Are we getting all the "oxygen" we might for the big tasks before us?

"Let us wait," we are told, "till we solve this cussed labor problem. Then we'll have the leisure to do great things."

But suppose that while we wait the chance for doing them is passed?

It goes without saying we should work upon the labor problem. Not just the matter of "capital and labor" but the *real* labor problem — how to reduce the day's drudgery. The toil and chore of life should, as labor saving devices increase, form a diminishing proportion of the average day and year. Leisure and the higher pursuits will thereby come to form an increasing proportion of our lives.

But will leisure mean something "higher"? Here is a question indeed. The coining of leisure in itself will create its own problem. As the problem of labor "solves," that of leisure arises. There seems to be no escape from problems. We have neglected to improve the leisure which should be ours as a result of replacing stone and bronze with iron and steam. Very likely we have been cheated out of the bulk of this leisure. The efficiency of modern industry has been placed at 25 per cent of its reasonable possibilities. This may be too low or too high. But the leisure that we do succeed in getting — is this developed to an efficiency much higher?

The customary approach to the problem of living relates to work rather than play. Can we increase the efficiency of our *working* time? Can we solve the problem of labor? If so we can widen the opportunities for leisure. The new approach reverses this mental process. Can we increase the efficiency of our *spare* time? Can we develop opportunities for leisure as an aid in solving the problem of labor?

AN UNDEVELOPED POWER — OUR SPARE TIME

How much spare time have we, and how much power does it represent?

The great body of working people — the industrial workers, the farmers, and the housewives — have no allotted spare time or "vacations." The business clerk usually gets two weeks' leave, with pay, each year. The U.S. Government clerk gets thirty days. The business man is likely to give himself two weeks or a month. Farmers can get off for a week or more at a time by doubling up on one another's chores. Housewives might do likewise.

As to the industrial worker — in mine or factory — his average "vacation" is all too long. For it is "leave of absence *without* pay." According to recent official figures the average industrial worker in the United States, during normal times, is employed in industry about four fifths of the time — say 42 weeks in the year. The other ten weeks he is employed in seeking employment.

The proportionate time for true leisure of the average adult American appears, then, to be meagre indeed. But a goodly portion have (or take) about two weeks in the year. The industrial worker during the estimated ten weeks between jobs must of course go on eating and living. His savings may enable him to do this without undue worry. He could, if he felt he could spare the time from job hunting, and if suitable facilities were provided, take two weeks of his ten on a real vacation. In one way or another, therefore, the average adult in this country could devote each year a period of about two weeks in doing the things of his own choice.

Here is enormous undeveloped power — the spare time of our population. Suppose just one percent of it were focused upon one particular job, such as increasing the facilities for the outdoor community life. This would be more than a million people, representing over two million weeks a year. It would be equivalent to 40,000 persons steadily on the job.

A STRATEGIC CAMPING BASE — THE APPALACHIAN SKYLINE

Where might this imposing force lay out its camping ground?

Camping grounds, of course, require wild lands. These in America are fortunately still available. They are in every main region of the country. They are the undeveloped or under-developed areas. Except in the Central States the wild lands now remaining are for the most part among the mountain ranges — the Sierras, the Cascades, and Rocky Mountains of the West and the Appalachian Mountains of the East.

Extensive national playgrounds have been reserved in various parts of the country for use by the people for camping and kindred purposes. Most of these are in the West where Uncle Sam's public lands were located. They are in the Yosemite, the Yellowstone, and many other National Parks — covering about six million acres in all. Splendid work has been accomplished in fitting these Parks for use. The National Forests, covering about 130 million acres . . . are also equipped for public recreation purposes.

A great public service has been started in these Parks and Forests in the field of outdoor life. They have been called "playgrounds of the people." This they are for the Western people — and for those in the East who can afford time and funds for an extended trip in a Pullman car. But camping grounds to be of the most use to the people should be as near as possible to the center of population. And this is in the East.

It fortunately happens that we have throughout the most densely populated portion of the United States a fairly continuous belt of under-developed lands. These are contained in the several ranges which form the Appalachian chain of mountains. Several National Forests have been purchased in this belt. These mountains, in several ways rivalling the western scenery, are within a day's ride from centers containing more than half the population of the United States. The region spans the climates of New England and the cotton belt; it contains the crops and the people of the North and of the South.

The skyline along the top of the main divides and ridges of the Appalachians would overlook a mighty part of the nation's activities. The rugged lands of this skyline would form a camping base strategic in the country's work and play.

SEEN FROM THE SKYLINE

Let us assume the existence of a giant standing high on the skyline along these mountain ridges, his head just scraping the floating clouds. What would he see from this skyline as he strode along its length from north to south?

Starting out from Mt. Washington, the highest point in the northeast, his horizon takes in one of the original happy hunting grounds of America — the "Northwoods," a country of pointed firs extending from the lakes and rivers of northern Maine to those of the Adirondacks. Stepping across the Green Mountains and the Berkshires to the Catskills he gets his first view of the crowded east — a chain of smoky bee-hive cities extending from Boston to Washington and containing a third of the population of the Appalachian drained area. Bridging the Delaware Water Gap and the Susquehanna on the picturesque Allegheny folds across Pennsylvania he notes more smoky columns — the big plants between Scranton and Pittsburgh that get out the basic stuff of modern industry — iron and coal. In relieving contrast he steps across the Potomac near Harpers Ferry and pushes through into the wooded wilderness of the Southern Appalachians where he finds preserved much of the primal aspects of the days of Daniel Boone. Here he finds, over on the Monongahela side, the black coal of bituminous and the white coal of water power. He proceeds along the great divide of the upper Ohio and sees flowing to waste, sometimes in terrifying floods, waters capable of generating untold hydro-electric energy and of bringing navigation to many a lower stream. He looks over the Natural Bridge and out across the battle fields around Appomattox. He finds himself finally in the midst of the great Carolina Hardwood belt. Resting now on the top of Mt. Mitchell, highest point east of the Rockies, he counts up on his big long fingers the opportunities which yet await development along the skyline he has passed.

First he notes the opportunities for recreation. Throughout the Southern Appalachians, throughout the Northwoods, and even through the Alleghenies that wind their way among the smoky industrial towns of Pennsylvania, he recollects vast areas of secluded forests, pastoral lands, and water courses, which, with proper facilities and protection, could be made to serve as the breath of a real life for the toilers in the bee-hive cities along the Atlantic seaboard and elsewhere.

Second, he notes the possibilities for health and recuperation. The oxygen in the mountain air along the Appalachian skyline is a natural resource (and a national resource) that radiates to the heavens its enormous health-giving powers with only a fraction of a percent utilized for human rehabilitation. Here is a resource that could save thousands of lives. The sufferers from tuberculosis, anemia, and insanity go through the whole strata of human society. Most of them are helpless, even those economically well off. They occur in the cities and right in the skyline belt. For the farmers, and especially the wives of farmers, are by no means escaping the grinding-down process of our modern life.

Most sanitariums now established are perfectly useless to those afflicted with mental disease — the most terrible, usually, of any disease. Many of these sufferers could be cured. But not merely by "treatment." They need comprehensive provision made for them. They need acres not medicine. Thousands of acres of this mountain land should be devoted to them with whole communities planned and equipped for their cure.

Next after the opportunities for recreation and recuperation our giant counts off, as a third big resource, the opportunities in the Appalachian belt for employment on the land. This brings up a need that is becoming urgent — the redistribution of our population, which grows more and more top heavy.

The rural population of the United States, and of the Eastern States adjacent to the Appalachians, has now dipped below the urban. For the whole country it has fallen from 60 per cent of the total in 1900 to 49 per cent in 1920; for the Eastern States it has fallen, during this period, from 55 per cent to 45 per cent. Meantime the per capita area of improved farm land has dropped, in the Eastern States, from 3.35 acres to 2.43 acres. This is a shrinkage of nearly 18 per cent in 20 years; in the States from Maine to Pennsylvania the shrinkage has been 40 per cent.

There are in the Appalachian belt probably 25 million acres of grazing and agricultural land awaiting development. Here is room for a whole new rural population. Here is an opportunity — if only the way can be found — for that counter migration from city to country that has so long been prayed for. But our giant in pondering on this resource is discerning enough to know that its utilization is going to depend upon some new deal in our agricultural system. This he knows if he has ever stooped down and gazed in the sunken eyes either of the Carolina "cracker" or of the Green Mountain "hayseed."

Forest land as well as agricultural might prove an opportunity for steady employment in the open. But this again depends upon a new deal. Forestry must replace timber devastation and its consequent hap-hazard employment. And this the giant knows if he has looked into the rugged face of the homeless "don't care a damn" lumberjack of the Northwoods.

Such are the outlooks — such the opportunities — seen by a discerning spirit from the Appalachian skyline.

POSSIBILITIES IN THE NEW APPROACH

Let's put up now to the wise and trained observer the particular question before us. What are the possibilities in the new approach to the problem of living? Would the development of the outdoor community life — as an offset and relief from the various shackles of commercial civilization — be practicable and worth while? From the experience of observations and thoughts along the skyline here is a possible answer:

There are several possible gains from such an approach.

First there would be the "oxygen" that makes for a sensible optimism. Two weeks spent in the real open — right now, this year and next — would be a little real living for thousands of people which they would be sure of getting before they died. They would get a little fun as they went along regardless of problems being "solved." This would not damage the problems and it would help the folks.

Next there would be perspective. Life for two weeks on the mountain top would show up many things about life during the other fifty weeks down below. The latter could be viewed as a whole — away from its heat, and sweat, and irritations. There would be a chance to catch a breath, to study the dynamic forces of nature and the possibilities of shifting to them the burdens now carried on the backs of men. The reposeful study of these forces should provide a broad gauged enlightened approach to the problems of industry. Industry would come to be seen in its true perspective — as a means in life and not as an end in itself. The actual partaking of the recreative and nonindustrial life — systematically by the people and not spasmodically by a few — should emphasize the distinction between it and the industrial life. It should stimulate the quest for enlarging the one and reducing the other. It should put new zest in the labor movement. Life and study of this kind should emphasize the need of going to the roots of industrial questions and of avoiding superficial thinking and rash action. The problems of the farmer, the coal miner, and the lumberjack could be studied intimately and with minimum partiality. Such an approach should bring the poise that goes with understanding.

Finally there would be new clews to constructive solutions. The organization of the cooperative camping life would tend to draw people out of the cities. Coming as visitors they would be loath to return. They would become desirous of settling down in the country — to *work* in the open as well as *play*. The various camps would require food. Why not raise food, as well as consume it, on the cooperative plan? Food and farm camps should come about as natural sequence. Timber also is required. Permanent small scale operations could be encouraged in the various Appalachian National Forests. The government now claims this as a part of its forest policy. The camping life would stimulate forestry as well as a better agriculture. Employment in both would tend to become enlarged.

How far these tendencies would go the wisest observer of course can not tell. They would have to be worked out step by step. But the tendencies at least would be established. They would be cutting channels leading to constructive achievement in the problem of living: they would be cutting across those now leading to destructive blindness.

A PROJECT FOR DEVELOPMENT

It looks, then, as if it might be worth while to devote some energy at least to working out a better utilization of our spare time. The spare time for one per cent of our population would be equivalent, as above reckoned, to the continuous activity of some 40,000 persons. If these people were on the skyline, and kept their eyes open, they would see things that the giant could see. Indeed this force of 40,000 would be a giant in itself. It could walk the skyline and develop its varied opportunities. And this is the job that we propose: a project to develop the opportunities — for recreation, recuperation, and employment — in the region of the Appalachian skyline.

The project is one for a series of recreational communities throughout the Appalachian chain of mountains from New England to Georgia, these to be connected by a walking trail. Its purpose is to establish a base for a more extensive and systematic development of outdoor community life. It is a project in housing and community architecture.

No scheme is proposed in this particular article for organizing or financing this project. Organizing is a matter of detail to be carefully worked out. Financing depends upon local public interest in the various localities affected.

FEATURES OF PROJECT

There are four chief features of the Appalachian project:

1. The Trail

The beginnings of an Appalachian trail already exist. They have been established for several years — in various localities along the line. Specially good work in trail building has been accomplished by the Appalachian Mountain Club in the White Mountains of New Hampshire and by the Green Mountain Club in Vermont. The latter association has built the "Long Trail" for 210 miles through the Green Mountains — four-fifths of the distance from the Massachusetts line to the Canadian. Here is a project that will logically be extended. What the Green Mountains are to Vermont the Appalachians are to eastern United States. What is suggested, therefore, is a "long trail" over the full length of the Appalachian skyline, from the highest peak in the north to the highest peak in the south — from Mt. Washington to Mt. Mitchell.

The trail should be divided into sections, each consisting preferably of the portion lying in a given State, or subdivision thereof. Each section should be in the immediate charge of a local group of people. Difficulties might arise over the use of private property — especially that amid agricultural lands on the crossovers between ranges. It might sometimes be necessary to obtain a State franchise for the use of rights-of-way. These matters could readily be adjusted, provided there is sufficient local public interest in the project as a whole. The various sections should be under some form of general federated control, but no suggestions regarding this form are made in this article.

Not all of the trail within a section could, of course, be built at once. It would be a matter of several years. As far as possible the work undertaken for any one season should complete some definite usable link — as up or across one peak. Once completed it should be immediately opened for local use and not wait on the completion of other portions. Each portion built should, of course, be rigorously maintained and not allowed to revert to disuse. A trail is as serviceable as its poorest link.

The trail could be made, at each stage of its construction, of immediate strategic value in preventing and fighting forest fires. Lookout stations could be located at intervals along the way. A forest fire service could be organized in each section which should tie in with the services of the Federal and State Governments. The trail would become immediately a battle line against fire.

A suggestion for the location of the trail and its main branches is shown on the accompanying map [not included here].

2. Shelter Camps

These are the usual accompaniments of the trails which have been built in the White and Green Mountains. They are the trail's equipment for use. They should be located at convenient distances so as to allow a comfortable day's walk between each. They should be equipped always for sleeping and certain of them for serving meals — after the fashion of the Swiss chalets. Strict regulation is essential to provide that equipment is used and not abused. As far as possible the blazing and constructing of the trail and building of camps should be done by volunteer workers. For volunteer "work" is really "play." The spirit of cooperation, as usual in such enterprises, should be stimulated throughout. The enterprise should, of course, be conducted without profit. The trail must be well guarded — against the yegg-man, and against the profiteer.

3. Community Camps

These would grow naturally out of the shelter camps and inns. Each would consist of a little community on or near the trail (perhaps on a neighboring lake) where people could live in private domiciles. Such a community might occupy a substantial area — perhaps a hundred acres or more. This should be bought and owned as a part of the project. No separate lots should be sold therefrom. Each camp should be self-owning community and not a real estate venture. The use of the separate domiciles, like all other features of the project, should be available without profit.

These community camps should be carefully planned in advance. They should not be allowed to become too populous and thereby defeat the very purpose for which they were created. Greater numbers should be accommodated by more communities, not *larger* ones. There is room, without crowding, in the Appalachian region for a very large camping population. The location of these community camps would form a main part of the regional planning and architecture.

These communities would be used for various kinds of non-industrial activity. They might eventually be organized for special purposes — for recreation, for recuperation, and for study. Summer schools or seasonal field courses could be established and scientific travel courses organized and accommodated in the different communities along the trail. The community camp should become something more than a mere "playground"; it should stimulate every possible line of outdoor non-industrial endeavor.

4. Food and Farm Camps

These might not be organized at first. They would come as a later development. The farm camp is the natural supplement of the community camp. Here in the same spirit of cooperation and well ordered action the food and crops consumed in the outdoor living would as far as practicable be sown and harvested.

Food and farm camps could be established as special communities in adjoining valleys. Or they might be combined with the community camps by the inclusion of surrounding farm lands. Their development would provide tangible opportunity for working out by actual experiment a fundamental matter in the problem of living. It would provide one definite avenue of experiment in getting "back to the land." It would provide an opportunity for those anxious to settle down in the country; it would open up a possible source for new, and needed, employment. Communities of this type are illustrated by the Hudson Guild Farm in New Jersey.

Fuelwood, logs, and lumber are other basic needs of the camps and communities along the trail. These also might be grown and forested as part of the camp activity, rather than bought in the lumber market. The nucleus of such an enterprise has already been started at Camp Tamiment, Pennsylvania, on a lake not far from the proposed route of the Appalachian trail. This camp has been established by a labor group in New York City. They have erected a sawmill on their tract of 200 acres and have built the bungalows of their community from their own timber.

Farm camps might ultimately be supplemented by permanent forest camps through the acquisition (or lease) of wood and timber tracts. These of course should be handled under a system of forestry so as to have a continuously growing crop of material. The object sought might be accomplished through long term timber sale contracts with the Federal Government on some of the Appalachian National Forests. Here would be another opportunity for permanent, steady, healthy employment in the open.

ELEMENTS OF DRAMATIC APPEAL

The results achievable in the camp and scouting life are common knowledge to all who have passed beyond the tenderfoot stage therein. The camp community is a sanctuary and a refuge from the scramble of every-day worldly commercial life. It is in essence a retreat from profit. Cooperation replaces antagonism, trust replaces suspicion, emulation replaces competition. An Appalachian trail, with its camps, communities, and spheres of influence along the skyline, should, with reasonably good management, accomplish these achievements. And they possess within them the elements of a deep dramatic appeal.

Indeed the lure of the scouting life can be made the most formidable enemy of the lure of militarism (a thing with which this country is menaced along with all others). It comes the nearest perhaps, of things thus far projected to supplying what Professor James once called a "moral equivalent of war." It appeals to the primal instincts of a fighting heroism, of volunteer service and of work in a common cause.

These instincts are pent up forces in every human and they demand their outlet. This is the avowed object of the boy scout and girt scout movement, but it should not be limited to juveniles.

The building and protection of an Appalachian trail, with its various communities, interests, and possibilities, would form at least one outlet. Here is a job for 40,000 souls. This trail could be made to be, in a very literal sense, a battle line against fire and flood — and even against disease. Such battles — against the common enemies of man — still lack, it is true, the "punch" of man vs. man. There is but one reason — publicity. Militarism has been made colorful in a world of drab. But the care of the country side, which the scouting life instills, is vital in any real protection of "home and country." Already basic it can be made spectacular. Here is something to be dramatized.

From "An Appalachian Trail: A Project in Regional Planning," by Benton MacKaye, *Journal of the American Institute of Architects,* 1921, as reprinted in *The Appalachian Trail Conference Member Handbook,* 11th edition, Appalachian Trail Conference, 1978.

NATHANIEL GOODRICH

It is somehow comforting to know that much of what is required to build a hiking trail is the same today as it was in 1917, when Nathaniel Goodrich delivered a paper on the subject to the New England Trail Council. We have highly efficient high-tech equipment—from the chain saw to clear the path, to the helicopter to deliver building supplies to remote mountain sites—to ease the burden of our labor today. Nonetheless, as in 1917, so in the 1990s, a great deal of trail-building work is tough hand labor, fueled by high-calorie breakfasts and equally high-octane enthusiasm. Goodrich put in over twenty years of service to the New England trail-building community.

The Attractions and Rewards of Trail Making

OF TRAIL MAKING THERE ARE THREE STAGES. THERE IS DREAMING THE trail, there is prospecting the trail, there is making the trail. Of the first one can say nothing — dreams are fragile, intangible. Prospecting the trail — there lies perhaps the greatest of the joys of trail work. It has a suggestion of the thrill of exploration. No one of us but loves still to play explorer. And here there is just a bit of the real thing to keep the play going. Picking the trail route over forested ridges calls for every bit of the skill gained in our years of tramping. There is never time to go it slow, to explore every possibility. Usually there is one hasty day to lay out the line for a week's work. For a basis there is the look of the region, from some distant point, from a summit climbed last year, perhaps. For a help, there is the compass, but in our hill country we use it little. Partly we go by imperfect glimpses from trees climbed, from blow-down edges, from small cliffs — but chiefly we feel the run of the land, its lift and slope and direction. The string from the grocer's cone unwinds behind — an easy way of marking and readily obliterated when we go wrong. We pay little heed to small difficulties, those are for the trail markers to solve. Only a wide blow-down, a bad ledge, a mistake in general direction, cause us to double back a bit and start afresh.

There is an edge, a tenseness, about this work. The day is a long strain of keen concentration, of quick decisions, of driving through scrub and blow-downs. The unexpected may appear at any minute — an outlook, a spring, a trail. It gets done at length, and so back to camp.

Making trail is the more plodding work; yet it has reliefs and pleasures of its own. Each day, as the gang works along the string line, problems of detail arise. Ours is no gang of uninterested hirelings. If the line makes a suspicious bend, the prospectors have to explain or correct. If it plunges through a blow-down, their intelligence and motives receive pungent criticism, and someone is likely to take a vacation for explorations of his own.

So there is scouting ahead and shouting back, running of trail lines in doubtful places, argument, decision. If we go through the blow-down, we lose much of the limited time in slow cutting; if around, we lengthen the trail. If we go over a hump in the ridge instead of slabbing around, we keep a straighter line, but cause posterity to climb up and then climb down again. And all is complicated by the requirement that the footing shall not be too rough for men under heavy packs.

Decision made, the gang scatters along the line, each to a rod or two, for we find working together is not efficient. Each then finds that he has in little the problems of the general line. He casts ahead over his section, picks his line over a bit of ledge, decides whether to loop around a small snarl of down timber or drive through, aware that few will ever know the difference whatever he decides, but thinking always of the future trail crank who might inspect his work with critical eye. In thick growth where it is impossible to see ahead it is sometimes necessary to break, head down, through a rod or two of country four or five times before the line is right. Then he settles to the job, and the odor of fresh-cut fir arises. He works in a remote little world of his own, a way through lengthening behind him, happy, intent, and oblivious, until quite suddenly he finds a fresh-cut way ahead — and that stint is done. He looks back and sees that it is good, looks forward up the next man's job and sees that it is very bad, shoulders tools and disappears up the line to start another section.

From *Mountain Passages: An Appalachian Anthology,* Robert Manning, editor, Appalachian Mountain Club, 1982.

MICHAEL FROME

For those new to the subject of the history of trail building in the eastern United States, there is hardly a better overview than Michael Frome's (written as the introduction to photographer David Muench's large-format book, his visual hymn of praise to the trail). Frome's numerous books and many articles explore the natural and social history of the American forests. Here he outlines each major step toward the AT we enjoy today: from prehistoric Native American paths to the legislation in 1984 that enabled the National Park Service to delegate to the Appalachian Trail Conference the day-to-day responsibility for maintenance of the trail.

The Evolution of Trails

*T*HE A.T., AS "A FOOTPATH FOR THOSE WHO SEEK FELLOWSHIP WITH THE wilderness," stimulates wonder about the evolution of trails. Indians of the eastern mountains and valleys were superb travelers on ancient boulevards and byroads, which they followed for barter, commerce, hunting, fishing, fighting, and friendship. The most famous of their routes was the Great Indian Warpath, or Warriors' Path, one of the oldest trails on Earth, running through the heart of Appalachia, associated with prehistoric human migrations and even earlier movements of endless herds of buffalo. With settlement, however, came roads, highways, canals, and railroads, transportation arteries of urbanizing society. The old trails were lost and forgotten— until late in the last century and early in this century, when walkers rediscovered old colonial paths and eighteenth-century woods roads through second-growth forests.

The walkers worked together in groups, opening new paths, not to go places, but to get away from them. The Appalachian Mountain Club (AMC), the oldest mountain club in the country, was organized in 1876 "to explore the mountains of New England and adjacent regions and in general to cultivate an interest in geographical studies." In those days, only a few peaks were named, but club members cleared trails, posted signs, and built a network of huts to shelter climbers on the Presidential summits in New Hampshire. The club actively supported passage of the monumental Weeks Law of 1911, by which Congress approved establishment of national forests in the eastern United States, including the White Mountain National Forest, the AMC's own stronghold, which remains to our day the largest, most visited parcel of public land in New England. Here, Mount Washington, elevation 6,288 feet, the highest peak in the Northeast, a huge mountain mass capped with a rock-strewn, windswept summit, is often shrouded in clouds, a hiker's challenge.

Hikers were also active next door in Vermont. In 1910, twenty-three charter members organized the Green Mountain Club. Pledging to "make the mountains play a larger part in the life of the people," they developed the Long Trail, "A Footpath in the Wilderness," extending 255 miles between Canada and Massachusetts; they also built the celebrated Long Trail Lodge at Sherburne Pass, near where the A.T. now swings south to join the Long Trail for more than 100 miles to the Massachusetts border.

In Pennsylvania, a Reading group in 1916 organized the Blue Mountain Eagle Climbing Club, gradually taking responsibility for maintaining 65.5 miles of the A.T. along their favorite mountain and establishing the Rentschler Arboretum near Bernville.

In the South, the Appalachian National Park Association (later renamed Appalachian National Forest Reserve Association) had joined forces with the AMC of New England to campaign for enactment of the Weeks Law. Passage did not come easily. Virtually all the land in the eastern mountains was privately owned and the powerful speaker of the House of Representatives, Joseph G. Cannon of Illinois, insisted, "Not one cent for scenery." Once the law was passed, however, and the Pisgah National Forest was established to protect the highlands of western North Carolina, the advocates turned to organized hiking and mountaineering. In 1920, a southern chapter of the AMC, shortly to become the Carolina Mountain Club, was established at Asheville.

Benton MacKaye worked for the Forest Service from 1905 until 1918. As part of his assignment, he surveyed the forest cover of the White Mountains in developing documentation for the Weeks Law. He was a pioneer in social and land reform. I treasure his slim volume, *Expedition Nine*, published by friends in 1969 as a tribute to Benton on his ninetieth birthday (six years before his death), as a guide to observing, understanding, and appreciating small things in nature and the relationship of community life to them. He retraces the expeditions of a boyhood year within walking distance of his home in Shirley Center, Massachusetts, exploring canyons, forests, and bogs, studying the shape, substance, and relationship of rivers, muskrats, kingfishers, and glacial effects, before reaching the climax of Expedition Number Nine atop Hunting Hill — showing how everyone can be an explorer and naturalist, reaching the highest hill, making their region a place for expeditions. Clearly, when he outlined his concept of an Appalachian footpath, he saw it as more than a recreational resource; he saw it as the means of making each metropolis a place of cultural individuality and unity, based on its own natural setting.

Scattered groups and individuals responded to MacKaye's article of 1921 when it was circulated widely by the Regional Planning Association. Within two years, hiking clubs of New York and New Jersey completed the first section of the Trail in Palisades Interstate Park and published the first edition of the *New York Walk Book,* destined to become a classic. In reviewing the history of the Hudson Highlands, citizen activism is not surprising. During the nineteenth century, settlements on the east bank of the Hudson north of New York City became cities, while on the west, towering prisms of rock, the Palisades, stood largely inviolate, like unconquerable monuments. But, once builders decided to crush those monuments into concrete, shocked citizens on both sides of the river reacted and rallied. In 1900, New York and New Jersey established the Interstate Park Commission to purchase and silence the cliffside quarries. Some of the wealthiest Americans, including J. P. Morgan and John D. Rockefeller, Jr., contributed to the cause, while the Harriman family gave 10,000 acres. Today, Bear Mountain and Harriman state parks constitute more than seventy-five percent of Palisades interstate Park, safeguarding twenty-one miles of the A.T., including its lowest point.

Just as volunteers were marking and cutting the Trail in Palisades Interstate Park, others were doing the same elsewhere. Early in 1925, leaders of the various groups convened the founding meeting of the Appalachian Trail Conference, in Washington, D.C., to coordinate their interests and activities. Major William A. Welch, general manager of Palisades Interstate Park and a prime mover in the Trail project, was elected chairman. Benton MacKaye outlined the philosophy he hoped would guide it. The route was generally accepted as extending 1,700 miles between Mount Washington in New Hampshire and Cohutta Mountain in Georgia, with potential extensions to Katahdin, Maine, and Birmingham, Alabama.

Various public officials and personalities prominent in planning and conservation addressed that first Appalachian Trail conference, but it was clear then, as it has been ever since, that local initiative and leadership count most. MacKaye felt it proper that government agencies administer the land but essential that volunteers, through the clubs, maintain and protect the Trail. That is how it works. Members of more than fifty affiliated clubs contribute time, talent, and muscle to labor on trail design, construction, and relocation and on shelters, huts, campsites, signs, privies, and bridges. Clubs schedule weekend or Sunday trips year-round and publish guidebooks and maps based on first-hand observation, thus ensuring a continuity of freshness and personal discovery.

Following the 1925 conference, individuals and groups along the Trail did wonderful things to advance its goals. In eastern Tennessee, Harvey Broome, Paul Fink, and others established the Smoky Mountains Hiking Club, to be responsible for ninety-seven miles of the Trail across the Smokies, then still wild and little known. Harvey, as a child in Knoxville, had been small and sickly. He told me that to build his strength his parents sent him to stay with an uncle in the Smokies and climb the hills. There he learned to honor the earth. Paul Fink, who lived in Jonesboro, one of the historic settlements of Tennessee, was a patriot of his state and a tireless researcher, who wrote (among other things) a booklet on the names and lore of the Great Smokies. In it, he recalls the list of elevations and names assigned in 1859 to key features of the mountains by Arnold Henry Guyot, the Swiss-born geographer, and how for seventy years it was impossible to reconcile the list with any existing map — until 1930, when Myron H. Avery, chairman of the ATC, discovered Guyot's long-lost map in dusty archives in Washington, solving the mystery at last.

In Virginia, George Freeman Pollock in 1928 welcomed Avery and the other members of the Potomac Appalachian Trail Club (PATC) on their first trip to Pollock's resort, Skyland. Pollock had headed for the hills of the Blue Ridge in 1894, when he was twenty-five, setting up a cluster of tents and inviting cash customers. In time, he built comfortable log cottages. A colorful host, he fed his guests well and led them where no trails existed. In 1926, Congress authorized establishment of a new national park — to be named Shenandoah — in no small measure due to Pollock's persistent promotion. He championed the treasures of the mountains but wanted to share them as well. "Polly" found a friend and ally in Harry F. Byrd, governor and later United States senator (who climbed every peak in the mountains and his favorite, Old Rag, every year), and another ally in Avery. Starting in 1928, PATC held conferences at Skyland and ran yearly trips. In those days, reaching the rustic retreat was an arduous journey, even though only seventy miles from the nation's capital, but PATC members adventurously placed directional signs on trails that Pollock had laid out.

Avery was an industrious trail-blazer, and more: He was founding president of PATC and chairman of the ATC for twenty-one years, 1931 to 1952, tirelessly recruiting, organizing, and writing, determined to complete the Trail even while holding a full-time federal position. Though living in Washington, Avery never forgot he was a native of Maine, site of what became the northern terminus of the A.T., located in superlative backcountry, the largest wilderness in the East, and virtually all of it in large, private holdings. It was a major challenge. His concern, luckily, was shared by Percival Baxter, governor of Maine from 1921 to 1925.

As a young legislator, Baxter felt the magic of Katahdin, rising 5,267 feet in solitary splendor among rivers and lakes of central Maine, and introduced a bill to create a state park. He failed then, and again as governor. On leaving office, however, he determined to act as a private citizen. In 1930, Baxter persuaded the Great Northern Paper Company to sell him 5,960 acres, including most of Katahdin, which he deeded to Maine as a park to be "forever left in the natural wild state." He continued to buy land, increasing the size of the park over the years to 200,000 acres. He resisted proposals in the

1930s to convert the land into a national park, for he wanted it "forever wild." As Baxter wrote the governor and legislature on January 2, 1945:

> Everything in connection with the Park must be left simple and natural, and must remain as nearly as possible as it was when only the Indians and the animals roamed at will through these areas. I want it made available to persons of moderate means who, with their boys and girls, with their packs of bedding and food, can tramp through the woods, cook a steak and make flapjacks by the lakes and brooks. Every section of this area is beautiful, each in its own way. I do not want it locked up and made inaccessible; I want it used to the fullest extent, but in the right, unspoiled way.

The protection of Katahdin in Baxter State Park fulfills the dream of a man ahead of his time. "The dream of a man" — yes, I have written so far only about men. That is true, but now I introduce a woman, as fearless and determined as any of them, who saved a critical fragment of Appalachian highland along the Trail, not for human needs, but for birds.

Rosalie Edge, a wealthy New Yorker, championed birds of prey at a time when they were generally despised. She deplored the wholesale shooting each fall of thousands of migrating raptors, principally hawks, passing over a particular mountain in Pennsylvania. When all other efforts failed, she bought the whole mountain herself in 1934, establishing Hawk Mountain Sanctuary as the world's first refuge for birds of prey. With Maurice Broun . . . who would serve for years as director of the sanctuary, Rosalie Edge campaigned to legally protect the birds and pioneered raptor education. Hawk Mountain today attracts each fall thousands of birders, including A.T. hikers, to observe bald eagles, ospreys, thousands of broad-winged hawks, followed by red-tailed hawks and golden eagles flying along the Kittatinny Ridge raptor-migration pathway.

Individuals and groups during the thirties spurred development and recognition of the Trail. The federal CCC and state agencies contributed manpower to help in construction. Cooperative agreements between the Appalachian Trail Conference and public agencies recognized the value of the A.T. — through eight national forests, two national parks (Great Smoky Mountains and Shenandoah), plus state parks, state forests, and wildlife-management areas — and the Conference's role in maintaining it. The agreements established protective zones, to be kept free of roads and timber-cutting, and authorized a system of campsites and shelters.

In 1937, with the opening of the last two miles on the northern slope of Spaulding Mountain in Maine, the Trail was declared complete as a continuous footpath. Complete, but not, however, safeguarded. Civilization in one form or another pressed against the Trail, requiring unending relocations. The most serious resulted from construction of the Skyline Drive in

Shenandoah National Park and the Blue Ridge Parkway, from Shenandoah to the Smokies, the very mountaintop boulevards MacKaye had warned, and warred, against. Then, after World War II, a plethora of public projects and commercial enterprises — ski resorts, mountaintop subdivisions, highways, clearcut logging — placed much of the Trail in jeopardy.

In 1954, *The Washington Post* published an editorial favoring a parkway along the Chesapeake and Ohio Canal, intruding into a section of the A.T. in Maryland. The proposal stirred the blood of Supreme Court Justice William O. Douglas, a celebrated hiker and wilderness champion. Douglas was a native of Washington state, frail and sickly as a child, who had found strength and purpose in the outdoors. He called the Cascades home but knew the mountains of the world and considered them all sacred. After climbing Katahdin to complete his hike of the A.T., he wrote: "We must multiply the Baxter Parks a thousandfold in order to accommodate our burgeoning population. We must provide enough wilderness areas so that, no matter how dense our population, man — though apartment-born — may attend the great school of the outdoors, and come to know the joy of walking the woods, alone and unafraid."

In what became one of the most famous letters-to-the-editor, Douglas challenged the author of the *Post* editorial to join in hiking the 185 miles of canal towpath between Washington and Cumberland, in western Maryland. "He would [wrote Douglas] get to know muskrats, badgers and fox; he would see strange islands and promontories through the fantasy of fog; he would discover the glory in the first flower of spring, the glory even in a blade of grass; the whistling wings of ducks would make silence of new value for him." Subsequently, Douglas and thirty-six others, the editor included, rode the train to Cumberland and started hiking down the towpath parallel to the Potomac River through rolling pastureland, Appalachian mountain gaps, and historic towns. The Immortal Nine, eight men and a woman, including Bill Douglas, Harvey Broome, and Grant Conway, averaging between twenty and twenty-seven miles a day, completed the full journey in eight days. It was a bit of Gandhian protest, as Douglas called it, and it worked. The parkway plan was discarded.

In 1958, the Georgia Appalachian Trail Club sadly reported the area around Mount Oglethorpe had become thoroughly overdeveloped, necessitating moving the southern terminus of the Trail twenty miles north to Springer Mountain.

In the 1960s, encroachments worsened. "We must open roads for visitors who are growing older. Many can't hike anymore," declared the superintendent of Great Smoky Mountains National Park in 1966, defending his agency's plan to construct a second transmountain highway across the park. It was a terrible idea that stirred nationwide protest. I remember the exciting Save Our Smokies Hike, with more than 550 people of all ages, including the Reverend A. Rufus Morgan, eighty-one and nearly blind, a true apostle of the southern mountains (and a Trail enthusiast until he died at the age of ninety-seven). Happily, the Park Service reviewed its plan and decided the park needed wilderness more than another road.

I remember another protest hike on the Trail. It was two years later, farther north, at Sunfish Pond in Worthington State Forest in New Jersey. I never imagined New Jersey held such natural beauty until I saw it while hiking at High Point State Park, at 1,803 feet the highest point in the state, and at Worthington. The elevation scarcely compares with the Rockies or even the southern Appalachians, but the A.T. in New Jersey leads through pleasing forests and parks, landscaped with pine, hemlock and oaks, laurel and rhododendron, waterfalls and glacial lakes, such as Sunfish Pond. it opens vistas of forests in neighboring New York and Pennsylvania and of the Delaware River winding and bending through its valley, with natural terraces, rolling hills, and mountains rising above it. Portions of this region have remained little changed since the time of the Lenni Lenape Indians and the Dutch, who began settling these environs before William Penn founded Philadelphia.

That was the point. The wealthy Worthington family had conveyed its estate, a wonderland above the Delaware Water Gap, to the state to ensure its lasting protection. But the state turned around and sold the major portion to the New Jersey Power and Light Company for the specific purpose of converting Sunfish Pond into a pumped-storage hydroelectric site, or sump hole, complete with dikes of rock and gravel, to be connected to the Tocks Island dam and reservoir, planned for the river below (but luckily never built).

The defense of Sunfish Pond was led by purely local groups, including the Lenni Lenape League and the Save the Delaware Coalition. One of the prime movers, Casey Kays of Hackettstown, was like scores of others everywhere along the Appalachian Trail, and everywhere in America, everyday people without prominence or portfolio who feel impelled to defend the rights of nature from the greed of technological supercivilization. Casey had researched the sale by the state to power companies in 1961 and wrote thousands of letters alerting people of all kinds to the breach of trust and the beauty of the glacial pond. In 1968, we walked from the campground of Worthington State Forest to the summit of the ridge. Some sections were fairly steep — the elevation rises about a thousand feet — but nothing is ever dull about marching with friends through a wild, mixed forest. I recall people of all ages, many in family groups, almost a steady stream. In the two-day weekend, the total number reached 2,213 — not counting pet dogs, of which there seemed an appreciable, and appreciative, number. It was a tough battle, but the dam was not built, and Sunfish Pond was rescued and later proclaimed a national natural landmark and is now in the A.T. corridor.

That same year, 1968, Congress responded to pleas from hiking organizations to help protect and enhance corridors of America's trails. Legislation had been introduced earlier, starting in 1945 and repeatedly thereafter. Now, at last, the National Trails System Act designated the A.T. as America's first national scenic trail. The National Park Service was assigned principal responsibility (while the Forest Service was given the same mission for the proposed Pacific Crest Trail).

The trouble was that very little funding went with the act, even while encroachments made land acquisition critical. Luckily, a young, energetic congressman, Goodloe Byron of Maryland, a committed Trail hiker, sparked Congress to respond anew with an amendment in 1978. Authorized funding for acquisition was increased from $5 million to $90 million, not simply to buy a pathway but an entire corridor. Unfortunately, despite his strong spirit, Byron died within a year. The Trail would become his lasting memorial.

Following the directives of the act, the National Park Service initiated a massive project of Trail route designation and land acquisition aimed at ensuring continuous and desirable locations buffered from development. The work at times proved difficult. The very notion of big governments taking little people's private property stirred spots of intense opposition, as evidenced in the Cumberland Valley, Pennsylvania, group called CANT (for Citizens Against the New Trail). The project would never have succeeded without the combination of patience plus principle. The solution in Pennsylvania came with acquisition of a greenbelt through the rapidly developing valley, providing the Trail with a new scenic route through its longest valley crossing. A cadre of committed, competent individuals helped, too. I think, in particular, of David Richie, a National Park Service veteran in charge of its A.T. office from 1976 to 1987, a true Trail person, an agent of the grassroots, working for a bureaucracy but never a bureaucrat.

Or, take the case of the Maine Appalachian Trail Club (MATC), a group of volunteers in a state of rugged individualism long resistant to federal intervention on any account. In 1968, the club reviewed its section of the Trail, covering 263.2 miles. Much of it was not in wilderness but on old roads; more than half needed relocation. The state owned 96 miles, with the remainder in private hands, controlled principally by a handful of major pulp and paper companies. Initially, the Maine club, hoping to induce these firms to make gifts of land or easements across their holdings, asked the National Park Service to concentrate its efforts elsewhere. That approach seemed to work, particularly when Maine passed its own Trails Act in 1973, including the A.T. prominently in the Maine Trails System, and when 1978 land-use legislation delineated a 200-yard buffer zone. But the largest portion of unprotected miles along the *entire* Trail was still in Maine, still subject to degradation. The turning point came in 1983, when the Park Service was asked to make direct acquisition. Another break came late that year, with the Park Service's delegating to the Appalachian Trail Conference authority for the management of the Trail lands and authority in turn being delegated to thirty-one local clubs, such as MATC.

David Field, University of Maine forestry professor and MATC president for ten critical years, starting in 1977, sparked an incredible program of land acquisition for preservation, the best because it was local, based on responsible citizen activism. The Trail corridor in Maine, the wildest part of the entire A.T., is now virtually complete. When the hiker enters Maine and passes through Mahoosuc Notch, he or she can look forward to tramping on to Katahdin through unbroken forests, across rugged mountains, passing clear brooks, ponds, within sight of wildlife, and with lots of distance between road crossings. The Trail corridor in Maine soon will embrace a total of more than 43,000 acres, including almost 31,000 acres of federal land administered for the National Park Service through the Appalachian Trail Conference. David Field made sure it happened, even while insisting it's been an all-club effort. To be sure, 400 MATC members build trail, signs, and steps of rock and log, tend campsites and privies, publish the *Guide to the Appalachian Trail in Maine,* and face plenty of challenge in developing and maintaining the relocated sections.

Over the entire length of the A.T., the Park Service, in coordination with the Forest Service and individual states, has acquired more than 2,500 separate parcels of land covering more than 141,000 acres, either through direct purchase, condemnation, or easements that leave productive farmland and woodland in private ownership. Where there is no feasible alternative, occasional short sections still follow sidewalks through towns, but no longer must the hiker compete with motor traffic on paved roads.

Growth in Trail popularity and problems inevitably led to growth and change in the Appalachian Trail Conference as well. In 1972, the conference moved from a townhouse office it shared with the Potomac Appalachian Trail Club off Dupont Circle in Washington, D.C., to headquarters of its own at Harpers Ferry, West Virginia, fittingly within a few minutes of the Trail crossing of the Potomac River. In 1975, Paul Pritchard, formerly a recreation resource planner in Georgia, became the second full-time executive director. Little did anyone realize that, two years later, Pritchard's old boss in Georgia, Jimmy Carter, would appoint him to a key position at the Department of the Interior, assistant director of the Bureau of Outdoor Recreation, where he would continue his involvement in advancing the Trail project.

In 1984, the conference structure stretched anew, to meet the delegation of responsibility from the National Park Service for day-to-day management of Park Service land in eleven of the fourteen Trail states. That arrangement is unprecedented, but it makes sense: placing people who know best and care most in charge.

From *Uncommon Places,* photographs by David Muench, introduction by Michael Frome, Appalachian Trail Conference, 1991.

GUY & LAURA WATERMAN

Benton MacKaye and the two subsequent leaders who took the helm of the Appalachian Trail Conference in the first decades of its life—Arthur Perkins and Myron Avery—receive a close, admiring treatment here by Guy and Laura Waterman. The Watermans' magnum opus, Forest and Crag: A History of Hiking, Trail Blazing, and Adventure in the Northeast Mountains, *makes great fireside reading for anyone curious about the details and the stories associated with the outdoor life in New England.*

All the biographers of the AT's founding fathers agree on one thing: there never would have been an Appalachian Trail had it not been for the single-minded devotion to the goal these three leaders brought to the task. The analogy to climbing a difficult mountain on a hot day is certainly apt. There were differences in philosophy, strong contrasts in personal styles, and more than once exchanges of blistering letters and memos. Somehow, the work went forward, almost as if with its own momentum.

On the Trail's Founding Fathers

THE ONE BIG SUPERTRAIL WAS INEVITABLE. BY AROUND 1920 PROMOTER James Taylor was hawking "blueprints" of a Quebec-New York City trail. Prof. Will Monroe was extending that to the Delaware Water Gap. Forester William Hall was musing at public meetings about linking up with the southern Appalachians. Trail-cutter J. A. Allis was mapping connections between Vermont and Harriman Park. Philip Ayres, Allen Chamberlain, and Albert Turner were all mulling over the idea. The Appalachian Trail from Maine to Georgia awaited only the right person to give the word in the right place. The surprise was that the person and place were both completely outside the Northeastern trail community as we have been watching it develop.

BENTON MacKAYE

Benton MacKaye was born in the urban confines of Stamford, Connecticut, on March 6, 1879. When he was nine, the family moved to Shirley, Massachusetts, 30 miles west of Boston, where he found wooded hills to roam. He and his childhood buddies formed a secret society called the Rambling Boys' Club. It is tempting to suggest that MacKaye's original concept of the purpose of the Appalachian Trail could scarcely be better summarized than by the stated purpose of the Rambling Boys' Club of around 1890:

To give to the members an education of the lay of the land in which they live, also of other lands, taking in the Geography, Geology, Zoology, and Botany of them.

Monadnock was the first mountain that MacKaye climbed. As a Harvard freshman, he made his first trip to the White Mountains in 1897. The summer after graduation (1900) he and classmate Horace Hildreth embarked on an extended hike through the Green Mountains, starting at Haystack on the southern end and working their way by trails, wood roads, cart paths, bushwhacks, and back roads across low land and high, over Stratton to Killington, and on northward as far as Mansfield — virtually the Long Trail-to-be ten years before Taylor had his vision. Thus a yen for long-distance hiking was part of MacKaye from his college days. Three summers later the concept of linking existing trail systems together was added to his fermenting ideas when he worked under James Sturgis Pray, scouting how to link the AMC's Mount Carrigain Trail to Waterville Valley. . . . Further study at Harvard gave MacKaye a degree in forestry in 1905, the year that Gifford Pinchot organized the U.S. Forest Service. MacKaye went to Washington, D.C., to work for Pinchot, who immediately sent him back up to the White Mountains to survey the forests — part of the groundwork for the White Mountain National Forest. During the 1910s MacKaye worked in Washington for the Forest Service and the Department of Labor, and his ideas on conservation, land use, and regional planning continued to evolve.

In Washington MacKaye grew into a "dignified, affable philosopher with the ever-present pipe clamped firmly between his teeth." He became one of those large-scale, imaginative thinkers whose vague idealism and facile way with words and ideas may change the world but are the nemesis of more precise thinkers or practical doers. At one agency he was provided with "an upstairs cubbyhole where he welcomed anyone in for a 'pow-wow'" Here he would sit, smoke his pipe, and think, except that

once a week, he'd come downstairs to the staff meeting and pep up the others with new ideas and diagrams and imagination, and then disappear upstairs again.

One perceptive MacKaye-watcher called him a "walking anachronism," in that he was

a nineteenth century New England reformer strayed into the Jazz Age. His political radicalism partook of pre-Marxist utopian socialisms, bucolic and spiritual, rather than the urban, gritty proletarianism of this century.

The modern reader looking at his articles, speeches, and reminiscences, is struck with the continental sweep, the glittering generalities, the quasi-mystical epigrams, the frequent minor errors of fact, arranged against an overall vision that stirs the imagination even now and changed forever the walker's world of 1921.

In late June 1921 MacKaye began noting down ideas for what he alternately called an "Appalachian Trail" or an "Appalachian Skyline." On July 10 he visited a friend, Charles Harris Whitaker, editor of the *Journal of the American Institute of Architects*, who introduced him to a community planner named Clarence S. Stein. The three men spent the day spinning philosophical notions, and Whitaker suggested that MacKaye put down in an article his idealistic ideas about the use of the Appalachian skyline. The piece appeared in the October 1921 issue.

MacKaye's original vision was much more than just an Appalachian Trail. It was a utopian plan "to develop the opportunities — for recreation, recuperation, and employment — in the region of the Appalachian skyline." With the trail and shelters along it, MacKaye imagined a series of "community camps" of one hundred acres or more, where families could live simply and cheaply, engaging in various pursuits of self-improvement; and ultimately the development of "food and farm camps" providing "permanent, steady, healthy employment in the open. " All this was to provide "a sanctuary from the scramble of every-day worldly commercial life." In later rhetoric, he portrayed the trail as designed "to preserve the primeval environment" and called on hikers to "organize a Barbarian invasion," first assaulting and capturing (through the AT) the ridgeline, to protect it from civilization, and then working downward: "Cabins and trails are but a line of forts." Thus, and much more, ran the grand vision.

With a product worth pushing, MacKaye began to introduce himself and his idea to the Northeastern hiking community. Heretofore MacKaye had been on the fringe of that community: as an occasional hiker and an interesting ideas-man, he had formed friendships with Allen Chamberlain and a few other prominent outdoors leaders in the region. These contacts were a good start. But he had not been active in any of the regional clubs or trail-building projects. Now he sought out influential leaders to sell them on the Appalachian Trail. He attended his first NETC meeting in 1921, where he talked with Albert Turner and Arthur Comey, both fellow global thinkers and long-trail proponents. Over the winter, in Cambridge, he conferred with Allen Chamberlain and with his old mentor, Sturgis Pray. In March, Stein introduced MacKaye to a newspaperman in New York whom Stein thought might be helpful: Ray Torrey. Four days later, in Flushing, he reviewed his dreams and schemes with Boy Scouts impresario Dan Beard.

In Torrey, of course, MacKaye won an invaluable ally. A "Long Brown Path" column soon appeared, providing "the first big broadside newspaper account" of the AT idea. On April 6, 1922, at the City Club in New York, Torrey brought Stein and MacKaye to the same dinner table with Major William Welch and J. A. Allis. MacKaye's vision perfectly suited the action plans of those two eminently practical doers: Welch was looking for trails to lay out through Harriman Park, and Allis had already been working on connecting that park with the Long Trail. From this meeting was launched the first concrete plan for the initial section of trail explicitly built as part of the Appalachian Trail. That summer Torrey and Allis scouted the route and stimulated the New York Appies (including a young trail worker named Murray Stevens) to begin cutting it.

MacKaye — like James Taylor, a celestial dreamer who left the dirty work to other hands — was off to Washington and more conferences. He also hit the banquet circuit in 1923, with talks to the NETC and a Bear Mountain Conference of New York trail workers. Finally, on March 1-3, 1925, he spoke at a specially convened meeting in Washington, held under a name that was to stick around from then on: the Appalachian Trail Conference.

The first Appalachian Trail Conference established a vehicle for getting the Appalachian Trail out of the hands of the global thinkers and into the hands of the doers. Except for what Torrey and Allis had achieved in New York, the trail was not making physical progress. The Community Planning Committee of the American Institute of Architects, chaired by Stein, had made some vague plans for building the trail, but it lacked the necessary contacts with real-life trail-builders. Allis was bogged down with his plans for eastern New York. MacKaye and Torrey attempted to enlist the support of the chairman of the Taconic State Park Commission, Franklin D. Roosevelt, without substantive success. MacKaye continued to spin his ideas at meetings, but the trail was not moving across the hills.

At the first meeting of the ATC, Major Welch was elected chairman but did not throw his proven talents for action into the AT. For another year or two, the trail plan drifted along without action. By 1926 it was "practically moribund."

ARTHUR PERKINS

The turning point came with the entry of two new men. The first was Judge Arthur Perkins of Hartford, Connecticut. Perkins had climbed the Matterhorn as a youth but otherwise had devoted himself to a law career until he was well along in his fifties. By then a distinguished barrister, Perkins began to give some time to latent outdoor interests. In 1923 or 1924 he spent the summer in Chocorua, New Hampshire, climbed that peak several times, and became a devoted hiker. By 1925 he was involved in trail work and was named to fill a New England vacancy in the ATC. In 1926 he was scouting possible routes both in his own state's northwest corner and, during a vacation at York's Twin Pine Camps, in the state of Maine. In 1927 he became trails chairman of the AMC's Connecticut Chapter. By the end of that year he was in very active touch with Welch and Torrey, pushing suggestions at them about the future course of the AT all up and down the East. Largely at his instigation, a second Appalachian Trail Conference was called in Washington on May 19-20, 1928. By this time Major Welch was ready to step down as chairman. Perkins was appointed, first, chairman of a committee on reorganization, and then, in late 1928, chairman of the ATC, succeeding Welch. During the late 1920s, Judge Perkins roamed up and down the trail corridor, enlisting workers, forming Appalachian Trail clubs, and plotting specific routes. Practical leaders began to emerge in specific localities. These were the true heroes of the Appalachian Trail, which in the end was built from the bottom up by those men who took on a section of perhaps fifty miles in length and got the job done. But the leader who, more than any other, originally found and motivated them was Judge Perkins.

MYRON AVERY

Among the trail groups that Judge Perkins encouraged to organize was the Washington-based Potomac Appalachian Trail Club, formed in 1927. The key figure in this outfit was a young maritime lawyer named Myron Avery. Though but twenty-seven years old, Avery seemed interested in the trail and a capable and effective organizer. Perkins asked him to serve as assistant chairman. With the work finally moving forward, and as the date for the Appalachian Trail Conference of 1930 approached, Perkins was stricken with an illness from which he never recovered; he died in 1932. Avery was made acting chairman for 1930, then chairman in 1931, and occupied that post in name and deed for the next twenty-two years.

If Benton MacKaye was indispensable to the creation of the Appalachian Trail, so was Myron Halliburton Avery. Two less compatible characters could scarcely be conjured. It is not surprising that they did not get along. Against MacKaye's rambling, pipe-smoking, airy visions, Avery displayed a pragmatic, no-nonsense dedication to results.

From *Forest and Crag: A History of Hiking, Trail Blazing, and Adventure in the Northeast Mountains*, by Guy and Laura Waterman, Appalachian Mountain Club, 1989.

Attitudes and Inclinations

MILES JEBB

While the equipment required for long-distance hiking has evolved enormously over the past century, the attitudes backpackers bring to the trail have changed as well. The results are mixed, according to the trail-tested British writer and walker Miles Jebb, whose hiking books describe long rambles through the Thames valley and the South Downs in England. Jebb sees the backpack, or rucksack, as a reflection of the walker's attitudes and intentions. After tasting the hiking experience on America's Appalachian Trail, Jebb recognized that not all walkers and hikers are stamped from the same mold, that indeed the typical North American long-distance backpacker brings some special attitudes and behaviors with him, or her, to the trail.

Backpackers

THE DIFFERENCES BETWEEN THE LONGER-DISTANCE WALKERS OF TODAY AND those of the past can be probed by a close examination of the use of the backpack, for the backpack has come to assume a centrality in the walking experience that it seldom had in the past. We have seen how many forms of long-distance walking were undertaken by people who carried very little beyond the clothes they wore. The pedestrian tourers moving from inn to inn typically carried only a change of underclothes, shaving kit and a couple of books, as well as perhaps some food and drink for the day, all stuffed into a small satchel. The ramblers and others on day trips didn't even carry a satchel but just put their gloves and sandwiches into their coat pockets. Englishmen walking in poorer countries or mountainous areas always assumed there would be others to carry their loads for them, and this is how it still is on luxury trekking holidays in the Himalayas or the Andes. But even when walkers did need to carry heavy loads the weight on their back was often peripheral to their general outlook and their expectation of the walk, a burden which had to be borne with the resignation of a mule or a donkey. This was true not only of soldiers but also of various voluntary walkers, such as the tramps of the Stephen Graham tradition or the walkers in mountains and hills who increasingly dispensed with porters and guides. John Ball, the first editor of the *Alpine Guide,* created something of a precedent in the Alps when in the 1840s he strode down the scorching Italian valleys bearing his own pack, and he was followed in time by a geometrical progression of rucksacked figures who found their way into remote places the world over.

The rucksack itself was deemed to be an advance on its predecessors, such as the two-shoulder-strapped knapsacks or haversacks (all words of German origin, incidentally; *haver* is the oats which cavalry carried for their horses, while *knapp* means close fitting and *ruck* means back). It was of Norwegian design and its merits were that it was capacious and framed and belted so that some of the weight was taken off the shoulders and shifted to the waist. Into its canvas cavity the rucksack brigade stowed their extra sweaters, blankets, primus stove and tins of bully-beef, sausages, butter, beans or whatever, and set forth with monstrous loads of 60 lb or more. The type is nicely satirised in Pat McManus's book *A Fine and Pleasant Misery:*

> The rule of thumb for the old backpacking was that the weight of your pack should equal the weight of yourself and the kitchen range combined. Just a casual glance at the full pack sitting on the floor could give you a double hernia and fuse four vertebrae. After carrying the pack all day, you had to remember to tie one leg to a tree before you dropped it. Otherwise you would float off into space. The pack eliminated the need for any special kind of ground-gripping shoes, because your feet would sink a foot and a half into hard-packed earth, two inches into solid rock.

The trouble was that the rucksack, though in some respects an improvement, was not only heavy in itself but was slung right down at the small of the back, thus weighting the body unnaturally and taking no advantage of the line of the backbone. It had quite escaped the attention of these modern men that primitive men and women the world over were accustomed to carry heavy loads either on their heads or at any rate with the use of a tump-line or head-strap, thus bringing into play the powerful muscles of the neck as well as the entire thrust of the spine. But then, the full significance of the backpack had escaped them also.

The heavy-duty backpack, as we now see it, is a symbol of self-sufficiency, and its bearer is proclaiming a message just as explicit as when clothes told of class distinctions. He is saying that he can travel without the help of anyone and, even if he is using his backpack for ordinary travel, at least that he is fit and able to walk when necessary within an urban environment. Once he is out in the country his pack tells us he is prepared for any eventuality — a change in the weather, an unforeseen delay, a sudden accident. The backpack is to the hill walker what the rope or axe is to the climber: a badge of intent, a membership card to a confraternity. At car-parks on the edges of the hills the backpacker is immediately distinguishable from the ordinary rabble of Sunday five-milers and, while they are joking and chattering and slamming the car doors, he is quietly gazing at the hills with a faraway look in his eyes.

He has taken great care what to put in his pack, selecting items with close attention to weight, taking or discarding according to experience in lengthy evening sessions at home with the aid of a check-list and the kitchen scales. He may have ultra-light 'new wave' items such as freeze-dried foods and vapour-barrier clothing, as well as his lightweight down-filled sleeping-bag, hoop tent, mini-stove, first-aid kit and pocket camera; and, as a result, his pack is much lighter than his father's was. But this consciousness of weight, this meticulous preparation, is just what makes the backpack more significant to him. With it he can be entirely alone in the wilderness. No need, as in the past, to live off the land to some extent, to collect brushwood for an open fire, to gather wayside herbs or fruit or fungi — practices that anyway are frowned on in many places. No need, therefore, to go to pre-arranged campsites: the night can be spent anywhere, with water perhaps the only further requirement. No need for companions. He is self-contained, able to be alone with nature though not subject to her. The backpack is his home, as much part of him as the shell of the tortoise. It is like a little house, for inside it are his bedroom, kitchen, clothes-cupboard and all other furniture and housekeeping items. When he leaves it, for example to take a side-trip up some hill, he feels exposed, vulnerable, worried, like a child away from mum. His backpack is smart, brightly coloured and clean-cut. It is cleverly designed and, though not actually on the head or attached to it, lies high above the shoulder-line. It is a source of pride, and all the little day-packs on the backs of the shorter-length walkers pay tribute to it, like small sailing boats saluting a tall-ship ocean racer: every walker feels he must carry at least something on his back. Only in the remoter parts of poorer countries, where to carry a burden on your back is to betray disgraceful poverty, do local people regard the backpacker with the same sort of contempt as was once accorded to the pedestrian tourers.

Whatever the merits of the backpack it brings with it a serious penalty in that the pure physical pleasure of walking is inevitably lessened when one has to carry any extra weight, on one's back or elsewhere. The joy of walking derives from the co-ordinated rhythm of the upright body, unencumbered by dead-weight of burdens, free-flowing and perfectly balanced. Even the lightest of backpacks has the effect of slightly impeding that flow, slightly upsetting that balance. The heavy packs, however well designed, force the body forward so that the head has to be held up to look ahead and the arms dangle in front like those of an ape. The added pressure on the legs tires them unnaturally and forces them down at each pace flatfootedly. Knees, hips and shoulders start to ache prematurely. The walk becomes an ordeal long before it would without the pack, and from the outset it is an exercise in which the legs protest at their handicap instead of rejoicing in their strength. Top-heaviness has to be counteracted, lack of agility to be anticipated. Footfalls have to be watched extra carefully, slipperiness has to be treated very cautiously. All the same, there is a special sort of satisfaction in walking with a heavy pack, a feeling of superiority over less-burdened walkers. Some hikers put stones into their packs for fitness training, others like to test their maximum weight-carrying capabilities. Volunteers taking summer provisions up to the hiking huts in the White Mountains of New Hampshire boast of carrying loads of over 150 lb for several hours. Besides, there are all the challenges and rewards of camping, the intermissions and destinations of the hike. But none of these are strictly speaking walking pleasures so much as pleasures which involve walking.

The nonchalance and frugality of earlier walkers are now seldom found, and safety first is the order of the day. The dire warnings issued to leaders of youth groups or adventure trainees, which should certainly be absorbed as a matter of course by serious mountain walkers, are often taken in an absurdly exaggerated sense by those just out for a two-hour walk on a sunny afternoon. To get wet is regarded as a dangerous misfortune, a likely prelude to pneumonia, and so everyone is clad in showerproofs or waterproofs often when there isn't a cloud in the sky, and many are the articles and discussions about the qualities of new materials like gore-tex and polypropylenes. Such excessive caution has earned a rebuke from the great populariser of fell walking in Britain, Alan Wainwright. In *Fellwanderer* he writes, "You are not making a date with death. You are not making a technical excursion into space. You are going for a walk, that's all, no different from all the other walks except that there is more up and down and the way is likely to be rougher." Another instance of this obsession with safety is the garish colours, the luminous scarlets and oranges, worn in the belief that if lost or stuck the wearer will be more easily found. Already in his mind, one feels, is the vision of the arrival of the mountain rescue team, the summoning of the helicopter, the winching-up of the stretcher, the arrival at the hospital. Sharp in his denunciation of those who make audio intrusions in the wild, whether with transistors or even shouts or singing, he is blind to his own visual intrusion. Such is the typical backpacking walker of today, in some ways so much more sensitive to and appreciative of the wilderness than were his predecessors, in other ways so much more insulated from uncertainty and adventure.

What is dominant in the backpacker's mind as he advances across the moorland or through the forest in insulated self-sufficiency? Like his predecessors he feels the spell of nature, but some aspects of it strike him more forcibly. The silence, for one: in his normal life he is constantly bombarded by sound — speech on the telephone or TV, music on the transistor or car radio. Assuming that he is not one of those who are so hooked on sound that they are plugged into their Walkmans throughout the hike, or unlucky enough to be walking in an area where low-flying aircraft or helicopters are active, the silence will come to him as a shock.

From *Walkers*, by Miles Jebb, Constable, 1986.

MICHAEL LANZA

Day-hikers on the Appalachian Trail now number over 4 million per year. In a group this large, "diverse" may be the only word to describe who they are. But those who hike the entire trail, in one year or over several, stand out from the crowd not only for their perseverance but for other less obvious reasons, too. Backpacker *magazine put writer Michael Lanza to the task of interpreting data about the thru-hikers, gleaned mostly from the research of interviewer Roland Muesser (who did the entire trail himself in 1989). Another storehouse of thru-hiker data is the Appalachian Trail Conference, which keeps careful notes about the hikers, almost all of whom register their thru-hike with the ATC headquarters in Harpers Ferry, West Virginia, and many of whom write a thru-hike report for the ATC when the adventure is done.*

A Breed Apart:
Appalachian Trail Thru-Hikers

YOU HAVE YOUR "YUPPIES" (YOUNG UPWARDLY MOBILE PROFESSIONALS), your "dinks" (double income, no kids), and your "baby boomers," all levels of the social strata that demographers have spent untold dollars and years analyzing and trying to understand.

Now a nomadic breed that had managed to evade census takers and transcend statistical profiles has finally been cornered by social scientists. "Thru-hikers" are at last being culturally defined.

While thru-hiking the Appalachian Trail in 1989, Roland Muesser, 66, conducted in-depth interviews with fellow long-distance trekkers. He convinced 137 of the 190 people he met along the way to answer questionnaires regarding their "trail histories." He restricted his sample to "serious" hikers, those who had been on the trail at least a week or two. The survey group ranged in age from 20 to 68. One hundred of the participants were men and 37 were women.

Here's what Muesser, a hiker and retired physicist from Mountain Lakes, New Jersey, found.

• The thru-hikers surveyed thought about the trip an average of 10 years before hitting the trail. Ten percent had contemplated the hike for 35 years before getting around to it, and 6 percent had given it virtually no thought before starting out. "The longest was 61 years, a man who talked as a small child about being taken on the trail," Muesser says, adding that he eventually made his hike after retiring.

•The average successful thru-hiker logs about 1,000 preparatory miles on other trails before setting out on the AT. A surprising 19 percent hadn't hiked at all. "They were totally inexperienced, not even a night in the woods. There was a wide range (of experience). The most experienced hiker had hiked about 10,000 miles. But there was one who said that before the hike he could hardly get from the bed to the coffee maker in the morning."

•A person's physical condition at the onset of the hike affects performance for just the first 30 days, and after that it doesn't matter. "The trail is the only real training for the trail," he says.

•Of the 100 men and 37 women surveyed, there was no difference in physical performance between the sexes, although women tended to carry packs that weighed a slightly higher percentage of their body weight than those that the men carried.

•The body weight of the men at the start of the trek ranged from 120 to 240 pounds, with an average of 162 pounds. Women were between 110 and 180 pounds, averaging 140 pounds. During the thru-hike, women retained more of their body weight than men, losing an average of 12 pounds, or 6 to 8 percent of their mass. The average male lost 17 pounds, or 10 to 15 percent of his body weight. "The bigger you are, the more weight you lose in percentage as well as in pounds," Muesser says.

•Another intriguing male-female observation: "Men on the trail, it appears, are much more apprehensive about snakes than women."

•While gender might not affect performance, age eventually does. Muesser found no appreciable difference in performance from age 20 to 60, but saw a sharp drop after 60. "And there are practically no thru-hikers over 70."

•Sixty percent of those interviewed made the entire hike the year they started. Ten percent did the trail in stages during two or more years, including one person who took 50 years to finish. Another 10 percent spent one or two weeks on the trail but didn't complete it. About 20 percent just "dropped out."

•A half dozen of the hikers traveled north to south.

•Twenty to 30 percent of those hikers in the survey group kept journals.

•The most successful thru-hikers are those who are naturally introspective and less social, although many said it was the people experience that was the most memorable part of the trail.

"The most important insight all this has given me is that it's not necessary to be an athlete or do special training to [thru-hike the AT]," observes Muesser, who's planning to write the "definitive" book on AT thru-hikers. "A number of people who have not trained properly and who make mistakes somehow are successful at this. The important word here is commitment. A large percentage of thru-hikers said they wanted to do the trail and were confident they could. It's kind of an egalitarian victory."

From *Backpacker*, December 1993.

PART TWO
VOICES ALONG THE TRAIL

Remote for detachment,
narrow for chosen company,
winding for leisure,
lonely for contemplation,
the Trail leads not merely north and south
but upward to the body, mind and soul of man.

—Harold Allen,
an Appalachian Trail hiker in the 1930s

THE SOUTH

Georgia, North Carolina, Tennessee, Virginia, West Virginia

Amicalola Falls, on the trail to Springer Mt., Georgia.

Northerners think of the South as hot, not cold. Southerners think of the North as cool, not sweltering. New Englanders think of their landscape as mountainous, rugged. They ignore Clingman's Dome and several other peaks in the southern Appalachians that are taller than most mountains in New England. An AT hiker in the southern highlands needs to forget all such assumptions.

There is a Cherokee injunction—sty-u!—that means "Be strong!" Every hiker heading northward from the AT's southern terminus on Springer Mt. in northern Georgia needs the help of this good wish and serious warning. Whether the trail runs uphill or down, the southern section, especially from Georgia to southwestern Virginia, is one tough hike. By the time the AT hiker reaches New Jersey, summer's heat may be oppressive. In the early spring, when thru-hikers leave Springer Mt., they may well trudge through snow and will certainly sleep through frosty nights. They won't have to wait until their autumn arrival at Maine's Mt. Katahdin to encounter winter face-to-face.

There are distinct features of an AT hike in the South. Botanically there is more variety in the Smoky Mountains of North Carolina and Tennessee than anywhere else in the East. The rhododendron of Virginia's Blue Ridge is in a class by itself. The dogwood of the Deep South is hard to find north of Connecticut. The lilting drawl of people encountered in southern AT trailside towns is a sure hint as to where you are, as are the red-eye gravy and biscuits served on every in-town breakfast plate.

Oddly, the southern AT offers stark contrasts, too. Consider a passage through the nation's most popular National Park (Great Smoky Mts.), whose shelters and trailhead parking lots are overtaxed by a tourist tidal wave. We once saw a clutch of women in spike heels "hiking" the AT from Newfound Gap in the park. They didn't get very far, and by the time we reached Charlie's Bunion, a rocky precipice a few miles to the north, we had the mountains and sky to ourselves. Here, and at dozens of other points in the southern Appalachians, such as photogenic McAffee Knob in Virginia, hikers lose themselves in rapt contemplation of the vast green valley undulating westward from the base of the mountains, a vision early pioneers, hungry for farmland, found intoxicating. And in the National Forests of North Carolina, Tennessee, and Virginia, there are long, isolated sections of the AT where no one but serious hikers and the occasional black bear use the trail.

It's a good thing Virginia is so beautiful, for it's the longest state on the trail, too: over 400 miles of footpath. For relief, the shortest state, in AT terms, follows immediately: West Virginia, where the highlight is the headquarters of the Appalachian Trail Conference in historic Harpers Ferry, home of the archive that supplied many selections in this book. In the ATC bookstore there is a massive raised relief map of the entire Appalachian Trail. If you need convincing that hiking 2,100-plus miles can take six months of one year or pieces of several years, this map will do it.

THE APPALACHIAN TRAIL IN
GEORGIA, NORTH CAROLINA, TENNESSEE

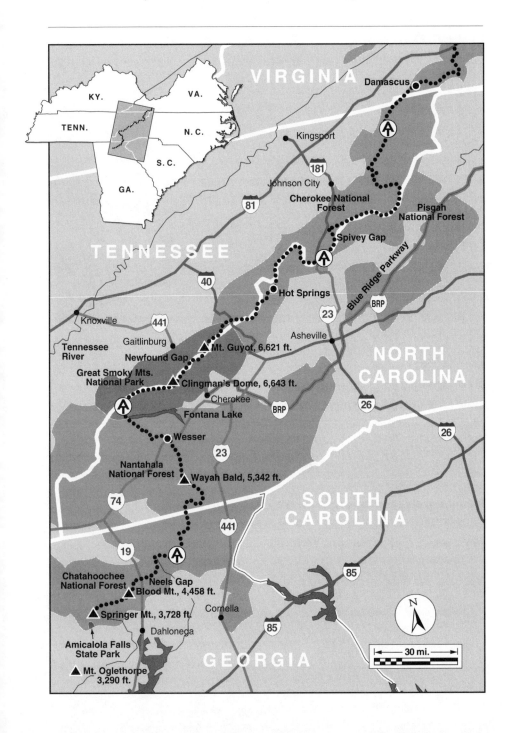

GEORGIA

Blooming shadbush and cumulus clouds, Blood Mt., Georgia.

Trail miles: 75.4

Trail maintenance: Georgia AT Club

Highest point: Blood Mt., 4,461 ft.

Features: Springer Mt. (3,728 ft.), southern terminus of the AT. Rugged wilderness, few towns, high elevation, lovely flowering plants (dogwood).

Parks, forests, and nature preserves: Amicalola Falls State Park, Chattahoochee National Forest, Vogel State Park

Most intriguing names on the trail: Chattahoochee, Slaughter Gap, Blood Mt.

Trail towns: Suches, Dahlonega, Helen, Hiawasee

JAMES DICKEY

As a terminus for southbound AT hikers, Springer Mt., Georgia, represents Mecca. As the launching point for northbounders, it's an odd place to have the official start because just to get there requires a challenging hike through Amicalola Falls State Park. Poet James Dickey, born in Atlanta, renders his climb of the mountain in words but without reference to the AT. Nonetheless, every hiker who passes by this way will know what the effort is all about. Many times honored, Dickey has won the National Book Award (for his collection Buckdancer's Choice)*, and he hit the big time with his novel* Deliverance *(which went to Hollywood).*

Springer Mountain

Four sweaters are woven upon me,
All black, all sweating and waiting,
And a sheepherder's coat's wool hood,
Buttoned strainingly, holds my eyes
With their sight deepfrozen outside them
From their gaze toward a single tree.
I am here where I never have been,
In the limbs of my warmest clothes,
Waiting for light to crawl, weakly
From leaf to dead leaf onto leaf
Down the western side of the mountain.
Deer sleeping in light far above me

Have already woken, and moved,
In step with the sun moving strangely
Down toward the dark knit of my thicket
Where my breath takes shape on the air
Like a white helmet come from the lungs.
The one tree I hope for goes inward
And reaches the limbs of its gold.
My eyesight hangs partly between
Two twigs on the upslanting ground,
Then steps like a god from the dead
Wet of a half-rotted oak log
Steeply into the full of my brow.
My thighbones groaningly break

Upward, releasing my body
To climb, and to find among humus
New insteps made of snapped sticks.
On my back the faggot of arrows
Rattles and scratches its feathers.

I go up over logs slowly
On my painfully reborn legs,
My ears putting out vast hearing
Among the invisible animals,

Passing under thin branches held still.
Kept formed all night as, they were
By the thought of predictable light.
The sun comes openly in
To my mouth. and is blown out white,

But no deer is anywhere near me.
I sit down and wait as in darkness.

The sweat goes dead at the roots

Of my hair: a deer is created
Descending, then standing and looking.
The sun stands and waits for his horns

To move. I may be there, also,
Between them, in head bones uplifted
Like a man in an animal tree
Nailed until light comes:
A dream of the unfeared hunter
Who has formed in his brain in the dark
And rose with light into his horns,
Naked, and I have turned younger

At forty than I ever have been.
I hang my longbow on a branch.
The buck leaps away and then stops,
And I step forward, stepping out

Of my shadow and pulling over
My head one dark heavy sweater
After another, my dungarees falling
Till they can be kicked away,
Boots, socks, all that is on me
Off. The world catches fire.
I put an unbearable light
Into breath skinned alive of its garments:
I think, beginning with laurel,

Like a beast loving
With the whole god bone of his horns:
The green of excess is upon me
Like deer in fir thickets in winter
Stamping and dreaming of men
Who will kneel with them naked to break
The ice from streams with their faces
And drink from the lifespring of beasts.
He is moving. I am with him

Down the shuddering hillside moving
Through trees and around, inside
And out of stumps and groves
Of laurel and slash pine,
Through hip-searing branches and thorn
Brakes, unprotected and sure,
Winding down to the waters of life
Where they stand petrified in a creek bed
Yet melt and flow from the hills
At the touch of an animal visage,

Rejoicing wherever I come to
With the gold of my breast unwrapped,
My crazed laughter pure as good church-cloth,
My brain dazed and pointed with trying
To grow horns, glad that it cannot,
For a few steps deep in the dance
Of what I most am and should be
And can be only once in this life.
He is gone below, and I limp
To look for my clothes in the world,

A middle-aged, softening man
Grinning and shaking his head
In amazement to last him forever.
I put on the warm-bodied wool
The four sweaters inside out,
The bootlaces dangling and tripping,
Then pick my tense bow off the limb
and turn with the unwinding hooftracks,
in my good, tricked clothes,
To hunt, under Springer Mountain,
Deer for the first and last time.

From *Poems 1957–67* by James Dickey, Wesleyan University Press, 1978.

COLIN FLETCHER

Surfeited as we are today with publications about the "how-to" side of hiking and camping, we may forget that this tsunami of information is relatively new. When Colin Fletcher's Complete Walker *appeared in the late 1960s, it established itself as* the *source, a kind of* Joy of Cooking *for the outward bound. Fletcher was also one of the first minimalist long-distance walkers, traversing California deserts, the Grand Canyon, and the north-south length of his native Great Britain with his pack weight pared down to the fewest ounces possible. En route he meditated on every piece of equipment and on every technique a hiker would ever need. Fletcher was tough as nails but gentle as a clown. His hard-earned hiker's wisdom and his wit have never been surpassed.*

Weight and
How Far Can I Expect to Walk in a Day?

Weight

When planning the house on your back, the weightiest matter is weight. The rules are simple:

　　1. If you need something, take it.

　　2. Pare away relentlessly at the weight of every item.

In paring away you will find that if you look after the ounces the pounds will look after themselves. Any good sports store that specializes in back-packing equipment will list in its catalogue the weight of each article to the nearest ounce, and will also keep an accurate arm scale handy. When shopping in other stores I often take along a postal scale and weigh every item like gold dust. I still like to remember the bewilderment of one sales damsel when I produced my scale and insisted on comparing the weights of two rival pairs of jockey shorts.

I find that the paring process never ends. At home, such foods as raisins that come in cardboard containers set repacked in plastic bags. At the start of a trip, margins and unneeded areas are trimmed off maps. And when I'm laboring along under a knee-buckling load I'm never really happy until I've eliminated the last eliminable fraction of an ounce. Once or twice, in really phrenetic moments, I've even found myself tearing the labels off tea bags.

Unfortunately it seems impossible to predict just what your load will be for a given trip. No matter how carefully you plan, you have to wait for an answer until you hoist the fully-furnished pack onto your back on the first day. The only thing you can be sure of is that it will weigh more than you had hoped. If you want a meaningful figure, don't rely on the way the pack feels; get it onto a trustworthy scale. And memorize the reading. When it comes to talking about the loads they carry, lamentably few backpackers seem to restrict themselves to confirmed, objective, unembroidered fact.

Men (or women),* such as Himalayan Sherpas, who have toted huge loads all their lives, can carry almost their own weight all day long. And even a half-way-fit, fully citified man can pack very heavy loads for short distances, such as canoe portages. Again, people whom I trust implicitly talk of having to carry eighty or one hundred pounds or even more on slow and painful approach marches of five or ten miles at the start of mountain-climbing expeditions. But this kind of toil is hardly walking, in our sense. The heaviest load the average man can carry with efficiency and enjoyment for a long day's walking seems to vary within rather wide limits, bur a rough guide would be "up to one third of body weight." Naturally, this figure assumes an efficient pack frame and a reasonably fit and practiced body. Practiced, mark you. The only way of getting used to heavy loads is to pack heavy loads.

One of the few occasions on which I have weighed my pack, operationally stocked, was at the start of the two-month journey I made through Grand Canyon. Then, with a week's food supply and two gallons of water, the pack turned the scale at 66 1/2 pounds. At the time I weighed 194 rather flabby pounds (twenty more than I did at the end) and the load felt appallingly heavy. But the start is always the worst of it. Each day you use up not only food but also such items as stove fuel and toilet paper. And beyond each refill point the water diminishes steadily, hour by hour. By the end of my first week in Grand Canyon, when I took an airdrop of food beside a big rainpocket in the rock, my pack must have weighed less than thirty pounds. And that made a tremendous difference.

It always does. People often say, "I guess you get so used to the pack that after a while it doesn't worry you any more." But only when the load falls below forty pounds can I sometimes forget it. At fifty I can't. At sixty it always feels desperately heavy. At 66½ it just about takes the joy out of walking. And short sidetrips with no load on my back are always like running into the sea after a hot and bothersome day in the city. . . .

There is one question that seems to haunt almost all inexperienced hikers when they are planning a trip:

How far can I expect to walk in a day?
For most kinds of walking, the question is wrongly put. Except along flat, straight roads, miles are just about meaningless. Hours are what count.

Naturally, there is a connection—of sorts. I have only once checked my speed with any accuracy, and that was more or less by accident. It was during my summer-long walk up California. One afternoon I followed the

*Everything I have to say in this book about men applies equally to women. Well, almost everything. And almost equally.

Atchison, Topeka and Santa Fe for nine arrow-like miles into the desert town of Needles. It so happened that I began at a mileage post and I checked the time and jotted it down on my map. I traveled at my normal speed, and I recall no difficulty about stepping on ties (as so often happens when you follow a railroad track), so it must have been straightforward walking on a well-banked grade. I took a ten-minute halt at the end of the first hour; and exactly one hour and fifty-five minutes after starting I passed the six-mile mark. I would guess that this three-miles-per-roughly-fifty-minutes-of-actual-walking is about my norm on a good level surface with a pack that weighs, as mine probably did that day, around forty pounds. In other words, seven hours of *actual walking* are roughly the equivalent of a twenty-mile day on the flat, under easy walking conditions.

But cross-country you will rarely come close to twenty genuine miles in seven hours. Even on good trails, two miles an hour is probably good going. Over really rough country the average can fall below half a mile. The nonsense that hikers commonly talk about mountain miles walked in one day is only equaled, I think, by the drivel they talk about loads.

But if you now ask the amended question, "How many hours can I expect to walk in a day?" it remains difficult to give a straightforward answer. The thing is seamed with variables. On any given day—provided you are well rested and not concerned with how you will feel next morning—you can, if you are fit and very powerfully motivated, probably keep going most of the twenty-four. But what really matters in most cases is what you are likely to keep up, fully laden, day after day. Even a rough estimate of this figure demands not so much a grasp of arithmetic as an understanding of human frailty. I have published elsewhere a table representing a typical day's walking on the desert half of my California trip—a day on which, beset with all the normal and quite fascinating temptations of walking, I pushed tolerably hard, though not even close to my limit. Mildly amended to fit more general conditions, the table may help to explain the difficulties of computation:

	Hours	Minutes
Walking, including ten-minute halts every hour	7	
Extension of half the ten-minute halts to twenty minutes because of sights, sounds, smells, ruminations, and inertia		30
Compulsive dallying for photography and general admiration of the passing scene—4 2/7 minutes in every hour		30
Photography, once a day, of a difficult and utterly irresistible object (this will seem a gross overestimate to non-photographers, an absurd underestimate to the initiated)	1	

	Hours	Minutes
Conversations with mountain men, desert rats, eager beavers, or even bighorn sheep	1	
Cooking and eating four meals, including tea	3	30
Camp chores		30
Orthodox business of wilderness traveler: rapt contemplation of nature and/or navel		30
Evaporated time, quite unaccountable for		30
Sleep, including catnaps	8	59
Reading, fishing, additional rest, elevated thinking, unmentionable items, and general sloth		1
Total	24	

From *The Complete Walker: The Joys and Techniques of Hiking and Backpacking*, by Colin Fletcher, Knopf, 1968.

EARL SHAFFER

For some time the only one of his kind, Earl Shaffer was the first person to walk the entire length of the AT in one season (April 4–August 5, 1948). In his day the trail began at Mt. Oglethorpe in Georgia. Choosing to go south to north set a precedent for thousands of would-be thru-hikers. Shaffer the diarist is as minimalist as is Shaffer the hiker. We read here his post-hike ruminations about what worked and what didn't and notes from his first few days. The notion of hiking the AT without detailed contour maps and guidebooks seems unthinkable today, but Shaffer was a tough and determined man with a goal clearly in mind. He made it to Mt. Katahdin, the northern terminus of the AT, which he "ascended . . . in leisurely fashion" in early August, having maintained a highly respectable pace.

Trail Diary, 1948

Equipment

Mountain Troop Rucksack (stripped of non-essentials): Marine Corps Poncho; Air Corps Rainhat; Mountain Troop Cookkit (2 nesting kettles, frying pan, with dish, cup and spoon added); Hand axe; One quart Canteen; Blanket (cut down with zipper added); Burlap Sack (acquired along the way); Sheath Knife; Pocket Knife; Waterproof Matchbox: Sewing Materials (thread, awl, needles); Toilet Articles (Straight razor, Barbasol, soap, tooth brush, washcloth); Camera (Retinna); Misc. Items in Ditty Bag; 2 T-shirts (replaced once); Navy Sweater (Replaced later by sweatshirt); Regular Shirt; 2 Pr. Mountain Cloth pants (one replaced once); 2 Pr. Part Wool Socks (Replaced twice); Russell "Birdshooter" boots (resoled twice).

Food

STAPLE—Cornmeal, oatmeal, flour, baking powder, salt, brown sugar, shortening, raisins, canned or powdered milk, tea or coffee.

OCCASIONAL—Powdered soups, canned soups, canned stews, spaghetti with meat balls, vienna sausage, jerked venison, potatoes, onions, wheat bread, candy bars, pancake mix, baking chocolate, bologna, dried beef, rice, cereals, fresh liver, canned fruit, fresh fruit.

All food, except initial supply, obtained at stores in the general vicinity of the Trail route.

General Observations

Weather troublesome with much cold rain. However, this kept snakes and insects to a minimum, Trail generally passable to good with some bad spots. Marking spotty in some sections. Existing shelters in fair to excellent condition generally.

The trip was planned and executed to have no exact schedule, but to be completed in approximately four months. Since some parts of the Trail were likely to be impassable or nearly so, I reckoned only on maintaining the approximate route.

Due to an error on the part of the mail service at York, I didn't receive a quantity of literature in time and was forced to set out with nothing but road maps to go by. This resulted in errors and straying from the Trail. By the time I received these pamphlets, I was already through the most difficult terrain and decided to continue without Guidebooks.

Such of the Guidebooks as I have seen seem too tedious and detailed regarding the trailway itself. My belief is that they should be simplified, retaining the maps, background about points of interest and details about unusual turns of the Trail etc.

For extended trips like mine, the Guidebooks are too cumbersome. I would prefer a set of contour maps, marked with shelters, springs and streams, points of interest, and nearby towns. Had such a set been listed among available publications, I would have been delighted to send for it. As it was, I did fairly well on roadmaps, and Park Service Maps obtained from Rangers.

The trip was a wonderful experience, even though the weather was often terrible. I feel that the Appalachian Trail is a very worth while project and is a credit to those who built it.

This report is brief and at times somewhat vague, mainly due to lack of information prior to starting and the turbulent weather conditions encountered which discouraged the taking of notes. In addition the signs designating place names were often missing or defaced, especially in the south. Ignorance of the location of shelters was particularly unfortunate since some of the leantos were off the trailway far enough to be unnoticed when fog reduced visibility to a few yards. Progress was very hectic, accordingly, until I reached Tapoco and obtained a map of the Smoky Park section. Words fail to describe adequately some of the hardships undergone during prolonged rainstorms and alternating cold spells. Gradually the Trail become a seemingly endless venture so that I was probably the most amazed of all when I finally reached Trail's end. I often pondered whether the difficulties provided me with the impetus to carry me along.

I am sorry that I cannot present to the Appalachian Trail Conference a record of a trip exactly planned and perfectly executed. I strayed at times and in getting back failed to cover every bit of the Trail route. Several times I found the Trail practically non-existent and was forced to bushwhack. Occasionally, as in the White Mountains, the A.T. was not specified on signs and I followed the wrong loop. However, I did maintain the approximate route and covered more distance than a precise trip requires.

In many respects my trail methods and camping techniques were in line with recommendations of Appalachian Trail Conference literature, though I differed in not setting aside rest days and in travelling alone. There is a good explanation for the latter. I had a very capable and congenial pardner who was killed in the war and I have never found another. His allegorical name for me is Lone Brave, and rightly so, for I would much rather take the risk of a lone expedition than chance a questionable companion. But I wouldn't have gone alone, in any event, had I not had varied experience in camping under diverse conditions including all seasons of the year. The risks involved require it.

To lessen the danger from poisonous snakes I wore nine inch boots, which also tended to prevent sprained ankles. I started early from the south to avoid hot weather so that snakes and insect pests would be less active. Food supplies were chosen for their healthful qualities as well as energy content and availability. Clothing was picked for durability, utility, and comfort. The rucksack was chosen for ease of carrying and adaptability. The poncho was used because of its versatility. Supplementing these items of equipment was my lifelong interest in efficient trail technique.

Lastly, I have a naturally hardy constitution, buttressed by the fact that I have never drunk alcoholic beverages or used tobacco in any way. I feel that these aggregate factors proved very helpful in making such an extended trip.

The following is a sketchy account of each day's progress:

Arrived at Jasper, Georgia April 3 after traveling most of the way by bus from Pennsylvania. Inquired of man near Post Office as to which of the nearby mountains was Oglethorpe. No one seemed to be quite sure. Talked to a boy who said another man had left one week previously on Easter Sunday. Located road leading in general direction and started walking. Got lift in truck and was warned about rattlesnakes. Walked several miles farther on then got another lift up to the top of the ridge. After considerable fumbling around finally got on the right track and arrived at Oglethorpe in early evening. The weather was cold and threatening rain so I went back down to the shelter at the old firetower to spend the night, keeping fire.

April 4—Started early from Mt. Oglethorpe, weather cold and raw, Made good time over fair trail till about noon. Met family of three having picnic near a water reservoir. Man said "Luck to ye". Lady said "I'se glad I got sense." Passed Amicolola Falls, and arrived at Frosty Mountain firetower. Had difficulty finding trail beyond, but finally reached the slope of Springer Mountain where I bedded down under a large fallen tree. Began to rain lightly.

April 5—Foggy, still raining. Passed Springer Mtn. firetower and came to a spring where I cooked breakfast. Made poor time due to fog limiting visibility to about fifty feet. Came to Cherokee Game Refuge No. 1 and due to indistinct marking turned the wrong way, arriving at the road near Diamond to the north before realizing the error. Talked to mountain boy who set me right. Backtracked and went on through pouring rain to Frying Pan Gap, where I pitched camp about sundown.

April 6—Weather still foggy with heavy rain. Arrived at Hawk Mt. lookout over brushy trail. Blazes badly faded. Continued on through Rock Gap to Cone Creek Gap at nightfall. Thunderstorm broke and wildcat howled nearby as I was chopping wood.

From "Report of Hiking Trip via Appalachian Trail From Mt. Oglethorpe, Georgia to Mt. Katahdin, Maine,"*Appalachian Trail Conference Report* by Earl Shaffer, 1948.

BRUCE OTTO

AT thru-hikers are leaving home and normal civilization for a good stretch of time. Today's portable cellular telephones weren't available in 1974 when Bruce Otto, a young man from Shelbyville, Kentucky, parted company with his father and headed into the woods, solo. Many AT hikers say their motivation for trying a thru-hike includes "getting away from society," but few are prepared for the extended periods of solitude the trail affords. Still, new trail friends are soon to be made, a new family awaits them.

Trail Diary, 1974

CHAOTIC CITY MORNING. THE FRANTICS OF LAST MINUTE TOUCH AND GO. The Kelty Tioga pack is readied: fifty-three pounds within, shiny nylon red without. Dad by gray car, a last picture he takes; Mom by front door, a last kiss she makes. Interstate 75 north soon places this scene and Macon, Georgia far behind. My mind is lost to a mountainous trail ahead and rests in observation that the best relaxation comes, not from doing nothing, but from doing entirely different things. To walk every step of this country's famous eastern wilderness pathway, the Appalachian Trail, strikes me as doing an entirely different thing. I grin in the awareness of riding with pleasure, soon to be walking with joy.

Georgia rural highway leads us northward through Monticello, Monroe and Winder. In Gainesville a lunch stop, I assumed, but Dad desires a farewell feast. The $15 husband borrowed from wife for those unexpected highway emergencies usher us into Clores Restaurant and a rib-eye steak. Never have Father and son been participant to a more pleasant highway emergency. Forty five minutes later we motor through Dahlonega on Georgia 52 west. Four miles to Grizzles store where we swing right. Passing Nimblewill church we pick up a dirt road which becomes Frosty Mountain Fireroad. Eleven crawling, jarring, lurching miles carry us into north Georgia mountains . . . and desolate Nimblewill Gap. Here all motors stop. To the right is the blue-blazed ascent trail which meanders up hill and through hollow 2.3 miles in summit approach to Springer Mt.

Dad laces his work boots. From stationwagon's rear I shoulder my pack. Everything in order we step onto the beaten approach path. So many have stepped here in approach to or departure from Springer Mountain, the southern terminus and southern thrust of the Appalachian Trail in Blue Ridge Province, Georgia.

Our intention was to achieve Springer's summit, snap a picture and bid the other adieu. But darkness is fast settling down amongst the hardwood hickory, fast settling down into our walk through Chattahoochee National Forest. Dark's descending curtain we know is soon to follow. Three paces ahead Dad pauses by a broken, fallen pine.

"I guess I better go back, Bruce." Dusk and awkwardness settle down about us, between us. How, in these moments, does one say farewell?

A word or prayer - a simple God bless you - the firm handshake - faltering steps forest us away - glances back over shoulder - the wave of hands - the disappearance into/behind tall trees - the Trail claims us. One goes south to home in the city. One goes north to home in the woods.

From "Stepping Into Joy: 142 Hiking Days, Spring to Fall, Georgia to Maine Along the Appalachian Trail," *Appalachian Trail Conference Report*, 1974.

ELIOT WIGGENTON

A thru-hiker on the trail in 1994 carried a tiny radio with an earplug, Velcro-strapped to his arm, "just to keep ahead of the thunderstorms." Eliot Wiggenton, author of The Foxfire Books, *a much-praised series of country living how-to guides, would have been aghast. No doubt Wiggenton, and many of the old-timers and hiking purists, would say it's to get away from conveniences like radios, and to rely on our own instincts and powers of observation, that we take to the trail in the first place. Those wanting to predict the weather may find Wiggenton's advice either helpful or charming. A look at the clouds works, too.*

Forecasting Weather

IT WILL RAIN:
within three days if the horns of the moon point down.
if leaves show their backs.
if cows are lying down in the pasture.
if there is a ring around the moon. Count the stars in the ring
    and it will rain within that many days.
if the sun sets with clouds.
within three days, if you see a black snake in a tree.
if an ant covers the hole to his ant hill.
if smoke goes to the ground.
the same time the next day, if the sun shines while it rains.
if earthworms come to the surface of the ground.
if birds fly low.
If it hasn't rained in a long time, and it starts before 7 A.M., it'll quit
    before 11 A.M.
If it rains on "Blasting Days" (the three longest days of the year),
        there won't be any "mast" (acorns, chestnuts, etc.) for animals like hogs
        to feed on. . . .
If it rains on Easter Sunday, it will rain every Sunday for seven weeks.
If it begins raining on the day the moon becomes full, it will continue
    raining until the moon quarters.
The first twelve days after Christmas indicate what each month in the
    next year will be like.
The weather will be fair if:
    you hear a screech owl; smoke rises; crickets holler.
    The temperature will rise.

From *The Foxfire Book,* by Eliot Wiggenton, Doubleday, 1972.

LARRY LUXENBERG

Larry Luxenberg ought to know: after thru-hiking the AT in the 1980s, he set about the arduous, imaginative task of interviewing hundreds of long-distance AT hikers on everything from equipment to blisters, to spiritual growth, to the sociology of the "linear community" along the trail. Luxenberg, a financial analyst in New York, offers one of the best slide-lecture shows about hiking the trail, with refreshing humor to put thru-hiking in perspective. Here he looks at the dark side of long-distance AT hiking, a subject wide-eyed enthusiasts starting out in Georgia need to face squarely.

Difficulties and Dangers along the Trail

THE A.T. IS NOT COMPLETELY SAFE, BUT DON'T BRING A GUN. MOSQUITOES are too small to shoot, and mice are too elusive. People worry about snakes and bears, but they shouldn't. It's possible to get mauled by a bear or bitten by a poisonous snake, but the odds of having a traffic accident on the way to the trailhead are much greater.

One likely will encounter other miseries or dangers on the trail. Possibilities include heat and cold, snow and rain, malnutrition, hypothermia, giardia, diarrhea, drowning, lightning, and pack snatching. Serious crime, while rare, has happened. There have been murders, rapes, and less serious assaults.

Cataloguing the physical challenges he overcame, Noel "the Singing Horseman" DeCavalcante wrote, "I lost forty pounds. I pulled knee ligaments, got blisters, shinsplints, twisted ankles, and a stress fracture. I hurt my Achilles, and lost my toenails. I pinched a nerve in my neck and got poison ivy and a million cuts, scratches, and lacerations. I had hurts I can't even remember."

Hypothermia, a potentially fatal drop in body temperature, is a common problem along the A.T., particularly for lone hikers. One is susceptible on rainy, blustery days when the temperature is above freezing. Those are precisely the conditions one frequently encounters in spring in the southern Appalachians. Actually, dangerous conditions can occur in any month, at any point along the trail. Keep in mind, also, that fatigue and hunger can aggravate the symptoms of hypothermia, which include shivering, lethargy, and confusion.

Sonie "Light Eagle" Shames recalls being on the verge of hypothermia when she arrived at a Georgia road crossing on her 1988 hike. Her teeth were chattering so hard she could barely talk. Fortunately, a woman came to her aid, offering her hot tea and warm clothes.

Paul "Bigfoot" Tourigny found himself approaching hypothermia at

Walnut Mountain Shelter in North Carolina. "I'd been wet, I'd been cold, and I kept plugging on. I was just wiped out. I still had my senses, but I was shivering. I wasn't hungry. Who comes to the rescue? Albie Pokrob." Albie arrived at the shelter soon after Paul got into trouble. He thawed him out with warm soup and drinks.

Defend against hypothermia by carrying enough warm clothes. Wool and synthetics are better than cotton at retaining body heat when wet. Leave the blue jeans at home.

Another defense is knowledge. Keep in mind that the weather can change quickly in the mountains. Most hikers who start in Georgia in March or April go through at least one big snowstorm. In the north, particularly in the Whites and the higher mountains of Maine, cold weather, including snow, is possible even in July and August. Hikers have made the mistake of mailing warm clothes home after a seventy-degree day, only to find it in the thirties a few days later. Syd "Not That Vicious" Nisbet, on his fourth thru-hike in 1990, made that mistake again. He, like other thru-hikers, mailed his warm clothes home after crossing the Smokies, but before climbing 6,200-foot Roan Mountain and the range beyond. Severe snowstorms can hit that area quite late in the spring.

One time, Ray Hunt got a personal lesson in why one shouldn't rely too heavily on weather forecasts. Holed up overnight in a Georgia shelter in heavy rains, Hunt's companions were four men from the long-range weather-forecasting bureau in Atlanta. They'd picked that weekend for a hike because the weather was supposed to be fine.

One part of the A.T. experience that Ray thought was among the most dangerous was crossing the bridge over the Susquehanna River at Duncannon, Pennsylvania. He had to walk on a narrow sidewalk next to a two-lane highway with 32-wheelers roaring past. When trucks went by with big mirrors, he had to lean away to avoid being hit. About ten years ago, a new bridge opened up with a wider, more protected walkway.

Giardia has become more common in the last decade. This waterborne parasite can cause intestinal problems for a long time, particularly if not properly diagnosed. Symptoms of giardia include diarrhea, nausea, and extreme fatigue. Generally picked up in drinking water, giardia was originally spread by animals; at one-time it was called "beaver fever." Roly Mueser believes that in the backcountry people spread it with poor hygiene. Roly found that, contrary to expectations, people who treated water were statistically as likely to get sick from water-borne illnesses as people who don't. But he, like most people, recommends treating suspect water. Hikers should treat at least some of their drinking water by filtering, boiling, or adding chemicals. Most hikers do not treat water that comes directly from an underground spring. Other than that, views vary, but most hikers treat at least some of their water and few treat all of it.

In 1990, five hikers traveling in a group in southern Virginia contracted giardia. They spent time in emergency rooms or clinics, and most spent at least a week convalescing before they could return to the trail. It's not always easy to diagnose giardia, but those who have it must receive medical treatment. If you experience lingering diarrhea, see a doctor.

Lightning is a real problem along the trail. Although reportedly no A.T. hikers have ever been killed by lightning, many have had close calls. Each year, lightning kills about one hundred people in the United States. On his 1977 hike, Phil Pepin had brushes with lightning in New York and the White Mountains. As he was walking along a road in New York, he saw a flash that seemed to come out of the ground a few feet from him. It sounded like jumper cables shorting out. He could feel the hair standing up on the back of his neck. Suddenly lightning struck thirty feet ahead of him. Then another bolt hit nearby. He raced ahead, found a building, and huddled out of the storm. "The lightning was like a shotgun blast," he said. "I have a healthy respect for lightning."

Paul Tourigny has developed a strategy that minimizes his exposure to lightning. He starts hiking early in the day and tries to be in a shelter by four P.M. He finds that most mountain storms hit later than that. Getting in early gives him more time to recuperate, wash, and hang up his sweat-drenched clothes to dry. It also improves his chances of finding space in crowded shelters.

Roger Brickner, the A.T.'s weather expert, confirms that in the summer, three quarters of mountain thunderstorms hit after late afternoon.

Open country and exposed places above treeline are the most hazardous for hikers caught in thunderstorms. Many hikers have felt vulnerable in the open stretch north of Roan Mountain. Roly Mueser, who is a physicist and was the Bell System's lightning expert for part of his career, says during a lightning storm, hikers should avoid the highest part of the landscape. Hair is raised by the electrical field preceding a lightning bolt. That's a sign —albeit a late one—to get off the mountaintop. Lying in a ditch is safer than standing, especially if you're the tallest object around. One also should avoid isolated targets like lone trees and mountaintop shelters.

Mary Jo Callan, the grandmother who repeatedly hiked the southern A.T., was on her first A.T. backpacking trip when lightning came calling. According to Jean Cashin, Mary Jo and her hiking companion were knocked across their tent by a lightning bolt. Mary Jo's companion decided she had better things to do with her time, but Mary Jo continued hiking.

A far more common danger for hikers is falling. Hardly anyone covers the whole A.T. without at least a few falls. Some cause broken bones or even death. Bill "the Orient Express" Irwin, the blind thru-hiker, must have the record with an estimated five thousand falls.

Mitch "Breeze" Keiler had one close call going up Kinsman Mountain in New Hampshire. "I didn't read how tough it was going to be. The guide-book said grab hold of any roots or rocks you can. Coming down, I did a complete somersault and landed in a fir tree on my pack." Luckily, he escaped serious injury. "In the Whites I fell every day," he said.

Foot, knee, and leg problems are among the most common hiker ailments. Dan Nellis, an outdoor-education instructor, stresses that you should wash your feet and socks often. He washes a pair of socks every day and hangs them on his pack to dry. He also suggests inspecting your feet every few days to see if serious problems are developing. He notes that it's human nature to hope that problems will go away. But if we treat minor problems before they fester, major problems can often be avoided. It's not uncommon for hikers to be driven off the trail because of, say, infected blisters, which could have been averted.

The most common cause of foot problems is boots that fit poorly or are not properly broken in. Some boots, especially lightweight models, are easier to break in than others. But bear in mind that just because boots feel good walking around your house doesn't mean they will hold up for full days of hiking steep, rocky trails with a heavy pack. If you have a problem, try to rectify it before it knocks you off the trail for good.

"I never really believed I'd make it," said Laurie "A Traveling Wilbury" Mack. "I'd had knee problems since I was young. I met a neuromuscular therapist at Trail Days in Damascus. Before we'd hardly said hello, he asked if I was having problems with my knees. He said, 'Your ankles are swollen.' I hadn't noticed. He did massage therapy on my legs several times, and it was incredible. I had one thousand miles pain free."

A less obvious source of danger is the confidence, almost hubris, that thru-hikers acquire. "I felt I was nothing but hard muscle and spring steel," said Dan Nellis. "It was exhilarating." But he believes that sometimes this attitude can lead to trouble. One instance he cited was sprinting down the trail, catching a foot on a rock, skinning a knee and denting a pack frame. "With my outdoor experience, I know that when we're real confident, the accidents happen," he said.

For the most part, following the trail now is not hard, but few hikers escape without getting lost at least once. Jean and Mortimer Weiser did the trail in sections, day-hiking as much as possible. They got through Mahoosuc Notch in Maine by noon. Because Jean was the slower hiker, she decided to get a head start on the steep climb up Mahoosuc Arm. Meanwhile, Mortimer became disoriented and went partway back through the notch, a narrow jumble of boulders that is the slowest, toughest mile of the trail. They were eventually reunited, but then it started to rain, and they still had the steep descent of Old Speck to do in the dark. They borrowed a flashlight and headed down, spotting only one blaze at a time. Sometimes, they had to sit down and feel their way. "Things kept going from bad to worse," Jean said. They finally emerged at 10 P.M.

It's not unusual to get disoriented on the trail, particularly starting in the morning from a shelter. Bill Irwin, the blind hiker, would always sleep pointed toward the next day's travel.

An unusual but painful problem struck Pete "Woulda, Coulda, Shoulda" Suscy and his partner at the start of the trail. Pete started in mid-May, and for eight straight days, it was bright and sunny without a cloud. Most hikers start earlier in the spring, when it's usually cloudy and rainy. The leaves still weren't out, and Pete had just gotten a short haircut. "My ears got really sunburned," Pete said. "I wore a baseball cap, but it didn't cover my ears."

Insects are often the biggest annoyance on the trail. Several hikers, including Grandma Gatewood and Paul "Lucky, Lucky, Lucky" Holabaugh, reported that wearing sassafras leaves in a band on their heads kept most bugs away.

In North Adams, Massachusetts, Dick "Lo-Tec" Cieslik found he had trickles of blood on his stomach from blackfly bites. He'd been wearing a net shirt. The bites eventually swelled to the size of half-dollars, lasting a month.

Another growing concern is Lyme disease. It is spread primarily by tiny deer ticks. The symptoms of the disease include a red, inflamed circle around the bite; fatigue; joint pain; and nausea. Since these symptoms are common in other afflictions, Lyme disease is difficult to identify without a blood test. If a doctor can't identify your illness, inquire about Lyme, reminding him that you've spent a lot of time in the woods. It can be effectively treated if caught early.

An unexpected, but nonetheless real, danger for hikers is their own equipment. They can impale themselves on their walking sticks, break their packs, and turn their stoves into fireballs. Frank "Red Blaze" Shea had been fiddling with his white-gas stove the whole trip. Every few weeks, it would clog up and stop working. He cleaned it and usually got it to work, but this time was different. He was sitting at the picnic table in front of the Rausch Gap Shelter, (also known as the "Halfway Hilton") in Pennsylvania. The stove wouldn't work. He cleaned it, tried again, then walked away to calm down. When he returned and lit it again, a flame shot eight feet into the air. "I jumped halfway across the valley in a second," he said. The fuel can, which had been full with thirty-two ounces of white gas, burned for ten minutes.

In the A.T.'s seventy-year history, seven hikers have been murdered, five since 1981. There is some debate about the efficacy of firearms for personal defense, but the ATC and most hikers discourage their use. Noel "the Singing Horseman" DeCavalcante wrote a letter to the *A. T. News* saying that as a former career military officer and lifelong hunter, he does not object to guns in general but feels they have no place on the trail. Others point out that four of the murder victims were attacked in their sleep, so what good would it have done to carry a gun?

As Maurice Forrester, Jr., put it in the *A. T. News*, the age of innocence on the trail is gone for good. The idea that the trail is a sort of haven, immune from the ills of society, is out of date. Still, the A.T. remains remarkably safe. "The Appalachian Trail may not be the paradise our fancies would like, but it is still a far better place than most others," Forrester concluded.

Every year, at least a few packs are stolen. Rape is a continual concern, particularly on the section of trail north of Elk Park, North Carolina, a high-crime area. Although many women do hike alone safely, they need to observe proper precautions, as do male hikers.

"It was brought home to me by Andy Coone, when his pack was stolen," said Jan "Sacajawea" Collins. "I came across his things on the trail. It was 1982, the year after the murders of a young couple at Wapiti Shelter, Virginia. I found Andy's sleeping bag and tent scattered in the bushes, but no pack. That's all I could picture—a copycat crime. We booked it [walked fast] to the road and tried to flag down a car. It was ninety degrees, and we looked like slimeballs. We were so distressed. Finally, I decided to stand in the middle of the road and get somebody to stop. I needed to know where Andy was. A nice couple stopped and rolled down their window a crack, just to hear what I had to say. I told them my friend was missing. They had a tremendous amount of trust to take us to the police. The police couldn't find his name because they had it spelled wrong. Finally, they told us he was okay. The couple drove us to his hotel, and there was Andy. He was so scared. He had been there a few days. He didn't want the incident to end his trip, and he asked us to go back with him to get his remaining things. He had been beaten up and had thought his arm was broken. No one would stop for him or let him into a house to make a phone call. Later, describing the attack in a shelter register, Andy wrote a courageous and humorous entry that closed with "People shouldn't pick on short people." He's continued to hike the A.T., completing five thru-hikes and working as hostel or shelter caretaker other summers.

Even veteran hikers are careful whom they tell about their travel plans or where they'll be staying. Women, especially, need to be attentive when crossing roads. Many pretend that they are with a group by using the plural ("we're going to do this"), and by looking down the trail as if they're expecting someone. Most advise that if you pick up "bad vibes" about a person or a situation, it's best to move on. "If somebody gives you the creeps, get away," said Susan Gall Arey. Often a person's senses pick up subliminal cues about a situation that are on target but don't readily translate to the conscious mind. Always be prepared to move on if you don't feel comfortable at a shelter. Some hikers try to avoid camping near a road or at an easily accessible shelter.

Still, the risks, while real, need to be kept in perspective. "I've done most of my 5,600 miles of backpacking alone," Susan Gail said. "If I didn't go alone, I wouldn't go at all. There are things that are a whole lot scarier than backpacking alone."

From *Walking the Appalachian Trail*, by Larry Luxenberg, Stackpole, 1994.

STEVE SHERMAN & JULIA OLDER

Steve Sherman and Julia Older thru-hiked in the early 1970s. Steve's obser-
vations about natural history and Julia's about people encountered en route
led to a valuable book, Appalachian Odyssey. *Julia's poems grace the nar-*
rative; a welcome candor colors the story, warts and all. Here they are start-
ing out, with too much weight and unhappy feet, "vulnerable as cacti in the
arctic." Other excerpts from Appalachian Odyssey *appear in the New Jer-*
sey and Maine chapters.

Georgia—78 Miles

O N SPRINGER MOUNTAIN IN NORTHERN GEORGIA WE SIGNED THE REGISTER,
a rusty metal pulpit with a stubby pencil and scraps of notebook
paper. Our signatures joined the scribbles of other conquerors: "Go
ing all the way"; "End to End!"; "Georgia to Maine on the AT."

Then, hoping to give back to the Appalachian Trail some of the new life
that we expected to gain by hiking it, we gouged holes in the still-hard dirt
and sowed the earth with zinnia seeds. A packet of marigold seeds we kept
to plant on Mt. Katahdin, the Trail's northern terminus in Baxter State Park,
Maine, fourteen states and two thousand miles away.

Exuberant, we followed the two-by-six-inch white paint stripes interspersed on tree trunks along the Trail. Our first day showed us what we
could expect in Georgia. Persephone and Spring had not yet risen from the
underworld. With icy invitation, the wind gusted through the barren maples
and oaks. Dead vines were rolled like barbed wire at the foot of skeletal
trees. The scant signs of color in the wintry landscape were rhododendron
leaves winnowing through the sunlight and a few chestnut-sided warblers,
brave vanguard of that cold April 11, 1973.

Before long we felt like this worn landscape. Our calves were throb-
bing, our feet sore, our backs aching. Two hours later we arrived at Big
Stamp Gap and the lean-to, a bare, three-sided enclosure with an earth-
gravel floor. We could not imagine anyone wanting to sleep on the slanting
ground under this rudimentary roof with the wind blowing down the valley into the open side.

Altogether, more than 230 shelters provided refuge for hikers along the
entire Trail. If the shelters were all like this one, to us the better choice seemed
obvious—a flat spot of Mother Earth. In minutes our man-and-woman tent
provided a waterproof, windproof home behind a giant fallen oak to protect us from the cold blasts.

We followed a blue-blaze trail to fetch fresh water flowing from a slab-rock crevice on a hillside about 150 yards from camp. Then, with wind-breaker hoods drawn tight around our faces, and wearing scarecrow brown gardening gloves, we gathered pieces of dry wood, built a fire, and pre-pared a hot chicken-and-rice dinner. Soon the Chicken Supreme, with a packet of sherry, no less, bubbled in the cooking pot. A standing rib roast and a bottle of Chateau Lafite back home in Hancock, New Hampshire, would not have tasted better.

That night, according to our pocket thermometer, the temperature dropped to eighteen degrees. We were as vulnerable as cacti in the arctic. Exhausted from the climb and the constant effort to keep warm, we got ready for bed. Most people get undressed for bed, but not us. We donned longjohns and thermal long-sleeve shirts. Over that we put on our summer sweat shirts, and over them sweaters and jeans. We put on two pairs of socks and cotton gloves. Then we crawled into our zip-together, newest-thing-on-the-market sleeping bags, and tied down the tent flap.

Whoever wrote "I've Got My Love to Keep Me Warm" never slept on the Appalachian Trail in Georgia in early spring. We trembled with the cold, squirmed and shivered, quaked and shuddered. We curled into each other, hugged each other, tossed and turned. We spent half the night playing single sack, double sack, sack in sack, all the while taking long swigs of Southern Comfort we brought to warm our blood.

We were discovering our first major mistake—the purchase of two French sleeping bags designed on the body-heat reflection principle. The bags weighed scarcely more than 1½ pounds each, a bonanza find in our pursuit of the lightest packs possible. They were specified to provide comfort in weather down to thirty-six degrees.

Through this long, freezing, first night on the Trail, we wondered why in-deed we had started from the south instead of the north. Yet from research and personal experience, we did know that April was far too cold to hike comfortably from Maine. Besides, we wanted to follow the unfolding fan of spring, hoping that the blackfly season of the north would be over by the time we reached Maine.

Part of our research back home had been to find exactly where Springer Mountain, Georgia, was located. Every atlas . . . ignored this first mountain peak. . . . Even on the day we boarded the Southern Railroad in Washington, D.C., for Gainesville, Georgia, we still didn't know exactly where Springer Mountain was. Willie, the train porter, added to our insecurity. "No, sir. That's a long way. Makes me tired just thinking about it. I don't even like riding that long way in a car. Now you watch out for snakes, hear? May is matin' season, you know. Two thousand miles. You ain't going to make it."

At the Greyhound bus station in Gainesville, we learned that no public transportation to Amicalola Falls and Springer Mountain was available. We hired a taxi, and an hour later watched the driver pocket two ten-dollar traveler's checks when he left us at the entrance to the ranger station of the Chattahoochee National Forest.

As we headed toward the ranger's cabin, snow swirled over the valley of bare trees. This was Georgia, the Deep South? Our decision to postpone the first climb until the snow let up was only one of many such decisions about the elements that we had to make along the Trail. We were not procrastinating, but we did not want to submit our bodies to the possibility of frostbite. Later, we heard stories of an older newspaperman who set out from Georgia in early March and suffered so badly from frostbitten fingers that he had to be treated by a doctor.

Biding our time, we rented a cozy cabin with plenty of hot water and a fully-equipped kitchen at Amicalola Falls. The National Forest maintains several of these cabins for tourists and hunters. All night the wind raged and rattled the glass. When we awoke it was cold but clear. We could get under way at last.

Up the steep, seven-mile approach trail we climbed to Springer Mountain (3,782 feet), the southern terminus of the Appalachian Trail, grandfather of all hiking trails in the United States, the longest continuously marked trail in the world. With the first five days of food in our packs, we signed the Trail register.

That had been the day before. Now, in our freezing camp at Big Stamp Gap, we awoke shivering. Fortunately, the wind had died down. Forgetting our exalted purpose, like zombies we stared at geysers bubbling up from our breakfast grits. Then the smell of sizzling bacon alerted our senses. Sunlight fell on our camp. An azure butterfly, like a flying violet, led us to the Trail. It was going to be all right.

We struggled up and down mountainsides these early days of the hike, stopping frequently to rest, catch our breath, and look at the tips of the great Blue Ridge Mountains corrugating the land as far as the eye could see.

This sub-range of the Chattahoochee Mountains was not an easy one for the novice hiker. Springer Mountain already proved that. Every two hours we stopped by a stream to wipe our faces with cool water. What a novelty not to have to turn a faucet. Water was everywhere, miniature waterfalls over rocks, thin rivulets meandering toward the valleys, hidden springs gushing as if from nowhere to form small clear pools in the moss-covered culverts. Our toes unsocked and cooling in one of those streams, we sat side by side eating raisins and Cracker Jacks, vying for the prize of a shiny bauble ring that Julia wore in her boot strap a few hundred miles. The raisins, we found, lasted longer in our stomachs: Every raisin a calorie, every calorie a step.

Our bodies stiffened early in the hiking day. Often, only the words in the guidebook kept us going, urging us on to the next shelter where spring water, firewood, and a flat tent site . . . awaited us for a comfortable night's sleep. A sleepless night was as bad as no water, two sleepless nights, disaster.

A quiet desperation set inside our psyches during these beginning days. We had not yet toned our hiking muscles or truly learned our pace and walking rhythms. We didn't know what we could do, and so the rush to move forward filled our heads with a drive to reach water before night. The thought of trapping ourselves somewhere in the unmanageable dark haunted us. Our backlog of experience was too scant to abandon ourselves to patterns not yet fully ingrained.

One day we kept seeing the distinct footprints of Vibram lug soles. We feared that the next shelter would be taken, not that we wanted the shelter, but already we had become accustomed to the silence of an unpeopled world. Fatigued, we climbed Hawk Mountain. Spurred on by yellow violets growing mysteriously every twenty feet, we reached the top and shaded our eyes from the brilliant sun. . . . A hawk swooped around the summit and glided overheard, neck craned, wings splayed, to eye the intruders.

We were right. When we reached Gooch Gap shelter, smoke lazed up through the treetops. Our shoulders slumped when we saw the lean-to already inhabited. The ground around the shelter heaved and swelled, rough sailing for a tent. Since the taciturn couple didn't appreciate us any more than we did them ("Well, have they gone yet?" the man whispered to the woman) we found a site farther on in a cozy grove of white pines that whistled in the wind.

While one of us got water, . . . the other built a fire, soon to be standard procedure. Whenever apart, we kept in touch by blowing dime-store whistles. One whistle meant: *Where are you?* Two: *Come here.* Three: *Help!* . . .

At dawn a phoebe came by the tent singing her friendly two-note name. The brisk morning called for something special. We sat in front of the fire warming our fingers, stirring our hash browns, and deciding what to get in Suches, the first grocery-town since the start of our hike four days ago. We walked 2¼ miles off the Trail on a gravel road that rolled through small country farms.

This one-telephone-booth town was the first stop for most long-distance Trail hikers. Like a crescent, Suches lined the banks of a lake surrounded with rounded hills and lush green meadows and pastures. The sky that day was as clear as the spring water we were drinking from the Appalachians.

The original general store was equipped with everything from shovels to soda pop. An iron pot-bellied stove squatted opposite the front door. The wooden floor creaked underfoot. Cooking pots and garden hoes hung on nails high on the walls. We bought what we could get from our list, the priority being moleskin . . . for blisters. We had to settle for hamburger buns in place of French bread, and macaroni and cheese instead of Quiche Lorraine.

"We get a lot of hikers round this time," the tall slim man in coveralls said from the cashier's counter. "Where you-uns from?"

"New Hampshire."

"Hiking the Trail, huh?"

"Yep."

"Well, anything you need, you just ask for it."

When we asked for hooch, he was startled. "Why, this a dry county." So we asked for pocket-size notebooks. He rummaged around and came up with just what we wanted—notepads advertising Bull of the Woods Chewing Tobacco and Dental Sweet Snuff. We bought a half-dozen fresh eggs, a pound of Cheddar cheese, two spoons (our experimental plastic ones broke), and four Eskimo Pies to eat on the spot.

The man couldn't find any flannel sleeping bag linings, so his wife telephoned the new general store across the lake. "You two go over yonder," she said, "and they'll fix you up with something."

We bought four yards of flannel material to make a floral mummy liner. Two local elderly women at the counter saw the material and, like blood grandmothers, unfolded the yardage and said, "Why isn't this perfect material. You could make a lovely dress with this, my dear. Is that what you're going to do?" . . .

Because it was the weekend, we met twenty-one people on Blood Mountain (4,458 feet), re-named Mt. Blood, Sweat, and Tears after the climb. At the top we stuck our heads into the windowless four-walled shelter. Three hikers were rolling up their sleeping bags on the dirt floor. The remains of a fire smoldered in the central stone fireplace.

"Have a good sleep?" we asked.

"Man, last night there were rats running around here as big as cats."

Tinfoil envelopes and tins from freeze-dried dinners were scattered in a pile near the dry kindling. This Skid Row on a mountaintop made us hurry back into the light and fresh air.

By noon of this, our fifth day on the Trail we were sweating in our summer shirts. The warmth was welcome, for it was resurrecting the earth. The spotted yellow trout lilies floated among the dark green galax leaves that covered the forest floor. May apple leaves unwhorled, fiddleheads uncurled. Congregations of bluets stared up bright-eyed as we passed.

The Neels Gap forest ranger, short, heavy-bellied, and loquacious, greeted us as we entered his way station. "You're numbers 63 and 64 this year," he told us after we signed the register. "That's how many Trail hikers are heading for Maine this year so far. You two look like you're carrying the lightest packs. No, I take that back. One hiker came in here with hardly anything. He said he wasn't carrying nothing except a five-pound bag of mixed nuts. Another girl and her dog came in. She was walkin' barefoot. Her blisters were so big she couldn't put on her boots. You know what? Only about five of those passing through here will make it to Katahdin."

We performed our ablutions in the lodge lavatories and washed our dirty socks and bodies with hot water. For lunch we lopped off slices of a one-pound salami and added them to cheese sandwiches on cocktail rye. Lunches were that simple. We sampled an assortment of candy bars from the vending machine, and set off to the woods again, our socks bobbing dry on our packs.

At an outcrop of granite and grass high on an unnamed rise, we rested and lolled in the sun to enjoy the expanse of Blue Ridge Mountains that gullied the earth below us. A black vulture eased his way on a thermal updraft toward us on a swoop of inspection. Perhaps our bright red nylon packs caught his eye. Perhaps he saw our Snickers candy bars. More than likely he was asserting his presence as the keeper of this dominion. He eased lower so that we could see the light patches on the underside of each spread wing. For a time we studied each other at eye level, a special treat that no downtown skyscraper affords. This bird, with its five-foot wingspread, was both command and beauty, a scouting warrior of the sky, a passing tribute to the wilds of the high mountains.

By the end of the first full week we were doing nine to ten miles per day instead of seven. We were learning that it paid to select a campsite early. One night we picked a moss-covered ledge, and, to insure double comfort, we pushed dry leaves under our poncho ground covering. The ponchos, we discovered, were far from waterproof in a heavy rain, but served well as ground covers, makeshift entrance roofs, pack covers, bathrobes in laundromats, pack padding when the portable pot handle stuck us in the back, windbreaks in high altitudes, rainwater collectors.

We were learning much about nature as well. The warblers, quick and small, defied identification, yet we spotted chestnut-sided and black and white warblers. In our plastic zip-lock offices, we carried paperback bird, flower, and tree books (minus the covers and several pages, which we thought added unnecessary weight). Dogwood was blossoming, not just white but yellow and pink. White bloodroot and scarlet wake-robins, bright harbingers of spring, advertised themselves against the drab forest floor. Still, the trees on the ridges refused to green.

Again we needed provisions. The sorghum syrup we poured from a plastic baby bottle onto our grits was nearly gone. Also, the ground Brazilian coffee we boiled camp style proved too much trouble. We were out of chipped beef and instant potatoes. The hickory-smoked ham bought in Suches disappeared in a day. Our appetites were growing as fast as the mountain dandelions. Each night . . . each morning we were famished.

Shortly afterward, two young hikers came through the gap, stopped, and talked. One had hiked many parts of the Appalachian Trail in the South and spoke with aplomb. He restrained his wonder at meeting people who were actually hiking the entire Trail in one season. "Well, if you make it through Stekoah to the Smokies in a couple of weeks," he said, the frown of authority creasing his forehead, ". . . then you'll make it the whole way."

We had heard about the twenty-five mile Stekoah section in North Carolina. Along with Mahoosuc Notch in Maine, it was considered one of the most challenging parts of the Trail.

The rains came again, this time spraying us under power of a mountain-high wind. We hiked up from Tray Mountain Gap and into a storm cloud thick with driving rain that struck us horizontally in the face. Visibility shrank to thirty feet. We reached the summit of the mountain and, according to the Trail guidebook, were to be rewarded with one of the most sweeping panoramas in that section of the country. Instead, we walked eye level with a cold April tempest. The rain soaked our jeans and shirts; the snaps from our ponchos had yanked loose. The only comfort about our ponchos was their color—bright yellow and orange. With the hoods up, we resembled a joyous holy order. Our brown cotton garden gloves turned into sponges, our socks blotters, our jeans candlewicks.

The sky was unkind to us that day. The Trail was, too, for it turned to mud and slick logs and rocks as dangerous as wet marble steps. We plodded on, if only to hike down from the driving rain and torment to relief in the shallow gulches where the woods, barren as they were, at least offered some protection.

We hoped for a motel and hot shower, but the next town turned out to be Browning's Gas Station. The store shelves were sparsely stocked with grits, antique corn flakes, pig hocks, and candy bars. The nearest head of lettuce was six miles away. Two tourist cabins out back were closed, but Mr. Browning offered us an old school bus converted to living quarters. Would we take that?

Browning owned the store, but Geneva, a small wiry old mountain woman who wore white cotton string in her hair and tattered tennis shoes, ran it. Browning offered us a lift into Hiawassee to pick up some fresh produce while he bought a tank of butane gas for the stove in the bus. Our quarters were somewhat less than we expected, but they were a piece of paradise out of the downpour.

From *Appalachian Odyssey,* by Steve Sherman and Julia Older, Stephen Greene, 1977.

DAVID BRILL

As Far as the Eye Can See *is one of the more thoughtful books on the AT experience. From the outset of David Brill's thru-hike in the late 1980s, the book shows candidly the author's progress from newly discovered fears and ineptitude to a relaxed attitude in the woods and the rewards of hard-won hiking competence. The AT passes for hundreds of miles through territory quite far removed from any convenient help, medical or otherwise. The strong recommendation is: don't hike alone. But even with a partner, and sometimes because of a quirky partner, danger can seem to lurk around every bend, and those strange sounds in the deep woods' black night can be decidedly unfriendly.*

Fear

JUST BEFORE A SPRING THUNDERSTORM HAMMERS THE MOUNTAINS, THE ANI-mals disappear. The songbirds stop singing. The chipmunks stop scurrying. The spring peepers stop peeping. The crickets stop grinding. And an eerie quiet settles over the woods.
When twisters accompany those storms and rip their own random trails across the landscape, you nestle down in the deepest part of your sleeping bag and hope that your luck holds.

You also swear that you will never, ever, camp in a mountain gap again. Tornados, like the pioneers of centuries past, often follow the gaps across mountain ranges. I know that now, but on April 24, 1979, as I lay under a nylon tarp in Tesnate Gap, Georgia, I didn't.

There was, however, one thing that I knew for certain that night. I was frightened.

I had watched the storm approach from the west in the late hours of the afternoon. Columns of cumulo-nimbus clouds lumbered into view above the faraway hills, erasing the sun. The air smelled and felt pregnant with moisture, and, as the first winds began to buffet my camp, the atmosphere took on a sick, green cast.

By 6:00 P.M., it was dark, and I lay ensconced under my rain fly, waiting, as the first peals of thunder rumbled a few miles away. I had learned that by counting the seconds that lagged between each lightning flash and peal of thunder, I could estimate my distance from the heart of the storm. A one-second lag meant the storm was roughly one mile away. At 6:30 P.M., the storm was four miles away and approaching fast.

By 7:00 P.M., the counting game ended when the storm enveloped my camp. The ground rumbled beneath me, and the wind and rain raged above.

I had experienced storms in the lowlands, secure inside four walls, but never in the mountains. At three thousand feet, I was wrapped in the low-slung clouds and, thus, inside the storm, and the thunder seemed to surround me before rolling away to the valleys.

Lightning bolts cast stark silhouettes of tree branches against the nylon of the tarp. First the flash, then immediately after, the resounding crack of thunder, like the slow splintering of huge bones. Then there was the rain, which fell so heavily at times that the tarp sagged under its assault and brushed against my face, and I could hear torrents of water channeling down-hill, carving away earth and stone.

The wind howled and churned like an errant locomotive, and its force all but deadened the sound of the thunder and falling rain. I could hear walls of wind originate miles away in the valleys, then thrash toward me gathering intensity. . . . They plowed through the gap, bowing the trees, scattering leaves, and snapping limbs. As each passed, the rain fly popped and bucked and surged, and I feared that it would tear from its tethers and disappear into the darkness, leaving me exposed and even more vulnerable.

I cowered under the fly, feeling utterly helpless, like a prairie dog trapped under the hooves of stampeding cattle, and I prayed for the storm to deliver me unharmed. Through the night I felt like a victim, as if all the storm's violent energy had been directed at me and as if raw vengeance bolstered the wind and powered the rain. Though I wouldn't realize it until the next morning, a twister had already cut a swath through another gap a few miles to the north. I had been spared.

When day broke, I surveyed the damage wrought by the night. Tree trunks had been splintered, severed branches lay scattered about, and uprooted trees crisscrossed the trail with gray clay and stone still clinging to their dying roots.

At that point, I was four days and thirty-seven miles into the Appalachian Trail. I had begun my hike at Springer Mt., the trail's southern terminus some sixty miles northeast of Atlanta, and I was determined to trek all the way to Mt. Katahdin, the trail's northernmost point, in central Maine.

A month earlier I had resigned my job as manager of a Washington, D.C., tennis shop and had committed myself and my meager $1,500 in savings to completing the trail. I wanted to become one of several hundred "thru-hikers" who had navigated the route from end to end in one summer, but other reasons, too, had drawn me toward the trail. Among them was the desire to confront and overcome my fears, but in the wake of the storm, I realized that I had only begun to identify them. Moreover, I acknowledged that I couldn't hope to banish my fears until I had pushed deeper into the eastern wilderness and probed much further into myself.

Though fear is a solitary condition, at least I had not had to endure the storm alone. I had shared my camp with Dan Howe, a twenty-three-year-old former architectural planner for a large oil corporation who had swapped his business suit and fast-track career for a pair of lug-soled boots, a back-pack, and 2,100 miles of adventure. When we had set out on the trail, we had known each other just over a month and had met face to face only a half-dozen times.

Dan and I had first met during a program on the Appalachian Trail at a Washington-area backpacking shop. The program featured Ed Garvey, a well-known thru-hiker and author who had hiked the trail in the early 1970s. I had arrived for Garvey's talk fully reconciled to the notion that I would begin and finish the trail by myself, despite the fact that my previous back-packing experience had been limited to four or five overnighters; the long-est duration had been three days. Over the previous months, I had tele-phoned every friend I had, and even a few casual acquaintances, in hopes of cajoling one or more of them into taking up the trail with me.

Most of them, like me, were in their first year out of college but, unlike me, had devoted their energies to charting career paths rather than ambling along wilderness trails. While they regarded the Appalachian Trail as a ro-mantic pursuit, they also recognized its potential for stalling a career climb, and one by one they declined my invitation. So I had attended Garvey's presentation with the dim hope of finding a partner there.

As Garvey concluded his presentation, he asked if anyone among the thirty people in the audience intended to attempt the trail that summer. Tentatively, I raised my hand and then quickly scanned the room. One other hand waved in the air, and it belonged to a sandy-haired, bearded man who appeared to be about my age. After the meeting disbanded, I approached him and introduced myself, trying not to seem too eager or needy and real-izing that to ask him abruptly if he would commit to spending the next five months with me was tantamount to proposing marriage on a first date.

Within a half-hour, Dan and I sat at a nearby tavern drinking beer and discussing our hopes, dreams, and expectations for our months on the trail. As we talked, I discovered that we had planned to begin the trail at about the same time—late April—and that we shared many common attitudes. Both of us had lived through the turbulent years of the late 1960s and early 1970s, and we both had emerged with a sense that if society failed to pro-vide the peace and stability we sought, we might find it in nature.

While I had begun the trail seeking nature's healing powers, over the first four days I had found only disappointment, discovering that nature was capable of more violence than I had ever experienced in civilization. I found disappointment, too, in discovering the fear that dwelt within me.

In the throes of the storm, I had lain awake, my heart thumping like that of a snared rabbit, while Dan slumbered peacefully beside me. Through the long night, my head churned a maelstrom of doubt and anxiety, and I began to suspect that I possessed neither the courage nor the stamina to reach

Mt. Katahdin more than two thousand miles to the north. I also suspected that I had invested my hopes in a folly that would break me the way the wind had cracked away the branches of the surrounding trees and that I would limp back home wounded by failure. Those feelings may have been amplified by the storm, but they had just as surely accompanied my first tentative steps on the trail four days earlier. . . .

Since I was a novice, my backpack burgeoned with expendable items that catered either to my fears or to my vanity but which served no purpose other than to occupy space with their bulk and stress my knees with their weight. While Dan's pack weighed a respectable thirty-five to forty pounds, mine surpassed fifty-five. I had read and reread backpacking how-to books, which sang the praises of lightweight packs bearing only the essentials. In the months before the outset of my hike, I had loaded the pack dozens of times, and each time I tried to assess honestly the merit of each item I slipped into the pockets. Gradually, I had pared the pack down to forty pounds. As the day of departure approached, however, my doubts and fears reversed the trend, and I found myself sneaking small items back into the pack until the scales again topped fifty-five.

On the eve of the hike, I had down-loaded the pack one last time, and I resolved to leave it just as it was. To assuage my fears, though, I had stashed the discarded items in the trunk of the car. As I wrestled the pack onto the ground in Nimblewill Gap and glimpsed them for the last time, each suddenly seemed essential, and I realized that once the trunk was closed, I would be forced to live without them.

Wouldn't the two-pound pair of binoculars in their leather case bring me closer to wildlife and help me identify the denizens of my new environment? Wouldn't the plastic egg-carrier and fifty feet of braided marine rope prove indispensable? What about the extra cook pot, aluminum plate, and oven mitt? Would one pair of long trousers be enough, and did I need a third pair of wool socks? Would the sheath knife, with its six-inch blade, protect me from wild beasts, or would my Swiss Army knife be sufficient? Would the package of firecrackers and can of dog repellent chase marauding bears from our camps? Would the metal pocket mirror, which doubled as a signal mirror, become an invaluable grooming aid or even save my life if I became lost? Wouldn't the one-pound hammock help make my leisure hours more comfortable? Would my health fail without the three-month supply of vitamins and the bulky first-aid manual? . . .

At the time, my pack, as heavy as it was, seemed far less burdensome than the emotional and physical challenge that awaited me, and as I glimpsed the trailhead, I first registered the full impact of what I was about to do. I had been raised by conservative and protective parents, who tended not to venture far from the cloister of their snug middle-class environment. From the time I was young, my life had been predicated on safe decisions. Now I was about to embark on a five-month journey through the unknown where I would face risks more real than any I had known before.

Fueling my fears was the knowledge that once I entered the backcountry I would leave behind the familiar trappings of the civilized world—electric lights to chase away the darkness, television sets and radios to help fill the idle hours, modern appliances to ease the chores of daily life—and the comfort they provided. I had fully enjoyed the morning's hot shower and the meal at the hotel restaurant. I felt no shame in ascending into the mountains inside the climate-controlled environment of the car, and I wasn't at all sure I could endure life without those and other amenities.

In some ways, the act of climbing from the car was tantamount to exiting the womb: I faced a strange and forbidding new world. At least in the first instance I had been blessed with conscientious parents who shepherded me clear of major pitfalls. Once I entered the woods, I knew that there would be nothing to shield me from hardship and danger except my own resources, which I had never really tested.

When the time to leave came, I embraced my parents and hoped they would offer some advice or guidance, yet I realized that I was about to enter a realm they knew little about.

"Be careful," said my mother, with tears welling in her eyes.

"Yes, and have fun," Dad advised, as I took the first of the five million steps that would lead me to Mt. Katahdin. After a few hundred feet, I turned one last time to see the white sedan disappear in a cloud of dust as it descended the gravel road. For the first time in my life, I was truly on my own. . . .

As the weeks passed, my blisters began to heal, and my thighs grew hard and strong. My camp routine became well enough ingrained that I could fetch water, fire the stove, cook and eat dinner, and hang my food without a wasted motion. My pack and its contents became more familiar to me than my dresser drawers at home, and I eventually discarded the spare socks, extra cook pot and plate, vitamins, firecrackers, dog repellent, and several other pounds of extraneous gear. I gave the extra trousers to a fellow hiker who had ripped the seat out of his own, and soon my pack dipped to a manageable thirty-five pounds.

From then on I carried only the essentials. As the load in my pack decreased, my initial fear of the wilderness mellowed, and I began walking my fifteen to twenty miles each day alone, fascinated with the process of spring awakening around me. I even began to regard thunderstorms, which weeks earlier had pitched me into panic, as among nature's most formidable and entertaining displays, more potent and grand than anything I had witnessed in civilization. Many evenings, as storms approached, I scrambled to an open perch on a ridge-line from which to watch them, as their charcoal-gray sentries floated across dusky skies stretching to the horizon. I sat captivated as their silver talons raked nearby mountain peaks and their thunder shook the earth. As I watched, I began to realize that my transformation from visitor to resident of the wilderness had begun and that there was much yet to learn about my new home.

From *As Far as the Eye Can See: Reflections of an Appalachian Trail Hiker*, by David Brill, Rutledge Hill, 1990.

Springer Mountain Trail Register Notes

In the trail registers at shelters all along the AT one discovers a strange brew of comments and quips. Some are pensive, some ribald, some informational, some a cheerful note to hikers who are soon to pass by this particular spot. Thru-hikers use the registers to communicate with friends behind them as the year's crop of long-distance walkers leapfrogs its way north or south. Day-hikers like to record their accomplishments or their complaints as well. The registers add up to legitimized graffiti; some entries run to a few carefully handwritten pages. In the registers at Springer Mt., Georgia, at Mt. Katahdin, Maine, and at other literal and figurative high points along the AT, colorful verbiage pours forth.

1/7/77 Tim Kearney, Reading, Pennsylvania
Maine to Georgia, Aug. 1, 1976 to Jan. 7, 1977.
It's been cold, raw, beautiful and long. The best thing has been that in the Appalachian Mtns. you can still kiss the creeks. Thank you Bob Strain (12-18-76) for the congratulations [Strain preceded Kearney at Springer and left him an encouraging note]. I was given so much from many to get me here; thank you.

3/19/77 Marty Gross, Great Neck, New York
So far, so good — In any case it beats Great Neck — Keep on truckin'.

3/18/76 Marianne Wiley [no town]
I'm 14, our troop is doing this. Our leader, Uncle Ed, begged us to come. The things we have to do to humor the older generation! You should build a bridge connecting Black and Springer Mountains. All I have to say is "Where's the water?!" [Later, on same page] Marianne again, "Notice to any backpackers. When you're here all hot and tired, I'll be in bed watching TV and EATING."

4/1/77 Bob Paradise, Old Greenwich, Connecticut

Going North, possibly all the way. I've heard stories about people giving up on the approach trail—now I can understand why. Was lucky to get a taxi ride up to the trail from Gainesville after a sixteen-hour ride on the train. Came with Tom "Fuzz" Phillips but he's taken off like a streak of lightning.

4/6/77 Laura Kane, Gaithersburg, Maryland

I turned 16 yesterday! / "There are those who worship loneliness, / I'm not one of them. / In this world of fiberglass / I'm searching for a gem." Bob Dylan, "Dirge"
[Another hiker wrote in the margin by the poem, "Bob Dylan is demon possessed."]

5/20/77 Andy Coone, South Carolina

Mt. Katahdin, Me.—to right here. Well, I am here. It's a satisfying feeling but I would be content to continue walking. At the start of the trip, 2050 miles seems plenty long but at the end not long enough. Good luck to everyone starting. I didn't dislike any part of it, even the roads. There's lots of beauty ahead. I was on the trail when the last U. of Conn. crew passed through and then I got sick of seeing there [sic] computer schedules scattered along the trail. I guess because I feel a big part of the joy of backpacking is carrying all of your own needs on your back, relying on yourself, and taking things day by day with a freedom that can only be found in the woods, that I think Warren Doyle's system of covering the trail is sacreligious [sic] and I'm sorry that he keeps corrupting others with his style of support vans and planned forced marches. I don't feel it's possible to organize an experience in living and gain from it. Bravo to everyone who made the distance, or plans to, on foot, using your own strength. *That* is an experience."

5/21/77 Steve Heimel, Johanna Eurich, Coudersport, Pennsylvania

As far north as compatible with enjoyment. We agree with the comments above about Doyle. [Johanna continues] We [are] moving North to settle and it seems like walking to our new home is about the best way to go. We're looking forward to taking the time to enjoy and contemplate our path for a good four months or whenever the snow starts falling on us or whenever we *choose* to call a stop to this walk. Question: How does one contemplate nature if one is making 20 or more miles a day? John Muire [sic] would certainly wonder and Thoreau might never have noticed his ants if he'd been traveling at that *rate*.

9/1/69 Steve Winter, Decatur, Georgia

Tired

From "Trail Registers—Springer Mountain," Appalachian Trail Conference.

NORTH CAROLINA

The undulating Nantahala Mts., from Wayah Bald, North Carolina.

Trail miles: 95.6 in North Carolina, 207.7 shared with Tennessee

Trail maintenance: Nantahala Hiking Club, National Park Service and Smoky Mts. Hiking Club (in Great Smoky Mts. National Park), Carolina Mt. Club

Highest point: Clingmans Dome, 6,643 ft. (highest point on the AT)

Broadest rivers: French Broad, Nantahala (bridge at Wesser over kayak racecourse), Little Tennessee (AT crosses 480-ft.-high Fontana Dam)

Features: The AT traverses most-visited national park in the U.S. (Great Smoky Mts.), with extraordinary variety of plant life (balsam fir, flame azalea) due to sustained high elevation and abundant precipitation. Extensive wilderness areas in national park and forests; over 70 miles of crest-line trail; spectacular vistas.

Parks, forests, and nature preserves: Nantahala National Forest, Great Smoky Mts. National Park, Pisgah National Forest, Cherokee National Forest

Most intriguing name on the trail: Licklog Gap

Trail towns: Franklin, Wesser (Nantahala Outdoor Center), Fontana Dam, Hot Springs

MICHAEL FROME

On a sunny day when an Appalachian Trail hiker rests on a Smoky Moun-
tain bald (a mountaintop natural clearing) to drink in the spectacular views,
the notion that all is right with the world is hard to resist, beauty and peace
being everywhere apparent. Yet these same hills carry a curse resulting from
the unconscionable forced removal, in the 1830s, of their native people, the
Cherokee. Michael Frome, chronicler of the history of American forests and
mountains, tells in chilling detail of the treachery used to displace and nearly
annihilate a great nation. Today's Appalachian Trail passes directly through
high Cherokee territory.

Genius of the Species

T HE CHEROKEE, MEANWHILE, DID NOT WANT TO DIE. THEY WANTED TO LIVE,
as do other natural species in the unending struggle to survive against
more powerful forces. Curiously, throughout the long history of the
earth, only one species, the human, has ever successfully perpetrated the
total destruction of another, and then of lower forms, like the passenger
pigeon, that once darkened the skies over the Great Smokies. But could one
race of man exterminate another?

The Cherokee did not believe it would be their fate to perish. They decided to accept the hand of hope held out to them by the Government of the
United States. They would place their trust in this Government, forsaking
the warpath and aboriginal hunting ways, living not in the forest but on the
farm, applying themselves to the use of plows, hoes, spinning wheels, and
looms which were distributed among them.

How well could they meet the test of peacefulness and practicality?
This is the story of the first thirty years of the nineteenth century and, indeed, provides an important key to understanding the Smoky Mountains
Cherokee down to this day. Whether it was a test based solely upon civilized rules is another question. As a historian, Theodore Roosevelt observed
the Cherokee were "a bright, intelligent race, better fitted to follow the 'white
man's road' than any other Indians," a statement which he intended as a
compliment. But essentially Roosevelt was a chronicler of expansionism, to
whom the frontier days were best defined as "the winning of the west" by
heroic pioneers specially chosen "to conquer the wilderness and hold it
against all comers." Like almost all others, he regarded the Indians as strangers, intruders in the path of national destiny.

The Cherokee, however, hung on and adapted their ways. Having already signed the first Treaty of Tellico in 1798, surrendering a portion of

their lands on the Government's pledge that it would "guarantee the remainder of their country forever," they were willing to concede the short
span of "forever" in the second and third Treaties of Tellico in 1804 and '05.
More important to them was to progress. They welcomed schools and mis-
sions; they professed the Christian faith, generally conducting themselves
by its tenets. In 1808 they adopted a written legal code and established their
own form of police, a system of patrols to "suppress horse stealing and
robbery." Two years later the National Council abolished the custom of clan
revenge, the primeval Indian order of justice. Before long they would write
a remarkable constitution and adopt a legislative form of government based
on that of the United States; they would achieve a written language, and the
publication of a national newspaper in their own tongue. In the measurement of human advancement it is quite possible that no nation has ever
made more sizable forward strides in so short a span of time.

By the 1830s, when elected representatives were conducting the affairs
of a republican government, most Cherokee dwelled on farms, in homes
ranging from log cabins to plantation mansions, and wore the frontier costume. Some of the mixed-blood offspring prospered, owned slaves, and were
well educated. But while the center of the new Cherokee culture had shifted
to northern Georgia, the tribal remnants in the high hills of Tennessee and
North Carolina, shut in from the outside world, clung to the older conservative beliefs; and only in the primitive hills would the Cherokee find the
spark of their survival. Many volumes have been written about this period;
the story here is designed to relate the principal events to the ultimate climax in the Smokies.

The Cherokee in the early nineteenth century were endowed with a rare
quality of national leadership and with representation from Washington that
genuinely endeavored to serve their interests--also a rare quality. Colonel
Return Jonathan Meigs, who arrived in 1801 at Tellico blockhouse as Indian
agent for the Cherokee and would suffer with them for twenty-two years,
faced the trying, contradictory assignments of guiding the Cherokee to become civilized while at the same time encouraging them to surrender additional land and to move to the vacant West. Unfortunately, he was not above
employing the secret weapon in Indian negotiations, the "silent consideration," or the bribery of chiefs. But Colonel Meigs distributed farming implements and household utensils while it seemed this course would help them
protect their country; he went with them to Washington, defending their
rights at treaty conferences; he encouraged them in the establishment of
their republic, and protected their land from invasion by troublesome whites
while it was still possible to do so. Today the proposal is often made that
Indians should be accorded the "full rights of citizenship" through the dis-
solution of their reservations, but in 1820, when the Cherokee were nearing

the peak of their greatness, agent Meigs learned through his own experience the fate of such a suggestion. When he proposed that, since the Cherokee were so far advanced that further Government aid was unnecessary, their lands be allotted to individual Indians and they be invested with citizenship, the generous states of North Carolina, Tennessee, and Georgia responded with vehemence—no Indian was welcome to live within their boundaries under any circumstance.

It was difficult for a white man on the frontier to be a friend of the Cherokee. Young Sam Houston, however, was one who could. Born in the Shenandoah Valley in 1793, he moved as a boy to Tennessee with his widowed mother, eight brothers and sisters, opposite the Cherokee territory on the Tennessee River. When he was sixteen, he crossed over to join the Cherokee and was adopted by Chief Oolooteka, or John Jolly. For three years he lived the Indian life, spoke the language, wore the dress, and bore the honored name Ka'lanu, the Raven. When he returned to civilization in 1812, he looked for a job in Maryville, near the Smokies, and became master of a log schoolhouse, an "old field school," where he was ridiculed at first as a graduate of the "Indian University." He charged eight dollars for a semester's tuition, one third cash, one third in corn, and one third in bright-colored calico for his shirts. The semester began in May, after corn planting, and ended in autumn, before the gathering and cold weather. Next spring he left Maryville to join the army and fight in the Creek War. But his heart would always be with the Cherokee. In 1829, after walking out on his unhappy marriage in Nashville and the governorship of Tennessee, he returned to his foster father, John Jolly, then living in Oklahoma, and married the chief's niece. In 1832 he served on a Cherokee delegation to Washington, dressed as an Indian, and remained one of the few political figures of his time who dared to fight for the Indian cause at the risk of his own popularity.

Despite local encroachment and abuse, the Cherokee continued to place their trust in the Government. During the War of 1812, they gave valuable support when hostile Indians went on the warpath in the British cause. The nearest to them were the Upper Creeks, who had been stirred by the eloquent Shawnee chief, Tecumseh, and his idea of an Indian confederacy to save the lands west of the Ohio River. From tribe to tribe, Tecumseh traveled to forge the confederacy, aided by his brother, Tenkswatawa, the Prophet, who filled a particularly important role with his "revelations" that the Indians must return to tribalism in order to preserve their existence. The Upper Creeks, responding with religious fervor, accepted Tecumseh as the leader who would restore the old life. There was much enthusiasm among the Cherokee as well, though when and where the message was brought to them is subject to conjecture. According to Smoky Mountain tradition, Tecumseh met an assemblage at the Soco town house, below Soco Cap, where his eloquence was well received until Junaluska, an influential patriarch, insisted that his people remain neutral. It is more likely the key decision was made at Ustanali, or New Echota, in Georgia, under persuasion from agent Meigs, and from Cherokee progressives led by John Lowery and The Ridge (later called Major Ridge), who warned that to join the attacking Creeks would invite destruction of the Cherokee by the United States.

Instead, the Cherokee sent hundreds of warriors into the field behind General Andrew Jackson, while those at home collected provisions for the American troops. In the final crucial encounter, the bloody battle of Horseshoe Bend, fought March 27, 1814, on the banks of the Tallapoosa River, Alabama, the Cherokee proved their value under fire. After Jackson was held at bay and no force could approach the Creek fortress without being exposed to cross fire, a group of Cherokee under Junaluska silently swam the river to the enemy's rear, captured a flotilla of Creek canoes, and used them to establish a beachhead. Sam Houston, young lieutenant of the Tennessee mountains and brother of the Cherokee, was among the first in the ensuing attack over the breastwork. When the day was done an estimated one thousand Creek warriors had been killed.

It was a high-water mark for the Cherokee in their relationship with the United States. They were credited with turning the tide. Among those in the ranks was Young Dragging Canoe, son of the fiery foe of Americans, and grandson of Attakullakulla. Others were Major Ridge, who had been instrumental in enlisting the Cherokee to join the war, and John Ross, of northern Georgia, who though one eighth Cherokee and seven eighths Scot would become the Principal Chief and the greatest figure of the Nation in the nineteenth century.

The time of travail called for great figures. Despite their efforts at peacefulness, the Cherokee were beset by the insatiable appetite of borderers for their land; and, in reward for their troubles at Horseshoe Bend, they returned to find their homes ravaged and despoiled by white troops; roads were built across their lands and five new treaties forced upon them by 1820. The Tennesseans, in particular, were anxious to be rid of them altogether. The Government pressed them to remove beyond the Mississippi; where earlier it had sent farm implements so they could follow the white man's path, it now told them of good hunting grounds and offered rifles if they would go.

But most Indians wanted to remain in the ancient homeland. They wanted to feel their trust was not misplaced in the Government. They wanted to taste the sweet American fruits of liberty that already had been transplanted to distant soils. So in 1819 they yielded nearly six thousand square miles, or one fourth of the land that still remained to them; they offered to accentuate the process of civilization to prove they were indeed worthy of remaining in the East.

By terms of the Treaty of 1819, they relinquished claim to the heart of the Smoky Mountains. The boundary line became the Little Tennessee. They had to move south and west of the boundary, which extended along the Little Tennessee to the mouth of the Nantahala River, then along the divide between the two rivers—the mountain crest our old friend Bartram had crossed—in a southerly direction to the South Carolina line. . . .

As to the mainstream of events centered in Georgia, the Cherokee proceeded with their forward strides. In 1820 they adopted a republican form of government, headed by a president, or Principal Chief. The Nation was divided into eight districts, each represented in the bicameral legislature; the upper house, of which John Ross was president, was called the National Committee; the lower house, of which Major Ridge was speaker, was the National Council. A system of district and circuit courts was established, and in 1822 the National Superior Court, later called the "Supreme Court of the Cherokee Nation." Laws were enacted for collection of taxes and debts, support of schools, road repair, for licenses to white persons doing business in the Nation, for the regulation of liquor traffic and the conduct of Negro slaves. To negotiate the sale of lands to whites without consent of the National Council was defined as the most serious of crimes, treason, punishable by death. In 1827 the establishment of the republic was climaxed with adoption of a constitution. John Ross, chairman of the constitutional convention and a principal author of the new document, was a student and admirer of Thomas Jefferson. The preamble reads:

"We, the representatives of the people of the Cherokee Nation in convention assembled, in order to establish justice, ensure tranquility, promote our common welfare, and secure to ourselves and our posterity the blessing of liberty; acknowledging with humility the goodness of the sovereign Ruler of the Universe, in offering us an opportunity so favorable to the design, and imploring his aid and direction in its accomplishment, do ordain and establish this Constitution for the Government of the Cherokee Nation."

The constitution, though intended to safeguard individual liberties and rights, in keeping with the American spirit, was poorly received in the surrounding Southland. To many of their neighbors the civilizing process, promulgated by the Federal Government, had gone too far. The Cherokee in their improved state were even more obnoxious than as savages.

But the pressures for survival evoke the genius of the natural species. The Cherokee not only adapted themselves to the white form of government but produced their own written language, an invention the more remarkable considering the status and character of the inventor, Sequoyah. He was not of the educated Cherokee, nor did he ever learn to read, write, or speak in English. Though now much idealized, he never abandoned the native religion for Christianity, nor did he invent the written language as the means of civilizing the Indian with white ways, but rather as the means of saving the Indian ways. He was a mountain Cherokee, probably born about 1760 in the Overhill town of Tuskegee, outside Fort Loudoun, who lived in matu-

rity at Willstown, Alabama. His name was Sikwa'yi, whose mother is generally believed to have been Wurteh, the niece of Attakullakulla and sister of
Old Tassel; his father may have been Nathaniel Gist, the white trader (or
possibly a soldier of the Fort Loudoun garrison). In his youth he was a hunter,
trader, and silver worker, known among the whites as George Gist, or Guess;
and from the whites be became intrigued with the ability to communicate
thought through marks on paper.

Between 1809 and 1821 he tried many approaches, including pictographs,
single signs for complete sentences, then signs for whole words. Finally, he
hit upon the idea of breaking words into syllables. After analyzing thousands of words of the spoken language, he discovered they could be classified into roughly one hundred syllables and subsequently devised eighty-
six signs, one for each syllable, sufficient to render all the sound combinations in the Cherokee language. He used characters in an old English spelling book, which he could not read, German printed characters and letters
out of a Bible, placing them right side up, upside down, adding a few strokes,
curlicues, and symbols of his own invention. Friends thought him unhinged
but harmless, while Cherokee neighbors around Willstown complained he
was a "witch" who should be put to death.

The accomplishment of Sequoyah belongs to the Nation as much as to
the man. When he announced his invention of the alphabet, or more properly the syllabary, the National Council gave him a hearing, with the critical
Alabama Cherokee sending a delegation to listen and be convinced. The
acceptance of the national language syllabary had an immediate effect—
within months almost all the savage people became literate, teaching each
other the system of the "talking leaves," in cabins and along the roads.

The national leadership realized that in Sequoyan print they held an
instrument with which to crystallize their institutions and culture. The proposed constitution and laws could be read by every Cherokee. They established a national newspaper, the *Cherokee Phoenix*, printed at New Echota
with hand press and type shipped from Boston by water to Augusta, then
two hundred miles overland by wagon.

How feverishly these people worked! Sequoyah had presented his syllabary in 1821 and less than seven years later, February 21, 1828, the *Phoenix*
appeared, printed in English and Cherokee, with editor Elias Boudinot ex-
plaining the title:

"We would now commit our feeble efforts to the good will and in-
dulgence of the public, praying that God will attend to them with his bless-
ings, and hoping for that happy period, when all the Indian tribes of America
shall rise, Phoenix-like, from their ashes, and when the terms 'Indian depredations,' 'war whoop,' 'scalping knife,' and the like shall become obsolete
and forever be buried deep in the ground."

They were believers in God and the syllabary was used in translating the Bible and hymn books. It was right that this should happen, for the most devoted missionary among them, the Reverend Samuel A. Worcester, was a moving spirit in advancing literacy and the publication of the *Phoenix*. Strangely and secretly, however, the new written word was seized upon by the old order, the conservative medicine men and conjurers, as the means of preserving ancient rituals and witchcraft formulas, which previously had been passed down only by word of mouth.

Unfortunately, God's message is variously received by His children. The missionaries taught the Cherokee the message of love. As forest primitives for centuries, they had already learned to know God in nature. On the other hand, God's word was not unspoken in the states of Alabama, Georgia, Tennessee, and North Carolina, nor in the Federal City, where the Houses of Congress opened their sessions with the customary daily prayer. But His image differed.

In 1828, Andrew Jackson, expansionist politician, Indian fighter, and Indian hater, was elected President of the United States, marking the beginning of the end of the Cherokee Nation in its hour of finest promise. Immediately he put through Congress the Indian Removal Act, placing in his hands the task of leading or driving all Indian tribes west of the Mississippi. His policy clearly understood, the sovereign state of Georgia advanced to claim first honors in persecution of the Cherokee.

Georgia had substantial reason for its course. In this same period gold was discovered in the mountain country. It is truly a beautiful parcel of this earth, the Georgia mountains, drained by the Chattahoochee River, which derives its name from the Cherokee word for "flowering rock," denoting the many tumbling waterfalls in the Appalachian highlands. It was considered much too good for Indians, better suited for 10,000 gold-fevered men, including many driven to lust and lawlessness, who gorged themselves until lured West by better diggings in California. And those who remained would slaughter the wildlife until, after three quarters of a century, the last deer was dead.

So Georgia proceeded to pass an act confiscating all Cherokee lands; it declared all laws of the Cherokee Nation null and void, forbade Indians to testify in any state court against white men, to dig for gold on their own land, to hold councils or to assemble for any public purpose; it distributed their lands to whites by lottery, and unloosed a bloody reign of terror by armed bands who brought plunder, torch, and terror. From the White House, Old Hickory cheered the proceedings. He favored leaving the "poor deluded Cherokees to their fate, and their annihilation," and denounced Reverend Worcester and the other missionaries as "wicked advisers."

He helped further by pushing through Congress the Removal Act of 1830, providing "for an exchange of lands with the Indians residing in any of the states or territories, and for their removal west of the Mississippi." The vote was close in both houses. A storm of protest was stirred by speakers and writers throughout the country. There was far more public appreciation and debate of the Indian plight then than now, when the survivors of the Cherokee and other Indian tribes have been reduced to the status of historical curiosities, with scant awareness of their problems in the contemporary world.

Because the Cherokee were helpless, the missionaries prepared to sacrifice themselves in their behalf. When Georgia demanded they either leave the state or take an oath of allegiance to its laws, eleven of them refused. Worcester was the strongest holdout; he insisted that he was a citizen of Vermont, living among the Cherokee with their consent and the consent of the Indian agent. He and Elizur Butler were sentenced to four years of hard labor in the penitentiary. Subsequently, the case of Worcester *vs.* Georgia was heard before the Supreme Court of the United States. To the joy of the Cherokee and their supporters, the Court finally ruled in their favor. The decision was based on the time-honored principle of the sanctity and sovereignty of small nations, a principle which the United States has since held aloft many times in circumstances relating to distant continents. The Indian tribes or nations, declared the Court, had "always been considered as distinct, independent, political communities, retaining their original natural rights . . . and the settled doctrine of the law of nations is that a weaker power does not surrender its independence—its right to self-government— by associating with a stronger, and taking its protection.

"The Cherokee Nation, then," concluded the Court, "is a distinct community, occupying its own territory, with boundaries accurately described, in which the laws of Georgia have no right to enter, but with the assent of the Cherokees themselves, or in conformity with treaties, and with the acts of Congress."

The Cherokee rejoicing was short-lived. Georgia defied the Court. The Reverend Worcester languished in jail almost another year at the Governor's pleasure. President Jackson interpreted the decision as part of an effort by his enemies to embarrass him during an election year. The classic remark attributed to the man of the people was, "John Marshall has made his decision; now let him enforce it."

The rush of thousands of whites into Cherokee territory heightened the turmoil and confusion. The Cherokee were nearly spent by constant battle. In May 1834, the *Cherokee Phoenix* breathed its last. On a glowing note of faith in God and in tomorrow's inevitable dawning, the editor signed off:

"To our Cherokee readers, we would say, DON'T GIVE UP THE SHIP; although our enemies are numerous, we are yet in the land of the living, and of our clearly recognized right. Improve your children, in morality and religion, and say to intemperance now growing at our doors, depart ye cursed, and the JUDGE of all the earth will impart means for the salvation of our suffering nation."

By 1835 some Indians, headed by Major Ridge, came to the realization their troubles must end with removal and that the best they could do was to hope for favorable financial terms. The majority, however, supported the national party of John Ross and were determined to fight for home and national existence. They clung to the trust in the Federal Government, presenting memorials and petitions to Congress, and appeals to the White House. Up until the very end it appeared that favorable action might forthcome from Washington, so vigorous were the efforts of Ross and so intensely was the Cherokee removal question debated. The Jackson Administration played the trump card by dispatching to the Cherokee no ordinary emissary but a clergyman, the Reverend J. F. Schermerhorn, of New York, who extorted the infamous 1835 Treaty of New Echota by deceiving both the majority and minority and gaining acceptance by a handful of the people. Neither President Ross nor any officer of the Nation was present or represented at the signing. By this document, written on the darkest day of American diplomacy, the Cherokee were to receive $5,000,000 for their seven million acres in return for lands in the West, plus allowances for the cost of removal. When the Senate ratified the fictional treaty, it did so with a pledge of perpetual peace and friendship, guaranteeing, of course, the western lands to the Cherokee Nation "forever."

The Cherokee did not want to go. They were hard to budge, despite a wave of brutality in Georgia, which saw them flogged with cowhides, hickories, and clubs, the women as well as the men stripped and whipped without law or mercy. Councils were held in protest all over their Nation; resolutions were adopted declaring the treaty null and void and denouncing the methods used to obtain it. Three years passed, they were still on their land, while in Congress Henry Clay, Daniel Webster, and the old Tennessee frontiersman, Davy Crockett, fought for their right to remain. Colonel Crockett risked the fates by denouncing the treatment to which the Cherokee were being subjected as "unjust, dishonest, cruel, and short-sighted in the extreme." He had been threatened to support removal or face the finish of his public career; after this interlude, Jackson's influence led to Crockett's political undoing.

By May 1838, the expiration of the time fixed for departure, only about 2000 of the 17,000 Indians had removed, despite all the pressures brought against them. Here and there efforts were exerted locally in their behalf. In 1837 a memorial to Governor Edward B. Dudley of North Carolina from twenty-four citizens of Haywood County stated the belief that Cherokee neighbors were "fast improving in Civilization, knowledge of the arts and agriculture, for sobriety not surpassed by the same number of whites in any part of the state." The memorial pleaded that the Indians were qualified to make useful citizens, since they had lived in peace and friendship. Except for the signatures, this document was in the handwriting of Will Thomas. Nevertheless, the following year General Winfield Scott was dispatched to force their eviction with infantry, artillery, cavalry, and eager local volunteers, totaling 7000 in number. A chain of twelve stockaded concentration camps was erected throughout the Cherokee country. There were five in North Carolina; the closest to the Smokies, Fort Lindsay, could hardly have been closer, being on the south side of Little Tennessee River at the junction with the Nantahala (now under the waters of Fontana Lake). There were five concentration camps in Georgia, one in Tennessee (Fort Cass, at Calhoun, on the Hiwassee River), and one in Alabama.

Cherokee men, women, and children were seized at bayonet point . . . and without notice removed to the concentration camps. Livestock, household goods, and farm implements went to the white camp followers, who burned the homes and dug the Indian graves for silver pendants and other valuables. In the stockades, hundreds died. Hundreds of others waited their chance and escaped. Within the stockade walls they set up preaching places. Native ministers like the Reverend Jesse Bushyhead and the Reverend Stephen Foreman preached constantly and baptized children.

In October 1838, the main procession of exile began, the old, the young, the sick, and the small, 14,000 of them; having stowed blankets, cook pots, and trifling remembrances in their six hundred wagons, they bid adieu to their ancestral land, and marched across the Tennessee, across the Ohio, across the Mississippi in the dead of winter, averaging ten miles a day over the frozen earth, stopping to bury their dead who perished of disease, starvation, and exhaustion and to conduct Sabbath worship to the Great Spirit, an army of strangers advancing over the Trail of Tears, while the new President, Martin Van Buren, advised Congress before Christmas that all had gone well, the Indians having moved to their new homes unreluctantly. The whole movement was having the happiest effects, he so reported with sincere pleasure.

From *Strangers in High Places: The Story of the Great Smoky Mountains,* by Michael Frome, University of Tennessee Press, 1980.

RANDY RUSSELL & JANET BARNETT

While hikers today may tell campfire ghost stories for the sheer fun of a scare in the dark, legends that live on in the hills of North Carolina had a more potent impact on earlier generations of Cherokee children, who no doubt took them more literally. Here is a tale from the Nantahala National Forest region of North Carolina, where the Appalachian Trail passes through deep-cut, lonesome valleys and tangled, shadowy woods.

The Wicked Witch of Nantahala

*I*N DAYS LONG PAST, THERE WERE MORE THAN SNARLING BEARS AND MOUN-tain panthers to frighten children in the hills of western North Carolina. There was Spearfinger, a woman-monster who fed on human livers. Spearfinger, a singularly nasty witch known to the Cherokee, feasted on unsuspecting children throughout the mountains. She was, however, particularly associated with Whiteside Mountain, a prominent peak at an elevation of 4,950 feet, one side of which is a highly visible 1,800-foot sheer cliff. This solid rock face is the highest exposed-rock cliff in the eastern United States.

In this part of the Nantahala National Forest just off U.S. Highway 64 between Cashiers and Highlands, the mountain woods are thick with towering hemlocks and spruce.

Banks of the stream near Whiteside are quilted with moss and criss-crossed with the delicate lace of thriving ferns. But it's the rocks that contribute most to the visual drama of Whiteside Mountain.

The area is littered with rocks. A jutting formation on the east side of Whiteside Mountain is known locally as the Devil's Courthouse, while a particularly large boulder about halfway up the same outcropping of rocks is claimed to be Satan's throne.

It was from these very rocks that the witch Spearfinger sprang. A terrifying witch, Spearfinger possessed the power to take on any appearance she chose, including that of the rocks. In her true form, Spearfinger looked something like an old woman, with some notable differences.

The ancient witch, who outlived generation upon generation of man, was yellowish in appearance. Her entire body was covered by a hard skin of rock, a skin so dense it proved impenetrable by arrow or ax. Spearfinger could best be identified by the form of her right hand, one finger of which was long and pointed, resembling an awl. The witch used her finger to fatally stab anyone unlucky enough to come within the range of her sharpened reach.

In her true form, the vicious witch also possessed a strong, horrible smell, which she could at times mask when people came near. Yet her natural malodorous state was so severe that Spearfinger was crawling with flies. Among the Cherokee, it was known that the hum of flies in the mountain forest meant that Spearfinger might be hiding somewhere nearby.

When hungry, Spearfinger altered her appearance to that of a sweet old lady, the flies vanishing, her stone skin disguised. The evil witch had enormous powers over stone and could easily move huge rocks. She could cement two stones together simply by striking one against the other. And she could turn herself into stone to keep from being found in the rocky terrain of the mountains.

To travel through the rugged country more easily, Spearfinger set about building a great bridge between Whiteside Mountain and a distant peak. The bridge was well under way when it was struck by lightning. The fragments of Spearfinger's stone bridge were scattered at the base of Whiteside Mountain. Pieces of her bridge are still visible today throughout the region.

Spearfinger favored hiding at the heads of mountain streams and in the dark passes and hollows of the Nantahala Gorge, where other Indian evils were known to lurk. She ventured throughout the area in search of her favorite food, however, and anyone who came across her in the mountains was a likely victim of her ferocious appetite for human livers. Spearfinger was especially fond of children.

At the time of Spearfinger, the rich bottomlands of the Nantahala National Forest were noted for their abundance of strawberries and other wild fruits and berries. Cherokee children were often sent into the hollows and grassy areas along the rushing streams to pick wild strawberries for their village. The children were especially vulnerable at these times. Many were snatched away by Spearfinger.

At other times, when no child could be found at the wooded edges of the rocky mountain forests, Spearfinger would venture closer to the villages, watching with hungry eyes from behind a tattered shawl for any child she might be able to seize.

Spearfinger would call to the children, referring to them as her grandchildren. There is no word for grandchild in the Cherokee language. Cherokee endearingly addressed their grandchildren as "my son's children" or "children of my daughter." The endearment was particularly alluring when spoken by a kind old lady with gray hair who hid her smile behind a shawl.

"Come," Spearfinger would call. "Come, my little girl, and let your grandmother dress your hair."

The witch hid her mouth because her teeth were made of sharp, broken pieces of stone that would scare the children away.

She was also careful to keep her awl finger hidden beneath her shawl. When one of the girls ambled over, the wicked witch laid the child's head in her lap. She petted and combed the child's hair with the fingers of her other hand until the little darling fell fast asleep.

Then, with her rock-and-bone finger, the hungry witch stabbed the napping child through the heart. Spearfinger quickly removed the child's liver with her blood-smeared awl finger and ate it on the spot. As the old witch chewed, she gradually returned to her true form, her skin hardening and taking on its yellow cast, the fetid smell rising as flies came to light upon her wretched, laughing face.

Warriors would follow the trail of buzzing flies and drying blood into the dense forest, but with no result. Spearfinger simply changed herself into a pile of rocks or a single boulder whenever anyone came after her. After the murder of village children, she was occasionally discovered in the form of stone by Cherokee warriors when a particular boulder or human-sized pile of stones was covered with flies. But the warriors could do little to harm the witch. Many arrows and spears were broken in an attempt to kill Spearfinger after she'd changed herself into a rock. Should the warrior touch the rock, he'd be tainted with the smell of the witch as if he'd been sprayed by a skunk, and he would have to sleep outside his home for at least four days before he was permitted to enter again. The unlucky Cherokee spent those four days fighting off flies.

Cherokee children were particularly vulnerable to attack in autumn. This was the time of leaf burning, when the Cherokee burned fallen leaves from the forest floor before shaking chestnuts from the trees. The old witch was always on the lookout for trails of smoke among the trees of the Nantahala Forest in autumn. She knew that the children of the villages would be gathering the nuts and wandering to the edges of the mountainside. The wrinkled crone would patiently wait, sharpening her appetite, waiting to change into a gentle old grandmother and surprise a hapless child who was accidentally separated from the others. Cherokee elders, the actual grandparents of the children, tried diligently to keep the children together as they gathered chestnuts.

The witch of Whiteside Mountain became a pronounced danger when she could find no children in the forests on whom to dine. She ventured progressively closer to the villages, watching with hungry eyes from behind her tattered shawl for any child she might be able to seize. Spearfinger might ultimately summon her powers and enter a village in search of a meal. She'd wait until she spied a family member leaving a house. Instantly, the hungry witch took on the appearance of the family member and entered the home. So swift was Spearfinger and so sharp her finger that at these times she could stab a child without the victim's even knowing it. The witch left no wound and caused no pain, quickly removing the liver and carrying it off into the night, where she could eat it in safety while slowly changing back to her yellowed form. The child who was her victim went about his affairs until all at once he felt weak and grew ill. Eventually, the child pined away and died. . . .

On rare occasions a solitary hunter spotted Spearfinger walking in the forest. Her hand was visible even from a distance, appearing at first glance as if she were carrying a knife. No hunter came too near because the strong odor of Spearfinger warned him off.

The witch was said to sing along with the hum of the flies that accompanied her as she walked among the rocks and trees, climbing carefully up the mountainside. It was rather a pretty song, sung in a low voice like a lullaby, but one that told of the many sweet livers of children Spearfinger had consumed. More than one hunter lifted his bow and arrow, his blood chilled by the words of the witch's song, and took aim at the dreadful creature, only to watch his arrow bounce off her hardened skin or break in two upon contact. The hunter would then hurry away in silent flight back to his village to tell his story of Spearfinger.

So many children died in the area of Whiteside Mountain that the Cherokee called a great council to devise a manner to rid the forest of the wicked she-monster before everyone was killed. Indians traveled from many villages to attend the council. After much debate, it was decided that the best way to kill Spearfinger was to trap her in a pitfall. Then all the warriors could attack her at once.

The pitfall was known among nearly all the Indians of the eastern United States, but was used only to catch especially large or dangerous game. A pit was dug along a trail and covered with underbrush. The animal was chased along the trail until it stumbled upon the pitfall and fell snarling into the deep trap.

The Cherokee dug a pit across the trail outside their village and covered it with leaves, twigs, and small, brittle branches. They were careful to line the trail with similar autumn leaves so that Spearfinger would not discern that the ground had been disturbed. To entice the witch, the Indians lit a fire on the other side of the trail before hiding themselves in the shrubbery.

Spearfinger saw the trail of smoke and smacked her lips. She believed the children had been sent out from the village to gather chestnuts. The witch made her way down Whiteside Mountain.

The hidden warriors waited. Eventually, an old woman wearing a shawl came along the trail. Several of the young men wanted to shoot her upon sight, but the closer she came the more it appeared that this old woman with gray hair might not be the wicked witch they meant to kill. In fact, she looked exactly like an old woman of the village they all knew well.

After some hushed debate, the warriors let the woman pass unmolested. If she were the woman from the village, she would know they'd built a pitfall, they reasoned. The Indians had already pointed out to each other that this elderly woman kept her right hand covered by her shawl.

With a loud crash, Spearfinger tumbled into the pitfall. Upon landing at the bottom of the deep hole, she changed instantly into her true, yellow form. A swarm of late-season flies followed her into the pit. No longer a feeble old woman, the stony-skinned Spearfinger snarled and raged in a rasping, terrible voice as the warriors encircled the pit, weapons poised. She ranted curses upon the Cherokee around the sharp, broken rocks that were her teeth. The odor of the witch was so strong that many of the warriors had to back away from the rim of the pit after firing an arrow at the yellow witch.

The battle had just begun. The savage liver-eater scrambled up one side of the pit, then the other, reaching out with her bone finger in all directions, looking for someone to stab. The warriors beat Spearfinger back by throwing large rocks, but they did no damage other than to cause the woman-monster to fall back down into the hole.

The warriors grew frantic. Though they fired their arrows straight and true and as rapidly as they were able, the weapons proved useless against Spearfinger's stony skin. The arrows broke and fell like snapped twigs all around the witch.

Spearfinger taunted the men, certain she would eventually climb out of the pit and get at them. A small bird the Cherokee call tsi-kilili, the Carolina chickadee, watched from a nearby spruce branch and began to sing to the warriors. The Cherokee know the chickadee as a truth teller. The bird swooped into the pit, singing, "Here, here, here." The chickadee bravely alighted on the yellow witch's deadly finger, and try as she might Spearfinger could not shake it loose. The warriors understood that tsi-kilili was instructing them to fire their arrows at her right hand. They did so, and as an arrow struck the witch's palm she let out a piercing scream. Her wounded hand poured forth a great quantity of blood.

The chickadee lifted in flight as the old witch withered and died.

Many demons and witches of the mountains were known to hide their hearts in secret places so they couldn't be killed. Spearfinger always kept her right hand clenched because she carried her heart in her hand. Tsi-kilili had somehow learned Spearfinger's secret, and the small bird remains a welcome friend among the Cherokee.

The witch was buried where she lay, at the bottom of the pit. Some believe Spearfinger turned herself into one of the rocks in the pitfall and lived to stalk today.

It is still considered a foreboding of bad luck when a fly is found buzzing around a rock in the Nantahala National Forest in autumn. Cherokee hunters will change direction to keep from hiking beyond such a spot. The warning is considered especially severe if the fly is seen in November, long after the killing October frosts have turned the leaves.

From *Mountain Ghost Stories and Curious Tales of Western North Carolina*, by Randy Russell and Janet Barnett, John Blair, 1988.

ANN & MYRON SUTTON

Atop several of the highest of the Smoky Mountains are strangely open areas, free of panorama-obscuring trees, as though designated by the gods as perfect scenic overlooks for passing hikers. A debate continues about why these areas remain "bald." The botanists say one thing, the foresters another, the Chero-kee legends yet another. In any case the pleasure of pausing for lunch or a rest on one of the balds, especially when the flame azaleas are blooming, is worth every step in the effort to climb up from the smoke-hazy valley below.

Gregory Bald

IN THE GREAT SMOKY MOUNTAINS, WEST OF CLINGMANS DOME ON WHAT IS now a side trail to the A.T., we climbed some years ago to one of the prime localities for observation of the flame azalea. Through humid mists in sheltered coves, and out along steep ridges crowned with unusu-ally luxuriant forests, we hiked to Gregory Bald, a 4,948-foot-high ridge-top meadow on the line between Tennessee and North Carolina. We must have lost a gallon of perspiration, but if the muggy heat had been twice as bad, the trip would have been worth the effort. If there were ever a Garden of Eden, it must have had a corner designed after Gregory Bald.

All around the fringes of this open meadow were shrubs of flame aza-lea. But natural hybridization had occurred in unusual proportions. Some of the flowers were white and some were yellow. Some were white and yellow combined. Some were salmon and pink. Others were yellow-orange and red-orange, red and deep red. A botanist of the University of Tennes-see, who was also on the hike, said that he had counted on this bald no fewer than twenty-one color variations—all forms of the same species. It is now believed, however, that not one but three species are represented. In any case, William Bartram would have been thrilled if he could have seen it.

And yet, in the dazzlement of the hour, there is a curious mystery in these mountains that tends to be overlooked by the hurried visitor or the photographer focused on color. The peculiar absence of trees and shrubs on these mountain ridges commands the attention of the hiker. He is accus-tomed to thick forest. He walks for miles through tunnels of foliage, en-closed within the fold of vegetation that covers these mountains so richly.

Thus when he comes to open ground, as here at Gregory Bald, he can hardly believe his eyes. He is not at tree line—yonder ahead and higher he sees a continuation of the rich vegetation. Here at Gregory Bald there is a profusion of shrubs all around, but the top of the ridge is clear and unclut-tered, opening to him extraordinary views of the lowlands in almost every direction.

This case of the empty summits is perhaps a mystery of little consequence to the highway traveler. But to the lover of wilderness who, like Bartram, is impelled by restless curiosity, it may become an all-consuming puzzle, especially as he hikes across one bald after another (there are eighty or more between Virginia and Georgia), each as inexplicable as the other.

Instinctively, the hiker looks for remnants of farm buildings because these balds resemble that type of "overgrown clearing," but there aren't any. Early settlers knew of Gregory Bald, however; it was here when they arrived, and for many years they grazed sheep upon it. The Cherokee Indians called it *tsistuyi*, the rabbit place, where the chief of the rabbits ruled.

The question is, in a region with more than 130 species of trees, of which some two dozen individuals reach record dimensions, where poplars and hemlocks thrive, and where on the highest slopes spreads a rich assembly of spruce and fir, why are there any open spaces? If the Appalachian balds arc not man-made, as apparently they are not, what then?

Tree line lies theoretically above 7,000 feet at this latitude, but no peak in the southern Appalachians attains that height, so there ought to be no mountains devoid of forest for purely climatic reasons.

Bartram, like other early explorers, made no mention of this situation, probably because the greater part of his travels were along less mountainous routes. Yet the balds are there, curious and conspicuous. They vary in size from a quarter acre to 100 acres, with the exception of Roan Mountain Bald, which has been enlarged by man in modern times to about a thousand acres. They are not completely barren; heath balds support a tangle of shrubs, and grass balds a carpet of grass. On Andrews Bald, in the Great Smokies, is a bog where sundews grow. Natural animal communities have developed. But the balds appear naked because they contrast sharply with the forests along their fringes.

Balds exist impartially over rocks of numerous kinds—igneous, sedimentary, and metamorphic. The soil is so deep, so black, and so homogeneous that it is likely to antedate historic times, perhaps even Indian times. Adjacent to the balds grow trees of considerable antiquity whose eccentric growth rings show that they have been standing on the weather-beaten edges of these montane meadows for more than a century.

Balds have a place in Indian legend. Cherokees called them *udawagunta* and believed that in ancient days they were occupied by a hornetlike monster that swooped down from the heights, scooped up children, and vanished swiftly. Defenses and subterfuges against this monster, or *ulagu*, as it was called, never seemed to succeed, and the depredations increased. At last the creature was traced to a distant cavern on a sheer mountain slope. In desperation, the people convened a council and begged the Great Spirit for help. He was pleased to have been asked, and promptly sent a lightning stroke that sheared off the side of the mountain.

There lay the *ulagu*, stunned. The Indians attacked with spear and ax and soon put an end to it. The Great Spirit then decreed that the summits would remain unforested so that the people could station sentinels to keep lookout for other *ulagus*. Perhaps in our time an *ulagu*, along with various unidentified flying objects, will be sighted, and the devotees of the Cherokee theory will gain in strength. In the meantime, botanical science has yet to produce a thoroughly successful explanation. Could the balds be simply burned-over areas? Perhaps—but if fire were solely at fault, there ought to be more balds than there are today. Windthrow is evident on a number of balds, and gall wasps kill oaks by the thousand; could the vegetation have been destroyed by heavy winds or rampant disease?

As the hiker treks across them, he may be entirely unaware of the mystery that has risen in an almost legendary fashion around the Appalachian balds. There is little help in seeking to explain the mysteries of balds in other places. Balds exist in Nevada where shrubby and herbaceous areas lie lower than forests of limber and bristlecone pine (there are more than a dozen "Bald Mountains" and "Bald Peaks" in Nevada). Tundra grasslands happen to exist below tree line in Wyoming's Medicine Bow Range. On the South Island of New Zealand, grasslands occupy the summits and upper slopes of the Maungatua Range, and the grass there, called *Danthonia*, is closely related to the dominant Appalachian species.

Scientists still hike to the balds in search of a solution to this seemingly simple phenomenon. They are tending now to think that the balds are bare of trees because there have been no seeds to reforest them. In the wake of the last glacial epoch there existed a warming period that nearly eliminated spruce and fir from the lower summits of the southern Appalachians. When the climate cooled again, spruce did not recover on these summits because of the absence of a nearby source of seeds. Severe attacks by wind and ice and insects have probably hindered recovery, too.

But these are theories, and the balds remain as enigmatic as when the *ulagus* surveyed the southern highlands. The hiker who scans the uplands from these open summits enjoys a major benefit of The Appalachian Trail— access and viewpoints unparalleled in the heart of a wilderness of extraordinary beauty and mystery. And at Gregory Bald, the rabbit place, he may think of these balds, blazing with flowers in June, as floral epaulets on the shoulders of the mountains. But their beauty is a fragile beauty. Within the national parks and forests, these wild and natural gardens are reasonably protected; but even here, danger approaches: we pause on a high point of The Appalachian Trail and our gaze goes from freshly glistening banks of rhododendrons and flame azaleas down across the forested ridges, over pinnacles and into hollows where the haze of the valley hangs. Beyond the river, we see the smoke of industry seeping through the trees and among the shrubs, pushing a layer of haze and acid into the forest, filling the coves, crowding closer against the upland ridges. . . .

From *The Appalachian Trail: Wilderness on the Doorstep*, by Ann and Myron Sutton, Lippincott, 1967.

CHARLES KONOPA

Benton MacKaye—who urged AT walkers to slow down—would have been happy with this hiker's method of traveling on the trail. Konopa started at Springer Mt., Georgia, on June 6, 1964, and finished the entire trail at Mt. Katahdin, Maine, on September 19, 1970. Taking it in stages, Konopa gave himself time to acquire and digest a vast amount of information—botanical, historical and otherwise—and his self-understanding deepened too. Here we travel with Konopa through the botany of the Appalachian Mountains.

The Botanical Garden

W HEN HERNANDO DE SOTO AND HIS COMPANY OF ADVENTURERS PROBED the Appalachians over 400 years ago they came upon a treasure that was greater than the gold they sought—and sought so single-mindedly and vainly.

In Georgia, the invaders saw wild roses blooming 'just like those in Spain." They gorged on plums in Tennessee as juicy as the ones ripening in the warm sun of the Estremadura, the poverty-ridden province from which most of them hailed, and with their pikestaffs cracked black walnuts that were "much better" than the walnut which grew back home. In actual fact, nearly all the plants were different. Botanists were one day to find that not a single native species of tree is common to both Europe and America. And where Old World forests may brag two or three dozen species of trees, this silva numbered more than a dozen times a dozen.

Though none suspected it at the time, the conquistadors were traveling in the corridors of the greatest hardwood forest in the earth's temperate zones. All about them was the treasure they failed to perceive.

Unlike rare metals and gems, it was renewable and capable of providing endless bounty in the form of lumber, shade, streams of sparkling water, flowers, nuts, fruits, and pharmaceutical products. (There is not a drug store on the globe but which stocks medicines made from the herbs of this forest.) It was, and it still is, in spite of reckless, even contemptuous, treatment, a magnificent botanical garden.

Not once in its 2,000 miles does the Appalachian Trail leave the confines of this garden. Only where asphalt, concrete, and buildings cover the land does the garden—for the moment—fail to prosper. But let the buildings crumple into ruin, let the roadway fall into disuse and from the cracks and between the boards and bricks its seeds will germinate and plants rise. Within several decades all will have surrendered to a virile botanical embrace.

When North America was still largely uncharted wilderness, European mapmakers gave this silva a name: The Great Forest of America. Later, the name would be forgotten as the intricate pattern of woodland Indian culture and the mute plants and animals was shattered, like a glass of crystal abused by unappreciative hands. Today, the forest is known more for its parts, rather than as a whole. We speak of the Green Mountain Forest, the Cherokee Forest, the George Washington Forest, and others.

Francis Packman, the nineteenth century historian, described the Great Forest of America as a vast kingdom of trees which "shadowed the fertile soil, covering the land as the grass covers the garden lawn, sweeping over hill and hollow in endless undulation, burying mountains in verdure, and mantling brooks and rivers from the light of day. Trees overlaid nearly all of the country from ocean strand westward to Arkansas and north to Minnesota, Manitoba, and southeastern Canada. The forest's boundaries were the Atlantic on the east, the open prairies and grasslands of the West, the swamps of Georgia and the Gulf Coast to the south, and in the north the horizon-filling stands of spruce commonly known as the North Woods. The Great Forest sprawled over one-third of the United States.

Half of the Great Forest's original one million-plus square miles is now taken up by farms and fields (the word "fields" means "felled" woods), cities, highways, factories, mines, airports, reservoirs, and the backwaters of a plethora of hydroelectric dams. And cemeteries and trash dumps. The remainder has largely become a managed forest — 95 percent is second, third, and fourth growth trees and subject to constant, if generally supervised, cutting. To the unknowing, rushing through it to the throb of gasoline engines, this remnant may seem impressive. Some of it is. But it is merely a pale shadow of that which once graced the land. The height of the trees has been reduced to 50 percent or less of what it was when nature was still unblessed by European civilization, while their trunks are certainly no more than a third of their forefathers' girths.

Only a small portion is virgin, and most of that is on summits where terrain makes logging difficult. But few trees grow tall on mountain peaks; there, maturity finds them stunted, if hardy, from exposure to cold and the buffeting of winds. It is in sheltered valleys, on gentle slopes, and well-watered lowlands that trees find encouragement to swell their boles and stretch their canopies.

But for all of that, the hiker on the Appalachian Trail will come upon tracts which are miniature copies of the original. In parts of the Great Smoky Mountains and Shenandoah national parks . . . and elsewhere are stands— seldom large and nearly always remote—of botanic nobility. These rare groves provide insight into the past. It is an awesome past which only rarely has been permitted to flourish into the present.

To walk through one of these green mansions is a compelling experience, such as might be found within an ancient cathedral of Christendom. Mighty columns soar to the vault, where their boughs intertwine as if they were hands clasped in prayer—the very inspiration of the Gothic arch. Like candles, slender beams of amber sunlight flicker in the medieval dimness. From the greenery comes a wafting of soft incense. Birds and bats flutter about distant niches. The traveler's footsteps slow and then halt on the mosaic of last year's leaves. He waits, listening in the hush for an unseen organ to crash into the *Te Deum*. This is the forest primeval, the climax forest, a state which takes hundreds of years of striving to achieve. An equilibrium in the total ecology has been reached. Unless some calamity occurs, as fire, plague, or human interference, the forest will perpetuate itself with little change. From the raw materials of rock, air, water, sunlight, and time, Nature has created a masterpiece.

Here, because of the shadows thrown by mighty trees, nurslings succeed only when an oldster topples from a murrain of bark or leaves, spears and tridents of lightning, spell of abnormal freezing, or violent storm. Every year the mature trees fling their seed to the winds and to the loam to ensure dominance of their kind. Long ago, captains of sailing ships plowing the waves out of sight of the American mainland would jot entries in their logs that decks were awash with brimstone: the power of Beelzebub was manifest. But the manifestation was an amazing example of generative, not destructive, power. The "brimstone" was yellow pollen borne on air currents which had stirred the stands of white pine scattered from northern Georgia to Newfoundland.

The white pine was one of the paragons of the Great Forest. Its wood helped to fire the American Revolution. Its tapering trunk rose string-straight for 150 to 200 feet; some even pushed to 250 feet. European eyes blinked to see stands of millions of these glorious spires, of a height and species of conifer undreamed of heretofore.

England's expanding navy saw in these long, flexible sticks the solution to its masting problem. Vessels, increasing in size, needed more wind power. Longer masts could hold more canvas and stretch higher for a breeze. In short order, white pine masts and spars from the Great Forest were soughing and swaying with the winds of the seven seas.

At first, 100 pounds sterling were paid for each great log landed in Britain. But not many years were to pass before the Crown virtually appropriated for itself the white pine stands of its northern colonies. Prison terms and heavy fines were meted out to illegal axmen.

The White Pine Acts, as they were called, blew up a gale of hard feeling among the colonists, who wanted the trees for their own clippers, for trading abroad, and for constructing homes and furniture. The wood is light, soft, and typically creamy white with few blemishes. It saws like butter and warps or swells but little. A first rate mast would fetch a useful sum, $500 or even twice that in today's money; on moonless nights many were rafted to foreign ships loitering nervously in colonial harbors. On a few occasions settlers donned Indian disguise (as if rehearsing for the Boston Tea Party) and chopped down trees in the King's Woods to demonstrate their pique.

The white pine became a symbol of colonial resentment. The ensign of America's infant navy, whose first fleet was assembled in 1775 to intercept a pair of British munitions ships, bore a pine and the inscription "An Appeal to Heaven." But the victorious citizens of a new nation were reckless with their forest patrimony, supposing it inexhaustible. By the 1920s, less than a century and a half later, the monumental stands of white pine were mostly a memory.

In Great Smoky Mountains National Park, botanists have counted 130 species of native trees, more than in all Europe. All but a few are hardwoods. On the park's list are the names of over 1,300 native flowering plants, about 2,000 species of fungi, nearly 350 mosses and liverworts, and 230 lichens. A hardwood forest provides wildlife with a greater quantity and variety of food than a conifer forest, and this riotous diversity of vegetation supports 50-some kinds of native mammals, from flying squirrels and the tree-climbing gray fox to bears, and 200 species of birds, from the tufted titmouse to the wild turkey. Visiting naturalists from many nations have expressed amazement at the flora and fauna of this relatively small preserve of 800 square miles. One fourth of the park is virgin—the largest such area east of the Rockies to escape the attention of the timber engineers. It is a microcosm of the Great Forest at its hospitable best. . . .

Man has existed in the Great Forest for perhaps 20,000 years. And for more than half of that period he has had a constant companion in the form of an almost unique wild plant.

This plant—today recognized as the oldest living thing—covers over 100 acres near Losh Run, a half-dozen miles north of the Appalachian Trail crossing at Duncannon, Pennsylvania. The low evergreen shrub, a species of box huckleberry, first attracted attention in 1790. Not until 1918, however, was it made the subject of extensive study.

Investigators found its small, oval, serrate leaves and edible dark blue berries to be uniform in shape throughout; moreover, tests showed it to be self-sterile, incapable of producing offspring. They concluded the patch is a single plant that is steadily enlarging.

Owing to the physical geography of its mountainous site, the *Gaylussacia brachycera* is 1¼ miles long, though limited to a width of a few hundred feet. Measurements indicate that its rhizomes or underground stem-roots which send up leafy shoots, are elongating at the rate of six inches yearly. So scientists believe this box huckleberry has been occupied in attaining its present length for over 12,000 years! . . .

Many of the trees of the Great Forest have uses in which they excel, and are not only used at home but exported by the shipload. Hickory smokes meat, is shaped into the shock-resisting handles of striking tools as axes and hammers, and provided spokes for the wheels of the pioneers' Conestoga wagons. American holly becomes piano keys and the resilient ash is worked into oars. The policeman's club is osage-orange. Tupelo makes wear-resisting factory floors. Furniture that defies time and knocks is manufactured of red maple. Black gum, which will not split even under assault by wedge and sledge, is favored for wooden machinery parts; the mountain ladies of the South select its twigs for "chaw sticks" to brush snuff, or pulverized tobacco, behind the lips—a tingly practice known as "dipping snuff" as opposed to the rarer "sniffing snuff." Flowering dogwood has long been used by weavers for shuttles. Thread seldom snaps on its smooth surface, and the closely-knit wood withstands great centrifugal force. Each spring this little tree heralds the new growing season with outsized immaculate white bracts; each October it enriches the autumn palette with small scarlet fruits which, it is said, sate the appetites of 93 kinds of birds.

And there is the tulip tree, a lordly tower of light, easily worked timber popular with cabinet makers since Puritan times. George Washington, who knew an aristocrat when be saw one, planted the tree on his Mount Vernon estate. Two of these *Liriodendron tulipifera,* now pushing above the 120-foot mark, are the tallest plants at this national shrine. The tulip tree (often, and erroneously, called the yellow poplar) has an unusual leaf which is most unlikely to be mistaken for any other species: it does not come to a point, but ends with a broad edge rather like a spade. The tree's bouquets of tulip-like flowers, each an exotic composition in pale green and orange, remind the onlooker of the Tahitian paintings of Gauguin. . . .

Of the world's 18 elm species, *U. Americana* is held to be the loveliest on reaching maturity. When its days as a stately lawn tree are over the strong, beautifully cross-grained wood is sought after for furniture and flooring. Sadly, those days are now numbered—it is being ruined by the Dutch elm disease. The disease entered the United States about 1926 as a fungus in a shipment of Carpathian elm burls which were to be sliced into veneering. D.E.D. is carried from tree to tree by two kinds of beetles and produces great masses of spores which crowd into the small vessels within the tender spring shoots, literally choking the tree to death. In recent years whole cities have lost their considerable populations of elms. Springfield, Massachusetts, is no longer the "City of Elms."

White oak, *Quercus alba,* has played a stirring role in American history. Its timber launched swift windjammers by the thousands to convey a new nation's produce to foreign shores. Good oak was resistant to the shock of minor bottomings and could absorb the stresses of hard naval duty without failure. For hundreds of years the sea power of many nations rested on oaken hulls. Britain seized Canada from the French partly in order to deny her ships the oak planking and pine masting of the Great Forest.

Prodigious amounts of oak were swallowed up by rival fleets. During the Revolutionary War, Massachusetts alone sent out more than 1,600 privately manned vessels to prey on British commerce. As another example, some 500 choice white oaks were hewn in Delaware in the 1920s to help reconstruct just one man-of-war, the U.S. Frigate *Constitution*. When an English cannonball bounced screaming off the *Constitution*'s staunch oak side in the War of 1812 she fought on to glory as "Old Ironsides." Her mainmast, three feet square and 112 feet in length, had been originally a white pine tree, but all the highest pines having been chopped down in the century that followed her triumphs at sea, a Douglas fir from Washington State was substituted when she was rebuilt.

The days of sail predated the widespread use of copper sheathing or closely spaced nailheads to thwart the borings of the toredo, the ravenous shipworm, below the saltwater line. The best wooden vessels lasted only a few years. Whole forests of *Quorcus alba* lie on the bottom of the oceans. . . .

There is no mechanical substitute for a tree. In addition to providing food and abode for birds and wildlife, trees offer shade and shield the earth from the sun's fire. Roots bind the soil, staking it down to prevent gullying and washing away. The spongy floor of a live forest holds tremendous reservoirs of fresh water; these are the founts of rivers. Insects tumble from branches into streams to feed hungry trout and catfish. Harmful noise, loud, incessant, startling, or irritating, is absorbed and muffled. Dust is held down and ruinous winds are tamed by trees—the taller the trees the better—to a mere whimper, a tenth or less of their force. Plants purify the air by breathing in carbon dioxide and returning oxygen. (Man and his combustion machinery do the reverse.)

Besides adding to the vital supply of free floating oxygen, plants moisten and cool the air. They accomplish this feat by breathing out vast quantities of water through the stomatal openings of their leaves. A mature apple tree, for instance, will lift three to four gallons of water every hour of daylight into the atmosphere during its green-leaf season; the transpiration of a great elm with perhaps eight million leaves might be 30 times that amount. One large, well-watered tree can produce cooling equivalent to over one million Btu.'s or 200 times that of the average room air conditioner. And the power source of the tree air conditioner is free—the sun. . . .

It is written that Gautama Buddha received the heavenly light as he sat in meditation beneath a pipal tree, the *Ficus religiosa*.

"The forest," Buddha said (among other pronouncements), "is a peculiar organism of unlimited kindness and benevolence that makes no demands for its sustenance and extends generously the products of its life activity; it provides protection to all beings, offering shade even to the axman who destroys it."

Having said this, Buddha glanced upward and smiled. The sun fondled the pipal tree and its leaves stirred dreamily in the gentle breeze. In its cool shadow was serenity.

From *Hiking the Appalachian Trail*, vol. 2, edited by James Hare, Rodale, 1975.

WILLIAM BARTRAM

Gore-Tex may have replaced oiled skins for rainwear, but the human eye delights today at the same colors and shapes as it did hundreds and thousands of years ago. Countless hikers take to the AT in springtime with one goal in mind: to see the spectacular flame azalea in bloom. Here we time-travel with William Bartram in the 1780s as he "discovers" and names the plant. Bartram was among America's first serious explorer-botanists.

Most Gay and Brilliant Flowering Shrub

THE EPITHET *FIERY* I ANNEX TO THIS MOST CELEBRATED SPECIES OF AZALEA, as being expressive of the appearance of its flowers, which are in general of the color of the finest red lead, orange and bright gold, as well as yellow and cream color; these various splendid colors are not only in separate plants but frequently all the varieties and shades are seen in separate branches on the same plant; and the clusters of the blossoms cover the shrubs in such incredible profusion on the hillsides that suddenly opening to view from dark shades, we are alarmed with apprehension of the hill being set on fire. This is certainly the most gay and brilliant flowering shrub yet known . . .

From *Travels of William Bartram*, by William Bartram, Yale University Press, 1958.

BENTON MacKAYE

That Benton MacKaye, outdoorsman, had an education in the classics is evident in a witty, enthusiastic bit of support he provided for a local hiking club in North Carolina. MacKaye calls himself "the Nestor of the Appalachian Trail," referring to a king of Pylos who as an old man served as a counselor to the Greeks at Troy. MacKaye was hardly an old man at this point (1933), but the work of creating the AT was already twelve years along, and the torch had been passed to other leaders by its founding father–philosopher.

Letter to Smoky Mountains Hiking Club

Knoxville, Tennessee
November 15, 1933

Miss Margaret Broome,
Chairman, Handbook Committee,
Smoky Mountains Hiking Club

Dear Margaret:

I am happy to respond to your kind request to write some words of greeting for your Handbook, especially so in view of my pleasing experience with so many of your Club members during my recent illness here in Knoxville. . . .

Friendship is a hard thing to define. To me it is a portion of creation held in common. Our special portion (yours and mine) we call the wilderness—the portion untarnished by act of man. Such is our common bond. To cherish it (even as human fellowship itself)—such is our common goal.

For we need this thing wilderness far more than it needs us. Civilizations (like glaciers) come and go, but the mountain and its forest continue the course of creation's destiny. And in this we mere humans can take part—by fitting our civilization to the mountain.

This, friend Margaret, is the thing that you are doing (you and your Clubmates)—you who have wrought your portion of the Appalachian Trail—you who cherish your strategic Smoky Mountains for yourselves and all America. To you, my age-old friends, go the depths of my fellow-feeling—for the good year 1934 and the coming happy years of action.

Your own,
Benton MacKaye
Nestor of the Appalachian Trail

From a Smoky Mountains Hiking Club handbook, 1933.

LINDA TATSAPAUGH

Thru-hikers and others going a long way commonly take on a "trail name" of their own choosing, though often the name is concocted in jest by a friendly hiking partner who puts a label on qualities one might not recognize in oneself. Linda Tatsapaugh called herself "Hunger Hiker" because she found sponsors who promised money for a feed-the-hungry project if she finished her hike. As it turned out, Tatsapaugh raised more than money. She raised her spirits as well.

Trail Diary, 1990

OKAY, OKAY! I GIVE UP! I WILL NEVER BE ABLE TO ENCOMPASS MY JOURNEY up the Appalachian Trail, its monumental effects on my life, the extremes of emotion, and all the minute anecdotes which filled each day, in one report. I can't even find words to adequately describe what I do attempt to share. But write I must, or no one will understand who I've become, or why (and I'll never receive my 2,000-mile rocker from the ATC). Besides, it is high time to bring this adventure to a retrospective denoument.

My decision to hike the AT grew from a long but casual relationship with it. I used to hike the Mount Rogers section with my father, brother, and several friends. Although I live in the piedmont of North Carolina, I began to think of the mountains as my home, and looked to a thru-hike as a homecoming. As a sophomore in high school, I began the planning that I knew would someday come to fruition. Two friends at different times agreed to go, but backed out because of other commitments. I delayed by a year, but once I held that first guidebook in my hand, I had no desire to do anything else until every one of those mountains was climbed. It didn't take long on the trail before I would have been satisfied with a few less, but I never questioned my decision or my goal.

I hiked for a cause, which I found was not unique among my '90 classmates. A supporter of hunger-fighting causes, I worked to raise sponsorship for a 2,100-mile CROP Walk (CROP Walks, generally 6-10 miles long, are held by Church World Service). I began preparations for the trail a year in advance. That's not necessary for a thru-hike, but I loved every minute of it! I was actually on the trail (in spirit or body) for two years that way.

After most of my contacts for sponsorship and speaking engagement were set, I turned to physical preparation. This involved training, schedule-planning, and food-gathering. Being somewhat of a pauper, I opted for bulk foods. I built a food drier out of wood, screening, and a light bulb. I experimented with drying various fruits and vegetables. The best candidates were peas, carrots, onions, mushrooms, apples, and bananas. Less successful were celery (there's nothing left once the water's gone) and green beans (probably because I used canned beans).

I bought 20 pounds of self-rising flour, 20 pounds of rice, and several bags of lentils, as well as an assortment of noodle dishes (ramen and macaroni and the coveted Lipton noodles), 48 Snickers bars, 40 packets of soup, 16 jars of peanut butter, tea, and other goodies. My post-trip comments? Flour is wonderfully useful. Get minute rice—taste doesn't matter at 9:00 on a cold dark night. Lentils are terrific nutritionally; however, I could never wait until they were fully-cooked. The more variety in noodle dishes, the more sane are one's food fantasies. The one food-staple-must-have-absolutely—peanut butter, peanut butter, peanut butter! And I never before realized how loudly my body could scream out for a Snickers bar!

I packed my supplies into 20 boxes and addressed them to myself at various points along the trail, spread out about 100 miles apart. My roommate, Sharon, volunteered to send them to me. Included were paper and pen, toilet paper, sno-seal, film, and guide books.

April 1st found me atop Springer Mountain, surrounded by four well-wishing friends and one who was to join me for a week. I chose April Fool's Day on purpose, in case I wanted to quit later and say, "Just Kidding!" But I had no doubt I would sooner or later arrive on Mt. Katahdin.

Erik and I began slowly, but averaged 10 miles a day. Looking back at the profile maps, I am impressed, especially considering that Erik had never backpacked before in his life! We ran into cold weather and rain, and developed our first blisters. But our adrenalin cast an excited blanket of oblivion to hardship over us. We ate with gusto, slept soundly, and rose early. Our breaks were short to compensate for limited daylight hours. All this changed drastically by the time I reached Vermont!

After leaving Erik beside his car at Unicoi Gap, I moved ahead to gain mileage toward my next rendezvous, in Wesser. During the first week, we had camped in my two-person (so they claim) Sierra Designs Flashlight tent, very warmly. Without company, I now sought out shelters for ease of set-up and to be sociable. I learned lessons in thermo-dynamics—wind is freer to blow through a shelter than a tent; tents retain more body heat than shelters; and you can make friends quickly by sharing your tent. That is how I met my first thru-hiking partner, Doug "Geronimo" Horne. After one night of freezing in a shelter, I asked for volunteer tentmates. I figured I could trust a Presbyterian minister. We hiked into Wesser together, and then did not meet again until Hot Springs, and did not hike together again until Damascus.

A word on the state of trails in the south: Georgia—up and down and up and down. The planners did not miss a single possible incline on the route northward. And they did not waste energy in constructing gradual paths. I do remember several switchbacks, but those were the exception rather than the rule. In contrast, North Carolina and Tennessee brought on higher peaks, but also an excellent system of switchbacks. I don't think it is necessary to find the most difficult route up a mountain in order to appreciate the peak experience. I do not mean this negatively, but as a suggestion for future trailblazing.

Georgia lay in winter slumber, with only the sprite violets to greet us. NC and Tennessee bloomed in front of my eyes. I saw my first blooming dogwood, and the first of many wildflowers to bless my travels. I was joined in the Smokies by a resident of the area, Jim Rugh, who pointed out significant sights from the many vistas along the ridgewalk. We reached Clingman's Dome in fog and Newfound Gap in the rain. But the magic of the Smokies captured my heart. It pained me to walk through many skeletal patches of infected woods, and I vowed to join the fight against acid rain.

A stop in Hot Springs was required. I welcomed . . . Elmer, Gretchen, Jason, and Freddie at the Inn at Hot Springs. I barely tore myself away, not realizing how many more times I would have to do that again. I completed North Carolina/Tennessee mainly by myself, making 18-20 miles each day; I was strong and in love with the trail life.

My first setback struck just south of Damascus—shin splints. But then I began hiking with Doug and Mitch "The Breeze" Keiler, and their support coaxed me through that pain and tendonitis. In fact, I hiked more miles while thus inflicted than before the pain. I ended up hiking about 1000 miles with these guys, and I believe they exponentially increased my enjoyment of the trip. Friends are important. . . .

New Hampshire offered the spectacular and forbidding White Mountains. Mark and I tackled them with the plan I would recommend to other hikers: work the huts. Skeptical at first, I found interesting staff and guests, good food, free lodging (I have problems with charging at campsites), and something to look forward to each day. We stayed at Lonesome Lake, Zealand Falls, and Madison Springs Huts. We worked one day at Dodge Camp, too. We ascended Washington in clouds. For the next two weeks, the summit was clear as a bell!

After a day's respite in Gorham, we attacked our final state—Maine! I admit exhaustion dampened my gusto for the trail by then, and the rough terrain added to my frustration. I don't think the trail needs to be so difficult. Many times we climbed boulder faces, and then looked to the side and found easier routes up. I'm not sure Mahoosuc Notch should be mandatory trail hiking either. It's exciting, but also dangerous. I would suggest an alternative route for those who don't choose to rock-climb on their hikes. Also, I saw potentially straight and beautiful sections of the old AT which were bypassed for more difficult and less scenic routes. I suppose the paper companies can do what they wish with their land, but it is a shame to keep moving the trail.

I don't remember much about Maine, except rocks, roots, and lots of water—at an average of every 4.7 miles, by my calculations. The Bigelows and White Cap were breath-taking—so were the streams we crossed! Trail magic found us a ride across the Kennebec via two Outward Bound members. At our first view of Katahdin, we weren't sure of what we saw. But the image haunted us again and again, until another hiker confirmed that we were looking at our goal of 5 months. We closed in on the Big K, excited, but mainly glad to be finally at the end. We met Mark's parents and Carol Moore, the Lagunatic, at Katahdin Springs campground. We climbed in clouds, but as we sat on the summit, they cleared for a few moments of picture-taking. I sat, mainly numb from having completed a dream of half a lifetime. I wanted to shout my victory, but all I could mumble was, "What next?" It is only through later contemplation that I can realize the extent of my journey; then it was just another mountain.

This report has chronicled the physical highlights of my hike. What I found on the trail, however, was that the experience was with people. I hiked 1000 miles each with three super men and good friends. I accepted the aid of trail people like Elmer, Rusty, the Garmans in Boiling Springs, PA, and Jan and Levi Long. I learned to depend on guardian angels in the form of Randy Huddle, Carol Moore, the Humphreys, and especially Charlie (with the red van) Rausa. I met thru-hikers and weekenders who offered me camaraderie and compassion when I needed it. And I gave back where I could. Without these people, the trail would have just been another wilderness adventure. They have affected my life immensely, and I thank them eternally for it. I will never be able to hike the Appalachian Trail again without remembering the generous, loving, beautiful people who brought it to life for me.

From "Hunger Hiker Hits the Trail," *Appalachian Trail Conference Report* by Linda Tatsapaugh, 1991.

SUZIE ROSENBLITH

A worker at the Hulbert Outdoor Center in Fairlee, Vermont, at the time of her thru-hike, Suzie Rosenblith was physically ready when the odds against her were suddenly upped by a springtime blizzard that left much of the East Coast, including the Smoky Mountains, buried under insurmountable amounts of snow. Willpower was the one thing not to leave at home.

Trail Diary, 1993

I T BEGAN AS A TRIP, SOMETHING FUN, A CHALLENGE A GREAT WAY TO SPEND 6 months. March 6, 1993 was a beautiful. Only a slight dusting of snow left on the forest floor, 65°—a perfect day to begin a long hike. Our packs were quite heavy. 60 pounds each—we would walk a half mile and have to stop and bend over—our backs hurt so much. But, with relative ease we made it up to Springer Mtn. I got this funny feeling in my stomach a feeling of question, and uncertainty. But it was too late to turn back. I was headed north: The first days were O.K. tough getting a routine down, getting used to the weight, aches & pains every night—my feet were begging for an explanation.

On the fifth day of our journey we could tell a cold front was coming in. The wind had picked up the days & nights were brisker. On March 13th we met a trail maintainer as we descended Unioci Gap (GA). He told us there was a forecast for 14-16 inches of snow. We thanked him for the information and continued on. When he was out of earshot we both laughed at him. I live in Vermont, my hiking partner Maine—we knew they didn't get that kind of snow in the south in the middle of March. So we continued on up to Tray Mountain for the night. When we got to the shelter the wind was pretty fierce and it was blowing straight into the shelter so we decided since we had a 4-season tent to set it up. It was probably our smartest decision ever— because the Tray Mtn. shelter (now aptly dubbed the Meat Locker) might as well not had a roof. The 5 people in the shelter were covered in 2 inches of snow Saturday morning. We added two more thru-hikers to our tent and waited out what we later found out to be the "Storm of the Century." The day after we began our trudge 10 miles to Dicks Creek Gap where the Blueberry Patch was waiting. It was the hardest 10 miles I'd ever walked both physically & emotionally. After making it to the B.P. I realized how strong my will is and you can have the finest gear, be in the best physical shape but without a strong will you won't make it the 2000 miles.

From Thru-Hiker Report to Appalachian Trail Conference by Suzie Rosenblith, 1993.

CATHERINE EICH

Injured and alone in the woods, with bad weather and darkness coming on: it's every hiker's nightmare. What keeps the thru-hiker going, against such odds? We might borrow Edgar Allan Poe's infamous character, the Imp of the Perverse, to explain it. The same curious energy that draws us to the dangerous brink of the waterfall, to peer into terrifyingly beautiful empty space, may draw the frightened hiker onward. Or perhaps it's the instinctive feeling that turning back means depression and defeat, while carrying on promises adventure, that strange brew of exhilaration and fear.

Trail Diary, 1984

TOOK A BAD SPILL ON THE ICY PATH BEYOND NEWFOUND GAP. PASSED OUT for a few minutes. When I woke, I was chilled to the bone. Briefly forgot where I was, why I was there, how I came to be there. I thought I'd just woke up from a nap and maybe I was still dreaming. Everything around me seemed a bit dark, with a greenish hue. The cold and the rain and the tearing wind soon brought to me the reality of the situation, and my aching arm and pounding head were telling me to turn back, wait at the road for a ranger, get a ride to Gatlinburg. Surely they would assist an injured hiker? But I had the "milage fever" that day, and the hiker in me answered "Keep goin', if I turn back now will I come back to this?" Not the sensible thing to do, I know, but neither is hiking alone.

From Thru-Hiker Report to Appalachian Trail Conference by Catherine Eich, 1984.

CLAUDE LEINEKE

Appalachian Trail diaries often include comments by one hiker about another. Sometimes a hiker whose own diary seems to be nothing but a list of objectively recorded data (weather, mileage, menus, expenses) emerges as a fully drawn character, body and soul, in another hiker's words. Claude Leineke, of Chicago introduces us to a small crowd of colorful characters who come in and out of view. See "Grandma Gatewood," under West Virginia.

Trail Diary, 1976

*I*N HOT SPRINGS, NORTH CAROLINA, I MET 68 YEAR OLD MARY JO CALLAN, WHO is doing the length of the trail in sections each summer. She carries a 35 pound backpack, a pocketbook in one hand and a small stuff bag in her other, and walks from five to nine miles a day. She is becoming another trail personality, second only to Grandma Gatewood who completed the entire trail three times after the age of 60.

Inside a shelter on a cold, windy, snowy morning, Indian Harry was snug in his mummy bag. He is a full blooded Sioux who commutes along the trail and takes jobs in towns along the way. Harry can give information ranging from how many mice in Curly Maple lean-to, to the best way of hopping a freight from Georgia to Illinois—he calls the train the Chicago Flash.

In contrast to tumbleweed Indian Harry, I met a well-rooted corporate lawyer also named Harry, who was hiking the whole trail on his free weekends. He was dressed for an afternoon on the golf course. He carried an Austrian walking cane, a crushed wax cup for water, and a small bag of jellybeans. Harry's technique was to have his wife drop him off in their air conditioned cadillac at one point, then pick him up in another location. Then off to an air conditioned motel for steak and scotch. . . .

Across the bridge and back in the hills, I met up with John Manard, or Crazy Injun as he likes to call himself. He is a Mohawk Indian and artist and writer who travels with his dog Snoopy—a strange cross between beagle and doberman. Crazy Injun had on blue jeans, blue chambray shirt, and beaded indian necklace, with a red bandana around his forehead. He had a bowie knife on one hip and a canteen on the other; an instamatic camera in one shirt pocket and a pint of Bacardi 151 proof rum in his hip pocket. He told me that all Indian braves must climb the sacred Mount Katahdin before they die. He had made two previous attempts but failed. This year, he was on his way again for the third attempt, but when we parted company he was heading, with determination, in the wrong direction.

From *"Your Feet Must Be Stronger Than Your Head!"; or Memories of an Appalachian Trail Summer,* Thru-Hiker Report to Appalachian Trail Conference by Claude Leineke, 1976.

WILLIAM O. DOUGLAS

Atop the Smoky Mountains, where the trail actually follows, snakelike, the North Carolina–Tennessee border, children, and some grown-up hikers we know, delight in hiking in two states simultaneously, a foot on either side of the line. Supreme Court Justice William O. Douglas took pleasure in this fun and in making informed observations on the natural world during his hikes in the Smokies. Douglas was a lifelong liberal, defending free speech and the natural world whenever a case bearing on these issues came his way. This passage from My Wilderness *begins its hike in Newfound Gap, just north of Clingman's Dome, the AT's highest point, and heads northward, past Charlie's Bunion, one of the best rocky precipices on the entire trail, with its extraordinary view westward into Tennessee—a sight that would have stunned and inspired pioneers spying the verdant valleys west of the Appalachians for the first time.*

One Leg in Carolina, the Other in Tennessee

O NE FALL, HARVEY AND I MADE A FOUR-DAY HIKE ALONG THE RIDGE OF THE eastern Smokies. We picked up the Appalachian Trail at Newfound Gap and followed it to Mount Cammerer, where we dropped off the mountain to the pleasant valley of Cosby.

The trail for the most part follows the ridge. Yet when it reaches a peak, it cuts under and around it. The ridge is the state line, the trail swinging back and forth across it. At times it is so narrow one can almost straddle it, having one leg in North Carolina and the other in Tennessee.

It is here I first saw the spruce-fir forests that thrive above the 5000-foot level. This is the red spruce with four-cornered needles that never lie flat. The fir is the aromatic southern balsam with needles in a horizontal plane. These spruce-fir forests cast a deep shade that is damp from the moisture which the tall trees collect from the restless clouds. These forests are so dark that the undergrowth of ferns is low. The forest floor is made up mostly of deep moss, oxalis, and lichens spreading in great profusion.

While a hardwood forest has a luminous glow, the spruce-fir climax forest shuts out most of the light. That is partly due to the dark shade of the foliage, partly to the density of the needles and boughs, partly to the way the upper branches interlock, making a closely woven canopy which lets little sunlight through.

Yet this upper zone is not completely spruce and fir. The yellow birch sometimes keeps them company. And the mountain ash too. Once the vegetation is free from the spruce-fir coverage, it grows lush. Rhododendron is here in quantity—both the high and low species. Open places are thick with high blueberries. And wherever the sun touches these ridges, the viburnum flourishes.

This was late September, and the viburnum was a spanking red. The mountain ash was pumpkin-yellow and heavy with bright red berries. A lone yellow birch, now a golden plume, lit up a gloomy stand of spruce and fir, as if it were aglow.

We stopped often to eat the blueberries. We had competition, for it seemed that every stand of these bushes was cover for a ruffed grouse that sometimes went out with a roar that made us jump. Wildflowers had long passed their peak. Occasionally, however, we saw the white snakeroot and the star saxifrage, as delicate as a Japanese painting. Goldenrod still bloomed; and now and then we came across mountain angelica, which resembles the wild parsnip.

The trees were still dripping from the night's rain, and mist touched the ridge gently. Fog-colored caterpillars with black streaks down their backs worked their way around spruce trunks.

We found Charlies Bunion (5375 feet) deep in fog. This favorite lookout of mine, where on a clear day one can see for miles, was surrounded by whirling fog that cut visibility to a few rods. Dry Sluice Gap—a narrow hogback that drops almost sheer on the Tennessee side—was also swallowed in fog. Then the wind came up and cleared the ridge. We heard a nuthatch sing and saw a Carolina wren leave a stand of mountain ash. Then came the familiar song of the chickadee.

The sun was now streaming down. We came across droppings of the red fox and scratchings of a bobcat. A dead shrew with a strong musk odor had been left by a fox. The floor of the spruce-fir forest showed bright green blankets of moss. Star moss lay thick underfoot. The trunks of the firs were covered with mosses, and their lower branches hung with a beardlike lichen. Little spruce trees—one inch high and one year old—had taken root in the moss of the forest floor. Oyster mushrooms grew like tiny shelves from the sides of down logs. High overhead—so distant we could not see it--a raven sang his song. It came over and again in clear, almost metallic notes, like a xylophone.

At Hughes Ridge camp we put up a tent, for rain was threatening. There is a spring of cold, bubbling water at this camp—a treasure on these ridges. For while there is abundant water in the canyons of the Smokies, there is not much on the ridges.

There is good wood for cooking wherever there is birch or beech. These trees have a reputation for making good fires. The red spruce is different. It has moisture pockets that sometimes explode with such violence, they put out the fire. That happened twice to Harvey one wet night.

This night we chopped out the center of some dead birch logs and got a brisk, crackling fire going. We were drinking hot soup when the moon came up in the east. A barred owl hooted in the distant woods, calling in a resonant tone, "Who cooked for you?"

The last sound I heard was the dripping of the trees. It was the first morning sound too. And when we awoke, the fog had enveloped us. But soon the sun came out—at first briefly, and finally in full glory. We took two hours of sunshine to dry the camp out, spreading our tent, sleeping bags, and ground cloths over bushes.

When we headed east, we came to a stand of beech rising in splendid isolation, their leaves turning gold. This tree does not produce a good crop every year. But this year the ground was fairly covered with its little triangular-shaped nuts.

We stopped short of Eagle Rock, where a protruding ledge offered comfortable seats. The sky was now mostly clear, and far to the west we could see the Cumberland Plateau, a dark green line in the distance. In between was Knoxville and Oak Ridge, surrounded with clearings that showed light green. Charlies Bunion was far to the left; and now that the fog had lifted, I could see that the crest trail we had traveled was shaped like a huge fishhook.

We dropped a few hundred feet to Copper Gap, a low point on the ridge where the spruce-fir forest, underlain with moss, grows thick. Then we climbed 600 feet or so to Mount Sequoyah, named for a chief of the Cherokees whose statue stands in Statuary Hall, Washington, D.C. Here we had lunch. The fog moved in, shutting out the sun. But the sky, as shown by our light meters, was still bright. Not a breath of air stirred. After lunch we lay in our shirt sleeves, discussing the soil under these hardwood forests.

The leaf fall in the Smokies averages perhaps two tons per acre each year. As the leaves become packed down they begin to rot, rebuilding the soil from which they came. This rotting process is caused by bacteria and fungi which require shade and moisture for their work. The decayed leaf litter gradually produces humus, the key constituent of topsoil. Now the earthworms go to work, passing the soil through their bodies and increasing its porosity. Mice, shrews, and moles move in, eating the insects and the earthworms. In the Smokies there are as many as a million earthworms in one acre of hardwood forest, and a hundred or more mice, shrews, and moles. All these animals tend to make the soil porous and spongelike, so that the water soaks into the ground.

As we hiked east, we came to down trees across the trail and saw how near the underlying rock was to the surface of the ridge. At places it was hardly a foot, never more than three feet. The steep slopes, the heavy rainfall, the thin soil make fast runoffs disastrous. Charlies Bunion and the other outcroppings of rock along the ridge where the tree cover has been removed are permanent warnings of what could happen to much of this country.

The second night we camped in a shelter at Tri-Corner. The next morning a thick fog possessed the ridge. We sloshed forward for several hours before it began to lift. As the first streamers of sun came through, a flock of blue jays met us. Now we came to thick stands of blueberries where ruffed grouse were feeding. We stopped for lunch where the trail overlooks a bowl-like valley on the Carolina side. This land, cut over thirty-five years ago, was showing new tree growth. Spruce twelve feet high was everywhere. Now and then a maple showed red and a birch yellow. One long finger of dark, somber spruce marked the boundary of an old burn. Somehow or other an ancient sourwood tree had escaped the ax and the fire and stood in all its scarlet glory. One ancient yellow birch shot up straight as an arrow. But the rest of the birch in this stretch of the mountains was bent and gnarled.

It rained again the next night at Cosby Knob shelter and a host of red-backed mice invaded our packs. The morning was foggy and the trail we walked was soggy. We were now dropping in elevation, Low Gap being only 4000 feet high. The change in elevation brought changes in vegetation. Oaks appeared, and their acorns covered the trail. Now we saw the hemlocks again on the northern slopes and sugar maples and silver-bell trees too. Here were cucumber magnolia trees whose pale yellow, fragrant flowers bring the woods to life, come springtime, and turn to dark red cucumbers that break open at maturity and expose the seeds on their surface. These trees that sometimes have a girth of ten feet were a splash of gold this September. Laurel and rhododendron grew in stands that seemed impassable, and they were intertwined with a vine called the *aristolochia*, or Dutchman's-pipe, whose stem was nearly two inches thick.

The wind was strong, the sky black. Thick clouds kept sweeping across the trail. The ridge would suddenly clear, then be enveloped again. When it was at last free of fog, I could see that we had left the spruce and fir behind. Now the red maples, birch, and beeches were thick. The fire cherry and blackberry showed on open slopes. We saw occasional striped maples, some thirty feet high. This tree, that the mountain folks call moosewood, showed the first touch of the golden color it would soon display. We found the touch-me-not in seed. I learned that its seed pods are under tension. For when I touched one, it would burst, sending its seeds out in a radius of eighteen inches or more. Its appropriate scientific name is *Impatiens*.

When we reached Mount Cammerer the wind was fresh out of the southeast and the clouds were high and broken. Mount Cammerer Lookout—a round wooden building on a pile of rocks—perched precariously on the narrow ridge. The Smokies have two seasons when fires are dangerous—Spring and Fall. Mount Cammerer then becomes an important observation post. This day it was empty. We picked some of the teaberry fruits, in abundance at Mount Cammerer, and chewed them for their wintergreen flavor.

The wind was so strong and cold, we did not stop long. We dropped directly off the mountain to Groundhog Ridge and the trail that would take us to Cosby.

We descended about 3000 feet in less than two hours. The first few hundred seemed almost straight down, though they probably were 80°. The slopes were covered with rhododendron, and I felt like a bear threading my way through it. Part of the time I was on my hands and knees, dropping my pack. Most of the time I was sitting down, sliding. The ground was soaking wet, the humus slippery, the rhododendron leaves slick. It made travel hazardous. Soon we were on gentler slopes and met Anne, who had walked up to meet us. The bottle gentian was making bluish streaks along the lower slopes. The galax, with shining green leaves, was turning bronze. The tulip trees and the buckeyes now reached to the heavens. And as we touched a stream, we found sycamores with their feet near the water. Wild grape hung like huge ropes from many of the trees.

The three of us had lunch by a creek at the foot of Groundhog Ridge and talked of the botanical history of these mountains. During the Ice Age the Smokies saved many species from extinction. The Smokies were one such refuge, eastern Asia another. The two have many plants in common—the tulip tree, trailing arbutus, Virginia creeper, some ferns, wild hydrangea, sassafras, persimmon, witch hazel, jack-in-the-pulpit, Dutchman's-breeches, shooting star, wintergreen. These and many others have close counterparts in China and Japan.

From *My Wilderness: East to Katahdin, Adventures in the American Wilderness from Arizona to Maine*, by William O. Douglas, Doubleday, 1961.

TENNESSEE

Day hiker and Catawba rhododendron in the mountains of Tennessee.

Trail miles: 69.5 in Tennessee, 207.7 shared with North Carolina

Trail maintenance: Tennessee Eastman Hiking Club

Highest point: Roan Mt., 6,285 ft.

Broadest river: Laurel Fork

Features: The AT follows the Tennessee border with North Carolina, frequently entering and leaving the state along the mountain crests in Great Smoky Mts. National Park. Spectacular views and rich plant life, including famous Roan Mt. wild rhododendron garden.

Parks, forests, and nature preserves: Great Smoky Mts. National Park, Cherokee National Forest, Roan Mt. State Park

Most intriguing names on the trail: Nolichucky, No Business Knob Shelter

Trail towns: Erwin, Roan Mountain, Hampton

MIC LOWTHER

We all have our favorites. Mic Lowther's trail narrative is one of mine. The combination of candor and crisp observation is a winning one. As in long-distance sailing, where the ship's tight quarters and constant demands on both body and mind can turn mild-mannered crew or captain into mutineers or tyrants, so a long hike, even a hike for fun taken en famille, *can range from blissful to grounds for divorce. The AT is an ever-patient teacher. Few trail narratives succeed as Lowther's does in articulating how the AT challenge brought out the best and the worst in the author. Mic Lowther's self-published book* Walking North *chronicles a 1978 thru-hike; we hike with him here—with his wife, Jerri, and daughter, Kyra—in Tennessee. Four other books of children's adventure stories followed his first writing effort.*

Walking North

WE REACHED DEVIL FORK GAP AN HOUR AFTER BREAKFAST. THE WALK through high, peaceful farmland was deceptively pleasant. We watched people hoe gardens in the distance and talked to residents where the trail passed near houses or yards. We were all set for a fast easy day. No such luck. Devil Fork Gap marked the start of nineteen miles of trail we would remember in great detail.

Billed as "numerous steep grades" in the guide, the trail crossed every fence in five counties and led us scrambling straight up and down every elevated piece of ground within range. We gasped along amid growing frustration, stopping more often than usual. I counted "steeply" twenty-two times in the directions before finding any sign of relief.

A patch of trout lilies and larkspur mercifully rescued us for a lunchtime photo session, then climbing and complaining resumed. Exhausted at day's end, we pitched our tent near a stream—and next morning began again.

Not until the top of 5,516-foot Big Bald did we find a scene of any interest. Curiously twisted trees dotted the weedy summit and followed the meadow-like ridge to the next peak. Bent and shaped by the wind, clutching at rocky soil, the widely spaced trees stood black and silent against low-hanging clouds. We passed through them slowly, now and then stopping to look back.

We were frothing again by mid-afternoon.

"The section between Whistling Gap and Spivey Gap proved to be totally absurd," I wrote in my journal. "They run you straight up a hill to see 'splendid views' of the same damn mountains you've seen all week, then dump you over the side for a descent so steep it's barely possible to stand up. The climb over High Rocks was unnecessary and pointless. We were all fairly sputtering."

Fortunately, relief wasn't far away. The cursed nineteen miles ended as the trail crossed U.S. 19W and leveled off for a quick run to shelter. We camped alone. Kyra gathered wood and helped lay out bags and find places to hang the packs. Jerri topped off the evening by baking a peach and apricot upside-down cake over the campfire. It was easily the high point of the day.

I paged through the guide, noting by flashlight we'd covered nearly forty miles in three days. Climbing had been difficult, even ridiculous, at times, yet we were doing the daily miles and more. We were getting tougher, it appeared. Persistence was paying off . . . perhaps we'd soon be a match for these mountains.

We reached the road to Erwin, Tennessee, the next day around noon. I chose the service road over the high-speed Asheville Highway and thumbed one car. I stood in the Post Office ten minutes later. The closed Post Office: it was Wednesday afternoon.

I banged on a door marked Private. The janitor answered and said everyone had gone to lunch—come back in half an hour. I asked directions to a grocery store: a mile and a half out of town. And I couldn't remember how to get back to the trail. Great planning. I went for a walk.

We'd changed our food supply system in Hot Springs. Instead of loading on ten days' food, walking as far as it would take us, then trying to fill in from stores along the way, we had turned to a more calculated approach.

We'd purchased food for 17 days, enough for 165 miles to Damascus, Virginia. After putting six days' worth in the pack, we'd mailed another six to Erwin and five more to Hampton, Tennessee. Assuming we could arrive during Post Office hours, we could resupply more easily and walk farther with lighter packs between stops.

No one else did it this way. Hikers traveling alone and walking fifteen to twenty miles a day carried food for several hundred miles. They would buy enough in Hot Springs, for example, to last till Damascus.

Some hikers purchased most of their food in advance or had mothers or friends to do their shopping. Their packages were mailed to them along the way; they only had to find the Post Office, load their packs, and move on.

I banged on Private again thirty minutes later and a genuine postal clerk answered. He regarded me with considerable distaste but retrieved the box. I loaded pre-packaged food into my pack, then walked in the rain the mile and a half to Erwin's discount supermarket. We hadn't mailed common items so I bought peanut butter, honey, gorp ingredients, and the like to complete our inventory.

I looked around, wondering what to do next. Damn . . . the whole afternoon was wasting away. Where was the trail?

The road across the field from the store looked familiar. I walked to it and thumbed a ride. The driver took me to where Jerri and Kyra sat under the tied-up rain fly.

"So much for our easy resupply," I said to Jerri.

"What's the problem?"

"The Post Office was closed and I wandered all over looking for a store."

"You got everything, didn't you?"

"Sure, but it took more than three hours."

"We have all day," she said. "Besides, we had a nice time writing letters."

"I hope the next stops go better."

"Such a rush you're in lately." . . .

We climbed quickly on a Forest Service road as rain held to a steady drizzle. We reached the mountain's crest and plunged into dense forest on a zigzagging path. The trail wove sharply in and out of narrow openings between close-packed trees. Light dimmed to near-dark as branches merged thickly about us. Rain dripped, misted, showered. Wind swirled fog through the trees and across our path.

I slowed my pace and looked about in eerie silence. Sky and mountain disappeared; trees and fog remained. Mountaintop syndrome again, but different. No rapturous "see the whole world" view; there was no world . . . only darkened tree trunks, tangled branches, wispy fog. Strange. Striking. Perhaps even . . . beautiful.

The interlude ended just across the crest and we began a long descent. Rain turned long sections of the trail to squishy, boot-slopping mud before we'd gone far. I followed Jerri at a considerable distance and wondered about Kyra, asking again questions that always came at such times.

Was she all right? Would she keep on, day after day, no matter what the weather? She'd dropped behind again and I stopped to look back. No ten-year-old cared to be seen with parents day after day, she'd said. She hiked behind us so she could be Kyra Through-Hiker walking alone. So she could be Walking from Georgia to Maine, not just tagging along.

I felt a stab of conscience as I watched the small figure bob along in shorts, orange rain jacket, and big red pack. Mud streaked and splattered her bare legs. I knew she must be freezing in cold gusts of wind. Why was she still doing this? Because we bribed her with chocolate bars? Hardly. Because other through-hikers treated her as one of them? Perhaps. Even so, was it worth it? Was slopping through the mud today any more fun than yesterday? As she approached, I started to ask. . . .

"Isn't that pretty?" she said, pointing out a red trillium blossoming near the trail. "And look at those Dutchman's breeches—they're getting all wet!"

Her eyes gleamed with the light of a child's discovery. She bent down to touch delicate white blossoms sprinkled with rain.

"That's what happens when you hang out laundry on a rainy day," I replied.

She looked up and smiled, then led the way down the trail. . . .

Next morning, we walked down the mountain into spring. The snow's grip weakened as we descended. Green grass and flowers began to show, then took hold. Looking back, we saw the dividing line above us, white turning to green. The sun shone. The air felt warm. There were no more 6,000-foot peaks until New Hampshire: this was it—spring! And this time, we knew it would stay.

Walking became easier and easier. Rain, snow, ice, high winds, and even steep trail were gone for a time, leaving a smooth path that wound across greening fields and invited us to follow. It seemed filled with promise, no less than if paved with yellow brick.

We walked in single file, Kyra in the middle for the moment. Jerri stopped to look at a flower from time to time, or to stand with her face in the sun, then we moved on. Kyra asked for names of flowers that stood above ankle-deep grass, and those just a touch of color in the green. Jerri supplied them, often with distinguishing marks and family names. I walked behind. My attention wandered. . . .

We had done well. Given the weather, the terrain, the conditioning we'd needed, we had done well. Counting mileage off the trail, thirty-five miscellaneous miles to towns and such, we'd averaged ten miles a day. Exactly according to plan. . . .

Rest stop. Jerri laid down in the sun and Kyra pulled out the canteen of lemonade. Ten minutes stretched to fifteen.

"Let's go," I said.

"Well, okay," Jerri replied.

Ten miles a day. Short days, too. Daylight lasted longer now . . . and nearly six weeks of walking had toughened us. We'd have no trouble making ten miles . . . or twelve . . . maybe fifteen. . . .

Jerri stopped. Something puzzled her.

"Get me the flower book, will you?" she asked. "I don't recognize that one."

I dug it out of her pack. Better keep it on top. . . .

"It's not in here, either," she said. "I'll get its picture and we'll look it up another time."

We moved on. Jerri walked slowly looking from side to side. Kyra followed closely.

Figure twelve . . . no reason why not. We were in shape. Walking would get easier through Virginia. We could really chalk up miles over summer. . . .

Then it hit me, something I hadn't quite seen. A walking distance measured in thousands of miles had always been absurd. Even a few hundred miles once seemed beyond reach. We'd covered four hundred miles now and conditions were improving. If we kept going . . . if we kept doing as well as we had. . . . And there, two miles into spring, I knew Mount Katahdin stood within our grasp. If we kept moving, if we stuck to our plan, we could make it. *We could really walk to Maine!*

Jerri stopped again. She began to joke with Kyra and they laughed and jostled each other for a moment. We walked on, lurching to a stop each time they noticed something new. An hour passed. We dawdled through less than a mile. Another rest stop dragged. Resting . . . from what? Jerri set down her pack again after walking ten minutes more.

"What now?" I asked, exasperation setting in.

"There are things here I want to photograph."

I stood around, waiting, stewing.

"Are we going to walk today?" I asked.

"Sure," she said. "Why?"

"We'll have three miles by nightfall at the rate we're going."

"We'll do better than that. But so what if we don't?"

"We finally have a nice day and easy trail. I'd like to cover some ground."

"These are the things I came to see," Jerri said. "I'm not going to race past them just to make miles."

"We're not *racing* past anything. We're poking along."

"But it's warm and sunny at last and there's new, growing things about. This is what it's all about as far as I'm concerned. Why don't you enjoy it? Breathe the spring air, lay in the sun, run your fingers through the grass. We've earned it!"

"I've been doing that every ten minutes."

"Don't be in such a rush. It's a good day to rest after what we've been through."

She took out her camera and focused on a cluster of purple violets. Kyra shed her pack and joined her. Bristling with irritation, I walked on, stomping away at top speed until Jerri and Kyra had fallen far behind.

I wasn't asking much . . . just a reasonable pace and a reasonable number of miles. I didn't mind stopping . . . I liked to see things, too. But why every ten feet? Was every flower that special?

I covered flat trail in a rush, feeling some urgent need to put miles behind. Feeling the freedom to walk, to go for miles and miles without being slowed by weather. Behind me, Jerri and Kyra felt new freedom, too—to stop and rest and loll in the sun-warmed grass.

After an hour I waited, sitting atop a fence and looking back over a wide meadow I'd crossed. Two figures appeared after a long while, moving slowly, seeming very small on a distant ridge. What would I say? I needed time by myself, perhaps. No . . . that was Kyra's line. I started to laugh: forty days in the wilderness and he wants to be alone.

Jerri and Kyra arrived.

"Were you hoping to get to Maine today?" Jerri asked.

"I just wanted to walk," I said, "and not poke."

"We'll get there," she replied, as I helped her over the fence. "But if we can't enjoy what we're passing through, I don't want to go.". . .

The trail led next morning through sterile woods with hardly a sign of a white blaze. We walked over stony ground, negotiating carefully among intersecting paths and roads. Scenery looked dull, both near and far. A good stretch to cover quickly, it seemed to me, but uncertainty about where we were going slowed us down. Surroundings had been pleasant the day before; I'd been content to mosey and take it all in. Now, with nothing of interest in sight, I wanted to move on.

We reached White Rocks Mountain Firetower about half past ten. Kyra had dropped behind again and was nowhere in sight. Ten minutes passed, then fifteen. She didn't appear. Suddenly angry, I started down the long hill to find her.

I found her a quarter-mile back, crying as she climbed slowly toward the tower.

"Where have you been?" I demanded.

"I . . . I got off . . . the trail," she sobbed.

"If you'd keep up like you're supposed to you wouldn't have that problem. What happened? Why are you crying?"

"I didn't . . . get lost really," she went on, her voice shaken by sobs. "But I . . . I thought I had."

"Give me that pack and let's get moving."

I slung her pack over my shoulder and set a brisk pace. She lagged just behind, still crying and seeking to explain.

"I got halfway . . . up this hill and thought it was wrong . . . so I went back down. At the bottom, I looked around . . . and decided I must have been right after all. But I still wasn't sure . . . and I didn't want to . . . to climb all the way up again for nothing. . . ."

"I thought this would happen sooner or later. You walk in the middle from now on."

"I'm *sorry*, Dad. I . . . was *being* careful. . . ."

"What's the matter?" Jerri asked as we neared the crest of the hill.

"Miss Pathfinder here got confused and thought she'd lost the trail."

"Is she okay? Why are you carrying her pack?"

"Just to get her up this hill. She's not hurt."

"Tell me what happened," Jerri said, putting her arm around Kyra and leading her to the firetower steps.

Kyra sat down and haltingly explained.

"It's all because she keeps dropping behind," I burst in before she'd finished.

"Maybe," Jerri said. "But don't be so harsh. She's scared and upset."

"If she'd keep us in sight she wouldn't *be* upset!"

"I know, but she needs comforting, not yelling."

"She'll walk in the middle now, that's for sure."

"SIMMER DOWN, will you?"

"Dammit, I don't know how we're going to get anywhere. We go slow when it's nice. We go slow when it's boring. Delay after delay. We'll still be poking through Virginia in *December*, if we ever *get* there. . . ."

"Hi," said a voice above us. I looked to the top of the tower stairs and saw Jeff. He'd been visiting the ranger on duty and could not have missed the disquieting scene below.

"I brought you a present," he said with a smile. He bounded down the steps and handed Jerri a bouquet of ramps he'd dug and cleaned.

"Happy May Day," he said with a smile.

I felt foolish and at a loss to explain. Jerri said something to Jeff, then we put on our packs and headed up the trail in silence. Kyra walked in the middle. I followed some distance behind. An hour passed. The scenery did not improve. Later, at our lunch stop, Jerri sought to describe the problem.

"We have different goals for this walk, it appears," she said, gently. "It wasn't obvious till the days got longer and nicer."

"What do you mean?" I asked.

"When the weather was so bad, we all worked together. We did our best and didn't worry about how long it took. Walking is getting easier and more interesting now. The things I came to see are growing and blooming all around, and I want to stop and see them. But you want to go, go, go."

"I don't mind stopping to see things," I said. "If we do our ten miles like we agreed, and maybe some extra to fill in short days, you can stop all you like."

"But that's the problem, don't you see?" Jerri said. "You're on a sched-ule: ten miles a day, seventy miles a week, three hundred miles a month. You're hiking to *Maine*, not to see what's here. I want to enjoy each day as it comes, watch the birds, smell and touch the flowers. You're turning this into a quest. *Gotta-Get-to-Maine*, that's what you've got!"

"If we plan a section for six days, and we bring six days' food, then we should try to do it in six days, right?"

"Sure, and we're doing that. But why get there early? Why carry food to town? Shouldn't we take time when we have it?"

"I guess so," I replied. "But we've been trying to get to shelters when we could. They'll be more crowded in the summer and we won't find space if we take all day getting there."

"Shelters are handy," Jerri said. "We can sometimes stretch a bit to reach one instead of putting up the tent. But why get there at three in the after-noon? Did we come to the woods to see shelters?"

"No, but that's where water usually is, and I'm tired of nights in a wet tent."

"What you're really worried about, I think, is winter hitting Maine before you get there."

"Baxter Park closes October 15," I said. "Two thousand miles in two hundred days puts us there October 6. Add a week because the trail's longer than that, and because we're a little behind . . . it doesn't leave much room."

"What are you going to do when you get there?"

"Well, when we finish the trail we can take our time driving home."

"What!"

"What I meant was. . . ."

"You have everything backwards. It's spring—the beginning. Flowers are growing, the sun is warm, and we can finally do what we came to do. You're thinking about the end. You want to rush through everything to be sure to be there for the *end*!"

"That isn't what I said. . . ."

"Isn't this a little early to be concerned about that? And does it really matter? Didn't every hiker's story we read say 'I wish I'd taken more time'?"

"I suppose."

"Look, I want to get to Maine too," she said. "It's too beautiful to miss, especially in the fall. But I want to live this whole experience and get there the last possible day. If snow starts to fall as we come off Katahdin, that will be perfect."

Jerri was ready for any argument so I took my medicine and agreed to be more patient. Sure, I wanted to go, go, go. Sure, I wanted to reach Katahdin and finish before winter shut the mountain down. Was that so unusual? What I'd tried to say was just what she was saying: let's enjoy the experience; let's reach the goal in time. But it came out different when I said it, like I wanted to race through the hike and relax when it was over. That wasn't what I'd meant. This was simply my approach to problems—set goals; work toward them at a regular pace. It had always worked before. . . .

The moment was lost, in any case. It seemed prudent to be more accommodating for a while. Perhaps we'd make better time as months went on. We'd kept to the plan so far; maybe everything would work out. I'd just have to wait and see. Meanwhile, I guess I could claim one distinction. I had possibly the earliest reported case: Katahdin Fever in Tennessee. . . .

It was obvious, even to me, just how differently Jerri viewed the world than I did. I saw the grand and the magnificent. I had to reach for smaller things, have them called to my attention, as if some interest threshold had first to be crossed.

Jerri had no such threshold. The color of reflections in a puddle, the touch of light and shadow upon a tree, might captivate her as much or more than a waterfall or superb mountain view. The natural world held her attention and she found everything in it of interest.

She'd paged through every flower book, bird book, or other field guide she could find as a child and was still doing so. She had great respect and appreciation for the land and the beauty it provided, and wanted to know all she could about it. That's why she stopped to follow birds and listen to their songs, she said. And why each familiar flower that jumped from the pages of her mind to appear suddenly at her feet made her want to stop—to see and touch and smell it, to remember it forever.

I had already logged more than fifty different flowers she'd seen. I'd entered common things—daffodils, buttercups, even dandelions—on up to the exotic whorled pogonia, the few known locations of which were kept purposely vague. She'd stopped for every violet since Georgia, I was sure, and those with beaded raindrops nearly guaranteed a stop for pictures. She'd photographed a false hellebore for an hour one morning, intrigued by patterns in its leaves. She felt no forward-driving urge to see something bigger, grander, more spectacular around the bend. The daisy or rhododendron leaf at hand was enjoyment enough. She seemed content with such things. As she put it, watching and seeing was what she did.

She walked into a bonanza after lunch at Turkey Gap. It started quite innocently with trilliums, the large-flowered kind. Off came her pack and out came the Nikon. We followed from flower to flower as she photographed delicate white blossoms that did everything in threes. Back on our way, we got maybe ten feet. She found more white trilliums and some in every shade of pink, lining the trail as far as we could see. We stopped again and again.

Lily of the valley joined in, then azaleas, yellow, pink, and orange. We all but crawled through a constant barrage of color that made those bleak, snowy days seem part of some other trip, so long before.

"Yellow lady slippers!" Jerri cried as we passed around another bend. She shed her pack again and got down on hands and knees to watch dozens of bobbing yellow slippers wave in the faintest breeze.

They were too lovely merely to be glanced at, Jerri said between pictures. We should admire each one for itself.

Kyra knelt down and lightly touched each blossom, saying, "You are beautiful . . . you are beautiful . . . you are beautiful. . . ."

"And look," Jerri said, pointing to one delicate, creamy bud bursting into bloom, "this one is just being born. Today is its birthday."

Kyra smiled and began to sing, "Happy birthday to you. . . ."

We stopped at a rocky overlook beyond Sugar Run for a look at our next few days' walk. Pearis Mountain, the next day's program, presented a long, level crest one valley over. It would drop us in Pearisburg on a Thursday afternoon. Peters Mountain, a distant lump in the haze farther on, would keep us busy the day after. Nothing ahead seemed unusual or formidable . . . just another selection of ups and downs. Trees had leafed out nearly all the way up the mountain slopes. Only summits and ridge crests had yet to be covered in green.

Many hot and perplexing miles followed. We stuck with the new trail but confusion between old trail, new trail, and segments of former trail scattered other hikers like dandelion fluff before the wind. We directed the lost and bewildered as though we really knew the way, but we were never quite sure.

A sign alleged Docs Knob Shelter to be 6.3 miles ahead. We walked more than ten miles and didn't find it. The five new miles had been inserted between the sign and the shelter, we concluded, but when evening came and the trail left the valley to take us up Pearis Mountain, we decided we'd had enough. We put up the tent and called it a day.

A car drove up at dusk and parked nearby. Two high-school fellows got out and strapped on backpacks in fading light as if getting ready for a hike. I walked over to say hello.

"We've been looking for Docs Knob Shelter all day," I said. "Is it around here somewhere?"

"Sure," one of the boys replied; "two hundred yards up the hill. We're headed there for the night."

It *had* seemed a strange time of day to start a hike. The news gave us no inclination to move, however.

Navigation problems were common in stories of hiking the AT. More than a third of the accounts published over the years mentioned walking in a circle or hiking the wrong way. Some hikers did so more than once. Others might have preferred not to say. When fog, multiple trails, and lumbered-off blazes made directions a matter of guess, even the most attentive hiker could retrace his own steps. But it would never happen to us.

That there were three of us accounts for this good fortune. Whenever we got off the trail, one would soon notice and we'd fan out to look. Whoever found the brush-covered blaze or not-obvious turn called the others with a whistle and we'd be on our way again. After a few hundred miles, we'd developed a feeling for where the trail would likely go. We found the right way even when markings disappeared altogether.

Our differing orientation methods helped as well. Jerri grew up in the Minnesota woods and learned to find her way as a child. She'd studied the positions of the sun and stars at different times of the year and could relate them to compass points in nearly any locale.

Kyra found her way in a different fashion.

"Where's north, Kyra?" Jerri would ask.

Kyra would look around, think a bit, and point:

"Squaw Peak is over there."

"Squaw Peak is in Phoenix," I might say.

"Uh-huh. And if *we* were in Phoenix, Squaw Peak would be over there, and that's north."

She'd usually be right on the mark.

I grew up in town and didn't know about north. My world went left and right. I could find north with a compass all right, but the significance faded once I put the compass away. I only used the information to get the map pointed right. Astronomy wasn't my strong suit, either. I first noticed the moon up in the daytime when I was nearly thirty years old. I figured it out mathematically one day, then went and looked. And if you asked me what direction I was going as I hiked into the setting sun, I likely wouldn't know.

But I knew left and right. If we came into camp from "this way" (Georgia), we should depart "that way" (Maine); never mind that we were walking due east.

"If this trail's going to get us anywhere," I might say, "it has to turn right pretty soon."

"North," Jerri would reply.

"Toward Squaw Peak," Kyra might add.

Soon the trail would bend to everyone's satisfaction. Seeing things in different ways helped us. We stayed on the trail, moving forward, and would till we sighted the last blaze.

AFTERWORD—1995

Kyra grew more confident and comfortable in the woods on her AT hike, she says, and more self-reliant, but she tells of her most lasting lesson this way:

"I remember watching you and mom make decisions, working with available data, considering options, deciding what to do on the fly. Children don't often see their parents making family decisions; I did and even got to take part. The most valuable lesson for me was learning the willingness to go on when you don't have all the information—learning to look at a situation, take your best guess, and go for it.

"The outcome of our hike was committed to those decisions. You made them and stuck with them. You were ready for opportunity when it came along and took it, saying 'Let's see what happens.'"

Wisdom from the so-much-talked-about ten-year-old.

I've been asked many times if I would hike the trail again. My feelings on that have changed over the years. At first I said my next adventure would be a cruise of some sort where I could sit down most of the time and have people bring me things. I did that, on the Alaska ferry between Juneau and Sitka, which was long enough. In Alaska I've taken to hiking again and think often about walking the AT or some other long trail. Some things would be different next time, however.

We were, I think, the best-equipped hikers on the trail that year. I've since replaced nearly all my gear with new products so would be even better equipped if I walked the AT again.

If I kept a journal I would write about different things—what I saw, who we met, what I was thinking and feeling, not what we ate for breakfast and our statistical rate of travel.

I would do about the same amount of planning next time: not so little I was caught unprepared, not so much the walk lacked adventure.

I doubt I would "take more time," as most hikers vow when asked; we took most all the time there was, 214 days, starting in snow and ending in snow. But I would try to use the time more profitably, thinking more about the moment, about what was happening now, rather than being so intent on how far we needed to get that day, how we would get through the White Mountains, or whether it was snowing yet on Mount Katahdin.

My reason for returning would be to recapture that view from Saddleback Mountain, that feeling of being at home, of being part of the natural world. I can't help but think that insight was just an introduction and that some wider vision lies beyond it.

From *Walking North* by Mic Lowther, self-published, 1990.

RAY HICKS

There is no better way to get to know a place than by talking with the locals. AT hikers lucky enough to engage an older Tennessee mountaineer in some story swapping, perhaps over coffee in a town along the trail, might well hear tell of mountain traditions and beliefs that seem quaint by city standards but are nonetheless heartfelt. Ray Hicks explains a local term ("haint") that refers to a walker's uncanny ability to find the way in the dark.

A Haint

WELL, NOW A HAINT, THE WAY THEY USED TO TEACH IT IN THE MOUNtains, what's called a haint, is when you're out at night—now this was back when you couldn't ride. You were always on foot, walking, and in the dark at night, no light. And you'd learn to walk of the durandum, they called it, of your body; of keeping on your bearings; the bearing that would grow in your body from walking. The gravity was on the planet, but people didn't know then what was doing it. Bearing, they called it. It's in your body, grows in it to follow those paths. It'd get dark as a dungeon.

Well now, a lot of times when the moon is partly shining, with the clouds running over it and hiding it and shaping it out and it'll go off. Well you'll be walking along what they call a hang, and you will see a rock or an old stump of a tree, or stuff like that; and if you're scary, now, scary of seeing something, you'll get to looking at that, and you'll imagine there's a pair of eyes. There's a head, and then when you see the head, there's a pair of eyes. Then you'll study a little more, and there's a nose with it. Then you'll study a little more and there's a mouth; then a little more and there's the body, hands. And then, you're running; most people run. And then, go off and tell they've seen a ghost. That's what they call a haint.

But, now a ghost is different. That's a spirit from where somebody that'd hidden their treasure, and God wanted somebody, poor people or somebody of the poor people to take it from God and not be skittish too much and not run, and stay there and talk with it and ask it what it appeared to them for, and it would tell them where it was hidden; and then they could go dig it out. That's a ghost. Now a haint like I told you is something you imagine. You imagine it. But a ghost is a real thing.

From *Mountain Voices*, Warren Moore, editor, Globe Pequot, 1988.

JEROME DOOLITTLE

Some people go to the Appalachian forest to hunt game. Others go to find themselves. Jerome Doolittle went walking on 4,500-foot Mollies Ridge and into Greenbrier Cove, near the Appalachian Trail, with his farmer-outdoorsman friend Zenith Whaley, in search of a giant. Doolittle notes that throughout the southern Appalachians loggers have cut enough forest so that most of the trees now, even in the parks, are second or even third growth, yet "there are stands of forest that look much as they did when Europeans first saw them." Whaley believed the giant tree was a yellow poplar, as local tradition had it. Technically, Liriodendron tulipfera *is a tulip tree. Capable of reaching heights of 200 feet, and adorning themselves with a profusion of blossoms in the sunny southern springtime, these are the tallest hardwoods in North America. Doolittle's scientific curiosity, in the tradition of famed 18th-century botanist William Bartram, is sweetly overwhelmed by the magic and majesty of his friend's old, familiar giant.*

Zenith's Tulip Tree

ZENITH HAD BEEN SILENT FOR A LONG TIME. WE HAD PASSED DOZENS OF tulip trees in our walk, but none of them was Zenith's tree. Suddenly he gave a sharp shout and pointed. Way up on the slope I spied a massive dark gray trunk, hulking in the dappled sunlight.

We scrambled up the mountainside, and only when we were right alongside the tree did I get the full sense of how enormous it really was. I held one end of Zenith's measuring tape while he worked his way around the trunk, disappeared from view and then reappeared on the other side. At chest height, the tulip tree measured 23 feet 1 inch around, or about seven feet through. It was probably 100 feet or more in height and for most of that distance the trunk swept straight up, clear of branches. I judged its age to be more than 300 years.

Zenith thumped on the dark, furrowed bark and I was startled by the dull, hollow sound. He told me to look over on the other side. There was an opening in the trunk at ground level just big enough for me to crawl inside. In old tulip trees such openings are common; they are caused by fungi that enter a wound and generate decay in the heartwood. They arouse in me a feeling of mystery—the mystery of childhood explorations for woodland spirits. . . .

When I crawled outside, Zenith and I stood for a moment, each thinking his own thoughts about this tree and the forest around it. For Zenith there was great satisfaction in finding his old friend still standing, a reaffirmation of kinship with the forest he had known since earliest childhood. To me there was some of the same, though this was my first time in this particular patch of woods. And I had another feeling, at once moving and companionable. This tree was more than three centuries old. It had been here when Bartram rambled through the Southern Appalachians, part of the forest that he had marveled at then and that I could marvel at now. A hundred years from now, with good fortune, it might still be here. And I hoped someone, way off then, would see the woods as the three of us have seen it—Bartram, Zenith and I.

From *The Southern Appalachians,* by Jerome Doolittle, Time-Life, 1975.

EDWIN WAY TEALE

A prolific naturalist, photographer, and writer, Edwin Way Teale, originally of Illinois, won a Pulitzer Prize for his book Wandering Through Winter *(1965). The following piece expresses what many botanists and hikers find inspiring and quietly dramatic in the forest—the sense that cycles of birth, maturation, decline, and death are inevitable and endless. Sometimes the moldering remains of a massive dying or dead tree are the most stunning sight the woods have to offer.*

It Rises Again

F OR A GREAT TREE DEATH COMES AS A GRADUAL TRANSFORMATION. ITS VI-tality ebbs slowly. Even when life has abandoned it entirely it remains a majestic thing. On some hilltop a dead tree may dominate the landscape for miles around. Alone among living things it retains its character and dignity after death. Plants wither; animals disintegrate. But a dead tree may be as arresting, as filled with personality, in death as it is in life. Even in its final moments, when the massive trunk lies prone and it has moldered into a ridge covered with mosses and fungi, it arrives at a fitting and noble end. It enriches and refreshes the earth. And, later, as part of other green and growing things, it rises again.

From *Dune Boy, The Early Years of a Naturalist,* by Edwin Way Teale, Dodd, 1943.

THE APPALACHIAN TRAIL IN
VIRGINIA, WEST VIRGINIA

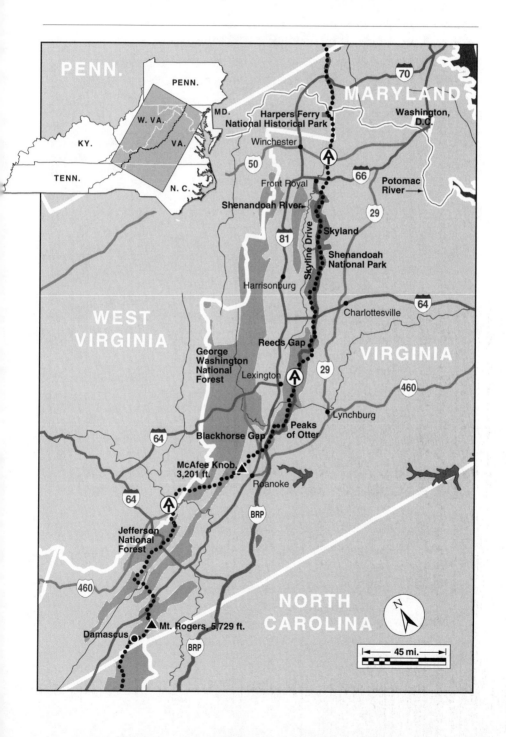

VIRGINIA

Punch Bowl Shelter, George Washington National Forest, Virginia.

Trail miles: 544.6 (including about 21.5 miles on West Virginia border) or about 25% of the entire AT, the longest section of the AT all in one state

Trail maintenance: Mt. Rogers AT Club, Virginia Tech Outing Club, Roanoke AT Club, Kanawha Trail Club, Natural Bridge AT Club, Tidewater AT Club, Potomac AT Club

Highest point: Mt. Rogers, 5,729 ft. (trail bypasses summit)

Broadest river: James

Features: Enormous wilderness areas and high peaks. Famous rhododendron and azalea displays in the wilds of Mt. Rogers region (southwest Virginia). McAfee Knob (3,201 ft.), perhaps the most photogenic rock outcropping on the AT.

Parks, forests, and nature preserves: Mt. Rogers National Recreation Area, Grayson Highlands State Park, Jefferson National Forest, George Washington National Forest (70 miles of AT), Shenandoah National Park (107 miles of AT), Sky Meadows State Park

Most intriguing names on the trail: Skyland, Deadening Nature Trail

Trail towns: Damascus, Troutdale, Pearisburg, Troutville, Waynesboro, Front Royal, Linden

THOMAS JEFFERSON

America's answer to the proverbial Renaissance man, Jefferson was a polymath. As if his political career, with contributions such as authoring the Declaration of Independence and serving as president of the fledgling nation, were not enough, he also was a noted naturalist, scholar, and architect. Jefferson carefully researched and meticulously wrote the first book about his beloved native state, Virginia. Rambling in the Blue Ridge west of Charlottesville, the site of his homestead, Monticello, Jefferson explored and documented the wonders that thrill Appalachian Trail hikers today as well. Had Jefferson been a man of our time, we can be sure he would be out there frequently, field glass, notebook, and imagination at the ready for the pleasures of climbing the forested mountains.

A Notice of Its Mountains
and *The Natural Bridge*

A Notice of Its Mountains

For the particular geography of our mountains I must refer to Fry and Jefferson's map of Virginia; and to Evans' analysis of this map of America, for a more philosophical view of them than is to be found in any other work. It is worthy of notice, that our mountains are not solitary and scattered confusedly over the face of the country; but that they commence at about one hundred and fifty miles from the sea-coast, are disposed in ridges, one behind another, running nearly parallel with the seacoast, though rather approaching it as they advance north-eastwardly. To the south-west, as the tract of country between the sea-coast and the Mississippi becomes narrower, the mountains converge into a single ridge, which, as it approaches the Gulf of Mexico, subsides into plain country, and gives rise to some of the waters of that gulf, and particularly to a river called the Apalachicola, probably from the Apalachies, an Indian nation formerly residing on it. Hence the mountains giving rise to that river, and seen from its various parts, were called the Apalachian mountains, being in fact the end or termination only of the great ridges passing through the continent. European geographers, however, extended the name northwardly as far as the mountains extended; some giving it, after their separation into different ridges, to the Blue Ridge, others to the North Mountain, others to the Alleghany, others to the Laurel Ridge, as may be seen by their different maps. But the fact I believe is, that none of these ridges were ever known by that name to the inhabitants, either native or emigrant, but as they saw them so called in European maps. In the same direction, generally, are the veins of limestone, coal, and other minerals hitherto discovered; and so range the falls of our great rivers. But the courses of the great rivers are at right angles with these. James and Potomac penetrate through all the ridges of mountains eastward of the Alleghany; that is, broken by no water course. It is in fact the spine of the country between the Atlantic on one side, and the Mississippi and St. Lawrence on the other. The passage of the Potomac through the Blue Ridge is, perhaps, one of the most stupendous scenes in nature. You stand on a very high point of land. On your right comes up the Shenandoah, having ranged along the foot of the mountain an hundred miles to seek a vent. On your left approaches the Potomac, in quest of a passage also. In the moment of their junction, they rush together against the mountain, rend it asunder, and pass off to the sea. The first glance of this scene hurries our senses into the opinion, that this earth has been created in time, that the mountains were formed first, that the rivers began to flow afterwards, that in this place, particularly, they have been dammed up by the Blue Ridge of mountains, and have formed an ocean which filled the whole valley; that continuing to rise they have at length broken over at this spot, and have torn the mountain down from its summit to its base. The piles of rock on each hand, but particularly on the Shenandoah, the evident marks of their disrupture and avulsion from their beds by the most powerful agents of nature, corroborate the impression. But the distant finishing which nature has given to the picture, is of a very different character. It is a true contrast to the foreground. It is as placid and delightful as that is wild and tremendous. For the mountain being cloven asunder, she presents to your eye, through the cleft, a small catch of smooth blue horizon, at an infinite distance in the plain country, inviting you, as it were, from the riot and tumult roaring around, to pass through the breach and participate of the calm below. Here the eye ultimately composes itself; and that way, too, the road happens actually to lead. You cross the Potomac above the junction, pass along its side through the base of the mountain for three miles, its terrible precipices hanging in fragments over you, and within about twenty miles reach Fredericktown, and the fine country round that. This scene is worth a voyage across the Atlantic. Yet here, as in the neighborhood of the Natural Bridge, are people who have passed their lives within half a dozen miles, and have never been to survey these monuments of a war between rivers and mountains, which must have shaken the earth itself to its centre.

The height of our mountains has not yet been estimated with any degree of exactness. The Alleghany being the great ridge which divides the waters of the Atlantic from those of the Mississippi, its summit is doubtless more elevated above the ocean than that of any other mountain. But its relative height, compared with the base on which it stands, is not so great as that of some others, the country rising behind the successive ridges like the steps of stairs. The mountains of the Blue Ridge, and of these the Peaks of

Otter, are thought to be of a greater height, measured from their base, than any others in our country, and perhaps in North America. From data, which may found a tolerable conjecture, we suppose the highest peak to be about four thousand feet perpendicular, which is not a fifth part of the height of the mountains of South America, nor one-third of the height which would be necessary in our latitude to preserve ice in the open air unmelted through the year. The ridge of mountains next beyond the Blue Ridge, called by us the North mountain, is of the greatest extent; for which reason they were named by the Indians the endless mountains.

A substance supposed to be Pumice, found floating on the Mississippi, has induced a conjecture that there is a volcano on some of its waters; and as these are mostly known to their sources, except the Missouri, our expectations of verifying the conjecture would of course be led to the mountains which divide the waters of the Mexican Gulf from those of the South Sea; but no volcano having ever yet been known at such a distance from the sea, we must rather suppose that this floating substance has been erroneously deemed Pumice.

The Natural Bridge

The *Natural Bridge*, the most sublime of nature's works, though not comprehended under the present head, must not be pretermitted. It is on the ascent of a hill, which seems to have been cloven through its length by some great convulsion. The fissure, just at the bridge, is, by some admeasurements, two hundred and seventy feet deep, by others only two hundred and five. It is about forty-five feet wide at the bottom and ninety feet at the top; this of course determines the length of the bridge, and its height from the water. Its breadth in the middle is about sixty feet, but more at the ends, and the thickness of the mass, at the summit of the arch, about forty feet. A part of this thickness is constituted by a coat of earth, which gives growth to many large trees. The residue, with the hill on both sides, is one solid rock of limestone. The arch approaches the semi-elliptical form; but the larger axis of the ellipsis, which would be the cord of the arch, is many times longer than the transverse. Though the sides of this bridge are provided in some parts with a parapet of fixed rocks, yet few men have resolution to walk to them, and look over into the abyss. You involuntarily fall on your hands and feet, creep to the parapet, and peep over it. Looking down from this height about a minute, gave me a violent head-ache. If the view from the top be painful and intolerable, that from below is delightful in an equal extreme. It is impossible for the emotions arising from the sublime to be felt beyond what they are here; so beautiful an arch, so elevated, so light, and springing as it were up to heaven! the rapture of the spectator is really indescribable! The fissure continuing narrow, deep, and straight, for a considerable distance above and below the bridge, opens a short but very pleasing view of the

North mountain on one side and the Blue Ridge on the other, at the distance each of them of about five miles. This bridge is in the county of Rockbridge, to which it has given name, and affords a public and commodious passage over a valley which cannot be crossed elsewhere for a considerable distance. The stream passing under it is called Cedar-creek. It is a water of James' river, and sufficient in the driest seasons to turn a grist-mill, though its fountain is not more than two miles above.

From *Notes on the State of Virginia,* by Thomas Jefferson (1787), University of North Carolina Press, 1955.

DAVID BATES

The Potomac Appalachian Trail Club is one of several, and one of the biggest, regional hiking associations in America. Founded in 1927, the club soon took a leading role in implementing the vision of an Appalachian footpath as articulated by Benton MacKaye (in 1921). David Bates, a native Virginian, joined the PATC in 1953 and soon became a trail overseer. Twenty years later he was appointed club archivist; eventually he wrote a sixtieth-anniversary history of the PATC. In two excerpts here, Bates shows us how the early AT plans grew out of existing shorter local trails, how camaraderie fueled the organizational process among a small cadre of enthused leaders, and how plans for the Skyline Drive along the Blue Ridge brought the Appalachian Trail Conference into crisis. Bates describes a bitter exchange of letters between MacKaye and PATC President Myron Avery, demonstrating that territoriality and ideological differences can degenerate into chilly conflict, even on a recreational project.

The Potomac Appalachian Trail Club and the Issue of a Skyline Drive

GETTING STARTED—1927-1930

In the autumn of 1927, Calvin Coolidge was finishing his elected term of office, after completing Warren Harding's term after the latter's sudden death. The Nation's economy was apparently strong, partially carried by a boom on the stock market. Prosperity seemed to have arrived to stay in the

United States. The evangelist, Aimee Semple McPherson, was drawing large crowds wherever she preached, promising salvation and gathering large amounts of money when the collection plate was passed. Charles Lindbergh had made the first non-stop flight across the Atlantic in April of 1927. In the rest of the world, the German economy was in a shambles, with inflation so high that a sack of deutschmarks was needed to buy a sack of potatoes, Mussolini had made the trains run on time in Italy, and Great Britain ruled the oceans with the Empire still intact. Asia was a place where Christian missionaries were needed to 'civilize' the ignorant, 'heathen' populations, and hardly worthy of notice otherwise. Comparatively few people in America knew much more about Africa than that it was the home of Edgar Rice Burroughs' fictional character, Tarzan of the Apes. America was in a definite isolationist attitude as far as the rest of the world went, and wanted very little to do with it. The country was so relaxed that citizens could stroll through the White House grounds, and exchange pleasantries with the few police on duty there.

On Tuesday evening, November 22, 1927, six men gathered in the Nation's Capital, in Room 519 of the old Metropolitan Bank Building, then located on 15th Street, N.W., between G and F Streets. This building was next to the famed Rhodes Tavern, both now gone because of redevelopment. A "Memorandum of Meeting of Washington Group of Appalachian Trail Workers" records this occasion. In attendance were "Messrs. Avery, Ricker, Schmeckebier, Schairer, Corson, and Anderson." It states that "Mr. Avery reported that Messrs. Matthes, Southworth and Cox could not be present because of conflicting engagements." One of the three missing men, Judge Joseph Cox, Myron Avery's uncle, was not a trail worker as the others, but was constantly in the background providing advice and encouragement in those early years. This memorable meeting had two main purposes: to consider the feasibility of a hiking trail in certain areas of Virginia and West Virginia, and to consider the formal establishment of a trail club in the Washington, D.C. area.

Reports from scouting parties were received. J. Frank Schairer and H.C. Anderson had gone south from Paris, Virginia to Linden, and Myron Avery and Homer Corson had gone north from Paris to Harpers Ferry, West Virginia. The first two reported that although sections of the area to the south were difficult, and more scouting and much work needed to be done, a trail was feasible. The way to the north had been found easier, with existing trails and old woods roads there which could be utilized. Mr. Southworth had sent a letter which reported that the Blue Ridge north of Weverton, West Virginia had an old road on the ridge with excellent views on both sides, and recommended that the main trail follow this route to South Mountain at Crampton's Gap. The immediate objective of the group was to complete the section of trail between Harpers Ferry and Bluemont, Virginia by April 1, 1928, so that the Wildflower Preservation Society of the District of Columbia could schedule a hike over it sometime in April. Their ultimate objectives were completion of a trail southward to Thornton Gap and to Stony Man Mountain, with a side trail leading in from Front Royal. It was considered feasible to have at least two open camps between Manassas Gap and Thornton Gap.

Having satisfied themselves that a trail was feasible, the group then moved to the business of the actual formation of a hiking club. Frank Schairer suggested the name of "Blue Ridge Trail Club", and letters from Benton MacKaye and Major William Welch (Honorary Vice-President of the Appalachian Trail Conference) suggested other names, but it was decided to name the new organization "The Potomac Appalachian Trail Club" (PATC). Myron Avery was named as President, a post he was to hold for the next thirteen years. P.L. Ricker was made Vice-President, H.C. Anderson the Secretary and J. Frank Schairer the Treasurer.

Initiation fees for joining were set at one dollar, in order to meet the general expenses of the Club. Scouting trips were planned for the next weekend for the Manassas Gap area, and for the weekend of December 10th for the Harpers Ferry area.

The "Memorandum" was signed by H.C. Anderson. This was the beginning of the PATC. The actions of these six men established an organization which has grown to be an active, respected, influential organization of 3,000 members in 1986.

From its beginning the PATC has always been a working club. The fact that there was a scouting trip of four men, two going north and two going south, to discover whether their hopes were feasible, before there was a meeting, is indicative of the kind of organization the PATC would be. There was something concrete to report on at the first meeting. There was a reason to organize. After the Club had been given a name, officers elected and a basic financial decision made, plans were made for two more scouting trips and then to blaze and clear trail between two points, with a time-table for completion. It was apparent at the very beginning of the group's existence, that although meetings were necessary to plan, to 'take stock', to sound off or offer opinions, and to keep the organizational structure going, the job of opening the trail was the important work. The PATC was to be a Club of achievement.

For many years, Benton MacKaye, a New Englander, had pushed his dream of building a hiking trail running the full length of the Appalachian Mountain Range on its crest. Originally he hoped it would run from New Hampshire to North Carolina, but later the dream grew, and Maine to Georgia became the goal. Some work had been done, especially in New England.

The Appalachian Mountain Club (AMC), founded in 1875, had many trails open in New Hampshire. The Dartmouth Outing Club had done some work in New Hampshire. There were trails in Vermont. New York State had trails on Bear Mountain. The Blue Mountain Club of Pennsylvania had started a trail on Blue Mountain. Trail had been marked and cut in the Great Smoky Mountains, but very little had been done in the Central and Southern Appalachians. There were no well-organized groups making any real effort to put a trail in those areas. The men in the new club in Washington knew this. They felt they had to be involved in the trail work in Pennsylvania and Maryland, to know its location and plan to hook up with it when they finished building the trail in northern Virginia.

The planned and barely started trail on Blue Mountain, where the Big Blue Trail is now, would have meant taking the C & O Canal Towpath southeast for 30 miles to connect with the Blue Ridge Mountains at Harpers Ferry. The six founders of the PATC and their colleagues felt they could build the trail down the top of the Appalachians on South Mountain in Maryland. The route would be closer to the population centers, where the future hikers would come from, and it would be easier for the trail builders to reach on their work trips. Benton MacKaye agreed to this alteration. Thus his dream came closer to reality. This matter settled, the new club began the work of building the central section of the Appalachian Trail.

Enthusiasm was great, but techniques were amateurish for trail building. Apparently no advice was sought from any other trail group. There are no records of any such requests or of any helpful tips offered by other groups. Officials of the Appalachian Trail Conference gave encouragement and moral support but apparently offered nothing concrete as to methods or tools. At the beginning, Boy Scout axes were used. They proved most unsatisfactory for work such as blazing trees and cutting brush. No funds were available to buy tools, so members bought their own pruning shears. In spite of all difficulties, including winter weather, the new trail was completed between the end of November and the next March, 1928. A "trail cutting party" for the completion of the trail between Ashby Gap and Manassas Gap was held on February 12, 1928. On February 18 and 19 there was a joint overnight trail clearing trip with the Wild Flower Preservation Society. February 22, PATC President Avery's birthday as well as George Washington's, was celebrated by a joint scouting and trail cutting trip, from Paris to Bluemont, Virginia, a distance of 12 miles.

The participants caught a commercial bus at 9th and Pennsylvania Avenue, N.W., at 7:30 A.M., and got off at Paris. At Bluemont, at 5:45 that afternoon the tired trail workers boarded the Washington and Old Dominion Railroad, a small but active line that ran between Bluemont and Rosslyn for well over 50 years, and returned to the city by streetcar from its Rosslyn depot. Additional overnight work trips going from Bluemont to Harpers Ferry were made on March 10 and 11 and 24 and 25.

To top off their winter of work, an inspection hike was made on April 13, 14 and 15, from Linden to Harpers Ferry. The full notice announcing this trip is quoted below, and gives the flavor of those early days.

Inspection Hike Over Trail from Linden to Harpers Ferry
April 13-15

> This hike is necessary, so far as the Club is concerned, in order to measure distances and complete the Trail description which is being prepared.
>
> The first part of the hike from Linden to Bluemont (26 miles), will be made on Saturday, April 14th, with Mr. Avery, as leader. The second part of the hike, from Bluemont to Harpers Ferry, (23 miles), will be made on Sunday the 15th by the Red Triangle Club with Bill Greenley as leader. The party taking the entire hike will leave Washington on 3:55 P.M. train at Union Station Friday, April 13th, arriving at Linden 6:45 P.M., stopping Friday night at a boarding house in Linden. On Saturday the 14th, the party will hike to Bluemont, where the night may be spent either at Morelands, some 2 miles beyond Snickers Gap on the Trail to Harpers Ferry, or at the Loudon House, where the Red Triangle group will stop. Those desiring to take the entire hike should phone Mr. Avery not later than Thursday, April 12th. Those desiring to take the hike from Bluemont to Harpers Ferry only should phone Mr. Greenley (Franklin 8243 between 6:00 and 7:00 P.M.) not later than Thursday, April 12th, who will make the necessary reservations, including dinner at Himes Cottage at Harpers Ferry. The Red Triangle party will leave Washington on the electric train from Rosslyn at 6:30 P.M. Saturday. While there is a good trail all the way, the hike will be strenuous, as there will be considerable climbing, especially between Linden and Bluemont. However, a moderate pace will be taken and there will be some fine views if the weather is clear. Total cost of entire trip about $10.00, cost of trip with Red Triangle Club $6.56.

One of the great necessities in building a viable organization is good communications, and PATC's leadership worked to build a good communication system. The BULLETIN began publication in early 1928; pamphlets, postal card notices, longer letter-sized notices, all sorts of printed matter were turned out by members assigned to or who volunteered for that sort of duty. A steady supply of information was directed to members almost from the very beginning. The first BULLETIN, dated February 12, 1928, gave notices of the work trips mentioned above and the second BULLETIN published the notice of the three-day inspection trip, shown above.

Work trips filled the Club's schedule, necessarily, as there had to be a trail, completed and inspected, before hikes for fun and exercise could be planned. The three-day inspection trip was proof that a little bit of Benton Mackaye's dream had been completed in Virginia.

The plan of the new Club, to fill in the gap in the Appalachian Trail from Pennsylvania to southern Virginia, was ambitious; its fulfillment would require many more than the original six men and those who had joined them immediately after the formation of the new Club. Where would the others come from? How were they to be recruited? Were there people who would be interested in such a scheme? If so, how many could be recruited who would work outdoors on weekends?

In a speech made at the Twenty-Fifth Anniversary of PATC, H.C. 'Andy' Anderson, one of the founders, discussed early recruitment efforts. "While small groups of members were soon making trips to the Blue Ridge nearly every weekend, we strongly felt the need of reinforcements. We circularized the members of the Wildflower Preservation Society and the Red Triangle Club and button-holed our friends. By May 10, 1928, our membership numbered 60 and by October 12, 1928, 112, but only a small percentage of this membership went on trail-cutting trips."

On March 29, 1928, President Avery wrote to Arno B. Cammerer, then Assistant Director of the National Park Service, concerning the creation of an Appalachian Trail. Mr. Cammerer replied to the PATC's President on April 2, saying that the idea of such a Trail was praiseworthy, but there were no funds available for the Park Service to help in its creation. This was the first of hundreds of letters that Mr. Avery wrote to officials of the National Park Service.

On June 22 and 23, 1935, the PATC again hosted the Appalachian Trail Conference at Skyland, in a conference that would have repercussions for a long time. The report in the October, 1935 BULLETIN does not tell of any trouble at the meeting. It mentions the reports of the Conference officers, and of the various Club representatives on their areas of the AT. Ernest Dench of *Nature Magazine* gave a good talk on publicity and PATC's Egbert Walker read a paper on the techniques of trail blazing. . . . Speeches were made, hikes taken, awards given for a photographic contest in which PATC's Fred Blackburn won the gold medal. Orville Crowder and Joe Winn entertained the gathering.

There are two items in the BULLETIN's resumé that may give a clue to the trouble that arose after the meeting adjourned. Both are quoted herewith. "Of the 130 delegates, half were from out of town and the other half were members of the P.A.T.C." The second was longer: "Numerous resolutions were passed, and a discussion centering around the subject of skyline drives resulted in the adoption of a resolution approving action taken to rebuild the Appalachian Trail where interfered with by parkways, recommending that each future project for the so-called "Appalachian Parkway" or recreational areas contiguous to the trail be considered on its particular merits, with instruction to the Conference officials to investigate each project and to advocate the construction of a foot trail at a suitable distance from any such project."

The controversy began not long after the Conference adjourned. The former Treasurer of the ATC, R.H. Torrey, wrote an article for the *New York Post*, in which he attacked both the PATC and the ATC, and complained of the PATC's "domination" of the meeting at Skyland. The PATC's Archives contain a twelve-page (single-spaced, letter-sized) document, unsigned, which refuted in detail the charges made by Mr. Torrey. The writing is very much in the style of Myron Avery.

Avery first wrote to a Mr. Hearmance of the New England Trail Conference denying Torrey's accusations of the PATC attempting to "dominate" the Conference.

Criticism of PATC's attitude toward the building of Skyline Drive was the subject of a memorandum of December 5, 1935, from Myron Avery to Dr. Schmeckebier. The memorandum discussed the articles in the magazine *Appalachia*, the official publication of the Appalachian Mountain Club of New England. These articles, including one written by Harold Anderson, a charter member of PATC, criticized the PATC's attitude toward such roads as Skyline Drive, and they demeaned the hiking facilities and scenery of Shenandoah National Park. Apparently the editor of this magazine had attacked the PATC because of its policy of adjusting to the building of the Drive instead of fighting it. The AMC felt that the PATC should have taken a strong stand against the National Park Service in this matter, and not cooperated. *Appalachia* condemned ALL roads through wilderness areas and the destruction of any wilderness in order to build roads, and was opposed to any policy of "adjustment" to such roads or to cooperation with authorities as regards these roads.

On January 8, 1936, Avery dispatched another memo to Dr. Schmeckebier, eight pages this time, regarding *Appalachia* and its article "What Price Skyline Drive." The PATC President was very bitter about the matter and he refuted the criticism of the PATC in the article and the charges that the southern Appalachians were damaged by the building and the existence of the Drive. Avery felt that the article injured the efforts of the PATC to increase hiking and camping in the Blue Ridge area. He seemed to feel that the AMC was trying to undermine the PATC and the other clubs in the area and all the work they had done in building the Trail and the shelters and lean-tos. His impression was that *Appalachia*'s article and attitude had denigrated the Virginia and southern areas of the Appalachians in regard to the scenery and the condition of the Trail and the camping structures.

Shortly after this, Avery published a 22-page article entitled "In The Blue Ridge Mountains of Virginia", extolling their virtues. This was undoubtedly for the purpose of attempting to counteract the effect of the AMC's articles.

The whole sad business was capped, but not closed, by an exchange of letters between Avery and Benton MacKaye in the winter of 1935-1936. Avery had written to MacKaye, criticizing his actions and attitudes in this matter. Avery felt that MacKaye had not supported the PATC and its leadership in a firm enough manner against some of the critical statements made by the AMC about the situation in Shenandoah Park and about the PATC's response to the Federal Government's activities there. On February 4, 1936, in a reply to Avery's long letter of December 19, 1935, the patron saint of the Appalachian Trail said that he had postponed his reply to Avery in "the hope of getting a better perspective than an immediate reply would have allowed." He then gave Avery a very strong reprimand saying that he had noticed a "self-righteous, overbearing attitude and a bullying manner of expression." He closed by breaking relations with him. It is a fact that the two men did not speak for many years.

In a visit to the PATC at the time of its Twenty-Fifth Anniversary, Benton MacKaye said, in an interview with Dorothy Martin (Mason), among his remarks, ". . . and while the '30's were still young, your Potomac Club, with the others from Maine to Georgia, all under the inspiring leadership of the valiant Myron Avery, placed the Appalachian Trail upon the map." Avery had passed on a few months earlier, and there is no record of reconciliation between the two men. One would hope that there had been one, for both had contributed very much to the establishment of the Trail.

From *Breaking Trail in the Central Appalachians,* by David Bates, Potomac Appalachian Trail Club, 1987.

CHARLES & NANCY PERDUE

How the national parks were carved out of remaining wilderness and gathered in from already developed land is generally an inspiring story, reflecting the best of the nation's instincts to preserve its wild lands and species. Exceptions to the generalization leap to mind, however. Similar to the early 19th-century expulsion of the Cherokee from the Great Smoky Mountains was a land-taking program in Virginia during the 1930s. Less bloody than the Cherokee Trail of Tears, it was equally disruptive to the agrarian culture and to the personal lives of mountain people forced from their homes in order to create the Shenandoah National Park. Hikers enjoying today's peace in these once-again-wild hills may want to pause to give thanks to those who were forced out to make room for essentially upper-middle-class recreation by visiting urban people.

Shenandoah Removals

T HE DEDICATION OF THE SHENANDOAH NATIONAL PARK BY PRESIDENT Franklin D. Roosevelt on July 3, 1936, was the culmination of an idea which had been extant since the turn of the century: to establish a national park "for the recreation of the people who lived in the thickly populated metropolitan centers of the East." However, the movement which eventually resulted in the creation of the Shenandoah National Park, encompassing about 200,000 acres on the slopes of the Blue Ridge Mountains, lying in eight Virginia counties, had not begun to take shape until early in 1924.

It is crucial to recognize that, from its inception, the idea of a national park in the East brought into sharp conflict the recreational needs and desires of a non-resident, urban population and the cultural/subsistence needs of a resident, rural population who held the land by right of private domain. Establishment of the Park resolved the conflict in favor of the larger, more powerful, urban interests and set a precedent by making use of the blanket condemnation forcibly to acquire privately-held land from persons, many of whom did not want to sell their land or to move from the area. It must also be understood that the movement to establish a park was composed primarily of middle- to upper-class entrepreneurs and politicians who were anxious for their own reasons and vested interests to promote tourism in the state. These persons were well organized, and their lobbying for a park was carried out in Washington, D. C., and across Virginia principally through a chamber of commerce type of organization set up in the

Shenandoah Valley and a business association set up by George Freeman Pollock, the owner and operator of the Skyland resort in the Blue Ridge.

The membership of these organizations, which eventually merged to work toward establishing the Shenandoah National Park in the Blue Ridge, included Pollock; Governor E. Lee Trinkle; then Senator (and later Governor) Harry Flood Byrd; editor of Byrd's Harrisonburg newspaper, John Crown; later Project Manager for the Shenandoah Park Homesteads, L. Ferdinand Zerkel; and "many prominent citizens" of the state of Virginia. These individuals may have been motivated by altruistic or conservationist concerns as well, but there is considerable evidence that economic interests and developing industrialization in Virginia were strong factors in their support of the Park.

Perhaps most important of all, the attitudes expressed about the mountain people of the Blue Ridge by park proponents and officials covered the range of stereotypes which has commonly been applied to the people of Appalachia generally, and which we referred to previously as the "culture-trait fable." By some accounts, the people of the Shenandoah area were the "sturdy people who have inhabited these mountains since the days when the pre-revolutionary adventurer advanced against this frontier." This view fostered and developed the "noble home life, strength of character and fine intellectual thought that characterized the whole process of the founding of our new Nation" and which "descended from the best blood of the British Isles."

On the other hand, George Pollock, who was said to have been sympathetic to the mountaineer and his needs, wrote:

> The Blue Ridge mountaineer was probably no different from any other Anglo-Saxon; but being ignorant, usually having a chip on his shoulder and being possessed of bulky strength, he had to go through a good many years of 'mixing' before he became the docile person he is today.

Other writers deplored the lack of "independence and resourcefulness" and the "dependence upon outside help" that characterized the people of Shenandoah. Some decried their lack of morality, citing the high incidence of venereal disease and of bastard children as evidence of their promiscuity. By the estimate of one author's sources, "in the strictly upland homes . . . ninety per cent of them would have bastard children." This same writer claimed that "'another bad moral feature is that of living together out of wedlock" and cited "their remoteness and the journey to the Court House to secure a license" and "the fact that there were no ministers at hand to perform the ceremony" as contributing to this condition.

Another view was expressed by two assistant editors of the *National Geographic* in the spring of 1930. They thought that the Park Service should let the people of Shenandoah and the Great Smokies stay on the land because "the mountaineers, not the scenery, were the real tourist attraction." Assistant Director of the Park Service, Arno Cammerer, replied that the editors were "all wet." Cammerer's assessment was that "the worthy mountaineers . . . would leave; the only ones anxious to stay were those anxious to make money from the tourists." He claimed further, "There is no person so canny as certain types of mountaineers, and none so disreputable." There is an irony in the fact that the same interest in tourism which motivated the businessmen and politicians touting the Park was seen as disreputable if it motivated the mountaineer.

Altogether, approximately 500 families were displaced by the establishment of the Shenandoah National Park in the period 1924-1936. Families who could afford to move on their own did so, often moving only a few miles away to nearby communities or lowland areas. Those families who had little or no resources by the time they had to move were relocated in subsistence homesteads provided by the Resettlement Administration. Some of the political, ethical, and cultural questions raised by the removal and relocation may be seen in stark relief in a letter from L. Ferdinand Zerkel to Hon. Wm. E. Carson, who had recommended that Zerkel become Director of a proposed Bureau to handle the resettlement of the Park dwellers. In his December 11, 1933, letter, Zerkel set forth his position concerning the job, the people, and the problems of removal and resettlement:

A seldom considered, if not largely unrecognized, phase of our problem is the need of informing the "outside" people carefully and accurately of the present and potential capacity, usefulness, habits, etc. of these "inside" people. It is very generally accepted that the poorer mountain folk, certainly the "squatters" in the inaccessible sections, must be guided into more civilized action and habits to become assimilable on the "outside." . . . Admittedly, these people are now improvident, listless and often undesirable from many angles. What the "outside" people must give these under-privileged hollow dwellers is wholehearted cooperation with the welfare agencies that seek to improve their situation. I cannot but believe that such will be forthcoming, particularly when it is more widely recognized that environment and lack of education, as much as laziness, accounts for such conditions as the following taken from Miss Sizer's tabulations in five hollows in Madison's park area: 132 families totalling 652 people—Only 22 families entirely self-supporting; 435 illiterate (over 6 years but neither read nor write) and near-illiterate (4th. Grade or lower); 389 persons with bad teeth and tonsils; 12 privies and 10 screens among the 132 homes and only 1 home provided with lime or ashes to cover excreta; 4 housewives, by name, out of the 132, alone scald their dishes (others using merely warm or cold water and usually no soap) and, almost universally in these hollows, the small patches of grain are still harvested with scythes or cradles and threshed with flails and the hauling is done almost entirely with sleds.

The colonization idea which I suggested to you and to Director Albright several years ago is today still in mind for the "squatters"; of whom, by the way, there are considerably more than is generally recognized—53 out of 132 families in five hollows in Madison County being without any property title and, consequently, without cash allowances under the Park condemnation awards.

Any "wholesale" colonization or group removal would, in my judgement, be very unpopular and prove later to have been ill-advised. A plan of re-estab-lishment on a "trade" or "exchange" basis, absorbing the evident differential in value between the abandoned cabin and the new home out of relief funds, is ideal in preserving greater self respect and pride of possession. It will pleas-antly camouflage the enforced transplantation of penniless and near-penniless families. I believe that small neighborhoods now inside the Park boundaries should be relocated in very similar but better small neighborhoods outside the boundaries, preserving isolation as far as possible and, assuredly, not group-ing many unacquainted families.

Zerkel's comment regarding small neighborhoods existing within the Park and the necessity of retaining those in the relocation process should be noted carefully. In 1935, Edward Steere commented that "the area of the Shenandoah Park is almost destitute of the remains of a mountain culture." Steere noted specifically, "The glens were too small to permit the develop-ment of a vigorous community life." Zerkel's statement in 1933 offers one bit of written testimony in support of the contention that communities had indeed formerly existed within the confines of the Park boundaries.

It is also important to know that Zerkel was a local man, who lived in Luray and dealt in real estate and timber before he began his rise through several positions associated with the construction of Skyline Drive and the supervision of Emergency Conservation Work camps in Shenandoah. Zerkel's involvement with the park project thus suggests that local people were not necessarily any more sympathetic and sensitive to the needs of the mountain people or understanding of their lifestyle and culture than were outsiders such as George Pollock. For Zerkel, class position and economic interests proved compelling. Although Zerkel may have had a genuine con-cern for what he called "this sociological problem," his concern was that of one of the "outside people" rather than of the "inside people," or of a supe-rior for an inferior. Because of his own personal background and social class, Zerkel could not differentiate between legitimate differences in technology and lifestyle (e.g., the method of harvesting grain) and elements of the widely generalized culture-trait fable (e.g., improvidence, listlessness, and laziness). He was a product of his times, caught up in what was represented to be a reform movement to help bring an illiterate, impoverished, and backward part of the population into the mainstream of modern society.

There was no single, consistent, or irrevocable policy with regard to removal of the people in the Shenandoah Park area until February 1, 1934, when Arno Cammerer, by that time Director of the Park Service, announced that the federal government would not accept any park lands from the State until all inhabitants had left the area. This announcement stemmed from problems the federal government had had with the people left in the Great Smokies Park and from the attitudes of the new Secretary of Interior, Harold Ickes. Cammerer's final removal policy statement set off an immediate and bitter controversy between federal officials, state officials, and local public opinion that has not been totally resolved even at this late date. Unfortunately, Cammerer had not heeded Zerkel's advice in the 1933 letter:

> One of the most important phases of the whole proposition; beyond the soul, mind and body salvation of the children particularly in the poorer cabins; is a guided publicity. With well planned press releases and developed sympathetic local newspaper propaganda, great assistance and no new ill will should be forthcoming. With possible haphazard news stories or any wild or sensational press reports tending to indicate eviction plans or methods, both the State and Federal agencies will face embarrassment and highly unwelcome publicity and a greatly handicapped process of moving the people.

For the 10 years of the Park movement preceding the final removal policy statement, various conflicting assumptions regarding removal had been current. In 1926, then Secretary of the Interior Hubert Work declared that the people would have to leave the park lands, but Col. Glenn Smith, head of the Geological Survey and secretary of the Southern Appalachian National Park Commission, disagreed. One writer states that "it is clear that Virginia officials were operating on the assumption of a removal policy as early as the winter of 1927-28." Some individuals supported the Park movement under the assumption that people would not have to move; others apparently found the idea of removal acceptable in the abstract, but were appalled by the action when it involved people they knew. At best, there was confusion and inconsistency regarding removal; at worst, there was outright deception.

In the intervening years since 1936, there has been little systematic inquiry into the nature or history of the people who were displaced by the formation of the Shenandoah National Park or into the socio-cultural consequences of their involuntary displacement. For the past nine years, we have been living in Rappahannock and Madison Counties, only a few miles from the Park boundaries, and have conducted research toward that end. We have been concentrating upon 160 or 32% of the approximately 500 families who were displaced. The 160 families involve only 10 surnames and are located in Rappahannock County and adjoining Madison and Page Counties. Neither the land area nor the population of the Shenandoah National Park was distributed evenly among the eight counties involved, and, in fact, these three counties contributed more than their proportionate share in both land area and in persons removed. Consequently, the 160 families that we are focusing on may safely be assumed to form a fairly representative sample of the total number displaced. We have been able thus far to trace all 10 family lines back in the general area to the mid- or late 1700's. . . . Even though the 10 family groups have diverse backgrounds and came into the area by way of various migration routes, their 175-200 year experience in the area makes it possible to talk about them as a stable, homogeneous population at the time of their removal.

From "Appalachian Fables and Fact: A Case Study of the Shenandoah National Park Removals," by Charles and Nancy Perdue, in *Appalachian Journal*, Vol. 7, No. 1–2, Autumn/Winter 1979–80.

KAREN BERGER

A whirlwind of hiking activity and writing, Karen Berger, of Bronxville, New York, took no ordinary honeymoon after her marriage to Daniel Smith. He proposed a walk from Mexico to Canada on the Continental Divide Trail, and Karen met the challenge. Their book, Where the Waters Divide *(1993), is a lively, well-informed narrative of that extraordinary adventure. Again with her husband, Berger took to the trail to walk from Georgia to Maine on the AT. In progress now is a book about that expansive journey, which Berger likens to a pilgrimage. The following excerpt finds her at a hilarious annual event on the AT where thru-hikers and other hiking aficionados gather to set a while, eat as though there's no tomorrow, and trade stories from their wilderness travels.*

Trail Days in Damascus

D AMASCUS—THAT'S DAMASCUS, VIRGINIA, NOT THE OTHER—CALLS ITSELF the friendliest town on the Appalachian Trail, and as if to drive home the point, a scruffy looking puppy writhed with excitement as we passed the first cluster of houses on the way into town. Hikers quickly become accustomed to free-roaming dogs who take a liberal view of their property lines and a conservative view towards sharing. Damascus being the friendliest town on the trail, this dog invited itself along on our walk.

Nor is the *bonhomie* limited to canine inhabitants; the first person we glimpsed, a middle aged lady in a print cotton dress and sensible shoes, waved her arm in a wide arc and called out across the street, "Welcome to Damascus. Are you having a nice hike?"

On a day like this, with a welcome like that, yes indeed, ma'am, we certainly were.

It's a small town, Damascus: one main street with a couple of sidestreets that spill a few stores maybe two hundred feet on either side. But to hikers, this unassuming hamlet is a mecca, probably because it is, more or less, the quarter-way point for northbound thru-hikers. Such are the things we celebrate, ticking off our progress by state lines and hundred mile increments. Fussy purists insist that Damascus is about 40 miles short of the "real" quarter way point, which is in the middle of the woods somewhere in the Mt. Rogers Recreation Area—inconveniently located if your idea of a celebration happens to involve some combination of a shower, a meal, and a beer. But those are the same joyless pedants, I expect, who will dourly, stubbornly insist that the millennium should be celebrated in the year 2001 even as the rest of us are sending up fireworks when the clock ticks past midnight into the year 2000. I admit to casting my lot with the heedless revelers: Damascus is the quarter-way mark.

And then there's Trail Days. Or, as the hikers call it, Trail Daze.

Think of any small town festival: You know the kind. Cotton candy and rubber duck races and baskets for sale, along with T-shirts and Kountry Krafts and the sort of overstuffed every-thing-on-it super-sized hot dogs that are found only at carnival booths and never in restaurants. There are thousands of small town festivals in thousands of America's small towns: corn festivals and potato festivals, and festivals for artichokes and sweet potatoes and for all I know, for garlic. In Damascus, where the white AT blazes go straight through the middle of downtown—all four blocks of it—it's Trail Days, complete with a Miss Appalachian Trail from the local school who rides in splendor in the parade down Main Street.

The thru-hiker grapevine—a remarkable construct that works as efficiently and inexplicably as an African telephone tree—is the only advertising, but the grapevine is enough. The communications system is simple: Its heart is the tradition of trail registers, in which hikers write poetry and complain about the weather and leave messages for their fellows. Next is the post office general delivery system, which almost everyone thru hiking the trail uses to receive food packages and mail. Then there's a network of hostels and inns that are hiker-friendly. And finally, word of mouth carries words up and down the trail, either with hikers going in the opposite direction, or with faster hikers who carry news ahead.

I don't think that most hikers start out planning to go to Trail Days. In the startling early days they have other things on their minds: blisters and aching muscles and whether or not their cranky stoves will light. It's quite possible that most hikers don't even know about the festival, and if they do, it resides in some far recess of their mind, an image swimming in a blurred jumble of places and events that mean nothing more to them than words from a guidebook. In Georgia, Virginia is a lifetime away.

But then, somewhere in North Carolina, there's a sudden click. Bodies harden, the process of living outdoors becomes routine. The hiker's mind shifts from the tyranny of muscles and mileage and malfunctioning gear. Now, there is time for views and ideas. The future is no longer unthinkable: Virginia, New York, and even Katahdin are places that can be walked to. Like the Velveteen Rabbit, the trip becomes real when it is no longer shiny and new, but routine and ragged and familiar and loved.

By the time Trail Days rolls around, half the hikers have dropped out. Those who are left sport a certain pride. Three states down, ten to go. Mileage in triple digits. Scuffs on their boots, dirt on their packs. The tables have turned: Now they look at home in the woods and out of place in a town. And now, the grapevine passes the message: Are you going to Trail Days? Anyone need a ride to Trail Days? Wanted: A ride to Trail Days. Groups form. Plans coalesce. And by the time the festival rolls around, the most popular hiking trail in the world is just about deserted, at least by those who purport to be walking its length.

Wednesday. The population of Damascus is 1200; during Trail Days it doubles. The hiker hostel sleeps about 50; if you add in floor space, couch space and tent space on the lawn, figure 200 in a pinch. We arrive at night in a car crammed with hikers and gear, looking like a college stunt of the fraternity-brothers-in-a-Volkswagen variety. The hostel is already full and the designated tenting areas down by the river look like a cross between a high-tech outdoor expo and a refugee camp. A town council member we met on a previous trip invites us to pitch our tents on her lawn, and if we'd like to sleep inside, that's okay, too.

Thursday. On the town green the mayor is fretting over which vehicle should park in which carnival booth, while the chief of police looks on, ready and willing to settle any disputes that need to be settled by the arm of the law. We've met the mayor before—on our previous visit, the hostel was closed for the season, so she let us sleep in the town hall and drape our drying laundry over the council's dais. She greeted us distractedly.

"I have to keep an eye on this. Otherwise they'll just park anywhere and I can't have that. They have to go into the spaces they paid for."

"You look busier than the last time we saw you."

"It's going to get even busier. Have you been down to the river? We've got more hikers than we've ever had. This event keeps getting bigger and bigger, and I have to keep it all under control."

Trying to imagine what it would take to keep a few hundred thru-hikers under control I don't envy the mayor her job. But she's prepared. She sets aside the paper showing which vendors go where and pulls a folded scrap out of her pocket.

"I'm carrying this with me the whole weekend," she announces. "Now you do me a favor and spread the word. We have an open containers law. This is a family event, and I don't want any trouble. You know those hikers, they get into town and they want a beer. Well, they can have all the beers they want down at Dot's but they can't have them outside in public. See, right here, I've got it written down: no open containers. I don't want to have to arrest anyone."

"I guess I can't offer you a beer, then," I joke.

"Oh, no, honey, I really wish you wouldn't," she says. "I'd have to put you in jail."

Friday. A hiker does go to jail, courtesy of the thru-hikers' contribution to the festivities, the in-drag Missed Appalachian Trail beauty pageant. It's safe to say that this parade of prancing, vamping, hairy-legged, unshaven, face-painted men in skirts is the raciest event to hit this small southern community all year. And the town turns out in force, all in good fun, to hoot and holler and point as the contestants strut their stuff around the gazebo in the center of the town green. One contestant, apparently, struts too much stuff, and the arm of the law is there to protect the cotton-frocked grandmothers and cotton-candy eating tykes from taking in another eyeful. It's all over so fast no one is sure exactly what did happen: "Did you see that?" "Someone got arrested?" "Who?" "I don't know." "Arrested for what?" "He was showing everything." "What everything? I didn't see anything." "He musta done something." "Who's on first?" "I don't know." "He wasn't wearing underwear!"

Saturday. The hiker is out of jail, the incident, if not forgotten, is set aside in the interest of enjoying the big day. The highlight is the parade, which starts across the street from Dot's, which serves breakfast and beer to a few hard core hikers—and a few locals, too—and ends at the gazebo, maybe a fifteen-minute walk away. It takes an hour or so to get organized: the fire department, the school band, representatives of the local trail clubs, and the open-topped car that transports a sequined, sashed, and smiling Miss Appalachian Trail (no relation to the "Missed" Appalachian Trail crowned the previous evening). And then come the hikers themselves, shuffling along to the accompaniment of a pots-and-pans percussion section under the wary eye of the law, who wants no more trouble. Today, the only infractions involve the wanton throwing of water balloons.

Sunday. The Methodist church owns and runs the hostel. During the Sunday sermon, the minister asks guests to introduce themselves, and one by one, hikers stand up, wearing their cleanest hiking clothes. I'm from Louisiana, from New York, from England. The congregation turns and looks at each of us in turn, welcoming us itinerant vagabonds from far-flung places, traveling on foot to what sometimes seems to us—and who knows, maybe to them, too—the ends of the earth.

"Dear Lord," says the minister. "Thank you for bringing these travelers into our community. Protect them on their journey and keep them safe from harm. Let them know your love and see the beauty of your creation."

To which all that is left to say is "Amen."

From *An American Pilgrimage,* by Karen Berger, manuscript in progress.

RODERICK PEATTIE

Those who look deeply see much. Natural history expert Roderick Peattie introduces us to a plant now quite uncommon in the southern Appalachians due to overharvesting. Its important symbolic status in several cultures (North American and Asian) may bear out the often extravagant claims made about its hidden powers. Hikers with lively imaginations and a curiosity about botany might want to keep an eye out in the deep woods along the AT for the plant known as "Little Man."

The Doctrine of Signatures
and The 'Sang Diggers

The Doctrine of Signatures

With the rediscovery of shortia, the strange story of the Asiatic-Appalachian floral kinships is still not exhausted. It has never been more practically demonstrated than in the colorful story of the ginseng trade. But before I tell of it I must explain, first, why the Chinese esteem ginseng so much, and to do so one must first understand the ancient "doctrine of signatures," which is at the root of almost all primitive medicine.

Put in its simplest form, this doctrine would hold, for instance, that to cure cardiac trouble one must seek a plant with a heart-shaped leaf. Hence Shakespeare's name of heart's-ease for the violet. To cure hepatic ailments, find a liver-shaped leaf. Thus do we get the name hepatica for a common spring wild flower. "In brewing medicines, look for an herb the same shape as the organ you want to cure," one mountain woman is quoted as saying, in that excellent book, *Cabins in the Laurel,* by Muriel E. Sheppard.

The Cherokees were ardent adherents of the doctrine. Thus a little orchid, the rattlesnake plantain, with net-veined leaves, looks enough like a snakeskin to suggest that it may be a "rattlesnake-master" or cure for snake bites. Another plant, the black cohosh, has a spike of button-like seed-pods, like an uplifted rattlesnake tail. So it too was deemed sovereign against the venom of the serpent. The mountain folk, having a deep respect for rattlesnakes, put credence in a whole list of other antidotes, mostly based on the doctrine of signatures. They are convinced, too, that their Indian predecessors here knew a great deal more than they told about the good points in the native flora—which indeed they did. It is remarkable that almost a third of the plants used in Cherokee medicine have held a place in the official *United States Pharmacopeia*, although only about half of these are employed for the same ills for which the Cherokees relied on them. Yet even a sixteen-percent agreement between the red medicine man and the white one is tribute to the Indians' centuries of experimentation, resulting in the beginnings of a genuine science of materia medica.

So the mountain people might not smile at the Cherokee belief that the tight-sticking burr of wild comfrey is a signature for a love potion boiled from the root—to make a lover stick to you. According to a statement I have read, a decoction of the root is still boiled in these mountains by some women and administered to husbands as a "manhood" medicine. The Cherokee woman ate plants with milky juice to keep her breasts full for her sucklings. And the old wives of the mountains today are not averse to taking, sometimes, a dose of squawroot for "female complaints," or of giving their teething children a little papooseroot.

The desideratum of all the ancient herbalists, just like the patent-medicine manufacturer of today, was a panacea, something that will cure anything that ails you. And what would the "signature" for that be? Why, a man-shaped root, of course. In Europe this was generally supposed to be the mandrake (an Old World member of the nightshade or potato family, quite unlike our American mandrake or May apple). With its bifurcated root, it sometimes remarkably reproduced also the head, arms and other external organs of a man, or, again, of a woman. Plainly this was an herb of the most powerful and desirable "vertues," as the herbalists said, and in order to keep the trade in it to themselves they beset its extraction with many difficulties. It was declared so dangerous that one who touched it might die. Hence it had to be encircled first with a chain of iron and then dragged out by dogs! It grew, according to some, only under gallows where it was fed upon human decay; according to others it "will give a great shreeke at the digging up." Besides curing "everything," it was thought by some to be sovereign in certain "loving matters, too full of scurrilitie to set forth in print, which I forbeare to speake of," says old Gerard primly.

The 'Sang Diggers

Now if our ancestors of Shakespeare's time believed in this sort of thing (even though Gerard himself was skeptical) it is not surprising that the Chinese had similar faith in one of their plants which they called jen-shen or root of life. A member of the English ivy family, it is rather an inconspicuous plant, growing about eight to fifteen inches high and producing three leaf-stalks at the summit of the stem; each of these bears five leaflets, arranged radially, like the fingers of the hand. And from the triple fork of the leaf-stalks arises the slender little flower-stalk bearing a tight head of six to twenty little greenish flowers, followed in autumn by bright red berries. Such are the outward and visible signs of the underground parts that for thousands of years the Celestials have held in almost holy awe. For the root is a spindle-shaped affair having a manlike or womanlike form and, sometimes as in the case of mandrake, the semblance of head, arms, legs and the like. To the Chinese this root bears the supreme signature and must be fit to cure every ill and prolong life. Mixed with the powdered antlers of a buck, it is also believed by the hopeful to be a sovereign aphrodisiac. And though I must draw over its further specific effects the veil of reticence, like Gerard, it is plain that such a root would be in high demand. When we consider how many Chinese have lived in China since the doctrine of signatures was first accepted, we can readily see how jen-shen has been uprooted from every last nook and cranny of the Flowery Kingdom.

European traders soon became aware of the exorbitant prices paid for jen-shen. But when they asked their own herbalists for the root, there was none to be found on the whole continent. Then, in 1715, jen-shen, or ginseng as we call it, was discovered in Canada. For it was another of the ancient Tertiary types that grows only in eastern Asia and eastern North America. And naturally such a plant would be found abundantly in the Southern Appalachians. It is said that it was Michaux who taught the mountain folk how to recognize it, when to collect it and how to prepare it and find a market for it. Indeed, the first American ship ever to set out to engage directly in the Chinese trade was the "Empress of China," which sailed in 1784 for Macao with a load of ginseng to exchange for tea, ginger, silk and camphor. The American species proved acceptable to the herbalists of Cathay, and so was begun the colorful trade which was to enjoy more than a century of profit. Thus grew up here in the mountains a special profession, that of the 'sang diggers.

The Indians too have engaged in 'sang digging, at times. In 1877, for instance, the price paid them by the wholesalers was fifty cents a pound—or equivalent to three days' wages. It is notable that in the ancient Cherokee "magic formulas," ginseng root had always been reckoned as of human form and called "great man" or "little man," though the name of the plant—as a whole, in Cherokee, is Atalikuli, meaning "it climbs the mountain." The

Cherokees employed it for headaches, cramps and female complaints.

The retail price of ginseng in America has fluctuated, going as high as twelve dollars a pound, and when war breaks communications, there is sometimes no market for it. But though nobody ever grew rich out of 'sang, many a mountain family has been kept from starvation by it, for after all Nature produces it; it costs nothing in cash to harvest it, and though much skill is required to dry it properly, this too involves little outlay. It must be dug in autumn for if collected at any other season it shrinks more on drying and, because appearance is everything under the doctrine of signatures, this would impair the market value.

'Sang digging is an essentially nomadic affair, for the diggers must range far over the mountains and into the uttermost depths of the forest to find their quarry. So whole families may be engaged in the hunt; they work fast because there is just the one season and an immense territory must be covered in it. A mountain man once described to me a party of 'sang diggers. He was no timid soul himself, but: "They was the most terrifying people I ever see," he confessed. "I was over in the Balsams, near the Pink Beds, when I see them coming down through the woods—men and women with eyes that didn't seem to see nothing, and their clothes all in tatters, and their hair all lank and falling down on their shoulders. They humped along through the woods like b'ars, muttering to themselves all the time, and stooping, and digging, and cursing and humping on and digging again."

I can't say if all 'sang diggers were like this; the only mountain people I have met in the 'sang business today were growing their own, as a crop--a slow process (with a seven-year wait for maturity!) and woefully subject to theft. I must confess indeed that I have seldom in all my wanderings in the Southern Appalachians seen any ginseng. It is more plentiful in my experience in the northern suburbs of Chicago! The 'sang diggers seem to have worked themselves out of a job, like their Chinese brothers.

From *The Great Smokies and the Blue Ridge: The Story of the Appalachians*, edited by Roderick Peattie, Vanguard, 1943.

FREDERICK COTTON, M.D., & RALPH LARRABEE, M.D.

"Emergencies." It's hard to imagine a contemporary wilderness rescue training program—covering such crises as exhaustion, insomnia, hysteria and homesickness, sunstroke, unconsciousness, and convulsions—going at it in the quaint, sexist, and chatty style of the trail guides of yesteryear. Even a small taste from a fine but long out-of-date edition of a Blue Ridge trail guide shows how much attitudes have changed, even if basic emergency medicine has not.

First Aid in the Woods

E XHAUSTION AND FATIGUE CALL FOR REST FIRST AND FOOD AFTERWARD. Alcoholic stimulation may enable a discouraged and exhausted man to rise superior to his environment, but it is brief in its action and is to be avoided if exposure to cold must continue. If possible stop the party, or a part of it, give the man a rest and if possible a short nap. Afterwards some easily digestible food—say some hot tea and crackers—and cheer him up. Of course relieve him of his pack and get him leisurely home by the easiest route.

Insomnia is a habit which probably deters more people from enjoying woods life than anything else. Treat it with contempt, or read the chapter on "Lying Awake at Night" in White's "The Forest." There is no objection to taking ten or twenty grains of sodium bromide (always dissolved in water). But always remember that *it does no harm to lie awake unless you let it get your goat!*

Hysteria and homesickness are more serious, often complicating the forced inaction of a prolonged rainy spell. Tact, kindness and plenty of work may avoid the need of returning to civilization. The proper procedure in cases of delirium or mental aberration is obvious.

Sunstroke is uncommon in the woods. If the skin is pale, cold and clammy, simply keep the patient quiet. If he is flushed and the skin is hot take any available means to cool him off, such as removing heavy clothing and bathing with cold water.

Unconsciousness, it need hardly be said, may be very serious. Lay the sufferer at full length, with the head low, loosen the clothing, and await developments. If it is merely a faint he (or more probably she) will promptly recover. If he does not you can only carry him, as best you may, to the nearest shelter, near water if possible, where he may be protected from exposure until plans for his removal to civilization, after sending for necessary help, may be made. It should perhaps be added that a physician, under such conditions, can do little more than a layman. Vigorous efforts to restore consciousness, or the administration of alcohol and other stimulants, is unwise. The rule is *let him alone.*

From *Guide to Paths in the Blue Ridge,* by Potomac Appalachian Trail Club, 1934.

BOB BARKER

One man with perfectly good legs will sit home, vegetating in front of the television. Another, with a constant uphill battle against multiple sclerosis, will thru-hike the Appalachian Trail. Bob Barker, of Sandston, Virginia, walked south to north on the trail, starting March 11, 1983, and finishing September 16, 1984. Twice his progress was interrupted by his disease, but he came back and finished the marathon. Where such determination comes from remains one of the great mysteries among long-distance wilderness hikers. In Barker's matter-of-fact report, there isn't a hint of self-pity.

Trail Diary, 1984

D URING THIS PERIOD OF TIME I EXPERIENCED ALL KINDS OF WEATHER FROM rain, sleet, snow, hot, cold, cloudy, sunny, windy (30-50 miles per hour and 38° on Mt. Washington, N.H. July 7 and 8) and beautiful calm days.

I was on the Trail a total of 182 nights.

104 nights at shelters
31 at hostels, homes, motels, etc.
25 nights camping in tent
11 days and nights resting
8 days day hiking
3 nights riding bus home

I wore out 6 crutch tips. Used 6 bottles of 100% DEET. Bought supplies at local stores untill I got to Gorham, N.H. here I started using freeze dried dinners. I meet several south bound hikers 3 times, they started at Katahdin and skiped south because of the black flies and hiked back north then hitched south and started hiking again. During this time I didn't get any ticks or poison ivey or blisters on my feet. But the palm of my right hand was a different story.

I figure that I averaged 12.26 miles per hiking day. The longest was 26.4 miles and the shortest only 3.8 miles.

From Thru-Hiker Report to Appalachian Trail Conference by Bob Barker, 1984.

CINDY ROSS

It's a shame we can't reproduce here the actual pages of Cindy Ross's book about her 1981 thru-hike. Ross, from Pennsylvania and nowadays a contributing editor for Backpacker *magazine, hand-wrote the book with nearly calligraphic beauty and accompanied her text with lovely pen-and-ink drawings of wildlife and landmarks observed en route. Her story is like so many others: the alternating rhythm of ebullience and despair as the long days on the trail bring new friends, new sights, injuries, and loneliness. It's a long walk from Georgia to Maine, and Ross's narrative suggests that sometimes the spirit can ache as much as a broken foot.*

Trail Diary, 1981

I'M LYING HERE OBSERVING ALL THE FOREST CREATURES. CHIPMUNKS SCURRY closer when I'm alone and quiet. I can observe a deer's habits for hours if I sit motionless and keep silent; even watch a millipede lazily weave himself in and out of twigs by my side.

I notice these pieces of life when there's no one to talk to. I begin to feel like a wild animal—unhuman, especially when I don't see other humanoids for days on end.

It's our nature though, to look and long for others of our own kind to share and communicate with.

Like the animals, we need our own around us.

I don't concern myself with wants. I turn my energy into NEEDS. I seem to be quite happy and satisfied when my basic human needs are fulfilled.

Back home I can get caught up in acquiring "things"—unnecessary trivia that clutters up my life and my mind.

Out here, I just want to quench my thirst, crawl under a rock in a storm and have the sun come out to dry me off.

Everything besides this is a special blessing from God . . . a cool breeze on a mountaintop, a brilliant blue sky, a deep pool to swim in on a hot day. Nothing . . . is taken for granted.

One learns to make-do. One learns to make the best of very little.

I use sticks to hold my bun together, large smooth leaves for toilet paper, baking soda for deodorant and tooth paste; and glowing candlelight in place of electricity.

I actually SEW my underwear . . . mend the elastic, patch my pants, darn my socks. Nothing is thrown away. Even when my clothes literally fall off me, I recycle it and use it as rags. My washing machine is a stream and my dryer is the sun, as my clothes hang on the back of my pack.

I can learn to make-do and do without nearly everything, except people. People who care and love me. People whom I can hug.

We have a very technologically advanced system of communications on the trail. There is a network of registers along the trail; tablets and note-books for hikers to sign in. News travels from one state to the next in a matter of days. Faster hikers passing by take news ahead up north; south bounders take it to those behind.

We can follow someone's entries for months—knowing their handwrit-ing, their adventures, their souls. When we finally meet up with them, it's like a reunion with an old, old friend.

Through these registers we learn which springs are dry, where stores are, which lakes have leeches and which shelters have porcupines. They even serve as a lost and found.

Once an entry read, "Has anybody seen my Mom? I lost her on the trail 2 days ago." He had *everybody* looking for his Mom, people that he's never even met. When they finally were reunited he neglected to sign it in, and many a concerned fellow hiker was still looking for dear Mom several days later.

Flat ridge walking seems like a dream come true. The elevation map reads ⌐⌐ . . . a "cruising trail." But usually there's some catch. This ridge has no water, and boasts hundreds of blown-down trees. There was a ter-rible ice storm here in Virginia last spring, knocking hundreds of trees down. A good 30 a day I must walk around, doubling the mileage as I travel com-pletely around their branches . . . stepping over limbs, into limbs. My legs are so scratched and bloody that they look as if they were beaten with whips.

It hasn't rained for days and days and all the springs have dried up. I am so thirsty that I resort to licking the moisture off the leaves of the trees that have fallen across the trail. My mouth is parched. My body is weak-ened. Never before did I long for water as badly as I do now.

I think back to other hard times that I found myself in. They never seem as bad when you have someone to share them with . . . to lighten the load. I approached such encounters light-heartedly, found amusement in them. Alone it is different. Alone I take life so much more seriously. I know now that life isn't meant to be lived alone.

I didn't always feel this way. When I was younger I used to believe my ideal life style was to live way back in a cabin somewhere—isolated and completely cut off from society. . . .

Not anymore. I realize now that *people* are everything. The woods are beautiful and I'm in love with every tree and animal and bit of moss, but they just can't love me back.

One consolation I have is God. We speak out loud to each other. He's my buddy. There *is* no one else. Once I tripped going down this steep de-scent. I was zooming down this eroded creek bed, trying to make the shelter by nightfall and tripped, falling flat on my face, ramming my jaw into a rock.

"You could die out here STUPID and no one would ever know it," I said to myself. I hike like a maniac, trying to make a shelter by nightfall, in hopes of having the company of other hikers.

The rest of the evening I walked with my arm extended, clutching my hand tightly as though someone was grasping it and saying in between sobs, "Jesus, take my hand and walk with me, be with me."

I wake up in the morning and ask God how things are going so far in His day; if we earthlings are relatively good or bad today.

All day long we talk out loud. If we get lost I say "OK God, we'll stick together and get ourselves out of this; and when we find the trail, we'll sit ourselves down and take a good break."

Does all this sound dramatic and extreme? It isn't. You would never believe you could behave this way, before you left on this hike. You learn FAST how badly you need when you're alone . . . that it's universal and there is nothing at all wrong with admitting to your weaknesses. In fact, I find this newly acquired humbleness, can actually make you strong.

Something happened to me yesterday. I'm hurting. I got up at dawn to do my 18+ miles a day and I couldn't walk. I am crippled. Everytime I take a step a biting pain goes up my leg. I have to drag my foot to get anywhere. I walked about one mile and sat down and cried. Took off my boot to examine it and it was all red and swollen. What could I have done? I don't remember doing anything in particular to hurt it. A half mile more I try to walk . . . looking at the trail through my tears and trying to figure out if I should go home or not.

I am getting tired of the trail. I'm doing long days with no spare time to stop and enjoy. There's a kind of compulsion that overcomes me whenever I hike alone. I feel like a machine, cranking in the miles, not really living the trail.

Every view looks the same. Every rhododendron flower smells the same. Every piece of trail just turns the corner and there is another piece of trail. I want to paint. I want to be with my family. I just don't want to be alone anymore.

The verdict at the Waynesboro hospital was a stress fracture Doc said he could either cast it and send me home on crutches or wrap it and send me back on the trail. I chose the latter. Three days I hike ever so slowly and carefully until I ram it one more time, good and hard. I am broken.

I think that at least half of my injury was brought on by myself, by my own subconscious will to end my heart's suffering. My mind isn't in the woods. I'm not aware of my surroundings, so I'm certainly not going to be aware of the rocks at my feet.

Ramming and ramming my foot into those rocks . . . I am too tired physically and psychologically to care about picking my feet up.

I am empty and broken and my whole being needs the nourishment of love and human companionship. It is time to go home and heal.

From *A Woman's Journey on the Appalachian Trail,* by Cindy Ross, East Woods, 1982.

SCOTT HULER

In spring 1995 Scott Huler hiked much of the southern section of the AT as part of a team of reporters from several newspapers in eastern cities—his own base being the Raleigh, North Carolina, News & Observer. *His reporting from the trail was consistently colorful and candid. Summing up his AT experience, Huler tries, as have many other long-distance hikers, to find in the walking a metaphor for the voyage of his own life.*

Bringing the Trail's Lessons Back to Life

I OBSESSIVELY WATCHED THE WEATHER CHANNEL FOR NEARLY HALF AN HOUR before the thought crossed my mind: Who cares?

It didn't make a difference whether it was going to pour all week; if it was going to be chilly, I didn't need to carry those gloves one more week before shipping them home. I live in a house now, with a closet filled with clothes and a supermarket full of food a mile away. The weather didn't make a difference.

I was crushed. I felt disconnected from my surroundings, disoriented to the point of dysfunction.

I was off the trail.

People who have through-hiked the Appalachian Trail talk about the difficult adjustment when they return to what they often call "the other real life," and now I can understand why. I was on the trail only seven weeks, but the return to civilization has me stunned and hesitant, blinking as though I've just awakened.

Of course I miss the friends I made on the trail. Like summer campers, through-hikers form a tight community. We have shared something special and intense; we have formed a brotherhood, and I miss them. Less seriously, I am working hard to remember that body function noises are not as acceptable off the trail as they were out in the woods.

But what I notice most are the little details. For one thing, it is so *noisy* here. Sitting quietly in my backyard late in the day I hear traffic, lawn mowers, radios from nearby houses and passing cars. And this is not even a particularly noisy place—this is Raleigh, where if you hear a siren it probably means that somebody put out the recycling on the wrong day and the neighbors called 911.

I miss the silence of late afternoon on the trail, when the only sound was the dripping of rain from the trees, the burbling of a brook, or the laughter of a few companions.

I miss the peace of the mornings, when I could drink coffee and stare in a way that seemed perfectly appropriate to my solitary surroundings.

I miss the connection with my environment. For seven weeks I was an intimate with the sun—I saw it rise and set every single day. I set up my tent instinctively, orienting the door toward the east for the morning sun without a conscious thought. I was out in the woods all day—I just knew where the sun was.

Now, though I know the sun comes in my bedroom window in the morning, once I step outside the house I need a compass to find east. In my yard, it simply doesn't matter.

Most of all, though, I miss the rhythms of a day spent only walking. On the trail, each day had a certainty, a necessity, that made walking nothing more than a fact of life—and, when that was done, made sleeping peaceful and easy. I faced no choices: When following the white blazes is all you do every day, a certain peace will find you. It has to.

I now face a life that is, like everyone's life, filled with trail intersections, with unmarked spots where I don't know which way the trail goes, and with the awful uncertainty that accompanies a world where choice is infinite. And with all the beauty that infinite choice offers, I miss—more than I could have imagined—a world where my only choices involved where to stop for the night and which flavor of Lipton dinner to eat each meal.

If you picture me standing, a little sadly, on a wooded hilltop where dozens of trails wander in every direction, with several maps, each of which gives me inconsistent and incomplete information about only some of the trails, you won't be far off.

But even in that I find comfort. Art, literature and song are filled with the metaphor of the journey, of the quest. I've had a little quest now, and when I came off the trail I thought that my first job would be to find a new metaphor to live by.

But as I conceive of my life now I find that the metaphor hasn't changed: Like everyone, I'm still on a quest. I'm just on the next one, and my decisions now involve which way to go. If I've learned anything from the trail it's that if you trust the universe it will find a way to guide you. I may be separated from the Trail Magic, but I can commit myself to being open to whatever magic the universe wishes to send my way. If I have courage maybe I can even count on it.

So I address my life, I consider my metaphors, and I begin—by doing the same thing I did on the trail.

I put one foot in front of the other. And I walk.

"Bringing the Trail's Lessons Back to Life," by Scott Huler, in *The News & Observer*, Raleigh, North Carolina, May 22, 1995.

WEST VIRGINIA

View from Jefferson Rock, Harpers Ferry: the Potomac River, West Virginia, and Maryland.

Trail miles: 2.4 in West Viriginia, shortest one-state distance on the AT, with 23–24 miles sharing the border with Virginia in two places

Trail maintenance: Potomac AT Club, Harpers Ferry National Historical Park

Highest point: Peter's Mt., 3,484 ft. (southern West Virginia, near Lindside)

Broadest rivers: Shenandoah, crossable on auto bridge; Potomac, crossable on 600-ft.-long Goodloe Byron Pedestrian Walkway

Features: Lovely woodland stroll culminating at the tiny historic town of Harpers Ferry, home base of the Appalachian Trail Conference, the psychological midpoint for north- or southbound AT thru-hikers.

Parks, forests, and nature preserves: Harpers Ferry National Historical Park

Most intriguing name on the trail: Jefferson Rock

Trail town: Harpers Ferry

CONGRESS OF THE UNITED STATES

By 1968 the popularity of the Appalachian Trail had reached a level unfore-seen by the trail's pioneers and founders in the 1920s. The federal govern-ment stepped in to assist in the protection and management of the trail, and at the same time Congress adopted the National Trails System Act. The Ap-palachian Trail and the Pacific Crest Trail were the first two trails under its aegis.

Administered by the National Park Service, in the Department of the Interior, by 1996 the National Trails System *consisted of trails in three broadly defined categories:*

National Scenic Trails

National Historic Trails

National Recreation Trails

The Scenic Trails are generally continuous and protected corridors through the wilderness (with linkage through settled areas) for recreational use—hiking, camping and the like.

The Historic Trails trace the routes of the transcontinental explorers, the pioneers, the forced marches of displaced Native Americans, and of military campaigns. These trails are usually not continuous and are instead themati-cally linked sites and segments, visitable by automobile and some walking.

The Recreation Trails are previously established hiking trails now recog-nized by the Park Service as integral to the overall National Trails System. These trails receive some tax dollar support but are not promoted directly by the federal government as part of the National Trails System.

National Trails System, 1996

National Scenic Trails	*National Historic Trails*
Appalachian Trail	*Iditarod Trail*
Continental Divide Trail	*Juan Batista de Anza*
Ice Age Trail	*Trail*
Natchez Trace	*Lewis and Clark Trail*
North Country Trail	*Mormon Pioneer Trail*
Pacific Crest Trail	*Nez Perce Trail*
Potomac Heritage Trail	*Oregon Trail*
	Santa Fe Trail
	Trail of Tears

The following excerpt from the National Trails System Act, as amended in 1978, describes its purpose and begins to lay out the criteria for placing a trail under the National Trails program.

An Act to Establish a National Trails System

NATIONAL TRAILS SYSTEM ACT
as amended
(through P.L. 95-625, Nov. 10, 1978)

AN ACT

To establish a national trails system, and for other purposes.

Be it enacted by the Senate and House of Representatives of the United States of America in Congress assembled,

SHORT TITLE

Section 1.
This Act may be cited as the "National Trails System Act".

STATEMENT OF POLICY

Sec. 2. (a) In order to provide for the ever-increasing outdoor recreation needs of an expanding population and in order to promote the preservation of, public access to, travel within, and enjoyment and appreciation of the open-air, outdoor areas and historic resources of the Nation, trails should be established (i) primarily, near the urban areas of the Nation, and (ii) secondarily, within scenic areas and along historic travel routes of the Nation, which are often more remotely located.

(b) the purpose of this Act is to provide the means for attaining these objectives by instituting a national system of recreation, scenic and historic trails, by designating the Appalachian Trail and the Pacific Crest Trail as the initial components of that system, and by prescribing the methods by which, and standards according to which, additional components may be added to the system.

NATIONAL TRAILS SYSTEM

Sec. 3. The national system of trails shall be composed of—

(a) National recreation trails, established as provided in section 4 of this Act, which will provide a variety of outdoor recreation uses in or reasonably accessible to urban areas.

(b) National scenic trails, established as provided in section 5 of this

Act, which will be extended trails so located as to provide for maximum outdoor recreation potential and for the conservation and enjoyment of the nationally significant scenic, historic, natural, or cultural qualities of the areas through which such trails may pass.

(c) National historic trails, established as provided in section 5 of this Act, which will be extended trails which follow as closely as possible and practicable the original trails or routes of travel of national historical significance. Designation of such trails or routes shall be continuous, but the established or developed trail, and the acquisition thereof, need not be continuous onsite. National historic trails shall have as their purpose the identification and protection of the historic route and its historic remnants and artifacts for public use and enjoyment. Only those selected land and water based components of an historic trail which are on federally owned lands and which meet the national historic trail criteria established in this Act, are established as initial Federal protection components of a national historic trail. The appropriate Secretary may subsequently certify other lands as protected segments of an historic trail upon application from State or local governmental agencies or private interests involved if such segments meet the national historic trail criteria established in this Act and such criteria supplementary thereto as the appropriate Secretary may prescribe, and are administered by such agencies or interests without expense to the United States.

(d) Connecting or side trails, established as provided in section 6 of this Act, which will provide additional points of public access to national recreation, national scenic or national historic trails or which will provide connections between such trails.

The Secretary of the Interior and the Secretary of Agriculture, in consultation with appropriate governmental agencies and public and private organizations, shall establish a uniform marker for the national trails system.

From the National Trails System Act, as amended, November 10, 1978, United States Congress.

CHRISTOPHER WHALEN

Few start a thru-hike on the AT without a careful plan. Serendipity in the wilderness may be attractive to some, but it's not much to rely on when food is running low and your boots should have been put out to pasture a hundred miles ago. Most long-distance hikers spend a year planning their adventure, calculating costs and strategy so that the weight they'll have to carry can be adjusted seasonally and with reference to the actual landscape on each section of the Appalachian Trail. The operative concept is always "Less is more." Unless, that is, you foolishly forget to bring something essential, like bug dope or flashlight batteries. Christopher Whalen's practical handbook for planning a thru-hike covers the theme from soup to nuts, from equipment to food, shelter, safety, and entertainment. A key element is a series of mail drops at post offices on or near the trail, where sympathetic postmasters will hold packages for the soon-to-arrive hiker.

Maildrops

*A*MAILDROP IS A SUPPLY PACKAGE THAT YOU SEND TO YOURSELF THROUGH the mail. If used strategically, maildrops can take excess weight off your back and still keep you well-supplied throughout your hike.

The Appalachian Trail is more-or-less wilderness hiking, but you should remember that, particularly from Virginia to New Hampshire, you are never more than four days from a town. A mistake made by many fledgling long-distance hikers (myself included) is to begin by carrying far too much food between town visits. You'll be persuaded to make better use of the mail the first time you arrive in a town with four days worth of food still on your back and recall how many mountains you carried it over to get it there.

A common way to prepare a maildrop is to pack at home all that you will use during the trip and have a family member or friend mail the boxes on a predetermined schedule. Leave them unsealed until mailing, so items can be added or removed. It's important to get the current hours of the post office to which you want to send packages. It's worth sending a card to the post office yourself. ZIP Codes of Trail post offices always can be found in the *A. T. Data Book*.

WHAT TO SEND IN A MAILDROP

Generally, a maildrop can include nonperishable food, and the gear and guidebooks necessary to take you to your next planned maildrop.

Some thru-hikers, however, have completed the entire Trail without using any *food* maildrops. They have used maildrops to send gear, clothing, film, *etc.* but have relied totally on stores for food along the way. Some benefits of this: less work on packing before departure, money saved on postage (food is heavy), no worries about post-office hours. But, it has some drawbacks: Small-town groceries can be expensive and limited. On our thru-hike, the grocery in Fontana Dam, N.C., had been picked clean by hikers before us. We needed to buy food to carry through the Smoky Mountains (no easy resupply for almost 70 miles), and virtually all that was left in the store was some mac and cheese, Kool-Aid, and a large amount of rutabagas.

Many thru-hikers resupply through the mail by sending most staples (pasta, rice, *etc.*) and their favorite hard-to-find foods and using stores along the Trail to buy bread (check expiration), fresh fruits and vegetables, meat, beverages, Squeeze Parkay, ice cream, and other perishables. This method has many valuable benefits: You don't need to rely on stores that may not have products you need, and you can mail yourself just enough of some-thing—powdered milk, for example—prepackaged in Ziploc bags. (Think about it: You're in town and have only the option to buy a large box in a store—one that is too large, too heavy, and wasteful—and then you have to repackage it into smaller bags outside.) Many foods can be bought cheaply in bulk. Spaghetti, rice, and powdered milk can all be packaged into reus-able, single-serving Ziplocs. You can also mix all your ingredients for a meal (oatmeal, powdered milk, sugar, dried fruit) into one bag. It simplifies mat-ters greatly.

Hikers should beware of sending too much through the mail. At home, when you fill a box to be mailed, pick it up. Would you mind carrying this weight on your back for a few days, along with your other gear? I heard about two people who sent themselves a maildrop weighing 68 pounds. Think about adding that to 30-50 pounds you may already have in your pack, and you may be inspired to trim.

Look at the maildrop. What's in there? Are you sending yourself two flashlights? Ten pounds of rice for a 100-mile section of the Trail? Victor Hugo's 2,100-plus-page *Les Miserables?* A good time to show discretion is before you mail. Remember that postage is expensive; if you mail some-thing both ways, you're paying twice.

What to Send in a Maildrop: A Checklist

___ **food** (How many days till the next maildrop? How much do you eat?)
___ **clothing** as needed
___ **guides** as needed for the next stretch
___ **vitamins**
___ **film, film mailers** (it's often difficult to get the exact type of film you want at a small store)
___ **tea/coffee**
___ **candy bars** (buy in bulk beforehand—less expensive)
___ **gorp**
___ **powdered milk**
___ **jerky**
___ a **book** (for the literary minded)
___ **Sno Seal** in a film canister with small cloth (to keep leather waterproof—enough for two pairs of boots)
___ **paper** (for letters, journal)
___ a list of **what's in your next drop**

HOW MANY MAILDROPS TO SEND

Many thru-hikers sent between 12 and 18 maildrops; one sent himself 30. The factors involved are: how much resupplying you will do from maildrops, and how often you want to go into town for foodstuffs.

A good rule of thumb is: Don't send yourself a maildrop to a town farther than one mile off the Trail unless you were planning to stop there anyway. It's annoying to walk in and out of a town solely for a maildrop.

For emergency shipments of equipment, money, *etc.*, consult the *Data Book*—if you passed up this under-$4 bonanza, ask someone at the shelter—for the nearest post office (in boldface, with the ZIP Code and distance from the Trail).

3 Ways to Send a Maildrop

(1) To a post office: First class
(2) To a post office: Fourth class insured for $50 (cheaper, but takes longer)
Address it: **Your Name**
 General Delivery
 Town, State, ZIP Code
Write in corner of package:
 "Please hold for A.T. hiker"
(3) To a hostel or inn: UPS (cheaper)

Address it: **Your Name**
The Hostel, Inn, Whatever
FULL STREET ADDRESS
Town, State, ZIP Code
Write on corner of package:
"Innkeeper: Please hold for A.T. hiker"

SAMPLE MAILDROP

This drop is for Damascus, Va.
The next maildrop is Pearisburg, Va., 163.4 miles north.
Food stops are available at Atkins, Bastian, and Va. 606.

What to Send

eight days worth of food: breakfast, lunch, dinner
large bag gorp
bag of powdered milk
8-10 candy bars
tea/coffee
A.T. guide for southwest/central Virginia
film, film mailer (to send rolls already completed)
one pair new socks
extra pair shorts

What to Send Home from Damascus

some (but not all) winter gear—keep some until after Mt. Rogers
A.T. guide for Tennessee/North Carolina
journal since last maildrop (saves weight)
Look in your pack—what haven't you been using for a while? Send it home, or get
rid of it!

From *The Appalachian Trail Workbook for Planning Thru-Hikes,* by Christopher Whalen, Appalachian Trail Conference, 1993.

JAMES HARE

James Hare's two-volume compendium of Appalachian Trail thru-hiker reports and other writing about the trail may have been the first literary collection about the subject. It was certainly the longest, weighing in at over 2,000 pages. We owe Rodale Press a word of thanks for publishing these stories. Among the most colorful characters in anybody's book about the AT is Emma "Grandma" Gatewood, who thru-hiked twice and logged other substantial miles on the AT and other challenging trails as well. Clad in flimsy sneakers and carrying hardly anything we would consider essential for comfort or safety (no tent, no backpack, little food or water), this was a hiker on a mission to prove something, and only she could say whether her mission was benign or perverse. Perhaps it was both.

When the news media caught wind of this unusual thru-hiker, they saw the potential for good copy. Emma Gatewood did not disappoint them. During her first thru-hike, in 1955, Sports Illustrated *spoke with her at several points along the way. The variation of her moods matched the extreme ups and downs of the Appalachian mountains and valleys. To wit:*

> *Mrs. Gatewood is serenely confident that she can finish her trek. "I'll get there except if I break something or something busts loose. And, when I get atop Mt. Katahdin, I'll sing 'America, the Beautiful, From sea to shining sea.'" (Sports Illustrated, August 15, 1955.)*

> *I read about this Trail three years ago in a magazine, and the article told about the beautiful trail, how well marked it was, that it was cleared out, and that there were shelters at the end of a good day's hike. I thought it would be a nice lark. It wasn't. There were terrible blow-downs, burnt-over areas that were never remarked, gravel and sand washouts, weeds and brush to your neck, and most of the shelters were blown down, burned down, or so filthy I chose to sleep out of doors. This is no trail. This is a nightmare. For some fool reason, they always lead you right up over the biggest rock to the top of the biggest mountain they can find. I've seen every fire station between here and Georgia. Why, an Indian would die laughing his head off if he saw [that] trail. I would never have started this trip if I had known how tough it was, but I couldn't, and I wouldn't quit. (Sports Illustrated, October 10, 1955.)*

Emma Gatewood thru-hiked the AT a second time a mere two years later, in 1957.

Grandma Gatewood:
A Legend along the Appalachian Trail

Started at MT. OGLETHORPE on May 3, 1955
Finished at MT. KATAHDIN on September 25, 1955

Started at MT. OGLETHORPE on April 27, 1957
Finished at MT. KATAHDIN on September 16, 1957

Started at MT. KATAHDIN in 1954
Finished at RAINBOW LAKE, MAINE, in 1964

Mrs. Emma Gatewood, better known along the trail as Grandma Gatewood, is probably the best-known of all the hikers who have completed the 2,000 miles of the Appalachian Trail. Almost every through hiker has his favorite story about Grandma, which he has heard along the trail. She is the kind of personality about whom legends grow. The following story was obtained in an interview in January, 1973:

Grandma Gatewood climbed Mt. Katahdin for the first time in July, 1954. At the time she was in her late sixties, had born 11 children, was about five feet two inches in height, weighed around 155 pounds, and wore sneakers for hiking. Mt. Katahdin was the first mountain she had ever climbed, and this was her first extended hike.

When she reached the summit she put on a black wool sweater from the denim bag in which she carried her belongings and ate a lunch of raisins while she counted the lakes and ponds below. When she reached 100, she gave up counting, even though other ponds could be seen on the horizon.

At dusk Grandma was back at the foot of the mountain. She had hiked 10.5 miles, including 8,326 feet of rise and descent. People at the campground congratulated her, for many hikers who start out to climb Katahdin never make it to the top. A young couple invited her to share broiled hot dogs and pea beans baked with molasses and salt pork. Would she want a lift to Millinocket in the morning? No, Grandma explained, she intended to hike "a ways" down the Appalachian Trail.

By first light she was gone. That day the trail was fairly level, and she did about 14 miles. She spent the night in a stand of birch near a brook. In the morning the trail took her up the Rainbow Ledges and down among blueberry bushes to the shore of Rainbow Lake. Here she came to a weather-rotted sign at a fork in the trail, could not decipher it, and took the wrong turning. She didn't realize that she must follow the white paint blazes which mark the Appalachian Trail. By afternoon her "trail" had disintegrated into wild animal paths in the vicinity of a fair-sized pond, and Grandma Gatewood knew that she was lost.

For a minute she experienced a surge of panic, but a mother who has raised 11 children is experienced in panics, great and small. Grandma Gatewood took a firm grip on herself. "If I'm lost, I'm lost," she told herself. "But it's not hurting any yet."

In the motionless air the blackflies were becoming bothersome. She tied a scarf around her head and made a pillow of the denim bag. Then, rolled up in a woolen blanket, she tried to sleep on a dry flat rock that protruded above the damp grass from which insects were swarming. During the night it rained, and at daybreak she was dismayed to find that a lens in her glasses was badly cracked. Apparently the glasses had been stepped on during the rain. While patching the lens with a Band-Aid, she remembered the rowboat she had seen yesterday, suspended upside down on ropes between trees. She remembered that it was near the shoreline of the pond. She began to retrace her steps and in a short while she arrived at the upside-down rowboat.

On first coming to the rowboat she was jubilant, thinking that since she had been able to backtrack this far she might be able to keep on backtracking to where she had lost the trail. At about that time she became conscious of the drone of an airplane, and soon a small floatplane came into sight overhead. It was flying low. Presently another small floatplane appeared, skimmed the trees, and vanished.

Grandma was certain that the planes were hunting for her, although she had no idea why she should be missed. Later she was to learn that a fire warden at a camp on Rainbow Lake had seen her as she hiked through. He had radioed the camp eight miles away on Nahmakanta Lake and asked for a report when she arrived. When Grandma did not show up, a search was started.

At the pond Grandma kindled a fire. A couple of hours later, as the floatplanes flew over again, she sprinkled water on the blaze from a rusting tin can she had found. She had remembered from her reading that during the daylight hours smoke is more easily caught sight of than fire. However, the planes did not see the smoke.

Grandma had read that a lost person should stay put and wait for rescue, so she waited and kept the fire going. She finished her small stock of peanuts and chipped beef. A plane was heard along toward evening. She threw wood on the fire till it roared and then drenched it with water. A spout of smoke rose above the trees, but the plane did not approach. That night, bedded down under the upside-down rowboat, Grandma was scarcely troubled by a light drizzle. The black flies, however, persisted in their attacks until well after dark,

Next morning she ate a dozen raisins, all the food that was left. She looked for wood sorrel, whose leaves could be eaten, and teaberry, which could be steeped to make a refreshing drink. Both plants were familiar from

her childhood, but neither was in evidence here. It was too early for raspberries, chokeberries, blueberries, and cranberries that are plentiful in Maine
in season.

Somewhere out of sight aircraft engines could be heard. Grandma was
hungry, and became even hungrier as she realized that until she was rescued there would be nothing to eat. She thought the matter over. "If I'm
going to starve, Lord," she said, "I might as well do it someplace else as do
it here."

Having made her decision, Grandma packed her belongings and walked
away from the upside-down rowboat. In a little while she happened upon a
barely perceptible aisle in the forest. She followed it, and in a few hundred
yards the aisle became wider and showed signs of recent use. Then, without
warning, the aisle burst onto a lake. Cabins were clustered at the edge of the
water, and the scene was somehow familiar. She was back at Rainbow Lake.

She saw a knot of men consulting a map. As Grandma approached, blue
denim bag across her shoulder, they recognized her.

One of the men put a coffee pot on the stove. Grandma was given a
wooden chair at a table covered with a checkered oilcloth. Through the window she watched a plane taxi to the landing dock. A man in the uniform of
the Maine Forest Service stepped out of the plane and came to the cabin. For
a moment he studied Grandma in silence.

"Welcome to Rainbow Lake," he said at last. "You've been lost."

"Not lost," Grandma said, "just misplaced."

The ordeal had undermined Grandma Gatewood's confidence in herself. From Katahdin's peak to Rainbow Lake is 24 miles, barely more than a
hundredth part of the Appalachian Trail, so when the wardens of the Maine
Forest Service suggested with considerable forcefulness that she give up
hiking in the Maine wilderness until she was more experienced, she agreed.
She returned to Ohio on the bus.

Grandma Gatewood had learned about the Appalachian Trail two or three
years before from a magazine article. She remembered the description as
being on the idyllic side: a smoothed footway with easy grades, a yard-
wide garden path carefully blazed and manicured, with plenty of signs. She
resolved to hike it all. Site had always wanted to do something notable, and
no woman had ever hiked the Appalachian Trail in one continuous journey.
The length of the longest footpath in the world held an irresistible appeal
for her. Her imagination was fired. It was a challenge worthy of the pioneer
women of the last century, some of whom she had known well. She herself
had come of a pioneer family, born October 25, 1887, one of 15 children, on
a farm in Ohio. Most of her life had been lived on farms, where she had
hoed corn, raked hay, chopped tobacco, and raised four sons and seven
daughters of her own.

For her hike she had fashioned a bag from denim. In it she carried any clothing not being worn; food such as bouillon cubes, chipped beef, raisins, peanuts, powdered milk, and salt; items of first aid like adhesive tape, Band-Aids, and Mercurochrome; hairpins, safety pins, needles, thread, buttons, and matches in a plastic matchcase.

Her basic outer costume consisted of hat, skirt, blouse, and sneakers. She wore a single pair of socks, sometimes cotton, sometimes woolen. At night she would pull on a second pair of socks. She also had a scarf, a sweater, a jacket, and a light wool blanket.

Grandma had been a little cowed by the events in Maine; she knew it and she hated it. She traveled to California to visit with relatives, but as the months slipped by the pull of the trail became strong. One day in spring she boarded a plane bound for Atlanta, and a week later she signed the trail register on the summit of Mt. Oglethorpe in Georgia.

Her hiking gear had been increased by a flashlight, a Swiss army knife with nine miniature tools, a teaspoon, two plastic eight-ounce baby bottles for water, a rain hat and rain cape, and a plastic curtain. She had sewn a tail on the rain hat to shield her neck. The rain cape, made from two yards of plastic sheeting, protected herself and her denim bag when she walked in the rain. It was used as a ground cloth when she rested in some damp place or slept on the ground. The plastic curtain was used for shelter when it rained. A straw hat began the trip, but was lost when a stray wind blew it into Tallulah Gorge on the Georgia border. Other hats followed—a fisherman's cap, a man's felt hat, another hat with a green celluloid visor, and a knitted stocking cap. None lasted long before succumbing to some vagary of the trail, like being forgotten at a rest stop or falling into a mountain torrent. Grandma's pack seldom weighed as much as 20 pounds; 14 to 17 pounds were more usual.

A chilling fog was shrouding the famed rhododendron thickets on Roan Mountain on the North Carolina–Tennessee line when she arrived there at the end of a June day. She heated rocks in a fire, laid them on the grass, and went to sleep on top of the rocks, wrapped in her blanket. The rocks gave off warmth for hours and the night was tolerable. During a cold snap on another mountain she pulled a wide board from the ruins of a tumbledown cabin and toasted it over the embers. This became her bed, and if the board rather quickly lost its heat the night had at least begun cozily.

Like many a hiker before her, she made the discovery that picnic tables in forest and park campsites could be used as beds if the ground was soaked, and they were no harder than the floors of the lean-tos. She did not depend on lean-tos much; she was a woman and alone, and sharing such primitive accommodations with chance strangers was not always satisfactory.

Tiny wood mice pulled at her hair as she slept, no doubt regarding the strands as capital homemaking material. She thought of the mice as sources of amusement and company rather than as annoyances.

As she hiked through the southern hill country, Grandma soon learned that a stop at a home to inquire about the route or to fill her baby bottles at the hand pump in the yard was likely to make her the object of intense though well-mannered curiosity. She was often invited to stay for the night. While preferring the "company room" for slumber, she wasn't finicky; the hayloft would do nicely.

In Shenandoah National Park a black bear ambled onto the pathway. Its intentions seemed not unfriendly, although it was ambling her way. As the gap between them narrowed, Grandma let go with what she calls "my best holler."

"'Dig,' I hollered, and he dug."

The episode seemed to release a little extra adrenalin into Grandma's system. Up till then she had been doing from 12 to 16 miles daily, but by nightfall on this particular day she had logged 27 miles.

West Virginia and Maryland sped by under Grandma's sneakered feet. By now she had switched to men's sneakers, having decided that the soles of women's sneakers were too light and thin. The rocks of Pennsylvania, which on the narrow ridgetops stand on end like the fins of the dinosaurs, put her choice of footwear to a stern test. In its 200 miles of trail, Pennsylvania accounted for about one and a half pairs of the five pairs of sneakers she was to wear out on her journey. Usually a pair of sneakers was good for from 400 to 500 miles.

For almost three months she had managed without utensils other than jackknife, teaspoon, and baby bottles. At a spring in New Jersey she picked up an abandoned tin cup and liked it so well that she never hiked without it afterwards.

Where the trail precariously negotiated a cliff on Kittatinny Ridge, a blacksnake practically stood on its tail in a fighting attitude, but Grandma Gatewood knew all about blacksnakes from her years on the farm. She simply waited until the creature subsided and fled into a crevice.

In New York a rattlesnake made the mortal mistake of shaking its tail at Grandma. And near the summer community of Oscawana Corners a German shepherd leapt a hedge and nipped the upper calf of her leg. As the skin was hardly broken, she painted the teeth marks with Merthiolate and hiked on, but more warily. When she ran into a patch of nettles she changed her mind about wearing a skirt on the trail. Dungarees became her usual garb after that.

In the Mohawk State Forest in Connecticut a bobcat circled around and "squeaked infernally" while Grandma was snacking from a can of sardines. "If you come too close I'll crack you," she warned. The bobcat kept its distance.

Coming down that choice little precipice in the Berkshires which Yankee humor has named Jug End, Grandma Gatewood slipped on the rain-wet slope. She grabbed at a tree limb; it broke and she slid hard against a rock. For some minutes she was unable to move and wondered if a shoulder was paralyzed, but the numbness ebbed and she went on.

In Vermont the porcupine thrives. Its flesh is said to be as toothsome as pork or veal. On learning this fact, Grandma cornered a porcupine and gave it a crack with a pole. Mindful of the quills, she skinned it with caution, then spitted the carcass over a fire. The flesh smelled lovely as it roasted, but the first forkful was another matter. "My imagination got away on me," Grandma said. "All at once the porcupine meat filled my mouth. I just couldn't swallow."

She had been carrying a walking stick, flourishing it at hostile dogs and using it as a third leg to ford streams; in the White Mountains she found it of particular help in descending barren ledges where her legs weren't long enough to make the step down without extra support.

As Grandma hiked, word of her progress ran ahead. She had become news, and reporters from local papers popped up at the road crossings to get her story. Heretofore only the children of her children had known her as "Grandma." Now "Grandma" was to become a fixed part of her name—and a part of the vocabulary of the Appalachian Trail.

The Maine Forest Service was on the alert as Grandma crossed the state line. If the service was astonished at seeing her again, after having issued a virtual writ of banishment, it managed to keep the emotion to itself, and was ready when she reached the Kennebec River at Caratunk. Waiting with a canoe to take her over were Chief Forest Warden Isaac Harris and Warden Bradford Pease. A dozen miles in the rain had soaked Grandma to the skin, and they brought her in some haste to Sterling's Hotel where Mrs. Sterling dried her out. A few days to the north Game Warden Francis Cyr rowed her across Nesowadnehunk Stream, thus sparing her the 10-mile detour made necessary by the recent collapse of the cable bridge.

On Mt. Katahdin Grandma signed the trail register while the low clouds hugged the summit and sprayed her with icy mist. She was wearing a plaid lumberman's jacket she had found back along the trail. The date was September 25.

When she returned to Katahdin Stream Campground, limping from a sore knee that had plagued her for days, she was met by Mrs. Dean Chase, a correspondent for the Associated Press. Mrs. Chase drove her to Millinocket, where she became the guest of the Chamber of Commerce and was interviewed by a reporter from *Sports Illustrated.* Grandma's time on the trail had been 145 or 146 days, depending upon whether the starting and ending days are counted as half-days or as full days. Exactly one month later she turned 68.

Grandma Gatewood was the first woman to walk the complete distance of the Appalachian Trail alone as well as the first woman to walk it in one continuous trip, straight through from one end to the other.* It was an exploit that only five others, all men, had accomplished at that time. Her weight had dropped to 120 pounds, 30 pounds lighter than when she started, and her feet had enlarged one size in width, from 8C to 8D.

The goal had been achieved, but if there was a glow of gratification, there was also the letdown. She told the news media that she had "had enough" and went home to Ohio and started a scrapbook.

Only 17 months passed before Grandma Gatewood was back on Mt. Oglethorpe's peak, poised for another go on the trail. From April 27 till September 16, from spring through the summer and into the autumn of 1957, she trod the trail energetically, to the delight of the manufacturer of Keds (six pairs) and of the many acquaintances on farms and in rural settlements along the way who marveled to see the 69-year-old lady once more.

Her second through journey was made in 142 days, at a daily rate of 14.5 miles. It was a trifle speedier and "no tougher" than before. She was the first person, man or woman, to hike the whole trail for the second time. (Three other persons have now hiked the trail more than once. Charles Ebersole and Earl Shaffer have done it twice. Another woman, Dorothy Laker, has walked it three times. —ED.) As always, there were days when she had to steel herself to continue. Aside from the love for the woods and the exhilaration that was hers on the trail, Mrs. Gatewood's reason for the second trip was simply to "see some of the things I missed the first time." As on previous trips, she didn't keep her family posted on her whereabouts, and was not nagged by the thought that she should dispatch a score of postcards from every country post office near the trail. Nor did her family worry; Grandma knew how to take care of herself.

When she wasn't invited to potluck in some mountain home, she was often content to dine upon the food that others had left behind in shelters. Certainly she didn't carry much food. Her pack of fewer than 20 pounds was probably the lightest burden ever taken on a through hike of the Appalachian Trail. She cared nothing for tea or coffee, and on the trail seldom cooked meals or even heated up prepared food. Even at home she had been out of the habit of cooking for several years. "Cold food is good enough for

*The first woman to complete the Appalachian Trail was Mary Kilpatrick of Philadelphia. She accomplished the feat by a series of trips with her husband and friends. She finished in 1939. The second woman credited with completing the trail was Mildred Lamb, also of Philadelphia. Her trip, made in 1952 with Dick Lamb, was made south-to-north from Mt. Oglethorpe to the Susquehanna River and then north-to-south from Mt. Katahdin to the Susquehanna, and included extended trips on side trails. Emma Gatewood is thus the third woman to have finished the Appalachian Trail, according to the records of the Appalachian Trail Conference. However, she is the *first* woman to walk the complete distance alone, as well as the first woman to walk it in one continuous trip.

me," she said. "People eat things out of the refrigerator that are colder than just cold and think nothing of it."

Sometimes a fortnight would pass without a campfire. One of the few meals she cooked on the trail was a pancake supper. When the rafters of a lean-to in Maine yielded a box of Aunt Jemima pancake mix and some bacon she scoured off a piece of sheet iron that had been rusting in the weeds and greased it. The pancakes were turned with a piece of wood. There were even a few cold pancakes left over for breakfast.

Sassafras is a common plant in the Appalachians. She was fond of chewing its rich green leaves for their spicy taste. She also sampled ramps, or wild leeks, but judged them to be gamy.

The year after her second completion of the trail, Grandma began a series of walks that, added to her abortive attempt of 1954 in Maine (Mt. Katahdin to Rainbow Lake), were to lead to the completion of the trail for a third time. In 1958 she covered the distance from Duncannon, Pennsylvania, to North Adams, Massachusetts. The summer of 1960 saw her hiking between Palmerton, Pennsylvania, and Sherburne Pass, Vermont, and between Springer Mountain, Georgia (which had replaced Mt. Oglethorpe as the southern anchor of the trail), and Deep Gap, North Carolina. She made it from Duncannon back to Deep Gap in 1963. In a jaded moment she announced to her kinfolk (neither her husband nor her children were trail enthusiasts) that she was going to hang up her sneakers. The next summer, however, she laced them back on and in 1964, at the age of 77, finished what she had begun 10 years earlier by walking from Sherburne Pass to Rainbow Lake. She continued on to the top of Katahdin and then gingerly walked the Knife-Edge Trail, where in places the hiker, by merely leaning too far to either side, can risk a fall of 1,500 feet. Grandma Gatewood also tested her septuagenarian agility on other footpaths. There were the Long Trail in Vermont, parts of the Horseshoe and Baker Trails in Pennsylvania, the Chesapeake and Ohio Canal Towpath Trail in Maryland, and others.

Grandma always hiked by herself, rarely going with others for more than a mile or two, although one young lad, out on his first backpacking trip, kept her company for two days. She was comfortable only at her own pace, which included frequent pauses for rest, but was steady and generally began at five-thirty or six in the morning and kept on till three or four in the afternoon.

On none of her forays did she carry a sleeping bag, a tent, or a regular backpack with a frame, but remained faithful to her blanket (and didn't always take that), her rain cape and plastic curtain, and her homemade shoulder bag. Later she did add straps to the bag. Many times she was wet through from the plentiful Appalachian rain.

She used no guidebooks except once in New England, when a hiker who was leaving the trail presented her with his well-thumbed manual. Once she tried walking in leather boots, but they gave her the only blister of her career, and she was glad to get back into sneakers. Sneakers are not reckoned as suitable footwear for hiking by most people, and how her feet survived remains a mystery. A Boy Scout leader summed it up by saying, "Grandma, you've broken all the rules for hiking—but you got there just the same."

NOTE: Grandma Gatewood passed away on June 5, 1973. She was 85 years of age and had lived a full and colorful life. In addition to her hikes on the Appalachian Trail, Grandma Gatewood walked the Oregon Trail in 1959, at the age of 72, as a part of the I00th anniversary of the Oregon Trail. —ED.

From *Hiking the Appalachian Trail*, edited by James Hare, Vol. 1, Rodale, 1975.

JEFF WALKER

Is the wilderness safe? We all recognize that a hiker may fall and find himself in serious trouble, that something dreadful like appendicitis may strike when help is miles away, but we don't think of the AT as home ground for the crime or violence endemic to city life. In 1990 two hikers (Geoff Hood and Molly LaRue) were murdered on the trail. It could have happened anywhere. It did happen in Pennsylvania. Jeff Walker's 1990 thru-hike was inevitably colored by this tragedy, but he remarkably remained deeply moved by and satisfied with his own experience. For him, the trail provided time to pay attention to minutiae that gave back substantial rewards.

Trail Diary, 1990

D URING MY HIKE I GOT INTO THE HABIT OF KEEPING A DETAILED LIST, DUTI-fully recording each animal sighting and unusual event alongside random thoughts and assessments for the day, ostensibly as documentation should it ever be called into question I was in fact living such a fantasy—awaking one morning to three inches of snow at Little Laurel Shelter, stumbling upon a rattlesnake on entering the Shenandoahs, camping out under the stars—although in reality more as ammunition against my own disbelief; a tabular means of pinching myself, of providing reassurance that an ever-growing sense of fulfillment was real. Since returning home, I have fallen away from keeping such a list, having grown complacent with only groundhogs and opposum to look at, and a limited if scenic drive to work, but the same doggedness with which I came to pursue new things on the trail remains intact. Instead, it now centers around variation on the job, a book from the library or simply a new face, as opposed to a windy ridgewalk, a shaded swimming hole, a mom-and-pop style general store. A diminishment in adventure, perhaps, but certainly no loss of enjoyment. For even the most mundane of activities, it seems, appear to have taken on new luster.

While moving up from Atlanta, I was struck by the intensity of my reaction upon glimpsing a view of the trail. I was driving up I-81 and had just passed through the Troutville interchange when it came into sight, a stile first, and then the AT itself, gradually sloping downward so as to cross under the road. Suddenly I was awash in emotion, with memories of crossing that stile only a few months earlier, of resupplying at a Winn Dixie also visible, of moving on toward the James River. . . . Sentimentality? No question about it. But I've observed that same strength of response in a number of non-trail related situations since then.

Perhaps it is my surroundings here in Schuyler, a peaceful setting far enough away you can hear the Whipporwills and see the stars at night. Or the job, an interesting change to say the least. Or, if only just for now anyway, an AT-quieted soul?

With a thoroughness I did not anticipate, my 5-month sabbatical from workaday existence has rather decisively altered my conception of things; my priorities and objectives, my needs and wants, my understanding of the rules of the game. It is as if I were starting over with a clean slate, graced with the opportunity to begin again, yet armed I hope with an improved foresight not to repeat the same mistakes. It presents an interesting challenge, the prospect of beginning anew, a challenge not unlike the one with which I was greeted back in March as I stood atop a mountain roughly 800 miles south of here. I hope I can live up to the task.

From "High Adventure in Schuyler, VA," Thru-Hiker Report to Appalachian Trail Conference by Jeff Walker, 1990.

HARRY CAUDILL

There are two Appalachias, claims Harry Caudill in this essay about the sociology of the southern Appalachians. One belongs to the mountain people, most of whom were descended from land-poor immigrants from the British Isles whose economy there and in the United States leaned more toward subsistence than toward financial success but whose culture (music, dance, storytelling, preaching, and more) was rich beyond description. The other Appalachia is the one owned, exploited, and often snobbishly maligned by powerful banks and industrial interests within and outside the Appalachian region. It all depends on what you consider a valuable resource: people and their ways, or minerals wrenched from the ground and water power sucked from the rivers. Hikers on the AT, especially in the southern and south-central sections, are walking through woods that merely buffer but cannot erase a social history that, writ large, is a reasonable paradigm for the country itself in its widening gap between the rich and the poor, the empowered and the disempowered.

The late Harry Caudill (d. 1990) was descended from early settler stock. He practiced law, was elected to the Kentucky legislature, wrote fiction and nonfiction, and won national honors for his work on behalf of soil conservation.

O, Appalachia!

THE APPALACHIAN MOUNTAIN RANGE IS THE LEAST UNDERSTOOD AND THE most maligned part of America. In the last decade alone it has been the subject of scores of economic and sociological studies. Lyndon Johnson's Great Society made it a principal battlefield in the War on Poverty. And, yet, despite this there persists a monumental unwillingness to recognize the harsh realities of the Appalachian paradox.

"Paradoxical" is the adjective most applicable to that vast region embracing western Pennsylvania, western Virginia, eastern Kentucky, northeastern Tennessee, nearly all of West Virginia, northern Alabama, and bits of Maryland, North Carolina and Georgia. The very name of the region has become synonymous with poverty and backwardness. Arnold Toynbee sees its people and culture as serious internal threats to Western civilization. "The Appalachians," he wrote, "present the melancholy spectacle of a people who have acquired civilization and then lost it." As he sees them, our southern highlanders have reverted to barbarism and are the "Riffs, Albanians, Kurds, Pathans and hairy Ainu" of the New World.

But the land itself is rich in every respect that an ambitious people would find necessary for greatness. To assert that the Appalachian land is poor is to display the same ignorance so often imputed to the mountaineers themselves.

Appalachia is rich. Its heartland is a mere 480 miles from Washington, D. C., and is within easy reach of the populous eastern third of the nation. This huge, sparsely populated region thus lies close to the heart of the most highly industrialized continent in the world.

Its forest—the finest expression of the eastern deciduous—is the most varied and splendid of the globe's temperate zones. Fifty million years old, it contains almost every plant the glaciers shoved down from the north and many that later seeded up from the south. More than 2,000 seed-bearing plants are native to West Virginia alone. Although this forest still covers Appalachia like the folds of a mighty carpet, human greed has reduced it in many places to thickets and stands of new growth.

The bottomlands produce excellent potatoes, grains, berries, grapes and fruit, and a survey by the President's Appalachian Regional Commission disclosed that there are 9.5 million acres suitable for pasturage.

After a century of mining, Appalachia's coal veins still contain 250 billion tons of the world's best coal. Economists have declared one of its coal beds to be the most valuable mineral deposit on the globe. The first petroleum wells gushed there; its oil and gas resources still boom. And in addition the region ships out limestone, talc, cement rock, iron ore, clays, gneiss, gibbsite and grahamite.

Appalachia has beauty. The ancient crags, timber-cloaked slopes, rhododendron and laurel thickets, beds of ferns and flowers, and creeks and rushing rivers make it a land of stunning loveliness. The Great Smokies is the most visited of all U.S. parks, and it is not mere coincidence that two of the nation's greatest aggregations of scientific minds have been brought together within the shadows of the Appalachian hills at Huntsville and Oak Ridge.

Little credence is due the notion that the troubles of the mountaineers stem from the mountainous character of their habitat. Mountains and poverty do not automatically go together, as the little Republic of Switzerland so dramatically proves.

Nor does the mountaineers' failure stem from any genetic deficiency or some ill fortune at the beginning. The settlers—whose descendants are a majority today—were English, Scotch, German and Scotch-Irish, with a virility and toughness legendary on the frontier. In 1780 at Kings Mountain, South Carolina, an army of 30-day volunteers administered to a larger British force the most unequivocal defeat in the history of the empire. Of 907 British and Tory soldiers engaged, all were killed, wounded or captured. These backwoodsmen proclaimed American independence and liberty at

Mecklenburg Courthouse a year before July 4, 1776. Tough, sturdy stock had a promising beginning in a labyrinth stuffed with riches and bright with promise.

How, then, did it happen that more than a century ago the descendants of Kings Mountain were already so poor and ignorant they had become a matter of grave concern to President Abraham Lincoln and his friend, O.O. Howard, head of the Freedmen and the Refugees Bureau? The essential trouble lay in this reality: from the beginning Appalachian people nurtured a profound distrust of government, sought to elude its influence and consistently refused to use it as a tool for social and economic enhancement.

Appalachia's population was drawn almost entirely from the frontier of the revolutionary war era. The same qualities that made the frontiersmen effective Indian fighters and revolutionaries doomed them and their descendants as social builders. What Toynbee has described as a retreat to barbarism is actually a persistence of the backwoods culture and mores into an age of cybernetics and rockets—nearly two centuries after the frontier itself rolled westward and passed into history.

The Europeans whose descendants filtered into Appalachia were poor. They were landless younger sons, people swept from the farms by landlords, indigents who swarmed into the cities in search of work, disbanded soldiers and Ulstermen pauperized by parliamentary acts designed to protect the English wool trade. Many came as indentured servants too poor to pay a shipmaster for their passage. The quest for land took them to the backwoods. They shared a tenacious hatred of the English rulers whose policies had brought them only toil and bitterness. They soon shared another sentiment—disdain for the copper-skinned aborigines who presumptuously claimed to own the virgin lands the newcomers coveted. In their struggles to preserve their ancient domain, the Indians fought skillfully against the interlopers and through much of the struggle were supported by the crown.

In 1763 His Majesty's government proclaimed the Appalachian crest as the settlement line beyond which no British subject could lawfully build a cabin. Thus, reasoned the King's counselors, peace with the natives would be preserved until they could be civilized and turned into good servants of the crown, the fur trade would be stabilized, and the whites would turn the land east of the line into a vast expanse of orderly, English-style farms. The Proclamation caused the fast-breeding backwoodsmen to pile up on the border and provided the stock for a massive wave of settlers when the revolution shattered English power.

The Indian wars lasted more than 40 fiery years until Anthony Wayne's victory at Fallen Timbers in 1794. Raid and counter-raid, scalped corpses, burned crops, slaughtered livestock, stratagems, counter-stratagems and a perpetual all-pervading unease—these were the elements that etched into the backwoods culture an acceptance of bloodshed as a normal part of life. With no effective government to protect them, the settlers became supremely self-reliant, loyal only to the helpful clans who moved westward as they did. They learned, though, from the enemy; and Cherokee corn bread, parched corn and fondness for the hunt mixed with lively Old World fiddle tunes as part of the burgeoning culture.

Many settlers stayed abreast of the frontier, forming the keen cutting edge of the scythe that reached Oregon a mere 80 years after the Mecklenburg Resolves. But most were absorbed by the Appalachian maze. They stayed, steeping in the backwoods behavioral patterns with their quick violence, subsistence farming, hunting, antipathy to government and, after the revivalist movement of 1800, old-time Baptist religion. All the later migrants—Germans, Poles, Jews, Italians, Scandinavians—went westward without touching the hill people. Until the railroads began to reach out for the coal and timber, they simmered undisturbed, acquiring the characteristics that have led to the present plight.

Having no one else to learn from, they learned from their forebears, repeating the techniques and perpetuating the aspirations of their frontier past. They evolved a traditionalism that ruled out everything unsanctioned by time. The patriarchs cautioned against the untried, and the mountaineer became a conspicuous anachronism.

Like someone of a Swiss Family Robinson within his fold of the mountains and surrounded by foes real or imagined, the mountaineer was crankily individualistic. He tenaciously defended the ideals and freedoms that made his bizarre individualism possible. He became a loner to whom cooperative efforts were distasteful and strange.

The sun began setting long ago for the highlander. His fields eroded and he had to clear new ground, which became barren for the same reasons. The labor of clearing exhausted him, and his unremunerative cropping bound him to subsistence levels except in a few broad and fertile valleys. New waves of out-migration drained off the strong and energetic. The primitive economy generated little money for schools and the traditionalism did not encourage them. E. O. Guerrant, a Presbyterian evangelist, wrote that during the Civil War he crossed the mountains many times without seeing a schoolhouse or a church. The roads remained little better than the ancient buffalo traces. The simplest manifestations of government advanced with glacial slowness. For example, in 1799 all of eastern Kentucky was organized into a new county called Floyd. Sixteen years elapsed before the fathers could complete a log courthouse 22 feet square. And promptly after it was finished someone burned it to the ground.

Ignorant, disorganized, old-fashioned and poor, the people were perfect victims for the mineral and land buyers who came after the Civil War. The buyers knew from their geologists what was in the land. The mountaineers knew nothing and sold everything at prices ranging from a dime to a few dollars per acre. The already precarious plight of the highlanders then became desperate, because the deeds gave to industrialists in New York, Philadelphia and London the legal title to "all mineral and metallic substances." And with the ownership of the mineral reserves passed, also, the political mastery of the region.

Thus, as the West Virginia Tax Commission warned in its 1884 report, "the history of West Virginia will be as sad as that of Poland and Ireland." And indeed all the elements of the Irish famine were present: inadequate agriculture, absentee ownership of the landed wealth, incapacity to generate and follow wise leaders. With the Great Depression and postwar mechanization of the mines, the Appalachian social order collapsed, and large-scale death by famine was prevented only by the largesse of the federal government and the most massive out-migration in U.S. history. If contemporary Appalachia has viable symbols, they are the public assistance check, the food stamp and the ancient sedan wheezing its uncertain way toward Detroit.

Thus two Appalachias grew up in the same domain, side by side and yet strangers to each other. One, the Appalachia of Power and Wealth, consists of huge land, coal, oil, gas, timber and quarry companies that "recover" the minerals from the earth; rail, barge and pipeline companies that convey the minerals to markets; and steel, refining, chemical and utility firms that convert the minerals to marketable products. This Appalachia, headquartered in New York and Philadelphia, is allied to mighty banks and insurance companies. It is exemplified by Edward B. Leisenring, Jr., now president of Penn Virginia Corporation, who boasted (*Dun's Review and Modern Industry,* April 1965), that his company netted 61 percent of gross income.

The second Appalachia is a land devastated by decades of quarrying, drilling, tunneling and strip-mining. Five thousand miles of its streams are silted and poisoned beyond any present capacity to restore them, and as many more are being reduced to the same dismal state. Its people are the old, the young who are planning to leave and the legions of crippled and sick. Its lawyers thrive on lawsuits engendered by an ultrahazardous environment.

Government has never pretended to serve both Appalachias impartially. Appalachia One routinely raises money to persuade and bribe Appalachia Two to elect candidates acceptable to wealth and power. Until recent stirrings of revolt, Appalachia Two invariably elected "bighearted country boys" beholden only to the corporate overlords who financed their campaigns. Invariably, they gave a bit more welfare to the poor and enlarged the privileges and exemptions of the rich. The poor sank into apathy and the rich, all curbs removed from their arrogance, wantonly triggered such calamities as the destruction of towns on Buffalo Creek, West Virginia. On February 26, 1972, a total of 124 people perished after a mountain of mining wastes collapsed.

In 1862, Abraham Lincoln became the first president to pledge aid to the impoverished Appalachians. The war and John Wilkes Booth kept him from acting on his promise. Seventy years later Franklin D. Roosevelt rediscovered them in an even worse situation.

The New Deal spent hundreds of millions of dollars on relief projects. Some of the ugliest schools and courthouses the human mind has ever contrived sprang up as destitute men chipped, hammered and sawed on relief works. The Civilian Conservation Corps and an expanding army and navy lifted thousands of benumbed youths out of idleness and away from moonshine stills. National Youth Administration jobs kept threadbare students in school so that they could graduate into World War II. On the eve of that conflict the New Deal formulated plans to resettle a million highlanders, a goal the postwar coal depression accomplished with dispatch.

It is doubtful that FDR could have done more even if he had wanted to. There were ranks of senators dutifully determined to protect Appalachia One even if Appalachia Two starved to death, and a Supreme Court determined to hold unconstitutional anything that tampered with the vested rights of the Mellons, Rockefellers, Pews and Insulls. A firm commitment to Appalachia Two might have aimed at a TVA-like program designed to use Appalachia's bountiful resources in a job-generating cycle within the region. The Tennessee Valley Authority pioneered in an area with few rich vested interests to offend while the equally destitute hill people were never considered for a federally mandated Appalachian Mountain Authority.

When John Kennedy ran for the White House in 1960 he overruled the advice of his aides and challenged Hubert Humphrey in West Virginia's primary. To the amazement of the nation, he won and went on to the White House. In the mountain state, the young president had seen two million people within the ruinous grip of the Appalachian culture. To do something, Kennedy appointed PARC—the President's Appalachian Regional Commission—to study the paradox of Appalachian poverty in what John Kenneth Galbraith was pleased to call the "affluent society." PARC was chaired by another Roosevelt, FDR, Jr., who, whatever his father's feelings may have been, displayed little comprehension of his task and learned little at his carefully staged 'hearings."

In the bleak autumn of 1963 Homer Bigart of the New York Times came to eastern Kentucky and wrote about children so hungry they were eating mud from between chimney rocks, of people living in collapsing shacks, of a society that offered no alternative to the dole. The story roused the lethargic PARC to action. John Kennedy was in his grave when the pallid report went to the president's desk and the recommendations entered the U.S. Code in 1965. Lyndon Johnson signed it in a little ceremony in the White House Rose Garden, made it a part of his Great Society, and in a typical example of rhetorical overkill, declared that in Appalachia "the dole is dead."

The dole remains very much alive, and there is nothing in the much touted Appalachian Regional Development Act that can ever bring it to an end. ARDA was written to please—or at least avoid conflict with—Appalachia One. One of Kennedy's requirements was that it be tailored to gain the support of governors whose states had counties in the region. These ranged from George Wallace to Nelson Rockefeller, and a more safely square, establishmentarian bunch of non-reformers can scarcely be imagined. They tucked in a clincher that allowed a governor to veto for his state any proposal he found offensive. Thus the Appalachia of Wealth was formally secured in its capacity to strike down federal efforts to lift the Appalachia of Poverty.

The initial authorization for LBJ's project to eradicate poverty in a diverse territory as big as Great Britain was by no means so bloated as to alarm fiscal conservatives—$1,092,400,000. And if the financing was modest, the plans, too, were calculated to stir few objections in the most cautious soul.

In America roads are beloved of all men from Paul Mellon's globe-girdling corporations to the humblest welfare recipient in a floorless cabin at the head of Powderhorn Creek. And, since roads are so favored, the governors, FDR, Jr., and Congress agreed that more than 75 percent of the money—$840 million—should be spent to build new highways.

But these were not highways of the first quality like the Interstates then beginning to lace the country together. The governors and their highway commissioners decreed 1950-style two-lane affairs, with a third or "passing" lane at intervals. The roads that emerged as a result of this saddle Appalachia with an archaic transportation system of continuing obsolescence.

And though the new highways would be rammed through the endless string of towns that shelter Appalachia Two, the bill provided no homes for the dispossessed. Hundreds of men and women—most of them old and sick, and some helpless from senility—were handed small sums and told to clear out. They did, generally into house trailers strewn about the landscape like huge, oblong dice. And the roads were scarcely completed when immense and immensely overloaded coal trucks began pounding them to pieces. In some instances the last guardrails were not even in place when highway departments started calculating the cost of resurfacing.

Then the lawmakers prepared a small Band-Aid for the staggering devastation inflicted by the strip-mining of coal. They appropriated $36.5 million to patch up some of the worst eyesores. Next they acknowledged that long exploitation had ravaged the hardwood forests and that the owners of small tracts could be helped if their timber stands were improved. Five million dollars went into this task!

The mammoth erosion that was shaving mountains to the bedrock and choking streams in hundreds of counties was combated with $17 million. A study of water resources was financed with another $5 million. Sewage treatment facilities and vocational schools drew $6 million. Demonstration health facilities were financed with $69 million.

Finally, the Act provided for support to local development districts—but only after their "genuineness" had been certified by the governors.

In due time the rest of the Great Society programs were impaled on the horns of the same dilemma: How to aid the region's poor without distressing its rich? It could not be done and the efforts broke down in frustration and failure.

Transferred from the Peace Corps to head the Office of Economic Opportunity, Sargent Shriver sent platoons of young, idealistic VISTA (Volunteers in Service to America) workers into Appalachia. They started "community action" enterprises, summoning the poor to countless meetings and exhorting them to organize. For what? No one had told the volunteers the answer to that or even informed them about the existence of Appalachia One. They promptly perceived the outlines of the truth, however, and began telling audiences about them, whereupon a lively time in the hills ensued. Boards of education were beset by people demanding better schools.

It was all entertaining and encouraging while it lasted. But sleeping dogs were aroused at last and telephones began ringing in the offices of congressmen and senators. VISTA was decried as Communist and un-American. A few of the volunteers were jailed on charges ranging from reckless driving to criminal syndicalism. The Great Society withdrew its soldiers from the War on Poverty, and Appalachia One settled back to digest the region undisturbed.

Henceforth federal funds came down through safe, orthodox channels where the control was well established and the people involved knew how to play the game without causing discontent in powerful quarters. With Richard Nixon came even further routinization of procedures and approaches. All told, billions have been spent on Appalachian renewal in the last 12 years and only a gimlet eye can tell any difference in the homes and lives of that numerous citizenry I have referred to as Appalachia Two.

Except in Kentucky, where a severance tax was imposed in 1972, the endless outflow of natural resources goes almost untaxed to the markets of the world. The flow is so great that as many as 25,000 railroad cars of coal have piled up at Hampton Roads, Virginia, awaiting ships for Europe and Japan. Strip-mining shatters the ancient ecology, and "reclamation" is a sorry

joke. The out-migration continues, and new vocational schools supply plumb-
ers and typists to many cities in other states. Silt from mine spoils is ruining
lakes the Corps of Engineers has built at enormous costs. After a decade of
much publicized "anti-poverty" efforts in the Appalachians, relief rolls have
swollen ominously—in some counties to support 65 percent of the population. A whole new generation has come to maturity as public assistance
recipients struggle to qualify for a continuance of the grants for the rest of
their lives. In growing numbers of families no one has held a job in three
generations.

In September 1972, ARDA issued its annual economic report. Within
the tenacious hold of the old culture of poverty and of the great corporations that own its wealth and shape its destiny, Appalachia Two reflected
the following interesting facts:

(a) Eleven percent of the residents of Central Appalachia had departed
in the 1960s.

(b) Thirty-four percent of the homes lacked essential indoor plumbing.

(c) A third of the work force may be jobless.

On August 28, 1972, *Barron's National Business and Financial Weekly* characterized the entire Appalachian Poverty Program as a "costly failure."

The modem Appalachian welfare reservation makes few demands on
its inhabitants. They are left alone in their crumbling coal camps and along
their littered creeks to follow lives almost as individualistic, as backward
looking and tradition ridden, as fatalistic and resigned as in those days three
or four wars ago before the welfare check replaced the grubbing hoe and
shovel as pot fillers. Then a man needed to know the seasons and the vagaries of the bossman if he were to eat. But new skills are required in an age
when government is gigantic, when a few men with giant machines can
drag from the ground all the fuel a nation can consume, and when the poor
are of little use to the well-to-do. It pays to sense winners and vote for them—
and to let them know of one's intention in advance. And one must recognize
that there are powers that cannot be overturned or defied, and so one does
not resist. Once these concessions are made it is generally possible to enjoy
many of the freedoms and prerogatives of the nineteenth century without
its toils and dangers. Perhaps Toynbee's "barbarism" is actually a preview
of the twenty-first century, when the rich will be truly secure and the poor
will not work, aspire or starve. Appalachia was the nation's first frontier.
Now it may be foretelling America's final form. (1973)

From "O, Appalachia!" by Harry Caudill, *Intellectual Digest*, April 1973.

ANN & MYRON SUTTON

It's an odd habit we have of thinking that scientists don't rhapsodize and that poets have no eye for objective detail. Wrong on both counts. The Suttons effectively combine the close observation of botanists and bird-watchers with the enthusiastic reverie of a Wordsworth or a Whitman out on a ramble in the mountains. Early spring in West Virginia, especially near the confluence of the Shenandoah and Potomac rivers at Harpers Ferry, would lift anyone's spirits. The Suttons' book predates another glory of Harpers Ferry: the offices of the Appalachian Trail Conference, where Herculean efforts are carried out with good cheer on a daily basis to manage many facets of the trail's life—from protective land corridor acquisitions to guidebook editing, to archiving the written and other materials that constitute the trail's collective memory, and, most importantly, to providing a helping hand to long-distance hikers en route to or from Springer Mt. or Mt. Katahdin.

Like Walking on a Carpet

THE TRAIL ITSELF EVEN SEEMS TO HAVE A THERAPEUTIC VALUE, AS IF, BY touching it, by walking along it, we absorb the magic of its freedom, the freshness of its air, the inspiration of the forest rebirth. Like Antaeus, we are renewed.

One day in early spring we struck out north of Snicker's Gap, along the boundary between Virginia and West Virginia. It was like walking on a carpet. The pathway was softened by moss, by beds of last year's leaves, by needles of pine, and by rich, abundant humus that never seems to wear away. The air was redolent of wild onion. Serviceberry (*Amelanchier*) flowers expanded on the slender trees like bits of winter snow clinging to the limbs. Some were yellow-green, where growth was not so far advanced, but in warmer places others had opened fully and stirred the forest out of its winter grays.

There was a brilliant red there, too: the seeds of maples in crimson clusters, and fresh new oak leaves glistening like autumn foliage.

Bloodroot was budding, and May apple stood abloom in patches on the forest floor. Blueberry shrubs spilled down the slopes. The alert eye could catch jack-in-the-pulpit flowering unobtrusively in shady places.

Cat brier clutched at our trousers as we moved along. Somewhere off in the woods a whining, sputtering handsaw started up, its racket carrying long distances through the trees; or a truck on a highway geared down for a steep hill—reminders that homes and highways are not very far away.

The Trail entered a rocky region, where the path was not as soft as before. White and gray cliffs below the Trail exerted an almost overpowering temptation to explore for caves and secret caches. Here and there could be seen white veins of milky quartz in streaks beneath the lichen splotches on the rock.

Tall trunks of oaks and hickories, still leafless, rose overhead as though to form cathedral naves. But these great vaults had not a single stained glass window—only the blue and white of a sky filled with shifting clouds. Dead snags stood pitted with small holes as if sprayed with buckshot, or gouged with giant holes as if a fusillade of cannonballs had sailed through the forest.

The sound of our feet through the leaves had a disturbing quality, but then on a carpet of moss again we walked with silent footsteps. Either way, our entry into this community of life had had its effect upon the nervous tension of the animals. We sat for a while.

There was no timing, or even time itself. We had hardly settled down when a strange lament came to our ears, an almost doleful howl from above. The winds were gently pushing against two trees that were leaning on each other. Their music was like that of a hinged door turning slowly, or the plaintive cry of a child lost in the forest, or a violin being tuned before an orchestral performance. The sound was never quite the same. We sat spellbound as these arias were played out, like some mysterious ode sung by two trees to an Appalachian spring.

Somewhere through the trees could be heard the song of a brook. Butterflies, black, black-and-white, and yellow, flew by. Towhees perched in the treetops, calling. Jays squealed, and crows sang out as they flew over. The piercing notes of an ovenbird nearby came with startling suddenness. And in the background was the soft voice of the wind through the pines.

We came, after a while, to the Devil's Racecourse, a clear stream flowing over moss-covered rocks. An old log, grandly festooned with shelf fungus, formed a natural bridge upstream, and not far away a spicebush was breaking into yellow bloom. Ferns grew in nearly every crevice, their fiddlenecks opening with a rare display of natural grace and beauty. For additional color there were trilliums and yellow and purple violets scattered across the rocky slope. For richness there were the ubiquitous May apples.

Hardly a devil's racecourse, one would think, but rather a wild garden. Beyond it, the Trail climbed northward through dry forest along the ridge top. The woods grew less thick, opening to our eyes some enchanting views across the Piedmont country to the east, and the valley of the Shenandoah to the west.

Down there, the Shenandoah River meanders sharply northward until at last it arrives, together with The Appalachian Trail, at the Potomac River.

The old village of Harpers Ferry now lies here, and the historic Chesapeake and Ohio Canal passes by on its way to Cumberland, Maryland. Once more the hiker approaches sites of fabled events, and recalls such names as John Brown, Stonewall Jackson and Robert E. Lee.

Crossing the Potomac, a wide and rock-filled river, and traveling north to the Susquehanna, we are reminded that the Appalachians are a birthplace of rivers. The A.T. crosses nearly all the major ones of the eastern United States: in addition to the two above there are the Tennessee, New, French Broad, James, Lehigh, Schuylkill, Delaware, Hudson, Housatonic, Connecticut, Androscoggin, Kennebec and Penobscot West Branch.

From *The Appalachian Trail: Wilderness on the Doorstep*, by Ann and Myron Sutton, Lippincott, 1967.

THE MID-ATLANTIC STATES

Maryland, Pennsylvania, New Jersey, New York

Bear Mt. Bridge, crossing the Hudson River, New York.

*Despite the conspicuous absence of tall mountains (by Appalachian stan-
dards), the mid-Atlantic states through which the AT passes have made a
disproportionately large contribution to the trail's construction and survival. Long-established hiking organizations such as the Potomac Appalachian Trail Club and the New York–New Jersey Trail Conference have impressive histories of leadership and initiative on all fronts in the trail-building enterprise. All through the mid-Atlantic region, the AT is a walk on the
edge of megalopolis. The proximity of major cities to the trail in this region
(Washington, Baltimore, Philadelphia, Newark, New York, not to mention
cities to the west, like Pittsburgh) no doubt explains the high level of committed participation in hiking clubs. Just as AT founder Benton MacKaye
envisioned, the pressures of crowded urban life have produced ever greater
numbers of people restless and eager to get out into the hills for exercise and
rejuvenation. Hence the mixed blessing: strong regional hiking clubs and
frequently overcrowded, overused trails.*

The AT's passage through Maryland is brief, under forty miles, but along with neighboring West Virginia, it provides one of the greatest river crossings on the entire trail, where the Shenandoah and Potomac rivers join at Harpers Ferry. Maryland is also the symbolic bridge between the South and the North, the Confederacy and the Union, one climate and another, some would say one culture and another. Side trips off the trail into social history are richly rewarding here.

Pennsylvania's long, rocky miles more than make up for Maryland's brevity. Here geology conspires against hiking boots, feet, ankles, shins, and knees. Thru-hikers praise Pennsylvanians for their support and friendliness and almost universally lament the bone-jarring walk on the state's rock-strewn footpath. The hills here give on to sweetly rolling meadows and fields.

The Delaware Water Gap is the geological bridge into New Jersey, a state whose AT miles often pleasantly surprise visitors from farther south or north who mistakenly think that all of New Jersey is one big shopping mall. In the Poconos of western New Jersey the plant life is as rich as in many places along the AT.

New York is a state and a city by the same name where there is no such thing as too many superlatives. Blessed with a huge wilderness area up north (the Adirondacks), the state is graced with another range in its southeastern corner, a landscape so lovely and dramatic that it has inspired poets and painters for over two centuries. Within shouting distance of Manhattan, the AT crosses the big river, the mighty Hudson, in a region known as the Hudson Highlands, where palisades rise up at the river's edge and literary associations lurk around every corner.

THE APPALACHIAN TRAIL IN
MARYLAND, PENNSYLVANIA

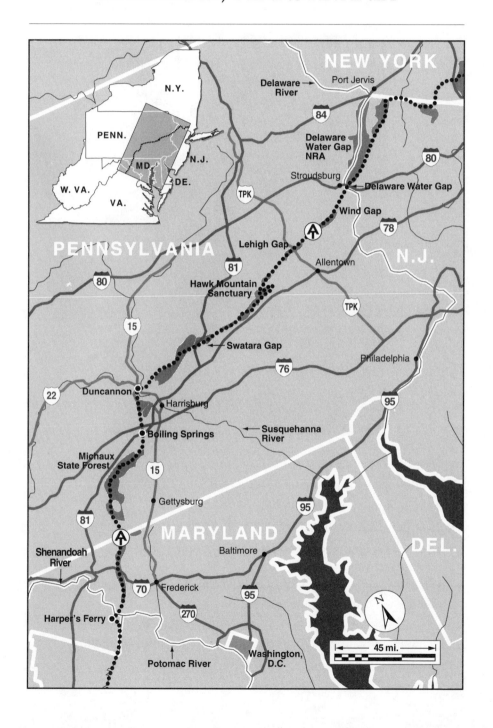

MARYLAND

Painting an AT trail blaze near Black Rock, Maryland.

Trail miles: 39.8, the second-shortest distance on the AT

Trail maintenance: Potomac AT Club

Highest point: Near High Rock, 1,880 ft. (Washington County)

Broadest river: Potomac, crossable on 600-ft.-long Goodloe Byron Pedestrian Walkway

Features: Largely a ridge walk at about 1,300 ft., through an area of intense Civil War historic interest.

Parks, forests, and nature preserves: Gathland State Park, Washington Monument State Park, Greenbrier State Park, South Mt. State Park

Most intriguing name on the trail: Devil's Racecourse

Trail towns: Boonsboro, Smithsburg

PAULA STRAIN

There is an endless and enjoyable debate about what is the finest vantage point from which to view the confluence of the Shenandoah and Potomac rivers where the AT crosses from West Virginia into Maryland. Is it at Harpers Ferry, West Virginia? Some say so, naming Jefferson Rock, a perch just yards outside the old village, which offers a view the illustrious president particularly loved. Others maintain it's on the Maryland side of the river, where the hills climb just as steeply from the swelling rivers' wide swath through the mountains. We situate this discussion of Jefferson Rock in the Maryland chapter because its author, Paula Strain, is a devoted Maryland historian and hiker, and a longtime member of the Potomac Appalachian Trail Club.

The Potomac, the Shenandoah, and Jefferson Rock

THOMAS JEFFERSON'S OPINION OF THE VIEW DOWN THE POTOMAC FROM THE rock bearing his name first appeared in his "Notes on Virginia," written in Paris to answer queries made to him by the French. In it he describes the view as seen from the rock, then claims:"This scene is worth a voyage across the Atlantic." When the book was published in the States, his critics said, scornfully, the view he described couldn't be seen in Harpers Ferry. Jefferson was incensed, pointing out his critics had not climbed the steep hill behind the Harper House tavern. Up there is where the view is.

Anne Royall, the journalist, made the same point in her more detailed description of the view in "The Black Book" (1828):

> From the summit of the hill which lies between the Potomac and Shenandoah, you have the best view of this grand curiosity. This is called Camp Hill, but is, now, more properly a mountain. As you stand on the hill, the Potomac is on your left, the Shenandoah is on your right. The mountain on the right runs up to the junction in a bold, perpendicular front of solid rock 1200' high; the mountain to the left, though 1400' high, slopes obliquely down to the water's edge. The Blue Ridge, on both sides the river, presents nothing but naked rocks. These resemble every figure in nature or art . . . some resemble houses with chimneys; others, ships under sail . . . One of these last is called the portrait of General Washington, in his uniform, even to his sword and epaulets. This is to the left and near to it is the figure of a huge bear.
>
> On the right stands a pile of rocks called a *chimney,* and has every appearance of a real stone chimney. It stands a little below the junction of the rivers and is seen very plain from the porch of Major Stevenson's tavern . . . When Mr. Jefferson said it was worth a trip across the Atlantic, he gave a very correct account of the assembly of mountains, rocks, and rivers. . .

I was on the celebrated Jefferson's rock, as large as a great house. It overhangs the Shenandoah, a few hundred yards from the chasm. But the best view is on top of the hill above the graveyard.

She did not see the rock as Jefferson knew it, because as Barry describes:

[In] 1799 — a bitter war existed between the Federalists and Republicans, and a certain Captain Henry, in General Pinckney's army is said to have taken his company, one day, to Jefferson's Rock and ordered them to overthrow the favorite seat of Jefferson, his political enemy. They succeeded in detaching a large boulder from the top which rolled down hill to Shenandoah Street, where it lay for many years, a monument of stupid bigotry.

Later, and exactly when can only be guessed at, workers at the National Armory put in stone pillars to support the balanced rock. A study by a National Park Service historian of the rock's history says that an aged resident reported watching workers lift the slab to put in new stone pillars; he said it was between 1855 and 1860. The stone used in the pillars appears similar to that used in the house and walk of the Master Armourer, which dates it to about 1855, during the Superintendency of Henry W. Clowe.

Visitors over the years, beginning as early as Washington Irving, carved their initials on the rock. Jefferson Davis added his, and so did many Union and Confederate soldiers.

In the last years of the nineteenth century, the Rock was a favorite site of picnics. Weddings were occasionally held there. An 1877 photograph shows visitors reclining on it. When postcards became popular about the turn of the new century, the Rock was a favorite subject.

All through the years people visited the Rock, but the first recorded improvement of the trail to it was in 1934 when the Civilian Works Administration did some work.

Grant Conway recorded in a note dated 1953 that a family living on Shenandoah Street had erected their television antenna on Jefferson's Rock for better reception. At that time, both Jefferson's Rock and the Stone Steps belonged to the town. Late in 1953, the town deeded the land to the state of West Virginia, then purchasing land for the National Monument. The television antenna was removed when the Monument came into existence. In 1956-7, access to Jefferson's Rock was again improved, by grading the path, installing some stone steps near the ruins and putting in logs to improve drainage. Today, the path is blacktopped, but nothing has been done about its steepness!

From *The Blue Hills of Maryland: History along the Appalachian Trail on South Mountain and the Catoctins*, by Paula Strain, Potomac Appalachian Trail Club, 1993.

PENNSYLVANIA

An intricate, antique wrought iron bridge, 1890, at Swatara Creek, Pennsylvania.

Trail miles: 232

Trail maintenance: Cumberland Valley AT Management Assoc., York Hiking Club, Susquehanna AT Club, Brandywine Valley Outing Club, Blue Mt. Eagle Climbing Club, Allentown Hiking Club, Philadelphia Trail Club, Appalachian Mt. Club (Delaware Valley chapter), Batona Hiking Club, Wilmington Trail Club

Highest point: Big Pine Flat Ridge, +/- 2,080 ft. (Michigan State Forest)

Broadest rivers: Susquehanna (Clarks Ferry Bridge); Delaware

Features: Extended ridge walk over ancient, sharply jumbled rocks, with pastoral valleys and historic sites (Civil War). AT follows northern end of Blue Ridge, crosses Cumberland Valley, traverses long Blue Mt. toward New Jersey. Hawk Mt. Sanctuary (birds!) and Delaware Water Gap National Recreation Area offer rich leisure activities. The Pinnacle, "the best view in Pennsylvania." Halfway point of the AT is 40 miles north of Pennsylvania-Maryland border (Mason-Dixon Line).

Parks, forests, and nature preserves: Caledonia State Park, Michaux State Forest, Pine Grove Furnace State Park, Swatara State Park, Hawk Mt. Sanctuary

Most intriguing name on the trail: Bake Oven Knob Shelter

Trail towns: Boiling Springs, Duncannon, Port Clinton, Delaware Water Gap

SCOTT WEIDENSAUL

Natural history writer and artist Scott Weidensaul roams widely in the Appalachian Mountains, keeping a sharp eye out for evidence of health and decline in the eastern forest. Here he tells about a walk on the Pennsylvania Appalachian Trail where he had an unusual encounter with a tree that most children growing up today will have no chance to enjoy: the American chestnut. We may still require school kids to memorize the famous Longfellow poem beginning with the line "Under the spreading chestnut tree," but we can no longer frolic in the gloriously dappled shade cast by the graceful branches of these giants, now lost to blight. The complex relationship between a natural process and human intervention is Weidensaul's theme in this well-informed eulogy for an old friend, Castanea dentata.

Castanea:
A Ghost Flowering in the Woods

I FOUND A GHOST TODAY, FLOWERING IN THE WOODS.

It was a chestnut tree, a spindly thing perhaps twenty feet tall and three inches wide at the trunk. Its leaves arched and drooped like green knives, long, finely tapered and edged with sharp serrations. The flowers were star bursts of white, narrow catkins that hung like the sizzling trails of a firework's demise, each strand more than six inches long and furred with tiny blooms.

In human culture, the act of blossoming has become synonymous with life. But for this chestnut, it was all but certainly wasted effort. Although there were other, equally stunted chestnuts scattered through the woods, none were old or healthy enough to flower, and the cascades of blossoms would probably go unpollinated. Worse, on the red-brown trunk of the tree was a gangrenous spot as wide as my thumbprint, the first sign of impending death.

Surrounding the trunk, in fact, were three or four dead stubs about the same thickness as the live sapling, in varying stages of decay. All were chestnuts, and all had risen from the same spot. They were the old hauntings of this ghost, and a portent of what it would soon become.

The American chestnut, *Castanea dentata*, was the crowning glory of the Appalachian hardwoods. A canopy species, it rose to heights of more than one hundred feet, with trunk diameters of four or five feet. Some exceptional specimens were eight feet across at chest-height; others were taped at thirty-four feet in circumference. In the forest it grew straight and tall; in the open, shading a farmhouse or a stone field wall, it stretched its arms magnificently, as if luxuriating in the elbow room.

Although the American chestnut's original range stretched from the southern coast of Maine to the shores of Lake Erie, and south to western Tennessee and central Mississippi, it was at its heart an Appalachian tree; the core of its homeland encompassed the mountains, plateau and Piedmont from southern New England to the Smokies. Chestnuts grew best in rich, well-drained soil, as high as five thousand feet in the southern Appalachians but on lower slopes elsewhere, usually in association with oaks and hickories, a triumvirate of nut-producers that flooded the forest with mast each autumn.

Chestnut wood was used for everything from cabins to cabinets, fence posts to bed frames, for it was light, easily worked and rot-resistant. As little prone to warping as to decay, it was also prized for floorboards and barrel staves, and more than one wit pointed out that chestnut sheltered a man from cradle to coffin. In late spring and early summer—long after most trees had bloomed—the chestnuts exploded with catkin tassels the color of cream, flowering so thickly that the canopy seemed to have been hit with a snowstorm. And in autumn came the product of that act: the sweet nuts hidden inside spiny burrs, like porcupines concealing a treasure.

That's all done. A fungus no one had ever heard of killed *Castanea* with an almost biblical swiftness and completion, leaving only the roots to send up these brave and pitiable saplings. But the blight bides its time, and before too many years pass the young tree breaks out in cankerous sores that spread and merge, choking it to death. Then the roots, if they have the strength, send up yet another sprout for a few years in the sun.

It is not hard to find a chestnut in the Appalachians. Almost any forest, particularly south of New York, will hold many of the runty, immature, trees. It is much rarer to find one that has lived long enough to bloom and rarer still to see a chestnut that has borne nuts.

I found one such tree five years ago, while I was walking along a portion of the Appalachian Trail near home. I was several hours into the hike and traveling with my eyes down, watching the rocky path with the sort of trancelike weariness that comes with a long trip and a heavy load. The brown burrs did not register at first, but after a few yards I stopped as if slapped, then turned and walked back.

There were dozens of burrs scattered on the ground, some still whole and spherical but most split into quarters. The tree was about twenty feet tall and as thick as my arm, one branch flung over the trail; when I looked around, there were even more burrs to be found.

My first thought was that I'd found an exceptionally large Allegheny chinkapin, a smaller relative of the American chestnut. But the dead leaves had the long, narrow silhouette of a chestnut, not the shorter shape of a chinkapin or a European chestnut. I scratched around in the leaves but found no nuts; it was late in the fall, however, and they may have been carried off by squirrels or eaten by deer—or, one hopes, hidden beneath the leaves, ready to sprout.

Two years later when I went back, the tree was deathly ill, its bark showing the ugly scars of the blight. But it was not dead, and although I have not made the long hike since to check on it, perhaps it has fought off the disease. If history is any gauge, the answer is no.

The chestnut blight took everyone completely by surprise. When it first appeared at the Bronx Zoo in 1904, no one recognized it; it was later surmised that the disease had been accidentally introduced around 1890 with a nursery shipment of Oriental chestnuts, which have a natural tolerance to its effects; another theory implicates a shipment of Chinese lumber. While the introduction of the chestnut blight led to the creation of plant quarantine laws to prevent future tragedies, the damage to the chestnuts was already done.

The blight is a fungus, its microscopic spores carried by wind, bugs, the feet of birds, even droplets of rain. It needs only the tiniest chink in the chestnut's armor to invade—a small crack in the bark, a tiny cut, a bruise. Once inside, the fungus spreads out like an inkblot, its filaments cutting off the flow of water and nutrients through the thin cambium layer as it breaks down the chestnut's tissues; outside, the bark develops a characteristic sunken canker, speckled with small, orange dots called pycnidia that bear the spores. Once the cankers encircle the tree, a process that takes about four years, the chestnut dies, choked by the invader. The spores, meanwhile, have been released to the wind, drifting toward another victim; in wet weather the cankers ooze with sticky tendrils, easily picked up by animals, like the woodpecker from whose feet scientists once washed nearly a billion blight spores. Only the rootstock of the chestnut is unaffected, since the fungus cannot survive beneath soil level.

H. W. Merkel, a forester working in the Bronx, is credited with first noticing the blight, and within a year he was fighting it, doctoring the infected trees and slicing away the cankers. But the blight needed a head start of only those few years, and Merkel's efforts were far too little, far too late. Probably nothing could have stopped it by that point. Because of its ease of transmission, the blight spread with wrenching swiftness up and down the Appalachians, rippling outward like the shock waves of an earthquake from its epicenter. By 1909 it had spread beyond New York City, and by 1915 Connecticut's chestnuts were going fast. New England was stripped of its chestnuts by the 1920s, and as early as 1918, dying chestnuts were found in the Peaks of Otter region of Shenandoah National Park.

The blight moved like lightning, spreading as much as fifty miles per year, despite such desperate measures as a mile-wide "firebreak" in Pennsylvania and programs (including one cold-bloodedly sponsored by a telephone pole company) that encouraged landowners to cut the trees before they died. Heaven only knows what genetic treasure was lost in the frenzy, including, perhaps, some trees with a natural resistance. The blight arrived in the Smokies in the mid-1920s, and by 1938, 85 percent of the park's chestnuts were dead or nearly so. By the 1940s, everything was finished except the grief.

Few people alive today can truly appreciate the sheer magnitude of the loss. I recall my great-grandfather, a timberman in his younger days, speaking with emotion about chestnuts—about going nutting with his family in the fall, about roasting chestnuts for the holidays, about cutting the second-growth chestnuts each winter for sale as mine timbers, skidding them down the mountains behind teams of mules. His affinity for (and knowledge of) trees was encyclopedic, but chestnuts were obviously something special to him.

In less than a generation, the Appalachians were robbed of their single most important tree—important both ecologically and economically. The toll has been estimated at some 4 billion trees equal to 9 billion acres of forest land, with a value of $400 billion, but even that awesome number does not convey the rending quality of the destruction. A species that made up a quarter of many eastern hardwood forests, and which produced an even greater percentage of its mast crop, had been rendered functionally extinct in an eye-blink.

Interestingly, many authors have glossed over the loss. "[T]he forest closed over the Chestnut's place, great as it was, and remained unbroken," Charlton Ogburn wrote, reflecting a general opinion that the Appalachian forests took the blight in stride. It is true that other trees grew up to take the chestnut's physical space, but no other species could fill its niche in the environment. Rather, I suspect, we simply do not understand enough about the intricacies of ecological linkage to comprehend the changes, large and small, forced by the chestnuts' deaths. Or perhaps, like someone who has lost a loved one, we are still denying it all.

It may be, too, that the Appalachians were such a radically altered ecosystem in the late nineteenth and early twentieth centuries that the effects of one more insult, however great, were difficult to distinguish from the background destruction. If, for example, the blight had struck a century earlier, when the eastern forests still supported billions of passenger pigeons, it is likely that the fungal assault would have caused catastrophic declines in the pigeon flocks, simply because the birds depended on chestnut mast to such a great extent. While oaks (which moved into preeminence after the chestnut blight) can produce tremendous nut crops, the chestnuts did so predictably, dependably, unlike the sporadic fruiting of oak trees and beeches. As it was, the pigeons were extinct, and mast-dependent big game like wild turkeys and black bears were nearly so—and when these last two recovered, it was with a newfound dependence on acorns.

When the chestnuts died, the most clearly noticeable effects were on people. In the southern highlands, the great trees were something of a cottage industry, combining the value of the lumber, the bark—which contained high levels of tannic acid, essential for leather tanning—and nuts. The nuts were the most immediately marketable product, and each autumn families took to the woods to collect them for shipment to the city, where in 1900 a bushel retailed for twelve dollars (the mountaineers, on the other hand, received pennies on the pound for them). . . .

For some mountain families at the turn of the century, the income from chestnuts was important, generating cash as winter was closing in; just as crucial, chestnuts (along with other mast crops) provided a rich diet for hogs, which were driven into the woods to fatten. The loss of the chestnut was a bitter one for some mountain communities.

The mass chestnut death produced some rather macabre situations. With the living supply exhausted, demand for dead chestnut increased, leading to a minor timber boom devoted to harvesting standing, dead wood. (This was possible because chestnut, being so decay resistant, seasoned nicely on the stump, and the posthumous insect damage gave "wormy chestnut" paneling its character.) Ironically, the wood that was once so common and cheap that it was relegated to the most menial of uses—shipping crates, "snake" fences around pastures and similar applications—became sought after, like the work of a recently dead artist that rises in value after the funeral.

Of course, *Castanea* isn't really dead. The tough old roots have continued to send up sprouts, in many cases for more than ninety years. This tenacity has long given hope to the legions of chestnut supporters that someday, somehow, a cure for the blight will be found, and the monarch restored to its Appalachian throne.

From *Mountains of the Heart: A Natural History of the Appalachians,* by Scott Weidensaul, Fulcrum, 1994.

J. PETER WILSHUSEN

For AT thru-hikers headed north, after too many Pennsylvania miles of bumpy ridge-top walking, stumbling over sharp-edged and often loose rocks, the green, soft valley of the Delaware River comes as more than just a welcome relief—it's a godsend. The valley, at the point where the river cuts through the Appalachian Mountains, is a National Recreation Area. Thousands of day visitors ramble through its hills and canoe or kayak on its waters. No one would come here if it weren't for the beautiful, intriguing form of the land itself. J. Peter Wilshusen, a geologist and Appalachian Trail enthusiast, explains how the Delaware Water Gap took on its characteristic shape.

Geology of the Delaware Water Gap

THE DELAWARE WATER GAP, THE NORTHERN TERMINUS OF THE APPALA-chian Trail in Pennsylvania, is a feature of national geologic significance. It is one of the best examples of a water gap in the United States.

The flowing water of the Delaware River has cut through erosion-resistant rock formations of Kittatinny Mountain to form the gap. This geologic action is related to a network of rivers and streams in the eastern United States that began to flow long ago on an upland surface (the landward extension of the coastal plain) before erosion carved out the present valleys and ridges. In time the rivers, which originated across the trend of the folded formations, cut the ridges, creating the water gap. At locations of most water gaps there is a weakness in the mountain due to a fault, flexure, or change in rock material, causing a ridge to be somewhat more easily eroded than in adjacent parts of the mountain.

The gap is cut through three rock formations: dark-gray shale (Martinsburg Formation, Ordovician age), quartzite (Shawangunk Formation, Ordovician and Silurian age), and red sandstone (Bloomsburg Formation, Silurian age). See the cross section below.

The dark-gray shale formation occupies the south end of the water gap. Some shale in the gap is covered by broken boulders and talus from the mountain above. The quartzite formation is the main rock layer visible in the gap and cliffs. The red sandstone formation underlies the north end. Excellent exposures of this red sandstone are found at numerous places along the Trail about halfway up Mount Minsi.

Continental ice sheets extended into northeastern Pennsylvania during a period of geologic time called the Pleistocene. They spread into land now occupied by the Trail from the Delaware Water Gap southwest for about 35 miles into Lehigh County. The rest of the Trail in Pennsylvania has not been glaciated.

Three periods of glaciation occurred, named for the areas of the country where they were originally found and described. The oldest is the Illinoian glaciation, which occurred 550,000 to 350,000 years ago: the youngest are two Wisconsinan glaciations which took place 75,000 to 12,500 years ago. During this Great Ice Age the successive glaciations sculpted the landscape. Bedrock was scratched and grooved by advancing ice and till, composed of gravel, sand, silt, and clay, which was deposited as hills and terraces by retreating ice. Most glacial deposits and grooved bedrock surfaces in the water gap area resulted from Wisconsinan glaciation. At its line of maximum advance south of the gap, a terminal moraine of poorly sorted, jumbled rocks and sediment was deposited. As the glacier receded, meltwater from it ponded behind the moraine to form an 8-mile-long, 200-foot-deep lake north of Godfrey Ridge, called glacial Lake Sciota. The original outlet for the lake was in the terminal moraine at Saylorsburg. As the ice front retreated northeastward, Delaware Water Gap was uncovered and the lake drained through it.

The thickness of the glacial ice here during the Pleistocene is not known. Early geologic investigators speculated that it rose high above Kittatinny (Blue) Mountain, and that there were waterfalls and plunge pools at the ice front. There is no evidence to support this, but glacial grooves and striations on the top of 1,200-foot-high Kittatinny Mountain indicate that the water gap was filled and the mountains overtopped by ice. Also, the variations in direction of glacial grooves and striations in this area indicate that preglacial topography had an influence on the direction of glacial ice movement.

On the east side of the Delaware River north of the water gap, old copper mines that date to the 1650's represent some of the earliest mining in the United States. Southwest of the gap, in the vicinity of Wind Gap and Lehigh Gap, minor occurrences of copper are present in red shales and sandstones north of the Trail. Nearby, Old Mine Road, which was the first long road to come into this area from the east in about 1659 reflects this past mining history.

At Totts Gap, 2.5 miles southwest of Delaware Water Gap, there is a short, abandoned mine opening. It is rumored that this was part of a gold-mine promotion deal in which stock was sold after gold-bearing rock was assayed. To make the assay impressive, gold dust was loaded in a shotgun shell and fired at the mine face. Samples from this face were then collected and assayed.

From *Geology of the Appalachian Trail in Pennsylvania,* by J. Peter Wilshusen, Pennsylvania Geological Survey, 1983.

THE APPALACHIAN TRAIL IN
NEW JERSEY, NEW YORK

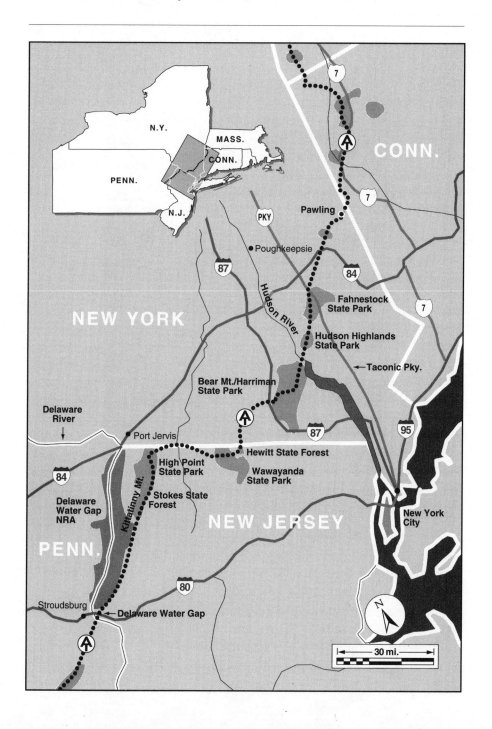

NEW JERSEY

Delaware Water.Gap, the Pennsylvania–New Jersey border.

Trail miles: 74

Trail maintenance: New York–New Jersey Trail Conference

Highest point: High Point, 1,803 ft.

Broadest river: Delaware

Features: Moderately challenging ridge hiking on Kittatinny Ridge at about 1,100–1,400 ft.; the Delaware Water Gap National Recreation Area at the Pennsylvania border.

Parks, forests, and nature preserves: Delaware Water Gap National Recreation Area, Stokes State Forest, High Point State Park, Wawayanda State Park, Hewitt State Forest

Most intriguing name on the trail: Mashipacong Shelter

Trail towns: Branchville, Glenwood, Vernon

RICHARD TURNER & ROBERT TURNER

Richard Turner was "Harpo" and his brother, Robert Turner, was "Home-spice" on their Appalachian Trail thru-hike in 1990. As a team, the two called themselves "the Mellow Woodsmen." The young men hail from Jackson, Mississippi. Their sweet and colorful report to the Appalachian Trail Conference offers a philosophical reflection on how the community-in-motion of AT thru-hikers takes on a special character out on the trail: there is little pretension and plenty of direct communication among those who realize, after walking hundreds of miles through all kinds of weather, that they all have the same needs, complaints, and aspirations. The Turners tell of a rare off-trail view, the Manhattan skyline from a New Jersey suburb, that puts the value of their thru-hike in perspective.

Trail Diary, 1990

O N THE 7TH DAY OF OCTOBER, SIX MONTHS AFTER CHECKING IN AT Springer Mt., Georgia, the two of us, Robert and Richard Turner, spent our final day on the Appalachian Trail. Our "thru-hike" was more honestly a "tour-hike" as the Philosopher's Guide recommends calling an AT hike interspersed with alternate routes. But we think this "blue-blazing" is no less an accomplishment. Perhaps we failed to resist the temptation, but we and many other hikers sooner or later discovered that the white blaze was not the kingdom for our deliverance.

This joint letter is hopefully representative of a shared experience we found along the trail, although we don't mean to take anything away from the individual growth we found which was an equally important aspect. However it seems that the most unexpected part of our experience and the most memorable was the community of people we found along the trail, not just with hikers but with all others who make the trail their home and are so important to its continuing existence. We look back on people and places like Rusty and his Hard Time Hollow, the Blackburn Trail Center, and the ATC headquarters along with its many daughter organizations, as well as the various church hostels, and the many friendly homeowners who opened their doors to us without question or judgement. To have made personal contact with these people and their different lifestyles affected us in a way that we can't ever forget. The dedicated work of the volunteer organizations connects these places to make an incredible journey like ours possible year after year. As blue-blazers we feel we must make a point of how much we appreciate your efforts, no less we believe than the purist does, and we hope that you are not offended by our need to make our own path every once in a while.

Though there was an obvious purist-nonpurist conflict on the trail, there also appeared a certain respect for each others ways that seemed to strengthen the trail community. On the trail individual opinions, ones that go far beyond the purist theme, seemed to come together and made for a more interesting and rewarding experience. And for us it seems that it is only when independent thought is respected that a community like this is possible. On a larger scale the Appalachian Trail and its success is a great example of how an individual's ideas, such as those of Benton Mackaye, can help to establish something that so strengthens the larger community.

At one point along our trek we took a ride with a friend into New Jersey and gazed at the New York City skyline from across the Hudson river. It was quite a site to see and such a contrast to what we had been used to in the past four months. The fact that these two lifestyles can exist so close to each other is amazing and seeing them like this made us appreciate what we were doing so much more. But we wonder about all the people stuck in the city who have no comprehension of our experience at all, or if they even could they might only think of it as a long vacation, a temporary escape from the real world. For us the trail became not a way to get away from reality, but a way to get to it, and a mere beginning to a life more directly focused on a better sense of reality.

After only a short while from leaving Springer Mt., the sense of urgency to hike every single white blaze left us, because we realized that in reality there shouldn't be any rules to limit our experience. We should do things our own way, letting the trail experience unfold day by day. We did keep a goal in mind, which was Katahdin, because we had set out for that goal and because our desire to find what it had to offer only got stronger day after day. Our purpose was to walk there, because in walking we found a unique and thorough method of discovery, seeing things around us and within us that we had never seen before. And of all those things we discovered these last six months there is one which we hope would apply to all people in all their lives, the blue-blazers and the purists, as well as the yellow-blazers and the Ward Leonards of the world. And that is that the best sense of accomplishment is to be able to look back on these days and say they were spent in happiness and harmony. Mobilis en mobile.

From *2,000-Miler Report to the Appalachian Trail Conference*, by Richard and Robert Turner, 1990.

STEVE SHERMAN & JULIA OLDER

There is a rule in many hiking groups that the one essential piece of equip-ment you must bring along on every hike is your sense of humor. Steve Sherman and Julia Older must work according to the same code. During a blistering heat wave in 1976, when road walking replaced the usual shady lane of the AT, these inveterate hikers nonetheless managed to wring insights and a good time from their sweaty experience. Sherman and Older tell of help offered along the way—a ride here, a cool drink there—reminding us that one aspect of "trail magic" is the unsolicited favor.

It's Too Damned Hot

*H*AD WE REACHED SUNRISE MOUNTAIN AT SUNRISE THE ENTIRE DAY MIGHT have been easier. As it was, the sweat of our brows, the rockiness of the Trail, the lack of ample fresh water in the oppressive heat doubled the burden of our packs. The sunlight fell on our backs like shovel-fuls of hot sand.

Our destination was High Point State Park, a mere 13½ miles away. We felt as if we were walking up a down escalator. What water we did cross was murky and so uninviting that we rationed our canteen until the next good source. All the lakes were in the valleys below, bright blue mirages.

The Trail wound over the tops of one false summit after another. Even our snacks failed to cheer us. Toward the end of the day we were covering only a mile to the hour. The unrelenting heat, the exposure from the leafless oaks, the slow hiking over loose, slab rocks dragged our bodies and spirits to a brown-out of enthusiasm.

We passed a few other hikers. One couple, experimenting with the out-doors, probably would turn thumbs down on this and all succeeding attempts in the woods. The overweight girl's overweight pack leaned at a forty-five-degree angle from her spine, increasing the impact of the weight on her droop-ing shoulders. Several carefree day-hikers passed, bouncy, full-breasted girls and gangly teenage boys out on a picnic. If only we had been picnicking.

At last we reached a rocky crest that overlooked Lake Rutherford. An exhausting mile later, we reached another crest overlooking Sawmill Lake. Then another sweltering mile more and we passed the American Telephone and Telegraph Company microwave installation and dragged down the mountainside to the gate house of High Point State Park. By the time we could see High Point Monument, the 220-foot lookout on the highest New

Jersey mountaintop (1,803 feet), we were too weary to care. Julia completely missed it, like missing the World Trade Center on the New York City skyline.

We sank into the red leather cushion seats inside the beam ceiling gate house, thankful to be out of the sapping sunlight. By a stroke of fortune, we applied for the last campsite. The next man in line was turned away and had to drive to another park.

"You look pretty tired," Ranger Rick Strain said. "You ought to be. It was ninety-five degrees in the shade down here. Probably hotter up there on the Trail. I'm off work in about fifteen minutes. Like a ride up to the campsite? It's about two miles."

As we were waiting for him, we read this newspaper clipping posted to the gate house bulletin board.

Camping in High Rise

Campsites, Incorporated, has announced plans to construct a twenty story campground in downtown New Orleans and is seeking financing for the project. "This will be unique," said Wesley Hurley of Hi-Rise. "It is designed for today's different brand of camping. People don't want the woodsy bit now; they want to camp in comfort near the city."

Plans for the four million dollar project call for eight lower floors of parking and twelve upper stories with 240 individual sites equipped with utility hook-ups for campers and carpeted with artificial turf. The campground will include a rooftop pool.

Ranger Rick, as they called him, drove us to one of the attractive sites adjacent Sawmill Lake. These campsites were a far cry from the high-rise concept of outdoor living. All sites were hidden in the trees far enough away from the lake to preserve a serene unpeopled shore. Water was available at easy walking distance. A clean beach awaited us. Our particular spot was a ground tent site with a small, clear stream that flowed under a plank-wood footbridge. Before leaving, Ranger Rick warned us that High Point had several bear families with young rapscallion cubs.

Our pre-dinner swim awakened our souls, the warm water embracing our tired bodies and spirits. A little boy stood up and rubbed his small fist into his eyes. "Hey, wait a minute, you guys," he called to his companions. "I got salt in my eyes."

In the morning Ranger Rick drove by in his pickup and took us on a tour of the High Point Lodge and the Monument. The restaurant of the Lodge now served as an entomological station for studies of the gypsy moth. The primary attraction, however, was a mascot black bear, affectionately called Mischa.

"Mischa became the mother of two cubs," he told us. "She tried to commit infanticide and the cubs were separated. Then one day the father became unnerved and attacked a small girl trying to feed them. The girl lost an arm and the bear was destroyed. Finally, the mother bear displayed such a hatred for one of the cubs that a decree went forth that the cub should also be shot."

Ranger Rick gave us a smile and a wink. "The night before the firing squad both cubs somehow got loose," he said. "Just don't know how that could have happened."

The Trail crossed the New York state line into Unionville, and then returned to New Jersey, a section entailing about eight miles of asphalt walking. Truckin' mile after mile in sparse shade during a summer heat wave was bad enough. Hiking the full glare of the sun along paved road was masochistic.

Too hot,
even too hot for God, Jesus and Mary.
Too hot in the Methodist Church.
Too hot in the public library.
Parking lot's bare.
Too hot in a car.
Too hot to cross the street without shoes.
Too hot to read the Vernon News.
Shades drawn
since dawn.

So touch me not, brother.
It's too damned hot.

We took asylum from the heat in the Vernon Public Library just off the Trail. Our propensity for libraries was boosted by the treatment we were given that day. For three hours we stayed inside. The librarian sent out an assistant who returned with ice-cold soda. Though we usually didn't imbibe soft drinks while hiking, in this heat we had no intention of exerting any of our 603 muscles. We would walk at twilight after the library closed. The soda was followed by glasses of ice water and then an offer to use the bathroom to freshen up. In this haven of kindness, we waited out the sun and wondered if Jesus, while walking the hills of Galilee, took salt tablets and postponed parables until dark.

From *Appalachian Odyssey*, by Steve Sherman and Julia Older, Stephen Greene, 1977.

HERBERT DURAND

Though almost as old as the Appalachian Trail itself, Herbert Durand's quaint guidebook for fern lovers, published in 1928, is as fresh as the sweetened air above a meadow of hay fern, a plant commonly seen along the trail (and used, dried, in the old days to stuff mattresses). In every AT state there are stretches of the footpath where ferns dominate the trailside greenery, and amidst a day's steep climbing or stumbling over punishing rocks, these elegant plants, often swaying in the breeze as if choreographed just for passersby, remind hikers of nature's capacity for the delicate and the tender.

Why Everyone Should Know the Ferns

T O VENTURE INTO A FOREST OR TO CROSS THE OPEN COUNTRY ANYWHERE, knowing nothing of the ferns, is like visiting an art gallery in which the finest paintings are turned to the wall. For there is nothing that grows or lives that can approach the feathery grace, the symmetry of form, or the lacy elegance of pattern of the Ferns: and to be blind to all this beauty is nothing less than calamitous.

This is a case where even a little knowledge is an excellent thing. I have been told hundreds of times by frequenters of the wild, that having learned by hook or crook to recognize and name half a dozen ferns or so, their outings, in consequence, became so rich in new zest and added interest, that they were not content until they had identified every species within reach. One enthusiastic novice said to me, " I can go over to Duden's Woods Sundays and call every fern I see by name. Why, it's like knowing everybody I meet as I walk down Fifth Avenue, and yelling at them, 'Hello, Jim!' 'Hello, Pete!' 'Hello, Annie!' A walk means much more to me now than mere physical exercise."

While a very marked and widespread interest in our native wild flowers, bushes and trees has developed of recent years, the ferns do not yet seem to be receiving the attention they deserve. One possible reason for this is the impression of many that their study is a difficult one, and that they are not easily cultivated.

Another is the attitude of a great number of people, among them not a few wild flower lovers, to whom a fern is a fern, simply that and nothing more. A recent visitor to my wild garden who knew and named a majority of the flowering plants, even those that were not in bloom, was dumb as an oyster when I showed her my fernery. Later, upon hearing that there were sixty species and over twenty varieties of ferns growing there, she said, "I was never so surprised in all my life. I have always thought there were only three kinds of ferns—Maidenhair, Brakes and just ferns!"

As for the vast multitudes of the unseeing, those who look upon all vegetation, except possibly things like cabbages and sunflowers, as a conglomeration of worthless weeds, their case seems hopeless. However, the introduction of Nature study into the schools may arouse in their children a better appreciation of the natural treasures of the wild, that will atone in some degree for their own ignorance and indifference.

Converts to the ranks of the fern lovers are easiest made from the second of these classes. When one knows a Maidenhair and a Bracken, it is not difficult to make him acquainted with the Christmas Fern, the Cinnamon Fern and other conspicuous kinds. And so he soon gets on speaking terms with a goodly number and is in a fair way to become an addict.

It is a little more difficult to persuade those of the first group that the study of ferns is really one of the simplest and most delightful pursuits in the world, and that they can be grown in the home garden and grounds as easily as one can grow Zinnias, but it can be done. All that is necessary is to tell them how to go about it, and induce them to make a start, if only with a few plants.

From *Field Book of Common Ferns*, by Herbert Durand, G. P. Putnam's Sons, 1928.

NEW YORK

New York Ramblers hiking club on Black Mt., Harriman State Park, New York.

Trail miles: 95

Trail maintenance: New York–New Jersey Trail Conference

Highest point: Prospect Rock, 1,433 ft., on Prospect Mt., near Greenwood Lake

Lowest point on the AT: 124 ft., near Bear Mt. Bridge

Broadest river: Hudson, crossable on Bear Mt. Bridge

Features: Surprisingly wild areas, with sharp climbs and descents, yet so close to New York City (views of Manhattan, 50 miles distant, at several points). First section of the AT was built in Bear Mt. State Park, 1922–23.

Parks, forests, and nature preserves: Bear Mt. State Park, Harriman State Park, Hudson Highlands State Park, Fahnestock State Park, Pawling Nature Reserve

Most intriguing name on the trail: Lemon Squeezer

Trail towns: Unionville, Greenwood Lake, Bear Mountain, Fort Montgomery, Pawling

WALT WHITMAN

In New York State's Bear Mt. State Park, right on the Appalachian Trail, is a statue of Walt Whitman, the dean of American poets. Hikers who know Whitman's poetry might well pause there, if not to genuflect then certainly to reflect on the way that great verse sets the tone for the culture as a whole. Whitman's magnum opus, Leaves of Grass, *published in several evolving editions from 1855 to his death in 1890, contains many poems celebrating the restless energy that drives us away from the farm, the factory, or the office—or at least out of the house—and into the refreshingly unknown wider world. Consciously or not, there's a little bit of Whitman's rambunctious spirit in every AT hiker.*

From "Song of the Open Road"

Afoot and light hearted I take to the open road,
Healthy, free, the world before me,
The long brown path before me leading wherever I choose.

Henceforth I ask not good fortune, I myself am good fortune,
Henceforth I whimper no more, postpone no more, need nothing,
Done with indoor complaints, libraries, querulous criticisms,
Strong and content I travel the open road.

The earth, that is sufficient,
I do not want the constellations any nearer,
I know they are very well where they are,
I know they suffice for those who belong to them.

(Still here I carry my old delicious burdens,
I carry them, men and women, I carry them with me wherever I go,
I swear it is impossible for me to get rid of them,
I am fill'd with them, and will fill them in return.)

You road I enter upon and look around, I believe you are not all that
    is here,
I believe that much unseen is also here.

From "Song of the Open Road," collected in *Leaves of Grass*, by Walt Whitman, 1855.

MARGARET KEATING

It's not for the faint of heart or those with a bad case of vertigo. Barring those problems, a walk across Bear Mountain Bridge, where the Appalachian Trail leaps over the Hudson River, is a greater thrill than many a carnival midway ride. Margaret Keating's appreciation of the bridge's technical achievement, and of its tortured history as a financial venture, makes crossing the river on foot, high above the powerfully flowing current, a more meaningful event. From a geological and cultural viewpoint, the eastern slope of the Hudson Valley (and thus the eastern end of the bridge) represents the beginning or ending of the northeastern watershed and, within a few miles, of the New England region—depending on the direction of your hike. Like the Mason-Dixon Line, dividing the Union from the Confederacy, the Hudson River clearly delineates the Mid-Atlantic region from New England. Thus for AT thru-hikers, the Bear Mt. Bridge is a true milestone.

The Bear Mountain Bridge

B RIDGING THE HUDSON IN ITS TIDEWATER LENGTH OF MORE THAN A HUN-dred miles is no ordinary feat of structural engineering. Not only width and depth, but more particularly the jealous governmental watchfulness against obstructions to navigation has dictated long and high spans calling for great technical skill and ample funds for construction. It was no human whim or regional desire, but rather an accident of topography which caused the first highway bridge over the river to be built in the Hudson Highlands and at the place where the gorge is narrowest between its tall rock cliffs, an ideal setting for a high, clear structure. But even the narrowest part of the Hudson is wide. At the time of construction, the Bear Mountain Bridge was the longest of suspension spans and was excelled in span length only by the Quebec and the Firth of Forth bridges, both of the cantilever type.

Prior to 1924 the only Hudson River bridge south of Albany was the one at Poughkeepsie built in 1887, which carried railroad freight trains to and from New England. In that long-past era another railroad bridge was projected at the precise location of the Bear Mountain span. Reported in 1889 to have been under construction, the project was soon abandoned, leaving no trace except a level roadbed carved out of the rock on the north slope of Anthony's Nose toward Manitou, at the present bridge level. Well hidden in the woods, this shelf was known only to a few hikers prior to 1925 and has since been obliterated by the new highway to Garrison. But its existence confirms the thought that, for the bridge engineer, this location is a "natural."

As cross-country motor traffic on a large scale sprang suddenly into existence, highways quickly supplemented railroads as the prime urge behind new bridge projects; and with the extreme congestion of motor traffic—as far back as 1921—at river ferries in the metropolitan region, all feasible locations for bridges on the Hudson were explored. Bear Mountain was certainly the most economical and was not without advantage from a traffic viewpoint, but the State had not acquired its present passion for bridge and parkway construction, and the matter was left to private financing. We may credit the Harrimans, who offered to and did put up the money, with a sentimental interest because of their family connection with the Bear Mountain Park and because of their own large estate nearby.

In any event, February, 1922, witnessed the introduction of a bill in the New York State Legislature authorizing the erection of a privately owned toll bridge across the Hudson River from Fort Clinton on the west bank to Anthony's Nose on the east bank. Construction began in April, 1923, and was completed on Thanksgiving Day, 1924.

Bear Mountain Bridge was designed by Howard Baird of New York City. Plans were approved by State engineers, the War Department, and the Palisades Interstate Park Commission. The total length of the central span was to be 1632 feet and the length between abutments 2258 feet. This was the longest suspension bridge in the world up to that time. No sooner had sketches been filed, however, than a hue and cry was raised by esthetically-minded groups who claimed that one of the beauty spots of the Hudson Highlands was being defiled. Their objections were not merely to the erection of a bridge at this particular scenic spot, but more particularly to the unsightly piece of engineering thus selected to mar the landscape.

No one denied the need of a bridge, but the site chosen, combined with the strict utilitarianism of the structure allegedly at the expense of good taste, aroused considerable opposition. It was even charged—when protests became hottest—that some members of the Palisades Interstate Park Commission had been given stock in the new venture to win their approval of the design. This charge was subsequently proved false. . . .

In 1927, three years after Bear Mountain Bridge was opened, the Holland Tunnel began giving the new bridge distant but keen competition. In 1931 George Washington Memorial Bridge just about sealed the financial fate of the Bear Mountain venture. . . .

Thus after sixteen years in private hands, Bear Mountain Bridge was acquired as a publicly owned facility. The State recognized the competitive situation, and toll rates under public ownership have been twice reduced. It is now possible to drive a car and all its occupants across Bear Mountain

Bridge for only 35 cents, which compares favorably with the 50 cents charged by the vehicular tunnels and the George Washington Bridge. But pedestrians must still pay a dime each.

This structure is notable as marking the return to popularity of suspension bridges. Despite their successful use for the three Manhattan-Brooklyn spans, designers had generally avoided them, probably because they lacked the rigidity desirable for railroad support. But for highways this disadvantage is negligible, and Bear Mountain started the boom in cables which was maintained by Detroit, Narragansett, San Francisco Bay, Golden Gate, Mid-Hudson, George Washington, and others. Simultaneously, it revived the highway toll gate, a prime nuisance of our great-grandfathers' era which some had assumed, with mistaken thanks, to have vanished forever.

From "The Bear Mountain Bridge," by Margaret Keating, collected in *In the Hudson Highlands*, Appalachian Mountain Club, New York Chapter, 1945.

JESSE BENEDIX

One of the rewards of climbing into the hills is access to plants that do not thrive in the valleys, where the climate and soil won't support them. Delicately beautiful alpine flowers abound above tree line in New Hampshire. Balsam fir perfume the air high in the Smoky Mountains. New York has no special claim on the mountain laurel, a large shrub that grows in the highlands from Canada to the American South, but naturalist Jesse Benedix, writing for the New York chapter of the Appalachian Mountain Club, surely produced one of the better hymns of praise to a beloved plant. When the mountain laurel blooms, its branches weaving a canopy of pink-white dappled light over a hiking trail, it's good to walk in the woods with the eyes and the mind wide open. Imagine the regal march of a king or queen. You just might find your heavy boots transformed into golden slippers.

Mountain Laurel

SYMBOLIZING AND EMBELLISHING THE FEATS OF THE ANCIENT ROMANS AND Greeks is a famous and lovely plant, the laurel. . . .

When America was first settled, interested colonists observed the laurel of our wooded hillsides. It was very much like the classical variety they had known, and so they gave it the same name. But the laurel of our hillsides is not the kind that was used to crown poets or conquerors in ancient Greece or Rome. The plant whose leaves were plaited into coronal wreaths, and used in various ways to thwart the evil doings of spirits, is the Sweet Bay or Noble Laurel, a tree-like shrub of southern Europe. The name is from the Celtic—*laur*, green—and refers to its evergreen qualities. The American Laurel, *Kalmia latifolia,* is a member of the heath family to which belong arbutus, wintergreen, azalea, rhododendron, and blueberries. It was named by Linnaeus in honor of his esteemed friend and pupil Peter Kalm. Kalm, a Swedish botanist, traveled in this country in the eighteenth century to study its flora. He greatly admired our laurel and sent several specimens and detailed descriptions to Linnaeus. *Latifolia* is from the Latin—latus, broad, and folium, leaf. There are several varieties of this plant, but the one with which we are familiar is the Mountain Laurel.

In spring and early summer, when the days are long and warm and the bright buttercups and sweet clover and fragrant tall grasses are gently riding the breeze, when the tulip trees are in bloom and the roses and lillies and honeysuckle fill the gardens with their perfume and color, then the laurel, with its delicate pink petticoats and perfect symmetry of form, rivals the more showy blossoms of civilization. It seems as if the climax of all that is dainty and lovely, simple and graceful, has been reached in the dignity of this beautiful American wild flower.

Laurel grows as a dense broad shrub from five to ten feet high with many stiff crooked branches and a round compact head. It is found from Newfoundland and Hudson Bay and along the highlands and mountains southward to Georgia. It grows all over the United States except in the central prairies and southwest plains. It blooms with greater abundance in the open or in open sunny woods than in dense ones.

When laurel leaves emerge from the bud they are pale green, slightly tinged with pink and covered with glandular white hairs. When full grown, three to four inches in length, they are thick, rigid, a dark lustrous green above and pale yellow green beneath. They remain green the year round and fall the second summer. Consequently the plant has only about half as much foliage in winter as in summer. The leaves grow alternately or in pairs or in threes in a crown and along the stem.

The flower buds are developed the previous summer and appear in the axils of the upper leaves as slender downy green cones. As the scales open, tiny rose pink buds emerge. These grow and open to become dainty, pink, star-like chalices which blanch into a crispy whiteness. The corolla is bowl shaped with five lobes or connected petals. There are ten dark red depressions or pockets in the sides of the corolla in which the tips of the anthers are securely held. The filaments form a series of taut arching spokes from the tiny crimson starred center of the flower in the pocketed anther. So delicately is the mechanism adjusted that the slightest jar will release the anthers. One has only to touch the hair trigger with the end of a pin to see how exquisitely delicate is this provision for cross fertilization. The velvety bodied bee abets this process in her wanderings. Her slightest pressure, as she approaches the nectary of the flower, releases the stamens which spring back to shower white pollen over her fuzzy body. The sticky pollen of *Kalmia* is connected by webby threads and is specially adapted to cross fertilization. The blossom next visited by the powdered worker probably has a ripe stigma to which the pollen strings quickly adhere. The flower stalks are hairy and sticky. This prevents unwelcome pilferers such as ants and beetles, who would be useless as fertilizing agents, from entering the blossoms and stealing the nectar. The flowers develop and ripen into dull red, five-lobed seed capsules which burst open during October and November to scatter hundreds of minute seeds. The empty seed capsules sometimes remain on the plant for several years.

Perhaps as a protective measure Nature imbued the Mountain Laurel with a poisonous quality harmful to foraging animals. Most cattle and wild creatures know enough to let it alone, nevertheless some fall victims. This is especially so in spring when the tender young leaves are tempting. Even the intelligent grouse, overcome with hunger when deep snow covers their food, are sometimes found dead, their crops distended by these leaves. The pollen and nectar seem not to affect the bee, but in 1790 fatalities were recorded when wild honey from *Kalmia latifolia* was eaten. The American Indians knew this quality and when they wished to commit suicide, drank a potion brewed from *Kalmia* leaves.

The beauty of this plant, combined with its utility, causes it to be much sought after. Where it was once abundant it is rapidly becoming scarce or extinct. Hundreds of tons of its foliage are used for Christmas decorations and other festivities. Laurel leaves were the chief decorative element in the splendid arches through which George Washington rode to his inauguration at New York as the first president of the United States. All year round the foliage is used to decorate fruit stands, a needless waste. Its wood is sought for rustic furniture, tools, spoons, and as a substitute for brier-wood pipes. The rapid depletion of this plant has led to legislative protection in many states.

The Indians called it spoonwood since it served to make their simpler eating implements. This name has almost passed into disuse, although a few farmers in remote sections still refer to it as such. The Southern mountaineers often call it calico bush probably because of the pattern of its flowers. But no matter what it is called, we repeatedly thrill to the aurora-like flush with which it suffuses the rocky hillsides of its native haunts each spring. Nor are we less impressed than was Peter Kalm when he saw its glory reflected from the quiet pools of crystal streams and the serene depths of azure mountain lakes.

From *In the Hudson Highlands*, by Publication Committee, New York Chapter, Appalachian Mountain Club, 1945.

NEW YORK–NEW JERSEY TRAIL CONFERENCE

Plus ça change, plus ça reste la même chose. *Lest today's Appalachian Trail managers feel burdened by the few hikers whose disrespectful behavior may damage trailside property or who leave trash in what should be a pristine environment, the following small piece of AT history will set things in perspective. From the earliest days of the AT there have always been those hikers who just will not keep to the well-trodden path and whose carelessness may have negative consequences for all who follow them. As always, the campaign to educate hikers about appropriate behavior is a necessary element in the trail maintenance program. In New York in 1934, the sore spot was a section of the AT passing through Harriman State Park and through an adjacent piece of private property owned by a corporation.*

Barring of Harriman Section Threatened

C LOSING OF THE HARRIMAN SECTION OF THE APPALACHIAN TRAIL FROM Arden to Lake Mombasha was threatened by irritation arising from a dispute of walkers with a watchman of the Sterling Iron and Railway Co., in February, 1934, in which the former claimed "rights" to build a fire off the trail, on the shore of Little Dam Pond. Walkers must remember that they have no "rights" on private land; they have only the *privilege* when it is granted by landowners, subject to revocation without notice if undue use of such privileges is made. This incident followed others of similar disregard for private property.

Through the consideration of Mr. Benjamin Moffatt, President of the Sterling Iron and Railway Co., use of the Harriman Section will be permitted in 1934, but walkers must keep on the trail as laid and marked, they must not build fires on that section; they must not stray off the trail, particularly they must not cross the dam or overflow of Little Dam Pond. "Some hikers are careless and assume rights never intended to be given," says Mr. Moffatt. Permission to continue use of this section, after 1934, will be dependent on the good behavior of hikers and others, in that year. We hope that all using this part of the trail will conduct themselves properly, and urge similar action on others, lest it be permanently closed, and a troublesome and less scenic relocation be required.

From *Guide to the Appalachian Trail, From the Housatonic River in Connecticut to the Susquehanna River in Pennsylvania, Via the Hudson River at Bear Mountain, Delaware Water Gap and Lehigh Gap,* by New York–New Jersey Trail Conference, 1934.

BARTON BROWN

It took Barton Brown, of Metairie, Louisiana, almost six months to the day, from Easter to mid-October, to thru-hike the Appalachian Trail in 1976, walking south to north. He took only ten days off the trail, for a side trip to Washington. The dream of hiking the entire AT was born in his Boy Scout days in New Jersey, when Brown's troop camped on Kittatinny Ridge. Yet it wasn't until years later, in 1974, when Brown was an office worker in Washington, that he took up backpacking, getting his start on the AT near Harpers Ferry, West Virginia. One day he met a couple at Crampton Gap in Gathland State Park, Maryland; they had walked there from Georgia. On the spot Brown made up his mind to do likewise. As such his story is stamped almost exactly from the mold AT founder Benton MacKaye envisioned: urban worker seeks respite in mountain wilderness, becomes inspired by the challenge, and opts out of normal life for several months in a refreshingly different environment and a long, long walk. That Brown also took time to observe carefully the world he walked through is clear from his witty notes about dogs and diners along the way.

Trail Diary, 1976

WHEN COMING OFF THE RIDGE, IT WAS MY CUSTOM FOR A LONG TIME TO grab a stick in order to keep the barking dogs at bay. As I became more experienced, I was able to intimidate snarling canines with nothing more than body English. The proof was in the pudding because although threatened, I was never nipped, but I met other hikers less fortunate. Not all valleys had dogs of the same personality. "One can tell the health of a town by the meanness of its dogs. If they snarl and bark, down to the smallest runt, the town is mean and its inhabitants set a poor table for the sojourner. Well fed dogs are content to lie on their porches in the shade and make a ceremonial growl as the stranger passes. That town will have hospitality."

It is town day. High atop the ridge a hiker hears the wind chimes of civilization tinkling on the wind. He strikes camp, eschews breakfast and heads for town spurred on by the promise of "cokes and smokes just 99 more strokes" (from a trail register). But, woe to that hiker who arrives in a small southern town on Wednesday afternoon to find the Post Office closed and the sidewalks buttoned up until Thursday morning.

There is no greater joy in town than the excess of a pig-out. "Pawling, New York. *Earl Slocum's—a cookery and saloon.* Inside a sign reads, 'There are no strangers at Earl's, just people you never met before.' At Earl's, I had the best meal along the Trail yet. The dharma restaurant. A hustling waitress who brings us foaming bottles of ale, hot sandwiches, real french-fried potatoes and pecan pie with vanilla ice cream. Friendly and fast, the way one wishes the world responded to us always" (from a trail register).

From *2,000-Miler Report to the Appalachian Trail Conference*, by Barton Brown, 1977.

ELLEN COLETTI

Peaks and valleys: for an Appalachian Trail thru-hiker it's not just a matter of elevation gained or lost. The topography of the spirit has its own contour lines. Ellen Coletti thru-hiked in 1984. She tries hard to explain why the trail experience seems so rarefied, compared to the mundane workaday world. Her trail name was "Prunefeet"; her companion's was "Duck." On the AT they coped with near-disasters and benefited from their portion of trail magic. As so many thru-hikers report, Coletti agrees that one of the hardest parts of the hike is having it finally be over. Coletti mentions a generous man, whose full name she has forgotten, who gave the hikers garden vegetables in exchange for their AT stories—one kind of food for another, no doubt. Perhaps this man's generosity reflected the nature of the neighborhood. Coletti alludes to Greymoor, a monastery at trailside on the east bank of the Hudson River, where for many years the monks welcomed thru-hikers with a free bed and meals, as though the hikers were fellow pilgrims.

Trail Diary, 1984

P ERHAPS THE LONGING TO RETURN TO THE WOODS IS CAUSED BY A CERTAIN belief that I will never again do something as adventuresome, as challenging, as educational and as fun. Nothing in my life up until I hiked the entire trail filled me with the joy of the summit of Mount Katahdin, the excitement of walking into Damascus at 6:00 P.M. after a fast-paced 26 miles (our biggest day of hiking), the pure, sensual, hilarious pleasure of *hot*, running water at Shaw's Boarding House after 10 days of wilderness hiking. Perhaps what causes the disappointment, the unease, after coming off the trail (and staying off for a few months), is the absence of such pure and simple pleasures. Not that I am always disappointed. David and I (he is the

Duck and I am Prunefeet) have settled in Boston, found jobs, blah, blah. I only really notice how much I miss the Trail when I start thinking and talking about it. There seems no way to convey to people who have not seen it for themselves that special, instantaneous accord between people on and near the Trail. To tell someone that Carl Van —— on the Old Albany Post Rd. in New York—just north of Greymoor—gave us fresh cucumbers and zucchinis out of his garden doesn't seem to capture the spirit of the exchange, our stories for his ice water and vegetables. "I stepped out of the Stony Brook Shelter in Vermont and twisted my ankle" fails to illuminate the terror I felt, and neglects to include that first lightning-bolt phrase through my head "Can I hike?" (I could and did, the next day.)

From *2,000-Miler Report to the Appalachian Trail Conference*, by Ellen Coletti, 1984.

RICHARD SATTERLIE

The late Frank Zappa, of avant-garde rock music fame, named one of his children "America," but that's not half as clever or as well earned as the child's name that pops up in Richard Satterlie's report about a thru-hike he made with his wife, Donna, in 1978. Probably in a category by herself, Donna Satterlie may still be the only thru-hiker to have carried out the walk not only for herself but for a very special fellow traveler as well.

Trail Diary, 1978

MY WIFE, DONNA, AND MYSELF HAD THE PRIVILEGE OF HIKING THE "A.T." last summer. We started in Georgia on March 29th and reached Mt. Katahdin on Sept. 28th. We completed all the A.T. with the exception of 210 miles. Our story along the trail is quite unique because we found out in Hot Springs, N.C. that Donna was "carrying a child." Needless to say, Donna went all the way with me and when she climbed Mt. Katahdin she was actually 7½ months pregnant. I won't go into any more details but we had our child on Nov. 18th and in honor of the Appalachian Trail and what it has done for us we named our little daughter "Georgia Maine."

From *2,000-Miler Report to the Appalachian Trail Conference*, by Richard Satterlie, 1978.

NEW ENGLAND

Connecticut, Massachusetts, Vermont, New Hampshire, Maine

Mt. Katahdin from Daicey Pond, Baxter State Park, Maine.

New England is a region of extreme contrasts. The rolling, pastoral hills of western Connecticut, where a woodland hike may offer the sweetness of flowering dogwood trees and a quietly gurgling Housatonic River, is a far cry from the potentially deadly but always awe-inspiring alpine region of New Hampshire's White Mountains, where hurricane-force winds and snow can put a sharp edge on a walk above tree line in any month of the year. And there is the disconcerting fact that some of the wildest, most rugged places along the Appalachian Trail in New England are now the most crowded corners of the trail as well. For solitude on the New England AT, one seeks out not necessarily the most dramatic piece of mountaintop landscape but perhaps a lovely and less often visited valley.

The trail meanders in and out of countless villages where architecture speaks volumes about the development of the country, from the 1700s to today. Frequent church steeples poke up through the canopy of conifers and deciduous trees like so many towering remnants of a vir-

gin forest long since harvested out. Two of the nation's most venerable hiking associations—the Appalachian Mountain Club and the Green Mountain Club—are based here. These two clubs built many of the earliest hiking trails in the Northeast, setting a precedent of initiative and stewardship that is still a model in our time.

On the Connecticut AT we attend a wedding, walk in a bog, and rhapsodize with a philosopher about Mother Earth. In Massachusetts we reencounter AT visionary Benton MacKaye, here philosophizing about the importance of hiking trails. An historian recounts a bloody political uprising at a trailside site. Major 19th-century literary figures, Melville and Thoreau, praise Mt. Greylock, the highest peak in southern New England. Poet Richard Wilbur muses about abandoned stone walls in the woods. Both Vermont and New Hampshire claimed poet Robert Frost. We meet him here in a poem about the black bear seen occasionally by Appalachian Mountain hikers. A native American legend from Vermont reminds us that we are only the latest custodians of a land that belonged to others long ago, and naturalist Michael Frome explores the complex botany of the Green Mountain National Forest.

A close look at rare alpine flowers, lichens, and mosses appears in the New Hampshire section, which features the Presidential Range and Mt. Washington in particular. We hear about colorful characters who blazed the early trails, for fun and for profit. Failure in the mountains is not uncommon; of the two cases presented here, one is wryly comic, the other deadly.

The energy on the Appalachian Trail in Maine seems to flow toward the final ascent of Mt. Katahdin, northern terminus and symbolic Mecca for northbound thru-hikers. Yet the carefully crafted words of Myron Avery, first Appalachian Trail Conference president, take us southward, through dense Maine wilderness. Percival Baxter, governor of Maine, calls out for a vast protected state park of which we are the beneficiaries. Trail diaries and trail registers capture some of the high spirits of those who know the intense solitude of the Maine woods and the elation of adding a small rock to the cairn at the top of Katahdin. In closing we turn again to Henry Thoreau and to one of his spiritual descendants, Wendell Berry, for the final words of this literary thru-hike on the Appalachian Trail.

THE APPALACHIAN TRAIL IN
CONNECTICUT, MASSACHUSETTS, VERMONT

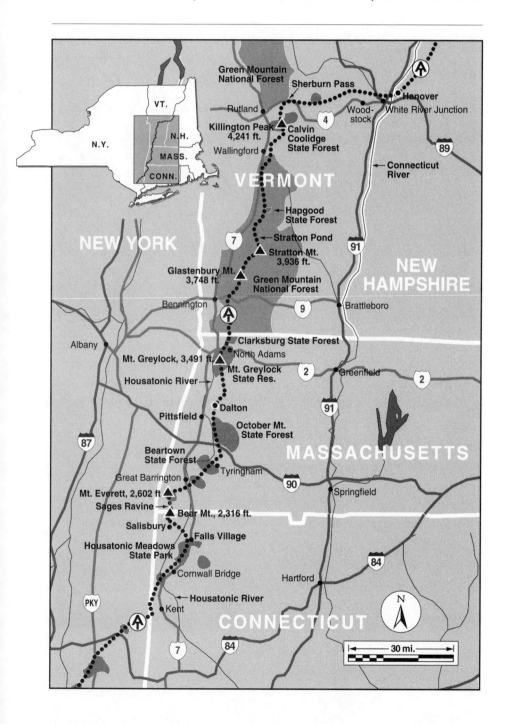

CONNECTICUT

In a shady pine plantation north of St. Johns Ledges, Kent, Connecticut.

Trail miles: 45

Trail maintenance: Appalachian Mt. Club (Connecticut chapter)

Highest point: Bear Mt., 2,316 ft.

Broadest river: Housatonic (two AT crossings)

Features: Lovely views of Housatonic River valley from the Taconic
   Range, one of the oldest geologic areas on the AT. Longest riverside
   walk on the AT, with miles of whitewater views (in season).

Parks, forests, and nature preserves: Housatonic Meadows State Park
   & Forest

Most intriguing name on the trail: St. Johns Ledges

Trail towns: Kent, Cornwall Bridge, Falls Village, Salisbury

RONALD FISHER

If it weren't for unfortunate blights that attacked hundreds of magnificent hemlocks and red pines, and a tornado as well, in the Housatonic River valley some years ago, Appalachian Trail hikers would still have the pleasure of walking through an area formerly known as "Cathedral Pines." (The trail has since been rerouted.) Ronald Fisher, out on the ideal journalistic junket, covered the entire AT in a book for the National Geographic Society. Trail magic serendipitously entered his workday in Connecticut when he received an invitation to an AT trailside wedding at Cathedral Pines. It made sense: the espoused were both hikers whose sense of the sacred was rooted not only in their love for one another but in their love for the outdoors as well.

An Appalachian Trail Wedding

*I*N CONNECTICUT, AUTUMN BEGAN TO CATCH UP WITH US. HOT DAYS AND muggy nights had dogged us all the way from Georgia, but now we noticed a subtle change. The night air was refreshing instead of oppressive; the moon, still a month short of harvest, shone so brightly it kept us awake and turned familiar forest shapes into dreamworld phantoms. And the unseen crickets and katydids, those harbingers of fall, began their nightly concerts — steady-pitched singing that flowed back and forth across the campground.

We came upon a beaver dam, by chance the first we had seen, although beavers live as far south as Alabama. In the bog behind the dam, quacking ducks paddled through a fuzzy maze of gray cattails. The beaver lodge was so symmetrical it might have come from an upended salad mold.

Near Cornwall, the trail passes through a virgin stand of white pines a hundred feet tall, appropriately called Cathedral Pines. Even the birds and chipmunks seem subdued in the quiet majesty of the place. Soft shadows and deep pine needles carpeted the forest floor.

Just beyond Cathedral Pines we fell into conversation with a couple on the trail—Mike Jacubouis, a thoughtful, pipe-smoking director of vocational education in the state school for delinquent boys in Portland, Maine, and tall, blond Cara Perkins, an outdoors enthusiast from Cornwall. We learned they were planning to be married at Cathedral Pines, and we gladly accepted an invitation to attend the ceremony.

The Saturday of the wedding, about 60 of us assembled in Mohawk State Forest, wearing "comfortable hiking clothes" as the invitation had suggested. The bride and groom were in denim shirts and sturdy knickers with bright red suspenders, and they both wore climbing boots; Mike's stainless-steel drinking cup swung at his belt.

In a small clearing beneath a pine tree, the Reverend Bill Kittredge of Lewiston, Maine—the "hiking preacher," the invitation had called him—read from Henry David Thoreau's *Walden*:

"We need the tonic of wildness—to wade sometimes in marshes where the bittern and the meadow-hen lurk, and hear the booming of the snipe; to smell the whispering sedge where only some wilder and more solitary fowl builds her nest, and the mink crawls with its belly close to the ground. . . . We can never have enough of nature. We must be refreshed by the sight of inexhaustible vigor, vast and titanic features, the sea-coast with its wrecks, the wilderness with its living and its decaying trees, the thundercloud, and the rain which lasts three weeks and produces freshets. We need to witness our own limits transgressed, and some life pasturing freely where we never wander."

Then we set out, up the gentle incline of Mohawk Mountain. I walked awhile beside Cara, and asked why she had chosen the Appalachian Trail for her wedding place.

"Simply because wilderness is so important to Mike and me," she said. "It's a very big part of our lives. We both hike a lot with the Appalachian Mountain Club, and occasionally lead hikes; so it seemed natural to us to have our friends join us in the kind of setting we both love, and to be married here."

We reached the summit of Mohawk, and the bride and groom and their families gathered on a low stone observation tower while the rest of us sat on the grass. As soon as several romping dogs could be quieted, the ceremony continued with melodies played on recorders, the flute-like tones lingering low and clear in the still air. For several minutes no one stirred.

After the company sang two folk songs, accompanied by guitar and banjo, the hiking preacher read these words of Thoreau:

"I never asked thy leave to let me love thee—I have a right. . . . O how I think of you! You are purely good—you are infinitely good. . . . I did not think that humanity was so rich!"

Again we walked. As we neared Cathedral Pines we met a troop of Boy Scouts from Pound Ridge, New York, who were thunderstruck to find themselves momentarily in the midst of a wedding party.

As we took seats on the fragrant pine needles and the guitarist strummed the chords of "God of Our Fathers," the bridegroom's 84-year-old grandmother joined us. She had made the short but steep hike from the opposite direction, and arrived scarcely out of breath, murmuring exultantly in a Polish accent, "I make it! I make it!"

Now Mike and Cara stood side by side, facing us, to exchange their vows. Above them the pines, moving gently in a slight breeze, sounded like someone's soft breathing as the service concluded:

> *May the silence of the hills,*
> *The joy of the winds,*
> *The peace of the fields,*
> *The music of the birds,*
> *The fire of the sun,*
> *The strength of the trees,*
> *And the faith of you —*
> *In all of which is God —*
> *Be in your hearts.*

Broadly smiling friends formed an archway of ice axes for the newly-weds as they left the grove. We walked the mile or so to the bride's home, and joined in a reception on the lawn.

From *The Appalachian Trail*, by Ronald Fisher, National Geographic Society, 1972.

HAL BORLAND

They threw away the mold after Hal Borland was gone. He kept a New York Times *column going for thirty-six years (1942–1978), always with a fresh look at the natural world and our sometimes damaging impact on it. Based in Salisbury, Connecticut, a town right on the AT, Borland knew the hiking trails well. Were Borland leading the hike, the pace would be slow, the pauses for close observation many. It's not only what he can see or hear that fascinates him, but what he can imagine as well, as though this were the mythic primeval swamp and through its mists a large creature might step forward out of time itself.*

The Bog

WE STOPPED AT A SMALL BOGLAND THE OTHER EVENING AND PARKED the car and went on foot to look and listen. It was just at sunset, and on the hillside beyond the swamp a barred owl was hooting softly. It was quite a way off and at first I thought I was hearing a mourning dove. But it was an owl, all right. Sometimes, at a distance, an owl will sound like a dove, and the doves have been calling so much and the owls so little that I was confused.

In the meadow that sloped down to the bog were a few patches of bluets,

Houstonia caerulea, which some call Quaker Ladies and some call Innocence. They were like little patches of fog in the grass, for they grew close and bloomed generously. The tiny four-petaled flowers were so white, so sparsely touced with any shade of blue, that I wondered again why anyone ever called them bluets. And down at the wet margin the swamp violets were full of deep purple blossom, one of the richest colors that early May has to offer.

But it was the bog itself we had come to see.

Red-wings challenged us, a small flock of them. They circled and scolded and flashed their crimson epaulets, and they perched on the stalks of last year's cattails, swaying precariously. The old cattails were fluffed into smoky-looking tufts, ragged out by wind and winter and perhaps by the early nest builders too. But at the base of each stalk rose the bright green of new growth, the blades that will make the bog a green jungle by July. Among them was the darker green of blue flag, the wild iris, which will color the swampland in another month with its big blossoms. At this stage the blades of iris and cattail look much alike, except that the cattails are somewhat narrower and a lighter, yellowish green. And among them were still narrower blades of one of the bur reeds, I couldn't be sure which but guessed at the variety known as *symplex*, the smaller one. The blades looked like rank grass.

On and around the little tussocks that were above the water were marsh marigolds, nearly all of them in bloom. Some were up to their ears in water, the leaves seeming to float and the blossoms only a little higher. They are web-footed cousins of the common buttercups and the Latin name, *Caltha palustris*, means marsh-cup. Botanically, they are also cousins of the columbine; but that is one of those things I have to take on faith. I don't really believe it, though I know it is true. I do believe that the marsh marigold flower is one of the loveliest golden yellows I ever saw anywhere.

And on the tussocks themselves were great masses of skunk cabbage leaves, big as elephant ears, gaudy, extravagant and primitive. And among them I could see others of the *Arum* family, with their dark-striped spathes, a number of light green, plantain-like leaves of sweet flag, and an occasional dart-shaped leaf of the arrow arum.

On the far margin of the little bog were two tall elms, trembling on the verge of leaf, still lacy in tufts of young seed, and beneath them were clumps of willow brush where the inch-long leaves had already begun to hide the finished catkins. And alder brush was tufting out in leaf, still hung with the little cone-like seed cases from last year. From somewhere nearby a hyla shrilled and I thought he was the last member of the peeper chorus that was so loud two weeks ago. But from down at the other end of the bog came an answer in a voice so high it sounded like falsetto. No chorus, though.

The water caught the glow of sunset and turned from pewter gray to opalescent. The opalescence was fire-dappled with specks of lettuce-green that caught some lively light and almost glistened. Duck-weed, finer than the finest confetti, drifted in the luminous water.

There was a dark movement back among the cattails. As we watched, a big brown muskrat swam into the open, the V of ripples from his nose like long, silvery whiskers. He swam toward the bank where we stood, quietly as a shadow; and suddenly he saw us and dived with a plop and left only a swirling of the opalescent water.

We turned and went back to the car. I always feel close to beginnings in a bogland; especially at dusk. I feel as though I stood on the brink of ancient days when warm seas washed the first land and aquatic life was making its first venture away from the mother element, Water. Even here in the Berkshire Hills, bog life has a primitive aspect, a sense of elemental change. The very smell of a bog is fecund and fertile of mysterious and fundamental change.

I get the feeling, particularly at dusk, that anything can happen on the margin of a swampland. Outlandish things. There have been dusks when I was sure that if I waited on such a margin only another hour I would see a 30-foot Stegosaurus, complete with armor-plate scales, come wading out from among the reeds and cattails, trailing a million centuries behind him. I never have, but I still wouldn't bet that I never shall.

From *Hill Country Harvest*, by Hal Borland, Lippincott, 1967.

ODELL SHEPARD

Selections for a literary anthology come to the editor's desk in odd ways. The name Odell Shepard was unknown to us until we found him in a personal classified ad in the back pages of AMC Outdoors, *the magazine of the Appalachian Mountain Club. A hiker advertised for walking companions to join a two-week reenactment of a sojourn Shepard himself had enjoyed in the 1920s, rambling through northwestern Connecticut, ending up in the corner of the state that is still fully wild today, where the Appalachian Trail crosses into Massachusetts. The advertiser called Shepard's book a "minor classic," and it is—perhaps a bit gushingly romantic for contemporary tastes but not at all at odds with the spirit of Bartram's, Muir's or Thoreau's similarly rhapsodic voices. Shepard subtitled his work "A Book of Digressions," and isn't that just what a walker's journal should be? Digressions into seldom seen quarters of the woods, into feelings and ideas that get short shrift when set against the distractions of the regular workaday world. Shepard tells us here, from a perch affording an inspiring view of Mt. Riga (also called Bald Mt.), a high point on the Connecticut AT, what he thinks about God, nature, and the good life.*

Mother Earth

THE HAPPINESS I FIND IN MY EXPERIENCE IS THAT OF UNACCUSTOMED ALERTness. During the hours I have spent here on Wells Hill my thoughts and memories have not become entangled with the trees and the odors of the fields and the blue of the sky; rather I should say that I have taken all these things up into myself and that they have been thinking and feeling through me. So far as these words are concerned, or any other words that I might find, this may seem to be a distinction without a difference, yet I know that the difference is really profound. It is the difference, indeed, between a passive and an active mood. I admit that when I began my walk, two weeks ago, at Brooklyn, I took whatever came and was glad enough to let my thoughts simply bask in the sun, for then I was a tired man; but more and more, as the miles and the days have gone by, I have resumed control, until now I seem in some sense to create the landscape as I go along. I am no longer a mere bundle of traveling senses, but rather Francis Bacon's *Homo additus Naturae*. Prospect Mountain over yonder is not merely a thing to be looked at: it is also a thought. I find that I cannot put my whole meaning into clearer words than these, but that is no reason why I should distrust the exultation, celebrated by Santayana himself, which is felt 'when the mind and the world are knit in a brief embrace,' when earth is transfigured by human thought and Nature is raised to the human level.

One who lives in his faith may have a higher vision and a deeper serenity than any that I am acquainted with among the Connecticut Calvinists— barring such men of religious genius as Jonathan Edwards—who once ruled all this land that I look out across. My theology is far less definite, my notions of good and evil are much less precise, than theirs; they were quite certain about many things which I am content to leave in the shadow of mystery; they derived from their doctrine an iron discipline of will and reason which I shall never be able to find in mine; and yet I do not bow before them as my spiritual superiors. I can praise them for many things, but not for this, that they were strangers in the fair world where I am every year more and more at home. I cannot praise the love of God that expresses itself in contempt for God's fair handiwork. If we may trust their own account, they knew pathetically little about simple happiness: I have spelled some words in its primer. They had a keener and more abiding sense than I of a God outside the world He made: I have a keener sense than they of a God inside that world. They looked back upon a Revelation completed long ago: I look out upon a Revelation now in progress, never to be complete. . . . These are some of the differences to be considered in a preliminary test of the religion of earth. Of course I know while I write them down that if one of their mighty men, say Cotton Mather or Richard Hooker or Thomas Shepard, should come up the road just now to discuss these questions, he could cite a thousand texts to confuse and entangle me; but the logic of the heart would be against him.

The sun is descending now upon the summit of Mount Riga, and the colors of the hills are deepened as he goes down the sky. The evening of my last day in the country is drawing in. What, now, shall I save to remember out of this final day and out of the two golden weeks to which it has been the appropriately quiet climax and close? Colors of sunrise and sunset, colors of trees, the song of the wind through the pine — a thousand sights and sounds. But even more than these things I should like to remember my present thought or mood as the goal of my fortnight's wandering. Free for a few hours yet from the clutch of circumstance, glad for the days that have been and gladly facing the days to come, I sit here in the last rays of the sun fulfilled with such a love of the brown earth, my Mother, as I have seldom known before. And it comes to me, as I sit here in this devotion of quiet thought, that all the vast toil of Nature struggling upward to this moment has here reached one of its terms. Earth sees now, through my eyes, the vision of her own beauty. Earth knows herself at last, and knows that she is divine.

From *The Harvest of a Quiet Eye,* by Odell Shepard, Houghton Mifflin, 1927.

MASSACHUSETTS

From Tyringham Cobble, the peaceable Tyringham Valley, Berkshire County, Massachusetts.

Trail miles: 90.4

Trail maintenance: Appalachian Mt. Club (Berkshire chapter)

Highest point: Mt. Greylock, 3,491 ft.

Broadest river: Housatonic (one AT crossing)

Features: Colorful mix of rugged mountains, pastoral valleys, and quintessential New England towns in the Berkshire hills. Highest mountain in southern New England (Mt. Greylock), crowned by full-service Bascom Lodge, staffed by Appalachian Mt. Club.

Parks, forests, and nature preserves: Mt. Everett State Reservation, East Mt. State Forest, Beartown State Forest, October Mt. State Forest, Mt. Greylock State Reservation, Clarksburg State Forest

Most intriguing name on the trail: Jug End

Trail towns: Sheffield, Great Barrington, Dalton, Cheshire, North Adams

WALTER PRITCHARD EATON

Walter Pritchard Eaton (1878–1957) was a man perfectly cut out to be Benton MacKaye's friend. MacKaye was a Harvard grad, Eaton went to Yale. MacKaye the land-use planner and advocate for an Appalachian footpath was matched in skills and enthusiasms by Eaton the literary critic, professor of playwriting, and sometime poet and essayist. At his Berkshire Hills home in Sheffield, Massachusetts (eventually to be an AT town), Eaton heard about MacKaye's bold hiking trail proposal from his friend R. R. Bowker. Bowker, a New York publisher of reference books, owned a home in Stockbridge and was active, with Eaton, in the Laurel Hill Association there—the oldest community-based land trust in the United States.

Eaton's letter to MacKaye is typical of MacKaye's correspondence with scores, if not hundreds, of potential helpers on the nascent Appalachian Trail project. Eaton outlines his preferred route for the trail through the Berkshires. Initial plans called for an "airline" path straight up the Taconic Ridge from Mt. Everett to Mt. Greylock, along the New York State border with Massachusetts. The alternative recommended here by Eaton became in large part the actual route of the AT in Massachusetts—via Sheffield, Great Barrington, Monterey, and Tyringham. However, at that point on the map, Eaton proposed running the trail to the west of Pittsfield, via northern Lenox to the Hancock Shaker village, and then north again through Lanesborough and New Ashford, over Brodie Mt. and thence to Mt. Greylock. In fact the AT continues east of Pittsfield, via Dalton and Cheshire, to Greylock. The details of the discussion illustrate the thoughtfulness, preferences, and prejudices that went into planning the original AT.

Eaton sustained his interest in the Appalachian Trail over many years, joining other early advocates in writing about the project so as to inform a broader public. He reached a huge audience with an article on the trail in the July 7, 1928, issue of the Saturday Evening Post.

Letter to Benton MacKaye, June 23, 1922

Twin Fires
Sheffield, Mass.

Dear MacKaye,

Of course I've heard of your trail, and its a fine idea (and what is back of it in your mind is in mine, too). The Mass. crossing of course is what most interests me. I think I am rather opposed to the "air line" idea here, and for an excellent reason. The air line takes the trail from Mt. Everett & Graylock up the Taconic ridge, following practically the Mass.-N.Y. boundary. It will go over into N.Y. at one or 2 points. I think this would be a great mistake, 1st, because the sections of the trail between the 2 mountains would not be much used, as they would lie too far West of the vally towns; 2nd, and most important, this route would neglect the wonderful opportunity to open up 20,000 acres of state forest to the public for recreational purposes, or advertise the state forest idea, and to secure State aid & interest in helping make the trail.

If you'll look at a map of western Mass. you will see that the trail comes into the state from Conn. on the high Taconic Ridge, passing through state reservation over Mt. Everett Summit. I think it should then cross the Housatonic Valley, using perhaps a country road between Sheffield and Gt. Barrington, or through pine woods there if possible, and enter the 8,000 acre state forest on *Beartown Mt.* Thence it can cross the head of the Hop Brook valley near Tyringham, pass Goose Pond, and reach the new 10,000 acre state forest on *October Mt.* (the old Whitney Preserve). Here is wild, high country, in which there are *moose*. It could descend Roaring Brook & new Lenox, go over the ridge north of Lenox, and thence, passing north of Richmond and crossing the state road near the west Pittsfield Shakers, head up onto the Taconic Ridge again for its air line passage north. In this way you would open up 2 state forests, you would bring trampers close to the Berkshire towns of Sheffield, Barrington, Stockbridge and Lenox, where most of your help must be secured, and where your week-end trampers will want to get, and you will also make the trail one which will be used by local people, in which they will take an interest.

If it sticks to the air line ridge, nobody south of Pittsfield is going to know it exists. However, the opening of the state forests, and the opportunity to hitch them up with the recreational idea is the big thing. Think it over. *The state might build the trail & shelters & camp sites in the forest areas.* Also, the state (i.e. the commissioners) might be made to build the trail over Everett & Graylock. The Graylock commissioners will, I'm sure. The Everett Commissioners are old fogies. However, we may be able to shake 'em up.

Thine ever
WP Eaton

From correspondence of Walter Pritchard Eaton, Appalachian Trail Conference.

BENTON MacKAYE

MacKaye's campaign for the completion of an Appalachian Trail went on for years. At its outset we find in his correspondence evidence of his solicitations for moral and financial support. Gifford Pinchot, the first professional American forester (chief of the U.S. Forest Service from 1898 to 1910 and governor of Pennsylvania for ten years), was an ardent supporter. In 1921 he wrote to MacKaye, "I have just been over your admirable statement about an Appalachian Trail for recreation, for health and recuperation, and for employment on the land. Your giant certainly sees the truth. I am greatly interested, and I wish you the very best of success."

By 1927 MacKaye's thinking about the relationship between outdoor recreation and cultural health had evolved. It was no longer merely a matter of providing urban office workers with a respite from the mental strain of their desk jobs. Now MacKaye raised the level of the debate to new philosophical heights, though always with a wry humor so as not to scare away those less serious than himself. He delivered an address to the New England Trail Conference with the title "Outdoor Culture—The Philosophy of Through Trails." By "culture" MacKaye said he meant "the ability to visualize a happier state of affairs than the average humdrum of the regulation world." He confessed to having utopian visions, and he set out to explain how long-distance trails might be a part of an ideal world worth working to achieve. MacKaye's own training in classical Greek, Roman, and English literature shines through even the following brief passage from his witty address.

Outdoor Culture

I MIGHT HERE WAX ELOQUENT AND POINT OUT THE WARNING OF ANCIENT ROME. Then I might borrow a term from Brook Farm and describe the "Civilizee." From all accounts Rome must have been getting on toward the ultimate of over-civilization. But she was lucky: for she had the Barbarian at her back gate.

And now I am nearing the point of the philosophy of through trails. It relates to the development of a certain type of modern (or future) American. It is the opposite type from the Civilizee. As Roman civilization received ultimately its cleansing invasion from the hinterland, so American civilization may yet receive its modern counterpart.

What manner of man may be the coming American "Barbarian"? A purifier? Yes, perhaps, but not a Puritan. The Barbarian which I have in mind is a rough and ready engineer. He understands water pressure and he understands human pressure. He knows that each demands its outlet. You cannot dam up *all* the water. Water at high level forms a high potential pressure, and the result of its release depends upon the sluiceway. If this be intact the flow becomes controlled and its power made constructive; if weak and leaky the power peters out or spreads disaster. As with water pressure so with soul pressure: its "hydraulics" are the same. The Puritan would build a dam; but the Barbarian would build a sluiceway.

Let us compare our Barbarian with our Civilizee. Each is a tendency—an ultimate: perhaps no specimen of either character has yet been born, but the embryos of both are plain to see. Each has his own Utopia. Our Civilizee is content to be a vicarious Robin Hood. Our Barbarian demands to be a real (if diminutive) Magellan—a pioneer in the new exploration of a Barbarian Utopia. Our Civilizee is content with the throb of the jazz band; our Barbarian demands the ring and rhythm of the Anvil Chorus. One is content with exotic metropolitan splendor; the other prefers indigenous colonial color. The one sees in colonial revival merely the worship of our grandfathers; the other sees in it a future potential art to be developed by our grandsons. Our Civilizee sees in the mountain summit a pretty place on which to play at tin-can pirate and to strew the Sunday supplement; our Barbarian sees in the mountain summit the strategic point from which to resoundly kick said Civilizee and to open war on the further encroachment of his mechanized Utopia.

And now I come straight to the point of the philosophy of through trails. *It is to organize a Barbarian invasion.* It is a counter movement to the Metropolitan invasion. Who are these modern Barbarians? Why, we are—the members of the New England Trail Conference. As the Civilizees are working outward from the urban centers we Barbarians must be working downward from the mountain tops. The backbone of our strategy (in the populous eastern United States) lies on the crestline of the Appalachian Range, the hinterland of the modern "Romes" along the Atlantic coast. This crestline should be captured—and no time lost about it.

From "Outdoor Culture—The Philosophy of Through Trails," by Benton MacKaye, address to the New England Trail Conference, January 1927, in *From Geography to Geotechnics*, University of Illinois, 1968.

JAMES MacGREGOR BURNS

In Sheffield, Massachusetts, the Appalachian Trail runs right past a weathered stone monument commemorating a bloody political uprising in the post–Revolutionary War period. Pulitzer Prize–winning historian James MacGregor Burns, himself a resident of another Massachusetts AT town (Williamstown, where he was a professor of government for many years at Williams College), retells the tale of Daniel Shays's radical rebellion against a crushing tax system that had left many farmers and workers homeless. The story and the monument remind us that at many points along the contemporary trail, we walk in the footsteps of history. Forest that we enjoy today for recreation was used in 1787 by Shays's compatriots, men deep in debt and deeply in fear for their lives, as a hideout.

Shays's Rebellion

WESTERN MASSACHUSETTS, LATE JANUARY 1787. DOWN THE LONG SLOPing shoulders of the Berkshire Mountains they headed west through the bitter night, stumbling over frozen ruts, picking their way around deep drifts of snow. Some carried muskets, others hickory clubs, others nothing. Many wore old Revolutionary War uniforms, now decked out with the sprig of hemlock that marked them as rebels. Careless and cocksure they had been, but now gall and despair hung over them as heavy as the enveloping night. They and hundreds like them were fleeing for their lives, looking for places to hide.

These men were rebels against ex-rebels. Only a few years before, they had been fighting the redcoats at Bunker Hill, joining General Stark in the rout of the enemy at Bennington, helping young Colonel Henry Knox's troops pull fifty tons of cannon and mortars, captured from the British at Ticonderoga, across these same frozen wastes. They had fought in comradeship with men from Boston and other towns in the populous east. All had been revolutionaries together, in a glorious and victorious cause. Now they were fighting their old comrades, dying before their cannon, hunting for cover like animals.

The trouble had been brewing for years. Life had been hard enough during the Revolution, but independence had first brought a flush of prosperity, then worse times than ever. The people and their governments alike struggled under crushing debts. Much of the Revolutionary specie was hopelessly irredeemable. People were still paying for the war through steep taxes. The farmers in central and western Massachusetts felt they had suffered the most, for their farms, cattle, even their plows could be taken for unpaid debts. Some debtors had been thrown into jail and had languished there, while family and friends desperately scrounged for money that could not be found.

Out of the despair and suffering a deep hatred had welled in the broad farms along the Connecticut and the settlements in the Berkshires. Hatred for the sheriffs and other minions of the law who flung neighbors into jail. Hatred for the judges who could sign orders that might wipe out a man's entire property. Hatred for the scheming lawyers who connived in all this, and battened on it. Hatred above all for the rich people in Boston, the merchants and bankers who seemed to control the governor and the state legislature. No single leader mobilized this hatred. Farmers and laborers rallied around local men with names like Job Shattuck, Eli Parsons, Luke Day. Dan Shays emerged as the most visible leader, but the uprising was as natural and indigenous as any peasants' revolt in Europe. The malcontents could not know that history would call them members of "Shays's Rebellion." They called themselves Regulators.

Their tactic was simple: close up the courts. Time and again, during the late summer and early fall of 1786, roughhewn men by the hundreds crowded into or around courthouses, while judges and sheriffs stood by seething and helpless. The authorities feared to call out the local militia, knowing the men would desert in droves. Most of the occupations were peaceful, even jocular and festive, reaching a high point when debtors were turned out of jail. Most of these debtors were proud men, property owners, voters. They had served as soldiers and junior officers in the Revolution. They were seeking to redress grievances, not to topple governments. Some men of substance — doctors, deacons, even judges — backed the Regulators; many poor persons feared the uprisings. But in general, a man's property and source of income placed him on one side or the other. Hence the conflict divided town and country officials, neighbors, even families.

Then, as the weather turned bitter in the late fall, so did the mood of the combatants. The attitude of the authorities shifted from the implacable to the near-hysterical. Alarmists exaggerated the strength of the Regulators. Rumors flew about that Boston or some other eastern town would be attacked. A respectable Bostonian reported that "We are now in a State of anarchy and confusion bordering on a Civil War." Boston propagandists spread reports that British agents in Canada were secretly backing the rebels. So the Regulators were now treasonable as well as illegal. The state suspended habeas corpus and raised an army, but lacking public funds had to turn to local "gentlemen" for loans to finance it. An anonymous dissident responded in kind:

"This is to lett the gentellmen of Boston [know?] that wee Country men will not pay taxes, as the think," he wrote Governor Bowdoin in a crude, scrawling hand. "But Lett them send the Constabel to us and we'll nock him down for ofering to come near us. If you Dont lower the taxes we'll pull down the town house about you ears. It shall not stand long then or else they shall be blood spilt. We country men will not be imposed on. We fought of our Libery as well as you did. . . . "

From *Vineyard of Liberty*, by James MacGregor Burns, Knopf, 1982.

Berkshire County Trail Register Notes

Notes written in trail registers at Springer Mt., Georgia, or at Mt. Katahdin, Maine, justifiably indulge in hyperbole and effusiveness. Why not? Those terminal points of the 2,150-mile-long Appalachian Trail catch hikers at a peak of excitement and/or relief. At quieter, less dramatic points along the way, the trail registers provide outlets for exclamatory remarks by young and old, for the practical note as well as the sweet scribblings of those on an emotional or physical high. It is particularly good to see that children out on the trail are free to express plain facts or true feelings, without fear of the censor's or the teacher's red pencil.

Guy in white van. Your lights were on. Red Nissan has jumper cables. Will be back about 3 p.m. —*Sea & Sky*

I'm hiking with my Dad on a ½ day of school. —Best wishes, *Eric & Glenn from Lee.*

Just got married two days ago and now I am enjoying the beautiful foliage with my new wife. We are looking for the perfect spot to consummate our marriage. —*Aimee & Glen, Ocean Grove, NJ*

I am never, never, never, NEVER doing this again! This has been more of a workout than Jane Fonda for 24 hours straight, but it's been fun. —*Nicole, Monument Mt. High School*

Wet! My pants haven't felt this way since I was a baby. —*Rita*

If you add an 's' to 'Mt. Everett,' then we can say we climbed the highest mountain in the world. *—Adam Selzer, age 8, Stockbridge*

Out for the day. Great views. God is everywhere. —*Pied Piper, Runner of the Woods*

In for a mid-morning break [at a shelter]. Have run out of cynical and elliptical comments. —*Cosmic Limey*

From Appalachian Trail Registers, Berkshire Section, Appalachian Mountain Club, 1993–1995.

DAVID EMBLIDGE

Perhaps it's the presence of astonishing numbers of wildflowers along the Appalachian Trail in the Tyringham Valley of Berkshire County that makes the hike I describe here one of my favorites. Yet it's also the sense that in these meadows and woods echo the voices, now long gone, of the Shakers, a people whose industriousness and spiritual discipline I respect. To some extent my determination to produce The Appalachian Trail Reader *took root on a summer of weekend hikes like this one, none more than an hour from home. This piece is from a series of articles on the AT "in our own backyard" written for the* Berkshire Eagle, *our regional newspaper.*

Hiking beside an Eerie Presence

*I*F YOU LOVE A HIKE THROUGH A UNIVERSE OF WILDFLOWERS AND THE EERIE, if silent, presence of history, then get on board.

Route: Beartown Mt. Rd., Monterey, to Main Rd., Tyringham
Distance: 6.3 miles.
Elevation +/-: About 840 ft. down

The trailhead—north side of Beartown Mt. Rd., on your right as you came in—is actually an inconspicuous AT road crossing in the shady depths of Beartown State Forest, an 11,000-acre spread abundant with wildlife, including exotics such as bobcat, coyote and black bear as well as all the more familiar creatures (deer, fox, beaver, and many birds). The first half mile or more of the Appalachian Trail corridor here, heading northwards, is dominated by running- or beaver-dammed water. Minor acrobatics may be required to keep your boots dry as you skip from rock to log to footbridge to rock.

Soon though you're on slightly higher, level ground, in a mature stand of hemlocks. Then, at a striking convergence of three long, mossy stone walls, you leave the state forest behind. All through the beech and hemlock groves, the muscular stone walls—some perfectly upright, others tumbled by frost heaves—make stoic declarations of borders and delineations, something walled in or walled out by farmers and herdsmen of a century or even two centuries ago. The occasional ancient apple tree (always a domestic plant) signals the likely presence nearby of a cellar hole on an abandoned farmstead, now smothered in moldering needles and leaves. If you fancy yourself an archaeologist, you may want to explore. Hereabouts there's an eerie feeling of trespassing on someone's sacred though dormant land.

Gentle ups and downs and a wide, clear path make for surprisingly quick momentum over the next mile (following the stone wall crossing). If you bend down to re-tie a hiking boot, keep a sharp eye out for a diminutive salamander, most likely the shy red eft, which likes the moist woodlands and is one of few who wander in the daylight. Easy walking, such as you have on the portion of the AT, is an opportunity to pay more attention to the surroundings—rocks, plants and animals—but I remember succumbing once here to another delicious temptation. I experimented with music to accompany my walk: Yo Yo Ma lifted me heavenward on the ascending notes of Bach's unaccompanied cello suites and brought me back to ground on the descending scale. The Walkman is a great toy, but I found that I missed the sounds of birds and wind up above in the trees and the crackling of twigs underfoot, the music I was really out to hear.

At about 2.3 miles you reach the lip of the hill forming the southern side of the Tyringham Valley (800-1,000 ft. below), and here you get your first glimpse, through the hemlocks, of this incomparably pastoral hidden gem, decidedly off the beaten track. Down you go, and quickly now, surrounded by vast expanses of delicate wood ferns, as you clamber amidst the boulders and fallen, twisted trees of a cool, darkened gulch that looks promising for spelunkers (at 2.6 miles). The trail loses considerable altitude here, as you switchback down the southern slope of the valley and soon cross aptly named Fernside Rd. (unpaved; 3.1 miles). From Mt. Wilcox, up and behind you in the state forest, to the valley floor, the AT descends about 1,300 ft. Those with full backpacks or kids in tow will see here why the South-to-North direction is preferable: it avoids this climb.

On a summertime hike here, in these shady, private woods, we once heard someone laughing, downhill ahead of us, not far off the trail. It was a he and a she, entwined upon a blanket, hiking shoes still on but not much else, doing what comes naturally, and we weren't quite sure what etiquette should apply. Somehow, issuing the couple a hearty "How're ya doin?" seemed a bit intrusive. We walked on, more amused than disconcerted.

The guidebook indicates three distinct, if small, brook crossings in the neighborhood of 3.4 miles. You may have trouble identifying all three on the ground, but the trail itself is clear. There is said to be a "scenic waterfall and old homestead foundation" 100 yds. upstream. Wander up brook number one if time allows, and the discovery may be yours . . . , if you're hiking in wet season.

Now and then you'll meet thru-hikers or other somewhat less ambitious types, doing three or four states' worth of the AT, going North to South. When you do run into them, plunge right into conversation. They may look a bit woolly or bedraggled (dress for the AT is nothing like those Ralph Lauren Polo or Timberland ads . . .), but usually they're gregarious. Solo hikers are often especially hungry for a chat.

Here at the three brook crossings, we once met two young AT thru-hikers with slow-as-molasses Georgia drawls that belied the obviously high energy of their 20-miles-per-day pace. We chewed the fat. I tried to keep them talking, for their accent was lyrical to New England ears more accustomed to flattened r's and swallowed vowels. One fellow's boot toe had split open, despite valiant salvaging attempts with glue. He planned to rescue his feet with a new pair of boots when the twosome reached South Egremont (extreme south Berkshire County)—where they also hoped to find mail awaiting them. We recommended Kenver Ltd. for hiking supplies but urged them to reprovision first in more well stocked Great Barrington, and indeed, within 48 hours, I saw them again outside the Price Chopper supermarket on State Rd. in Great Barrington, their shopping cart brimming with dried foods. They were discarding every bit of packaging—to eliminate unnecessary weight, even fractions of ounces—and were transferring everything to zip-close plastic bags.

At 3.7 miles you reach the Tenneco Gas Co. pipeline crossing (a fifty-yard-wide swath) which offers another good overlook, to the north, of the Tyringham Valley: a great lunching spot, and if you're lucky you'll sit amidst freshly mown hay and buzzing bees, drunk with pollen. A sweet sequence of hayfields and wooded sections follows the gasline crossing, leading to Hop Brook (at about 4.1 miles), a Housatonic River tributary. With its sun-dappled twists and turns, and several miniature waterfalls, the brook pleases both eyes and ears. Don't rush through here; saunter, if you can.

Next, the narrow wooden steps of a stile climb over a barbed wire fence (4.3 mi.), bordering the Trustees of Reservations property known as Tyringham Cobble. The trail rises again, easily. In the dark woods—hemlocks, once more—fallen trees are home to extraordinary colonies of lichens. Branching off to the left, in another half mile (at 4.9 mi.), is the side trail to the top of the cobble, a fifteen minute (one-way) walk worth the detour but not counted as part of this hike. If you go up to the top, you'll want to linger, perhaps basking in the sun on the warm, exposed rocks. If you have kids who would love scrambling on the quartz, gneiss and marble that give the cobble its name (or if there's such a kid inside you . . .), by all means go on up. The fine views of the Tyringham Valley you have right here on the AT are measurably better at the top of the hill.

Carrying on, you follow the AT now through a botanist's paradise. Down the far side of the cobble, you cross Jerusalem Rd. and another stile (5.2 mi.) and march out across the valley floor, with Hop Brook always nearby. You swish through asters, Queen Anne's lace, goldenrod, juniper bushes, black raspberry patches, and stands of staghorn sumac while following hedgerows along narrow but generally stable bog bridges (one log wide) over squishy fields. If you have brought a wildflower or tree identification book along on this hike, you'll be flipping from pictures to index and back again frequently during this stretch. Wild thyme, often underfoot here, willingly yields its soothing perfume.

The hike climaxes at a striking wooden bridge over Hop Brook (6.2 mi.) that affords a summarizing view of all the colors in the palette of the cobble and low-lying fields of both wild and agricultural Tyringham. It's just .1 mile from the bridge to Tyringham Main Rd., your destination, but, in another sense, if you have surrendered by now to the beauty of this valley, you will have already arrived, not quite at your car but definitely in heaven. No matter the season, and almost no matter the weather, this enthusiasm still holds.

My friend Miriam drank it all in and resolved on the spot to return here as a little old lady to be a witch who spends her days making potions from the myriad wildflowers and herbs. And her nights, I asked? She said, "Well, of course, there'll be cable TV!"

From "Hiking Beside an Eerie Presence," by David Emblidge, *Berkshires Week, Berkshire Eagle,* June 25, 1993.

RICHARD WILBUR

U.S. Poet Laureate (1987–88), National Book Award winner (1957), and Pulitzer Prize winner (1957, 1989) Richard Wilbur lives just a few miles east of the Appalachian Trail in the Berkshire hill town of Cummington. Lines from a haunting poem by Wilbur evoke the spirit of what are today lovely but functionless deep woods boundaries: abandoned stone walls. Fellow Berkshirite Herman Melville commented a hundred years earlier that "the very Titans seemed to have been at work" building the crisscrossed web of New England stone walls.

From "A Wall in the Woods: Cummington"

What is it for, now that dividing neither
Farm from farm nor field from field, it runs
Through deep impartial woods, and is transgressed
By boughs of pine or beech from either side?
Under that woven tester, buried here
Or there in laurel-patch or shrouding vine,
It is for grief at what has come to nothing,
What even in this hush is scarcely heard —
Whipcrack, the ox's lunge, the stoneboat's grating,
Work-shouts of young men stooped before their time
Who in their stubborn heads foresaw forever
The rose of apples and the blue of rye.
It is for pride, as well, in pride that built

With levers, tackle, and abraded hands
What two whole centuries have not brought down.
Look how with shims they made the stones weigh inward,
Binding the water-rounded with the flat;
How to a small ravine they somehow lugged
A long, smooth girder of a rock, on which
To launch their wall in air, and overpass
The narrow stream that still slips under it.
Rosettes of lichen decorate their toils,
Who labored here like Pharaoh's Israelites;
Whose grandsons left for Canaans in the west.
Except to prompt a fit of elegy
It is for us no more, or if it is,
It is a sort of music for the eye,
A rugged ground-bass like the bagpipe's drone
On which the leaf-light like a chanter plays.

From "A Wall in the Woods: Cummington," by Richard Wilbur, *The New Yorker*.

RONALD FISHER

Appalachian Trail fame can come to those who walk the entire trail or to those who barely walk it at all but who give of themselves in remarkable ways to passersby who log the miles. Genevieve Hutchinson of Washington, Massachusetts, an AT town, was such a heroine (she died in 1974 at age ninety). Her generosity and quiet wisdom, shared with countless thru-hikers, are Ronald Fisher's subject here. The serendipitous presence of good Samaritans along the trail has redeemed many a difficult day for hikers whose energy, food, water, or spirits were running low.

On Genevieve Hutchinson

BEFORE LEAVING MASSACHUSETTS WE VISITED MRS. FRED W. HUTCHINSON, surely one of the state's most gracious citizens. Mrs. Hutchinson's home in the town of Washington is half a mile from a lean-to in the October Mountain State Forest, and she is mentioned in the trail guidebook: "Brook in rear of lean-to unsafe for drinking; obtain spring water from Mrs. Hutchinson's home 0.67 m. north."

The two-story frame house is very old, and sits beside what was once a route of the Boston-Albany Turnpike. A porch runs the length of the front of the house, which served turnpike travelers as a station for changing horses.

A small plaque near the front door reads *1811.* "That's not right," said Mrs. Hutchinson. "That's just the earliest record."

With a no-nonsense cordiality she hurried us into her parlor, out of the chill autumn weather. The flames snapped and danced hospitably behind the glass front of the pot-bellied wood stove. Lace curtains bordered the windows, and family photographs and watercolors of wild flowers—painted by Mrs. Hutchinson—hung on the walls. It was a cozy, delightfully pleasant room.

When she had served us coffee and cookies, Mrs. Hutchinson showed us the scrapbook and register she has been keeping since 1938. Hikers who stop for water are asked to sign the register, and those attempting the entire trail get a red star. The scrapbook held postcards, letters, clippings, and photographs, many picturing her with pack-laden hikers. "I don't see how anybody who lives along the trail can fail to be grateful for it," she said as she recalled the friends who had first come to her door as strangers. "It is a privilege to meet people with eyes to see beauty."

We had arrived at Mrs. Hutchinson's home because of a misunderstanding; we had incorrectly interpreted an entry in the guidebook to mean that hikers could find accommodations at Washington's town hall, and that Mrs. Hutchinson was the person to see about such arrangement.

"Oh, no," she said, "my, no. That's wrong." Not only was the old town hall not a hostel, but the Sons and Daughters of Washington had only recently succeeded in saving it from destruction and were beginning to restore it. Already they had given it a new coat of paint. She was pleased that they had been able in this case to foil "the modern mania" for tearing down old buildings. "If the wind takes it down, so be it," she said, "but let us not be the wind."

After some hesitation, Mrs. Hutchinson agreed to read to us from a memoir she had written called "Home on the Trail."

"It's not for publication," she explained, "not even for quotation. It's for my family, so they'll know what it has meant to me to live here on the Trail." In a low, steady voice, she read to us of the joys and trials of rearing a large and active family; of her husband, who had been dean of engineering at a branch of Northeastern University; of sons who had gone off to war; of hikers who had stopped for water and had become lifelong friends.

Hearing her account was a lovely and moving experience. It provided one of our fondest memories of the entire journey.

Had Mrs. Hutchinson ever hiked any of the trail?

"Just once," she smiled. "And then I wasn't really hiking. Just picking wild flowers on Bald Mountain."

As we took our leave, Mrs. Hutchinson followed us out onto the lawn and gazed affectionately and thoughtfully at her home.

"It will not last forever," she said. "Any more than I will. Or you. Or anyone else."

From *The Appalachian Trail*, by Ronald Fisher, National Geographic Society, 1972.

HERMAN MELVILLE

Pierre *was among the novels Melville wrote during his Berkshire years at the farm called Arrowhead, in Pittsfield, Massachusetts. Visitors to Arrowhead today (it's on the National Register of Historic Places) can enjoy the same view Melville had from his second-floor study, looking north to the massive humpbacked presence of Mt. Greylock, highest mountain in southern New England. Melville spent many a brooding hour locked in this room, in a struggle with the forces of darkness and light, as his masterpiece* Moby Dick *took shape. He saw in the mountain's outline and hoary summit a strong suggestion of the great white whale itself. No wonder that he later dedicated an entire book to it, though by that time his mood had brightened and his style was deliberately mock-heroic. We think Melville would have been pleased that Greylock has become the jewel in the crown of Massachusetts parks, for he, too, was a hiker and climber whose Berkshire ramblings included an ascent of Greylock along paths near today's Appalachian Trail.*

To Greylock's Most Excellent Majesty

*I*N OLD TIMES AUTHORS WERE PROUD OF THE PRIVILEGE OF DEDICATING THEIR works to Majesty. A right noble custom, which we of Berkshire must revive. For whether we will or no, Majesty is all around us here in Berkshire, sitting as in a Grand Congress of Vienna of majestical hill-tops, and eternally challenging our homage.

But since the majestic mountain, Greylock—my own more immediate sovereign lord and king—hath now, for innumerable ages, been the one grand dedicatee of the earliest rays of all the Berkshire mornings, I know not how his Imperial Purple Majesty (royal-born: Porphyrogenitus) will receive the dedication of my own poor solitary ray.

Nevertheless, forasmuch as I, dwelling with my loyal neighbors, the Maples and the Beeches, in the amphitheatre over which his central majesty presides, have received his most bounteous and unstinted fertilizations, it is but meet, that I here devoutly kneel, and render up my gratitude, whether, thereto, The Most Excellent Purple Majesty of Greylock benignantly incline his hoary crown or no.

From Dedication to *Pierre,* by Herman Melville, 1852.

HENRY DAVID THOREAU

Thoreau lectured at numerous lyceums on the subject of walking, its pur-
poses and benefits, and his viewpoint must have sometimes struck his audi-
ence of practical-minded Yankees as bizarre. In a journal entry of November
1858 he wrote, "I know of but one or two persons with whom I can afford to
walk. With most the walk degenerates into a more vigorous use of your legs,
ludicrously purposeless, while you are discussing some mighty argument . . . ,
spoiling each other's day." He yearned instead for a "silent but sympathiz-
ing companion." On a long walk ten years earlier, Thoreau had had the per-
fect companion—himself—although his thoughts at the time may have been
troubled, with a failed romance and financial worries dogging him as he rambled
across northern Massachusetts toward a rendezvous with Mt. Greylock.

Primed he was, then, for an ecstatic experience to blow away the interior
clouds. Thoreau got his wish and made the most of it in the moment, and
later in the book that recorded this journey. The story of his night alone on
the summit of Greylock, right where the Appalachian Trail crosses the moun-
tain today, is one of the most rhapsodic passages in American literature on
the subject of wilderness and spirit.

Alone on Greylock's Summit

I HAD COME OVER THE HILLS ON FOOT AND ALONE IN SERENE SUMMER DAYS, plucking the raspberries by the wayside, and occasionally buying a loaf of bread at a farmer's house, with a knapsack on my back which held a few traveler's books and a change of clothing, and a staff in my hand. I had that morning looked down from the Hoosack Mountain, where the road crosses it, on the village of North Adams in the valley three miles away under my feet, showing how uneven the earth may sometimes be, and mak-ing it seem an accident that it should ever be level and convenient for the feet of man. Putting a little rice and sugar and a tin cup into my knapsack at this village, I began in the afternoon to ascend the mountain, whose summit is three thousand six hundred feet above the level of the sea, and was seven or eight miles distant by the path. My route lay up a long and spacious valley called the Bellows, because the winds rush up or down it with vio-lence in storms, sloping up to the very clouds between the principal range and a lower mountain. There were a few farms scattered along at different elevations, each commanding a fine prospect of the mountains to the north, and a stream ran down the middle of the valley, on which, near the head, there was a mill. It seemed a road for the pilgrim to enter upon who would climb to the gates of heaven. Now I crossed a hayfield, and now over the brook on a slight bridge, still gradually ascending all the while with a sort of awe, and filled with indefinite expectations as to what kind of inhabitants and what kind of nature I should come to at last. It now seemed some advantage that the earth was uneven, for one could not imagine a more noble position for a farmhouse than this vale afforded, farther from or nearer to its head, from a glenlike seclusion overlooking the country at a great elevation between these two mountain walls.

It reminded me of the homesteads of the Huguenots, on Staten Island, off the coast of New Jersey. The hills in the interior of this island, though comparatively low, are penetrated in various directions by similar sloping valleys on a humble scale, gradually narrowing and rising to the centre, and at the head of these the Huguenots, who were the first settlers, placed their houses quite within the land, in rural and sheltered places, in leafy recesses where the breeze played with the poplar and the gum-tree, from which, with equal security in calm and storm, they looked out through a widening vista, over miles of forest and stretching salt marsh, to the Huguenot's Tree, an old elm on the shore, at whose root they had landed, and across the spacious outer bay of New York to Sandy Hook and the Highlands of Neversink, and thence over leagues of the Atlantic, perchance to some faint vessel in the horizon, almost a day's sail on her voyage to that Europe whence they had come. When walking in the interior there, in the midst of rural scenery, where there was as little to remind me of the ocean as amid the New Hampshire hills, I have suddenly, through a gap, a cleft or 'clove road,' as the Dutch settlers called it, caught sight of a ship under full sail, over a field of corn, twenty or thirty miles at sea. The effect was similar, since I had no means of measuring distances, to seeing a painted ship passed backwards and forwards through a magic lantern.

But to return to the mountain. It seemed as if he must be the most singular and heavenly-minded man whose dwelling stood highest up the valley. The thunder had rumbled at my heels all the way, but the shower passed off in another direction, though if it had not, I half believed that I should get above it. I at length reached the last house but one, where the path to the summit diverged to the right, while the summit itself rose directly in front. But I determined to follow up the valley to its head, and then find my own route up the steep as the shorter and more adventurous way. I had thoughts of returning to this house, which was well kept and so nobly placed, the next day, and perhaps remaining a week there, if I could have entertainment. Its mistress was a frank and hospitable young woman, who stood before me in a dishabille, busily and unconcernedly combing her long black hair while she talked, giving her head the necessary toss with each sweep of the comb, with lively, sparkling eyes, and full of interest in that lower world from which I had come, talking all the while as familiarly as if she had known me for years, and reminding me of a cousin of mine. She at first had taken me for a student from Williamstown, for they went by in parties, she said, either riding or walking, almost every pleasant day, and were a pretty wild set of fellows; but they never went by the way I was going. As I passed the last house, a man called out to know what I had to sell, for, seeing my knapsack, he thought that I might be a peddler who was taking this unusual route over the ridge of the valley into South Adams. He told me that it was still four or five miles to the summit by the path which I had left, though not more than two in a straight line from where I was, but that nobody ever went this way; there was no path, and I should find it as steep as the roof of a house. But I knew that I was more used to woods and mountains than he, and went along through his cow-yard, while he, looking at the sun, shouted after me that I should not get to the top that night. I soon reached the head of the valley, but as I could not see the summit from this point, I ascended a low mountain on the opposite side, and took its bearing with my compass. I at once entered the woods, and began to climb the steep side of the mountain in a diagonal direction, taking the bearing of a tree every dozen rods. The ascent was by no means difficult or unpleasant, and occupied much less time than it would have taken to follow the path. Even country people, I have observed, magnify the difficulty of traveling in the forest, and especially among mountains. They seem to lack their usual common sense in this. I have climbed several higher mountains without guide or path, and have found, as might be expected, that it takes only more time and patience commonly than to travel the smoothest highway. It is very rare that you meet with obstacles in this world which the humblest man has not faculties to surmount. It is true we may come to a perpendicular precipice, but we need not jump off, nor run our heads against it. A man may jump down his own cellar stairs, or dash his brains out against his chimney, if he is mad. So far as my experience goes, travelers generally exaggerate the difficulties of the way. Like most evil, the difficulty is imaginary; for what's the hurry? If a person lost would conclude that after all he is not lost, he is not beside himself, but standing in his own old shoes on the very spot where he is, and that for the time being he will live there; but the places that have known him, *they* are lost — how much anxiety and danger would vanish. I am not alone if I stand by myself. Who knows where in space this globe is rolling? Yet we will not give ourselves up for lost, let it go where it will.

I made my way steadily upward in a straight line, through a dense undergrowth of mountain laurel, until the trees began to have a scraggy and infernal look, as if contending with frost goblins, and at length I reached the summit, just as the sun was setting. Several acres here had been cleared, and were covered with rocks and stumps, and there was a rude observatory in the middle which overlooked the woods. I had one fair view of the country before the sun went down, but I was too thirsty to waste any light in viewing the prospect, and set out directly to find water. First, going down a well-beaten path for half a mile through the low, scrubby wood, till I came to where the water stood in the tracks of the horses which had carried travelers up, I lay down flat, and drank these dry, one after another, a pure, cold, spring-like water, but yet I could not fill my dipper, though I contrived little siphons of grass stems, and ingenious aqueducts on a small scale; it was too slow a process. Then, remembering that I had passed a moist place near the top, on my way up, I returned to find it again, and here, with sharp stones and my hands, in the twilight, I made a well about two feet deep, which was soon filled with pure cold water, and the birds too came and drank at it. So I filled my dipper, and, making my way back to the observatory, collected some dry sticks, and made a fire on some flat stones which had been placed on the floor for that purpose, and so I soon cooked my supper of rice, having already whittled a wooden spoon to eat it with.

I sat up during the evening, reading by the light of the fire the scraps of newspapers in which some party had wrapped their luncheon — the prices current in New York and Boston, the advertisements, and the singular editorials which some had seen fit to publish, not foreseeing under what critical circumstances they would be read. I read these things at a vast advantage there, and it seemed to me that the advertisements, or what is called the business part of a paper, were greatly the best, the most useful, natural, and respectable. Almost all the opinions and sentiments expressed were so little considered, so shallow and flimsy, that I thought the very texture of the paper must be weaker in that part and tear the more easily. The advertisements and the prices current were more closely allied to nature, and were respectable in some measure as tide and meteorological tables are; but the reading-matter, which I remembered was most prized down below, unless it was some humble record of science, or an extract from some old classic, struck me as strangely whimsical, and crude, and one-idea'd, like a school-boy's theme, such as youths write and after burn. The opinions were of that kind that are doomed to wear a different aspect tomorrow, like last year's fashions; as if mankind were very green indeed, and would be ashamed of themselves in a few years, when they had outgrown this verdant period. There was, moreover, a singular disposition to wit and humor, but rarely the slightest real success; and the apparent success was a terrible satire on the attempt; the Evil Genius of man laughed the loudest at his best jokes. The advertisements, as I have said, such as were serious, and not of the modern quack kind, suggested pleasing and poetic thoughts; for commerce is really as interesting as nature. The very names of the commodities were poetic, and as suggestive as if they had been inserted in a pleasing poem — Lumber, Cotton, Sugar, Hides, Guano, Logwood. Some sober, private, and original thought would have been grateful to read there, and as much in harmony with the circumstances as if it had been written on a mountain-top; for it is of a fashion which never changes, and as respectable as hides and logwood, or any natural product. What an inestimable companion such a scrap of paper would have been, containing some fruit of a mature life! What a relic! What a recipe! It seemed a divine invention, by which not mere shining coin, but shining and current thoughts, could be brought up and left there.

As it was cold, I collected quite a pile of wood and lay down on a board against the side of the building, not having any blanket to cover me, with my head to the fire, that I might look after it, which is not the Indian rule. But as it grew colder towards midnight, I at length encased myself completely in boards, managing even to put a board on top of me, with a large stone on it, to keep it down, and so slept comfortably. I was reminded, it is true, of the Irish children, who inquired what their neighbors did who had no door to put over them in winter nights as they had; but I am convinced that there was nothing very strange in the inquiry. Those who have never tried it can have no idea how far a door, which keeps the single blanket down, may go toward making one comfortable. We are constituted a good deal like chickens, which, taken from the hen, and put in a basket of cotton in the chimney-corner, will often peep till they die, nevertheless; but if you put in a book, or anything heavy, which will press down the cotton, and feel like the hen, they go to sleep directly. My only companions were the mice, which came to pick up the crumbs that had been left in those scraps of paper; still, as everywhere, pensioners on man, and not unwisely improving this elevated tract for their habitation. They nibbled what was for them; I nibbled what was for me. Once or twice in the night, when I looked up, I saw a white cloud drifting through the windows and filling the whole upper story.

This observatory was a building of considerable size, erected by the students of Williamstown College, whose buildings might be seen by daylight gleaming far down in the valley. It would be no small advantage if every college were thus located at the base of a mountain, as good at least as one well-endowed professorship. It were as well to be educated in the shadow of a mountain as in more classical shades. Some will remember, no doubt, not only that they went to the college, but that they went to the mountain. Every visit to its summit would, as it were, generalize the particular information gained below, and subject it to more catholic tests.

I was up early and perched upon the top of this tower to see the daybreak, for some time reading the names that had been engraved there, before I could distinguish more distant objects. An 'untamable fly' buzzed at my elbow with the same nonchalance as on a molasses hogshead at the end of Long Wharf. Even there I must attend to his stale humdrum. But now I come to the pith of this long digression. As the light increased, I discovered around me an ocean of mist, which by chance reached up exactly to the base of the tower, and shut out every vestige of the earth, while I was left floating on this fragment of the wreck of a world, on my carved plank, in cloudland; a situation which required no aid from the imagination to render it impressive. As the light in the east steadily increased, it revealed to me more clearly the new world into which I had risen in the night, the new *terra firma* perchance of my future life. There was not a crevice left through which the trivial places we name Massachusetts or Vermont or New York could be seen, while I still inhaled the clear atmosphere of a July morning — if it were July there. All around beneath me was spread for a hundred miles on every side, as far as the eye could reach, an undulating country of clouds, answering in the varied swell of its surface to the terrestrial world it veiled. It was such a country as we might see in dreams, with all the delights of paradise. There were immense snowy pastures, apparently smooth shaven and firm, and shady vales between the vaporous mountains; and far in the horizon I could see where some luxurious misty timber jutted into the prairie, and trace the windings of a watercourse, some unimagined Amazon or Orinoko, by the misty trees on its brink. As there was wanting the symbol, so there was not the substance of impurity, no spot nor stain. It was a favor for which to be forever silent to be shown this vision. The earth beneath had become such a flitting thing of lights and shadows as the clouds had been before. It was not merely veiled to me, but it had passed away like the phantom of a shadow, *skias onar,* and this new platform was gained. As I had climbed above storm and cloud, so by successive days' journeys I might reach the region of eternal day, beyond the tapering shadow of the earth; ay,

> "Heaven itself shall slide,
> And roll away like melting stars that glide
> Along their oily threads."

But when its own sun began to rise on this pure world, I found myself a dweller in the dazzling halls of Aurora, into which poets have had but a partial glance over the eastern hills, drifting amid the saffron-colored clouds, and playing with the rosy fingers of the Dawn, in the very path of the Sun's chariot, and sprinkled with its dewy dust, enjoying the benignant smile, and near at hand the far-darting glances of the god. The inhabitants of earth behold commonly but the dark and shadowy under side of heaven's pavement; it is only when seen at a favorable angle in the horizon, morning or evening, that some faint streaks of the rich lining of the clouds are revealed. But my muse would fail to convey an impression of the gorgeous tapestry by which I was surrounded, such as men see faintly reflected afar off in the chambers of the east. Here, as on earth, I saw the gracious god

> "Flatter the mountain-tops with sovereign eye,
> Gilding pale streams with heavenly alchemy."

But never here did 'Heaven's sun' stain himself.

But, alas, owing, as I think, to some unworthiness in myself, my private sun did stain himself, and

> "Anon permit the basest clouds to ride
> With ugly wrack on his celestial face" —

and embraced my wavering virtue, or rather I sank down again into that 'forlorn world,' from which the celestial sun had hid his visage,

> "How may a worm that crawls along the dust,
> Clamber the azure mountains, thrown so high,
> And fetch from thence thy fair idea just,
> That in those sunny courts doth hidden lie,
> Clothed with such light as blinds the angel's eye?
>> How may weak mortal ever hope to file
>> His unsmooth tongue, and his deprostrate style?
> Oh, raise thou from his corse thy now entombed exile!"

In the preceding evening I had seen the summits of new and yet higher mountains, the Catskills, by which I might hope to climb to heaven again, and had set my compass for a fair lake in the southwest, which lay in my way, for which I now steered, descending the mountain by my own route, on the side opposite to that by which I had ascended, and soon found myself in the region of cloud and drizzling rain, and the inhabitants affirmed that it had been a cloudy and drizzling day wholly.

From *A Week on the Concord and Merrimack Rivers,* by Henry David Thoreau, 1849.

VERMONT

Stratton Pond, at Stratton Mt., southern Vermont.

Trail miles: 146

Trail maintenance: Green Mt. Club, Dartmouth Outing Club

Highest point: Killington Peak, 4,241 ft. (trail bypasses summit)

Broadest river: Connecticut (shared with New Hampshire)

Features: The Long Trail, completed in 1931 (Massachusetts to Canada), contiguous with the AT for about 100 miles from Massachusetts to Sherburne Pass in central Vermont. Vast forests, lovely villages, lofty peaks, some offering hikers off-season ski lift rides into the valleys below.

Parks, forests, and nature preserves: Green Mt. National Forest, Hapgood State Forest, Calvin Coolidge State Forest, Gifford Woods State Park

Most intriguing name on the trail: Maine Junction

Trail towns: Manchester Center, Peru, Wallingford, Woodstock, Norwich

WILLIAM HAVILAND & MARJORY POWER

Appalachian Trail hikers walking the ridges of Vermont's Green Mountains are treated to tantalizing glimpses of distant rolling fields rich with the queen of the late-summer harvest: sweet corn. The corn plant was unknown to Europeans until early Spanish explorers brought its seeds home as a gift from the native peoples of America. The Appalachian Trail meanders through forest that was the hunting ground of the Abenaki people, who lived in present-day Vermont, Maine, and Quebec. Their culture was rich with legends, including this one about the silken hair on the ripening cornstalk.

Corn Legend

A LONG TIME AGO, WHEN INDIANS WERE FIRST MADE, THERE LIVED ONE alone, far, far from any others. He knew not of fire, and subsisted on roots, barks, and nuts. This Indian became very lonesome for company. He grew tired of digging roots, lost his appetite, and for several days lay dreaming in the sunshine; when he awoke he saw something standing near, at which, at first, he was very much frightened. But when it spoke, his heart was glad, for it was a beautiful woman with long light hair, very unlike any Indian. He asked her to come to him, but she would not, and if he tried to approach her she seemed to go farther away; he sang to her of his loneliness and besought her not to leave him; at last she told him, if he would do just as she should say, he would always have her with him. He promised that he would.

She led him to where there was some very dry grass, told him to get two very dry sticks, rub them together quickly, holding them in the grass. Soon a spark flew out; the grass caught it, and quick as an arrow the ground was burned over. Then she said, "When the sun sets, take me by the hair and drag me over the burned ground." He did not like to do this, but she told him that wherever he dragged her something like grass would spring up, and he would see her hair coming from between the leaves; then the seeds would be ready for his use. He did as she said, and to this day, when they see the silk (hair) on the cornstalk, the Indians know she has not forgotten them.

From *The Original Vermonters: Native Inhabitants, Past and Present,* by William Haviland and Marjory Power, University Press of New England, 1994.

ROBERT FROST

In an unusual reversal of the American pattern, four-time Pulitzer Prize–winning poet Robert Frost (1874–1963), a native of San Francisco, went east to find himself, not west. His adopted northern New England was so intimately a part of his poetry that most readers took him for a native Vermonter or New Hampshirite. Frost spent periods in both states, situating himself always with a view of the mountains. He knew the wild woods as well as the domestic garden, and although sometimes his poetry is brooding, his dry sense of humor can generate delightful rhymes. Whether Frost ever hiked on the AT we do not know. His poem "The Bear," however, describes a scene that any AT hiker who spies this shy creature will recognize.

From "The Bear"

The bear puts both arms around the tree above her
And draws it down as if it were a lover
And its choke cherries lips to kiss good-bye,
Then lets it snap back upright in the sky.
Her next step rocks a boulder on the wall
(She's making her cross country in the fall).
Her great weight creaks the barbed wire in its staples
As she flings over and off down through the maples,
Leaving on one wire tooth a lock of hair.
Such is the uncaged progress of the bear.
The world has room to make a bear feel free;
The universe seems cramped to you and me.

From "The Bear," in *The Poetry of Robert Frost*, Henry Holt, 1928, 1969.

MICHAEL FROME

In a fascinating book whose title alludes to a Robert Frost poem ("Stopping by Woods on a Snowy Evening"), Michael Frome tackles the huge subject of the National Forests. Much of the Appalachian Trail in Vermont runs through Green Mountain National Forest, a heavily used but nonetheless largely wild area dense with a variety of plant life. Frome takes us on a stimulating guided tour of the northern forest's ecosystem.

The Tree and the Forest

THE GREATEST LYRICIST OF TREES, AND PROBABLY OF FORESTS, TOO, WAS NOT Joyce Kilmer but John Muir, who showed that appreciation of trees, like love, ambition and literature, is a thoroughly individual experience. Once he climbed a tree in the heart of California's forestland. It was in the midst of a windstorm and he described it so:

"The winds go to every tree, fingering every leaf and branch and furrowed bole; not one is forgotten; the Mountain Pine towering with outstretched arms on the rugged buttresses of the icy peaks, the lowliest and most retiring tenant of the dells; they seek and find them all, caressing them tenderly, bending them in lusty exercise, stimulating their growth, plucking off a leaf or limb as required, or removing an entire tree or grove, now whispering and cooing through the branches like a sleepy child, now roaring like the ocean; the winds blessing the forests, the forests the winds, with ineffable beauty and harmony as the sure result.

"We all travel the milky way together, trees and men; but it never occurred to me until this storm-day, while swinging in the wind, that trees are travelers, in the ordinary sense. They make many journeys, not extensive ones, it is true; but our own little journeys, away and back again, are only little more than tree-wavings—many of them not so much."

Anyone falling under the spell of this picture is likely to look for expressions of spirit in trees, which he may not quite find. For example, the procreation of trees bears a degree of similarity to the procreation of animals, even of human beings; that is, through the fertilization by a sperm of an egg in a female ovary. If this is so, and sex in humans reflects a psychic impulse, could it not be so in a tree? Alas, no. The biologist will explain that the tree, even though it is king of the world of plants, stands below the stage of development of the lowest animal. Our tree cannot move to water or shelter. It has no nervous system. It reacts unconsciously and unvarying to stimulus, the process known in botany as tropism.

Nevertheless the tree breathes, drinks water, nourishes itself and transmits qualities of heredity through reproduction. The tree and the forest around it fulfill wonderful natural functions beyond our capability. Moreover, they depict the sweep of evolution, spanning hundreds of millions of years of life on earth.

The forest is a community, or a whole complex of communities, in which millions of living creatures struggle for water, sunlight, soil nourishment, space in which to grow. Some survive as parasites and bandits. Some grow because others die, decay and decompose. The blight of one can be the blessing of another. Others benefit through co-operation or partnership, such as that between the fungus and alga in a lichen, or the tree and fungi whose vegetative portion becomes associated with the roots. Insects and animals benefit plants by carrying pollen. For man's part, the forester and wildlife manager benefit the trees and animals they cultivate and protect.

The lowest forest community is composed of the organisms of the soil: earthworms, ants, termites, bacteria, fungi and simple plant forms which do not contain chlorophyll. Above them are the world of liverworts, living on soil, rock, decaying wood or the bark of trees, mushrooms, moss, and fern, plants with roots, stems and green leaves that provide a nesting place for birds and food for higher animals like deer. Ferns are among the real enchanters of the forest, growing in 9000 varieties, including tree ferns with immense, lacy leaves such as you will see in the Rain Forest of Puerto Rico. Then the higher level of the plant kingdom, wildflowers and shrubs, capable of producing seeds, interplayed with bees, insects and rodents. Finally, the trees which furnish cover and food for the larger animals. In an area where fire has taken place you can see this whole process of plant succession, from the ground up.

Trees feed on materials from the forest soil and air. Within tiny cells of their leaves the green pigmentation called chlorophyll absorbs the light waves or energy of the sun. Through the magic process of photosynthesis this energy is combined with carbon dioxide breathed from the air and water drawn through the roots to produce nourishment and growth. It manufactures glucose, a simple sugar, and subsequently carbohydrates. These in turn combine with nitrogen to form more complex foods, which are transported throughout the tree. Then, as we release carbon dioxide in our breathing, the tree "exhales" oxygen as the by-product of carbon dioxide and water vapor; in producing glucose with the use of oxygen, it releases carbon dioxide and water vapor. How magic a process is photosynthesis! After a century and a half of study, science has yet to understand the exact process, let alone duplicate it—the only way in the world to manufacture carbohydrates. Thus far we have learned to compound chlorophyll. The next step would be a historic break-through in biology.

Tree growth is one of the few phenomena on the planet that successfully counter gravity. Roots go down and outward in the soil, but as the forest tree turns to the light it reaches ever *upward* so that leaves can synthesize food. Leafy crowns fill the space overhead, forming the "overstory" of the forest. Ideally, lower branches, shut off from sunlight, die and drop off. Through this self-pruning, the mature tree develops with a long clean trunk, by all odds best for timber purposes, and attractive to the eye.

Openings in the forest are often filled with little trees shooting up from the ground or sprouting from the stumps of old trees which have died or been cut. Some outstrip their companions and reach the sunlight first. Others lag; they become "suppressed" trees, and unless a fortunate break-through design of nature or forest management gives them more light and growing space they will develop unhealthy and crooked, perhaps die out altogether. Thus from beginning to end the life of a tree is a struggle for sun.

Although trees make demands on the soil, they also help to enrich it. The litter, or duff, on the forest floor is composed of fallen leaves, needles, branches, dead tree trunks and other plant remains. Through weathering and the interplay of insects and fungi, they decay and decompose into humus. Humus loosens compact soil—it is soil, providing the porous quality that opens the way for air and water, the elements vital for plant growth. And it combines with the interlacing roots of trees and other plants to influence the flow of streams.

Trees show their growth and age through the addition each year of a coat of new wood cells between the outside layer of the sapwood and the inner bark. This is the all-important cambium layer, through which water passes from roots to crown. You may admire a tree for *all* its magnificence, but only the leaves and cambium layer are alive; the center, or heartwood, is as dead as lumber at the mill. The cambium layer continues dying, reforming new wood on the inner side and new bark on the outer side, and being born anew. The layer it develops is the annual ring, which, once established never changes in size or place. This is detectable by using an increment borer, a kind of corkscrew that digs into the center of the tree and brings forth a slender sliver. Sometimes a scrawny little fellow, looking like a young tree, especially to the untrained eye, proves to be an old-timer with annual rings close together; a case of growing on poor soil or of a stunting disease somewhere in its lifetime.

All trees bear flowers, some with petals and some without, hardly looking flowery at all, as part of the process of reproduction. Most bloom in the spring, the season of romance, or at least of creation, in the forest, when pollen has ripened and its sac ruptures. Flowers are purposefully showy: to attract insects that carry pollen from male to female, and gather nectar or deposit their eggs within the flower at the same time. Other pollen is borne by the wind, alighting on the female stigma and moving into and fertilizing the ovule.

The net result in due time is a seed-bearing fruit. Some trees mature their seeds rapidly and scatter them early in the growing season. Others, like the nut trees, prepare them slowly for fall sowing. Red oaks and most pines take two years to ripen their seeds. The seed in pine is contained between the scales of its fruit—the cone. But in some species of pine the cones remain closed indefinitely. The seeds are freed only by decay of the cone, or a scorching fire, or by a hungry animal looking for food. Seeds of most conifers and other trees like the American elm are light and may ride the winds hundreds of miles from home before coming to rest. Maple seeds are heavier and do not wander from their parents. Nuts, acorns and berries are plucked and eaten by birds and animals but in many cases still reach their way remarkably and safely into the soil via the digestive system. Seeds of walnut, hickory and oak are carried off by squirrels and germinate where they are hidden if the squirrel doesn't eat them first. Most trees produce seed by the thousands, but chances are only one will take root and in its turn bear seed.

There are many hundreds of kinds of trees, divided into families, then subdivided into genera, and again subdivided into species. The oldest tree family is the conifer, which grew abundantly over the earth in the Jurassic Age, 175,000,000 years ago, and which retains a simple floral structure. More than 100 species of conifer, the needle-leaved cone bearer, also called softwood or evergreen, grow in the United States, including pines, firs, spruces, hemlocks, junipers. Conifers are the main strength of America's timber resources, comprising four-fifths of the large, saw-timber trees.

The largest tree family in the United States, the deciduous, also known as hardwood or broadleaf, include oaks, maples, sycamores, elms, all told about 650 species. Within these families are rule-breaking exceptions. Conifers with hard wood (southern pine). Deciduous trees with evergreen leaves (holly, live oak, sonic magnolias). Conifers which shed their leaves (larch and bald cypress). Douglas-fir, which is not a fir at all. The mixed-up yew, with coniferlike leaves but a berry instead of cone as its fruit.

Then there are the trees of the tropic and desert forests, the palm, yucca and cacti, some without a true cambium layer and others without leaves.

Trees, plants and animals group themselves by environment and react individually to it. If aspen and Englemann spruce were planted on the same plot, aspen might grow one foot in diameter while the spruce grew three inches, but the aspen would live fifty or seventy years while the spruce might live 300 years or longer. Aspen and cottonwood require full sunlight; they come in following fire, then are overtaken by other trees which are shade tolerant in growth and finally outdistance them. These are the "climax trees," which become dominant when a forest is left to natural progression. Douglas-fir may grow on one slope but not on a facing slope, for it is another tree requiring full sunlight. In the desert, where there is plenty of sunlight but not much water, cacti withstand drought by storing water and shedding leaves, if they have any, in dry periods to reduce transpiration, or exhaling. Water is one of the decisive factors in determining which tree grows where. In National Forests of the Southwest, for instance, within two hours you can drive from the desert floor to the subalpine life zone at 7000 feet and on the way pass through a piñon, juniper and chaparral area, with ten to twenty inches of annual precipitation ponderosa-pine area with twenty to twenty-eight inches of precipitation, and finally mixed spruce, fir and aspen area, about thirty inches of precipitation. There are other important environmental factors: temperature, light and wind, all related to climate; and factors relating to soil, physical and chemical composition, slope, drainage and water.

The modern forester strives to understand all of these. The goal in his managed forest is a healthy, growing environment for man, plant and animal. Timber cutting is a tool toward this end, and not just an end in itself. Systematic cutting releases competition and enables the remaining stand to grow stronger. Or it may be employed to open areas where animals can feed. Or a trail, vista or campground for human use. Or there may be no cutting at all: for example, along a streamside, where shade over the water maintains a cool temperature for fish; in places where animals will benefit from cover; in scenic and wilderness areas, where human visitors can experience the beauty of nature.

Virgin forest? If a virgin forest is one in which timber has never been cut, there is little left in the United States. Nearly all of it is in the West and coastal Alaska, with a potential harvest of up to 100,000 board feet per acre. In contrast, few Eastern stands can yield as much as 5000 board feet per acre. The expression of forest "untouched by the hand of man" tends to be misleading. The forests of the National Parks are said to "allow natural processes of growth and decay free play." But this is not completely so. Fire, insect and disease, three basic natural elements, are subject to control, as they must be; to say nothing of the effect of increasing human use. Whether it sounds proper or not from a sentimental point of view, the survival of fragile wilderness areas, which ten years ago had 100 visitors and may have 10,000 visitors ten years hence, depends on the extent to which they are managed as wilderness, with basic minimum improvements such as litter control, primitive campsites, clearing new trails to avoid congestion and planting additional meadows to provide forage for horses.

EDITOR'S NOTE: Michael Frome kindly updated his (1962) thoughts for us in a 1995 letter:

1) The idea that Douglas fir requires full sunlight to regenerate has been used to justify large scale clearcutting, but the species fares better by far in natural circumstances; 2) Timber cutting can in some ways enhance a forest environment, but only when conducted conservatively, which too often is not the case;

3) There may be little virgin forest remaining in the East, but this makes it more precious to protect; 4) Survival of fragile wilderness depends less on improvements to accommodate more visitors than on respect and restraint, and limitation on use; instead of providing forage for horses, in many cases horse use should be eliminated.

From *Whose Woods These Are: The Story of the National Forests*, by Michael Frome, Westview, 1962, 1984.

DAVID APPELL

Reflecting on his 1994 Appalachian Trail hike, David Appell of Tempe, Arizona, realized that a long walk is not at all the same thing as a cross-country automobile trip, with its rush of blurred sights and superficial human contacts. Appell's piece underscores a theme common to AT trail diaries: the "linear community" of the trail itself, which has a quality of camaraderie and openness hard to match when you get back to town. The location in this case is the skiers' village at Stratton Mt. in southern Vermont, accessible from the AT by ski lift gondola.

What I Really Saw

O N THE LAST NIGHT OF A SIX-WEEK A.T. HIKE, MY GIRLFRIEND AND I SAT ON the front porch of Spruce Peak Cabin in Vermont, talking to a dayhiker from Manchester. He wanted to know what we had seen, and so I tried to describe some of what we had observed since beginning our hike at Delaware Water Gap. I told him about the sunset from the top of Stratton Mountain, the graceful flow of the Housatonic River, the bears at Wawayanda Shelter, and more. He smiled as he listened, but, after he left, I felt dissatisfied with my answer, and, I thought, so did he.

Later, as we cooked our dinner and discussed our feelings about leaving the Trail the next day, I realized the limitations of what I had told him. He had asked his question as if we had been on an automobile trip, where you move along, seeing first a park and then a river and bridge, perhaps some snowy peaks in the distance. With my answer, I had validated this idea of the Trail. But, it did not begin to describe what I felt about our hike.

You see many things, beautiful things on a hike. But, I should have told him, you *feel* much, much more. You feel anew, you feel the wind and the rain, and the joy of sleep brought on by exhaustion. Every emotion you have is amplified and clarified, always shaped by the central, overriding task of walking. You learn how to somehow keep walking when you are tired and sore and wet and smelly, when you have to babble to keep your mind off all your aches and pains, and when you can't even listen to your partner's babbling because it seems you are walking on stumps. You learn the hard way that frustration will not help, you see how fear can make you fail, and you realize that weather and water and where you sleep, and how you live each hour, are the only things that really matter.

And then I remembered that I did see something—something simple that would not have satisfied the visitor's curiosity, but which summarized it all for me. Here is something I saw:

The day before, on the fourth of July, Sharon and I rode the gondola to Stratton Village, in search of real food and a telephone booth. While Sharon was making a phone call, I stood off to the side and noticed a man approach. He stepped toward the other phone, and our eyes met, and I began to nod and say hello. Then, I saw him quickly avert his glance and look away.

As the dusk settled in around Spruce Peak Cabin, I realized that, on the Trail, everyone says hello, and usually more. That is one of the things that makes it what it is, one of the best things. The rest of the world is too crowded, too busy, too often afraid to look directly at one another and say hello-too wary and cynical to worry about such unprofitable things as a sense of community, of participating in something common, and even, in its ways, wondrous. On the Trail, you see and feel everything, and you see yourself and other people in a new way, too.

This is not something you see from a car, ever.

From "What I *Really* Saw," by David Appell, *Appalachian Trailway News*, Nov./Dec. 1994.

THE APPALACHIAN TRAIL IN
NEW HAMPSHIRE, MAINE

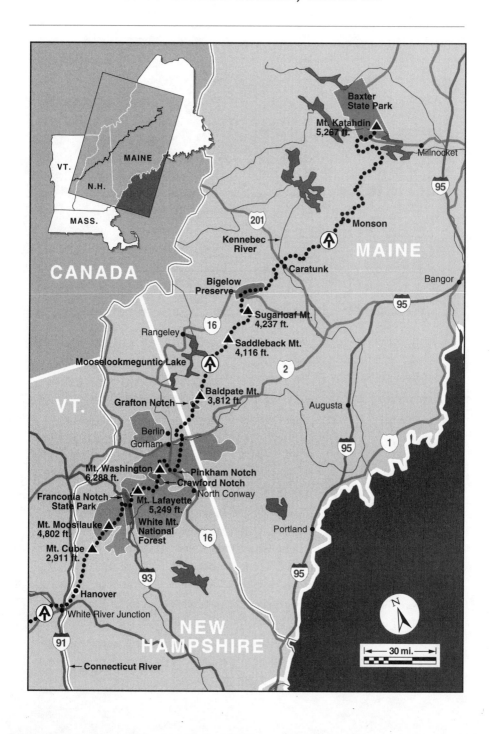

NEW HAMPSHIRE

Above tree line on Mt. Lafayette, in the Franconia Range, White Mts., New Hampshire.

Trail miles: 160.6

Trail maintenance: Dartmouth Outing Club, Appalachian Mountain Club

Highest point: Mt. Washington, 6,288 ft.

Broadest river: Connecticut (shared with New Hampshire), crossable by bridge

Features: Extensive hiking above tree line in the Presidential Range and Franconia Range of White Mt. National Forest. Wild, unpredictable weather. Many peaks above tree line and several over 5,000 ft. Hut system (lodges accommodating 36 to 90 guests). Fragile, beautiful alpine flowers, shrubs, lichens. Pinkham Notch Camp, at the eastern foot of Mt. Washington, a full-service outdoor recreation center staffed by Appalachian Mt. Club.

Parks, forests, and nature preserves: Franconia Notch State Park, Mt. Washington State Park, White Mt. National Forest

Most intriguing names on the trail: Velvet Rocks Shelter, Mt. Moosilauke, Lakes of the Clouds Hut

Trail towns: Hanover, Glencliff, North Woodstock, Gorham

MAURICE BROOKS

Above tree line in New Hampshire's White Mts., the common phrase "It's a different world up here" is loaded with meaning, some of which is almost too dramatic—or conversely too subtle—for words. The weather can be heavenly or deadly. The plant life is at once vulnerable and durable, the geology a delight to the eyes yet a painful challenge to muscle and bone. No one comes down from the alpine summits without a story to tell. My own hiking diary from a climb to Lakes of the Clouds hut at the foot of the treeless, rock-strewn, wind-whipped saddle around Mt. Washington reads: "Rocks everywhere, of every size, from tiny pebbles to house-size boulders. Above treeline, on the ridge, it's a lush moonscape of rugged delicacies." A traverse of some Appalachian alpine summits with a colorful expert guide, Maurice Brooks, follows here.

Alpine Summits

T REELINE ON A MOUNTAIN IS EXCITING, ESPECIALLY TO ONE WHO LIVES IN forested country. Here is a denial of the usual state of things, a place where timber struggles to maintain itself. It barely succeeds here; it loses the battle a few feet above. There are evidences of temporary successes, then of retreats as less favorable conditions develop. Farther downslope, trees grow easily and naturally, covering every available bit of the land. Warfare against the elements and the eventual loss of the battle seem unnatural. That, of course, is the forest man's point of view; I suppose trees are strange to an Eskimo.

There are two ways to reach timberline. One involves a long journey for most of us—say, to Fort Churchill on Hudson Bay. The other way is to climb a mountain, in one of a few possible places in the East; or to climb one of the many ranges and peaks in the West. Strictly speaking, there are timberlines wherever forest gives way to grassland or desert, but these changes usually come about by slow transition rather than with dramatic suddenness. Our concern is with Appalachian peaks high enough to approach or tower above the places where tree growth must give way to other plant life.

Not too many Appalachian summits meet these terms. In the Gaspé's Shickshocks, there are sizable areas above the trees, and even large stands of alpine and subalpine timber lower down. Mount Katahdin in Maine has an extensive treeless summit. The Presidential Range in New Hampshire has the East's most lengthy crest above treeline, a continuous ridge almost twenty miles in extent. Vermont's Mount Mansfield has a rocky crest that gives the effect of treeline. . . .

The Mount Washington toll road (and most of the hiking trails as well) begins the ascent in northern hardwood forest—birch and maple trees predominating. This is familiar woodland to anyone who knows the Appalachians, even as far south as Georgia. Wood thrushes, veeries, and rose-breasted grosbeaks sing, and redstarts constantly display their bright colors. Wildflowers in early June will include Canada violets, foam flower, red trilliums, and Solomon's seal. There is a variety of wild food, and deer like to browse around the openings.

The first noticeable forest change comes as coniferous trees—chiefly hemlock, white pine, and red spruce—begin to mingle with the hardwoods. In this woodland cover, northern warblers (black-throated blues, Canadas, magnolias, and black-throated greens) are more in evidence. Juncos become common, their tails suggesting animated pairs of scissors as they show, then cover the white feathers at their margins. New wildflowers appear, too. Northern clintonia grows in beds; dwarf dogwood (bunchberry) covers roadbanks; painted trilliums replace the red species.

This is good habitat for pink lady's-slippers; they seem to thrive in mixtures of decaying hardwood leaves and conifer needles. Near the base of the cog railway, Ruth spotted three of these flowers which were pure-white, strikingly beautiful orchids. I have seen the same variant along the Millinocket Tote Road leading to Mount Katahdin.

Somewhere near this level, the hobblebush, a major autumnal attraction in the Great Smokies, becomes common, and it will be with us almost to treeline. Its blossoms are surely among the whitest known in nature, and they are at their best in early June. I have not seen the fall foliage display here, but the handsome fruits are often photographed, and I can imagine that this is one of the region's finest September features.

Next above this mixed forest is a dense stand of almost pure conifers, largely spruce and balsam fir. Forest floors are carpeted with oxalis, whose three-part leaves may have been the original Irish shamrocks. Goldthread, so named because of its vivid yellow rootlets, provides delicate white flowers on mossy logs or roadbanks. Dwarf dogwood is still with us, perhaps even more abundant here than at lower elevations.

Winter wrens like the dark tangles of spruce as nesting sites and singing perches. Swainson's thrushes and hermit thrushes as well (at least until the latter became unaccountably scarce) are at home here, as are myrtle warblers and most of the species listed for the mixed forest just below this one. Kinglets call from the treetops, and yellow-bellied sapsuckers are much in evidence.

In the last forest below timberline, balsam firs are dominant, and often these trees occur in pure stands. Progressive dwarfing occurs as treeline is neared, and most trees will show the effects of wind, snow, and ice. There still are flowers in the ground cover—dwarf dogwood, Canada mayflower, oxalis, and goldthread. Logs may be overgrown with delicate, small, vining twinflower (*Linnaea borealis*).

For the first time in the ascent, there are now present a number of bird species that would not occur in the Appalachians considerably farther south, say in Pennsylvania or West Virginia. The gray-cheeked thrush lives in these stunted balsams and selects the topmost twig of one of them for its evening song perch. Boreal chickadees are here, as are gray jays. There is a chance of finding three-toed woodpeckers, and pine grosbeaks sometimes remain to nest. Spruce grouse occur, but the observer who sees one of these elusive birds is lucky indeed.

One of the most common summer residents is the blackpoll warbler, larger than many of its relatives, and somewhat slower in movement than most. These birds sing everywhere in the low balsams and spruces, but it is often amazingly difficult to see the author of this *tsi-tsi-tsi-tsi-tsi-tsi* song. Just under the thickest cluster of needles the males take their perches, and it may take a lot of looking to find this black and white bird.

As the tension [tree line] zone is neared, balsams and spruce become more compacted, more dwarfed, and more nearly horizontal, until finally the trees are prostrate, only a few inches above the ground, and one walks on top of the forest. To this point changes have come gradually, in slow transition that makes it difficult to draw exact boundaries. Not so at treeline: growth stops abruptly, there are trees here, there are none a foot above, and if arborescent vegetation creeps slightly higher in sheltered places, the line of demarcation is still dramatic.

It is to emphasize this climactic boundary that I have traced biotic changes up the mountainside. We may understand better what is above if we know what is below.

One bird species, the white-throated sparrow, was with us as we started, and another, the slate-colored junco, joined us soon after we began the climb. These will be the only two that regularly accompany us into the treeless zone; all the remainder of the mountain's rich avifauna is below us. Of course there are ravens, hawks, and other birds flying over at times; these do not count because they do not nest above the treeline. We shall not be much aware of birds at the heights.

Among the flowering plants, only a few species can make the transition. Most of the herbs we have seen below drop out; those that occur above timberline seldom penetrate far below it. We leave the trees and enter a new botanical world. Those who have not seen a natural alpine garden will be amazed at the richness, variety, and color that June's warm weather brings.

It is good to take a closer look at a few of these alpines, particularly those with showy blossoms. As a start, there is diapensia (*Diapensia lapponica*), a low evergreen herb, distantly related to galax, so prominent on southern Appalachian slopes (how these mountain plants do show similarities!). When we look at the bell-shaped white flowers of diapensia, another relationship is suggested: these alpine flowers resemble those of Oconee-bells (*Shortia galacifolia*), a classic among "lost" plants of the Southern Highlands. The resemblance is a natural one; the two plants are related. Diapensia is one of the cirumpolar plants, widespread in true arctic regions, and found on isolated mountain summits in Eurasia and North America. As far south as Newfoundland it blooms on exposed beaches; farther south it is found in the Shickshocks, on Mount Katahdin, in the White Mountains, and on a few Adirondack summits. On the upper slopes of Mount Washington it is common, growing in tufted whirls or in masses, often with bright-flowered arctic azalea and Lapland rhododendron. It begins to open its buds in early June; by the middle of that month it is in full display.

Lapland rosebay (*Rhododendron lapponicum*) has a range matching diapensia's and the two grow and bloom together. This dwarf heath has leaves of fingernail size, and its royal-purple flowers are larger than the leaves. A free bloomer, it is among the showiest of the alpines. Between it and the treelike rhododendrons farther south there are many similarities, but the dimension of flower parts and leaves is certainly different.

Third member of this closely associated trio is arctic azalea (*Loiseleuria procumbens*), whose hemispheric range is similar except that it apparently misses Adirondack peaks. It reappears in the Canadian Rockies. The matted leaves of this alpine gem are oval and only a quarter of an inch long. So closely does it hug the earth that when its lovely rose-colored flowers are open they are scarcely an inch aboveground.

It would be hard to find more pleasing gardens than these three make. Fortunately for the car driver or the hiker, they are not shy and hidden—they are in full view along the automobile road and the trails. Down to treeline they extend, and there they stop.

Here may be as good a place as any to offer a special word for Mount Washington travelers. The mountain's peak is not the place to look for these arctic plants; slopes are too steep and too rocky, and wind is too severe even for them. The alpine gardens are down below, in the saddles that join Washington to other peaks in the range, or on benches that relieve the steep pitch of the terrain. A famous place to look for flowers is along the Appalachian Trail as it skirts around the head of Tuckerman Ravine on the route to Lakes of the Clouds hut. . . .

Toward the end of June, when Lapland rosebay is near the end of its flowering, two other heather-like plants come into bloom. They also are of hemispheric distribution in arctic and alpine situations. In the western mountains of North America they are simply called "heathers." There are no appropriate English names; we shall have to call them *Phyllodoce* and *Cassiope*. The first has white flowers that turn blue as they age; the second bears white or rose-colored bells. Both plants are low matted evergreens, and both are true alpines.

Another handsome heath that grows at treeline, and sometimes above it, but is not at all restricted to this zone is rhodora (*Rhododendron canadense*). There are plants of this heath on Mount Washington, but it is particularly abundant near the top of Cannon Mountain, where an aerial tramway serves visitors to the Franconia Notch region.

It would not do to omit the little three-toothed cinquefoil. It begins in the Arctic and follows the Appalachians to the balds in Georgia. On all the White Mountain summits it is common. I know of no other plant that so favors the heights, and dwells on so many of them.

Willows and birches are not stopped by treeline, although as they extend beyond it they become low shrubs, often with creeping, vinelike habits. Botanists have a field day with the very difficult dwarf species on Mount Katahdin and in the Shickshocks. They are so near to each other in many characters and yet so tantalizingly different. Are they good species, hybrids, strongly marked races or just what? In any event, it is strange to see a prostrate willow creeping over a low boulder, opening its catkins where the sun strikes most directly.

Ferns and their allies are poorly represented in alpine regions, although a few of the clubmosses (*Lycopodium*) grew above treeline. On Mount Washington and other northeastern summits there is a stiff, bristly species which has been called *Lycopodium selago*. In the Shickshocks, on the fell-fields above treeline is alpine clubmoss (*L. alpinum*), a more truly arctic species. . . .

Save for insects, animal life above treeline in the Appalachians is disappointing. Those who know the western mountains above timberline will miss the constant movement of conies, marmots, chipmunks, and golden-mantled ground squirrels. I have seen groundhogs in the East at or near treeline on grassed ski slopes but no other larger mammals so high. . . .

I have mentioned juncos and white-throated sparrows above treeline on Mount Washington. On Mount Katahdin and in the Shickshocks another bird of high latitudes or mountain summits, the water pipit, joins them. This adds up to a scanty avifauna; students will not flock to treeless Appalachian peaks for bird study. Both plants and animals on higher Appalachian summits illustrate the biological principle that northward we find many individuals of only a relatively few species. Southward, the reverse is true: in the southern Appalachians at lower elevations there is a tremendous diversity of species. Note again the very wide distribution of most of the arctic-alpine plants we have discussed; the same thing holds for the water pipit. Balsam fir is continental in its extent, and many of the herbs just below treeline are found in suitable places throughout northern portions of this hemisphere.

On treeless Appalachian summits there is little or no true endemism—these mountain peaks have not produced plants and animals of sharply restricted distribution. The arctic butterflies previously mentioned might be listed as exceptions, but they are generally regarded as races of otherwise wide-ranging species. From Pennsylvania southward in the Appalachian ranges, endemism is common; many plants and animals have restricted ranges, some of them confined to relatively small mountain areas. And yet, with all these differences, how much alike the northern and the southern peaks are! The balsam forest on top of Mount Mitchell is remarkably similar to the forest just below treeline on Mount Washington. Juncos and winter wrens, kinglets and crossbills, wood oxalis and Canada mayflower, all are found in both situations. . . .

The towering mass of Katahdin has always held special interest for me. . . . I know why it has so attracted me, and perhaps the circumstances will cause some nostalgia in others of my generation. I am about to date myself.

Our home in West Virginia enjoyed three generations of *The Youth's Companion,* and its weekly arrival was an event: Homer Greene, James Willard Schultz—there were many stars among its contributors, but none so bright as C. A. Stephens. His stories of Maine—the Old Squire's farm, the winter frolics, the Big Woods—were unforgettable. In some of his early fiction (I never knew where fiction began and biography ended) four boys, Kit, Wash, Wade, and Raed, cast their vote for an education less formal than one they might receive in college. They planned a camping trip to Mount Katahdin, hoping that there they might find some mineral deposit which would finance their education by travel. The resident Indian devil of the mountain, Pamola, did his best to stop or hinder them; but right prevailed, and persistence paid off. They found a vein of graphite, sold it for fifteen thousand dollars, and were off to Labrador, Iceland, and the Amazon. Each trip inevitably resulted in a book, and I had them all.

This was my first contact with Katahdin. Maine was far away, but I knew I would get there some day, and, like my heroes, visit the peak. I have—several times—but I have yet to see the view from Katahdin's summit. Each time I have tried to, Pamola has spread a veil of clouds to keep his kingdom inviolate.

From *The Appalachians,* by Maurice Brooks, Seneca Books, 1965.

JEAN LANGENHEIM

If God is indeed in the details, as the cliché would have it, then writers like Jean Langenheim who put a highly specific subject under a literary microscope—here it's alpine lichens and mosses—must be looking toward heaven even as they peer at the ground. Towering trees and blossoming shrubs receive well-deserved applause, but there's a smaller world underfoot that can fascinate and charm as well. In fact, much of the color and texture of a walk, whether it's in the woods or above tree line, is given to us by tiny plants that barely reach a half inch in height. The Appalachian Mountain Club spon-

sored Langenheim's writing, as it has so many other useful books about the
mountain environment. Its 1995 illustrated Field Guide to the New England Alpine Summits *is aglow with the colors Langenheim describes here.*

Lichens and Mosses

*I*N ALPINE AREAS THE WORLD OVER, AS WELL AS IN ARCTIC ONES, LICHENS AND
mosses grow amid the colorful herbs, dwarfed shrubs, and tufts of
grasses and sedges. In the alpine areas in the Presidential Range, in particular, lichens reach greater abundance and play a more important role in
the development of the vegetation than in most other mountainous areas in
the United States. . . . The mosses, although they are of lesser importance,
are also fascinating when one's eyes are opened to their presence. In both
cases no attempt has been made to discuss other than a few of the most
conspicuous species, especially those that can be seen on Mt. Washington.

Because the lichen has such a distinctive plant body, pointing out a few
facts about its structure may be helpful in identifying these plants. The plant
body or *thallus* is a composite structure, made up of microscopic strands
(*hyphae*) of a fungus and usually a single-celled alga. This thallus, resulting
from the union of the fungus and alga, is entirely different from that formed
by either component when grown alone. The fungal hyphae for the most
part determine the shape, appearance and consistency of the lichen thallus.
The lichen fungi contain no chlorophyll and depend upon the photosyn-
thetic activity of the algae for their food. In fact, it has even been said that
the lichen in reality is a fungus that imitates a green plant by using another
plant to take care of its food manufacture. The algal cells, however, gain by
being surrounded by the fungal hyphae in protection against desiccation
and strong sunlight as well as in a supply of inorganic substances. Actually
the fungus is a controlled parasite of the alga. Because both organisms appear to derive mutual benefit from this relationship, however, it is called
symbiosis or consortism. As a result of this arrangement, lichens have a
truly remarkable resistance to drought and desiccation, which enables them
to occupy some of the most severe and forbidding habitats on earth. This is
one of the reasons that we see them so commonly in high mountain environments, where no other plants are sufficiently hardy to exist. Also, because an individual colony can attain a very old age, lichens are sometimes
described as "time stains." Certain lichens have been estimated to be more
than two thousand years old, which is more ancient than some of the oldest
redwood trees. Because they grow slowly and the rate of growth can easily
be measured, lichens provide evidence of the age of such geological phenomena as glacial moraines and lava flows.

Lichens are commonly divided into three groups based upon their growth forms. Those which form a crust which is firmly attached to the soil, rock, or bark are called *crustose*. The *foliose* types form leafy structures which are less firmly attached to their substratum than the crustose forms. The third type, known as *fruticose*, grows directly from its base in elongated stalks, which are either upright or pendulous.

The reproductive sacs which liberate spores are borne in various types of fruiting bodies. Some are globular or lumpy, whereas others are saucer-shaped. The spores come only from the fungal component. If they are to produce another lichen, they must come into contact with a free-living alga of the appropriate species. Unfortunately these species appear to be rare outside the lichens. Thus there is serious question as to whether the lichen depends to any extent upon this type of reproduction. It certainly appears that the most common type of reproduction is one which circumvents this complex problem of the fungal spore finding the right kind of algal cell. A fragment broken from any part, provided it contains algal cells and drops into a favorable habitat, may develop into another complete lichen. This breakage accounts for much of the dissemination of lichens. . . .

In identifying lichens, the nature of the growth form is important in separating genera. Fruiting bodies and spores are particularly important in determining species of the crustose types; isidia and soredia assume this role among the foliose and fruticose forms. Lichens secrete a number of unique organic compounds, called lichen acids, which are deposited in definite layers of tissue. The present trend in lichen taxonomy is to attempt to identify these lichen acids by color tests, crystal tests and chromatography. Many lichens with the same morphological form show different chemical strains. This appears to indicate to many botanists that biochemical evolution either precedes that shown in the form of the organism or maybe takes place independently.

Much beauty in our natural landscape would be lost without mosses because of the color, bright greens or rusty reds, which they add. This is especially true in alpine areas where, except for a short period of showy flowering, the aspect may be somber. They also play a significant role in moisture conservation. In some types of vegetation, such as sedge meadows, mosses provide seed beds as well as a subsequent favorable habitat for herbaceous and shrubby plants. They themselves seem quite independent of variation in climate. In damp weather they grow with amazing rapidity, and in dry or frozen periods they suspend growth. . . .

Mosses (particularly *Polytrichum*) and lichens (especially members of the fruticose genera *Cetraria* and *Cladonia*) are very conspicuous in meadows dominated by Bigelow sedge. Although the mosses become less significant, the lichens are still extremely abundant in plant communities containing a mixture of sedges and dwarf shrub heaths such as mountain cran-

berry, alpine bilberry and diapensia. *Cetraria* and *Cladonia* are also important elements in the three-forked rush-dwarf heath community. These lichens, as well as many other types, occur in most other communities; however, they are less prominent. The occurrence in such abundance of many of
these lichens and mosses on Mt. Washington, in particular, has been attributed largely to the exceptional weather conditions. The combination of ex-
ceedingly high winds, cloud cover, frequent fog, high precipitation and cool
summer temperatures results in a climate similar to that present today in
northern Canada and Alaska. It has even been suggested by some botanists
working on this flora that the luxuriance of lichens and mosses on Mt. Washington and north through Katahdin, Mt. Albert, and the Arctic reflects high
atmospheric moisture and frequent fog.

From *Mountain Flowers of New England*, by Jean Langenheim, Appalachian Mountain Club, 1964.

GUY & LAURA WATERMAN

*In the Watermans' history of trail building and mountaineering in the North-
east we meet the Crawford family, who built the first hostelries and trails in
what became Crawford Notch (cutting through the southern flank of New
Hampshire's Presidential Range of the White Mts.). This is a tale of trail
building in the days before either government or nonprofit outdoor recreation organizations were available to take the lead. The Crawford Path is now
a much-loved and heavily used stretch of the Appalachian Trail. The
Watermans are Vermont homesteaders who eschew most of the creature com-
forts the rest of us take for granted. It's no surprise they fell in love with
stories of the early pioneers.*

The Crawfords of Crawford Notch

A CCORDING TO THE OLD STORY, IT WAS IN 1771 THAT A HUNTER NAMED
Timothy Nash, in hot pursuit of a moose, climbed a tree on the southern flanks of Cherry Mountain hoping to get a better view of his
quarry. What he saw was of considerably more historical importance than
the north end of the southbound moose. Among the towering ridges of the
main chain of the White Mountains, there opened a deep defile that appeared to cut directly through the otherwise impassable heights. This was
the great Notch of the Mountains, later called Crawford Notch, a place destined to play a major role in Northeastern hiking history.

Nash followed this narrow vale, threading among some of the region's tallest peaks and more imposing cliffs, until he emerged into settled regions below—the towns of Conway and Tamworth. Then he went straight to Gov. John Wentworth to inform him about this notch and the use that could be made of it. The colonial governor was delighted and offered Nash a tract of land if he could get a horse and a barrel of rum through from Lancaster. Somehow Nash succeeded, with the help of a hunting buddy, though the rum, it was said, "was taxed heavily, in its own substance, however, to en- sure its passage, and reached [the other end of the notch] in a very reduced condition." We know nothing of how the horse came through the day, but the two hunters ended up with the land known today as Nash and Sawyer's Location, which extends from the notch northward to just beyond the site of the Fabyan House, near what is now the Bretton Woods ski touring center.

This was the widely told fiction of the nineteenth century—that Nash was the first person to see or pass through the White Mountain Notch. The truth is that the Indians knew of it, and it is most unlikely that earlier set- tlers were unaware of the passage. One source suggests that Nash "had noted the existence of an old Indian trail" through the notch. According to a local newspaper of the 1880s, this path was used by settlers at least as early as 1764.

It was also the quality of legend that portrayed Nash as a rustic hunter chasing a moose. In fact, Timothy Nash was a leading citizen of the town of Lancaster, New Hampshire, appointed to a committee of five charged with the responsibility "to look out and mark" roads that might improve that new town's contact with other areas. This committee was appointed in 1767, so Nash might have been looking for feasible routes at least four years ear- lier than 1771.

Discovery or rediscovery, 1771 or earlier, this event was important to the history of the mountains. Today we think of Crawford Notch as one of a triumvirate of coequal notches of the White Mountains, the others being Pinkham and Franconia. In the late eighteenth century, however, the route through Crawford Notch was peculiarly important as a vital throughway between the settlements of the upper Connecticut River valley and the sea- coast trading centers, principally Portland, Maine, then a port of consider- able commerce. . . .

In the wake of Manasseh Cutler's scientific expeditions, botanists be- gan to take a growing interest in the vegetation of the alpine zone. They were soon followed by other scientists, artists, writers, and the just plain curious. This trickle grew to a respectable flow of visitors during the 1820s, to a steady stream of tourists during the 1830s and 1840s, and to a flood of mountain vacationers by midcentury.

Before the botanists or anyone else could climb Mount Washington in great numbers, however, a more feasible ascent route was needed. Cutler's two climbs, like those of Field, had been bushwhack ordeals, through dense thickets, up the steep eastern or southeastern sides of the range.

The first path up Mount Washington was cut at the instigation of Col. George Gibbs, a mineralogist and one of the first scientists encouraged by Cutler to visit the White Mountains. Gibbs made more than one trip to Mount Washington, apparently around the year 1809. During one of these trips he arranged to have a path cut through the scrub growth, the belt of stunted fir and spruce just below treeline that is the most difficult obstacle to the higher Northeastern summits. A close reading of the sole direct reference to this path, by an 1816 party, places it most probably through Tuckerman Ravine. Local climbers used a path up from the east for the next generation or so; this could have been Gibbs's path, although it may have ascended Boott Spur from a point farther south.

Most visitors might have continued to approach Mount Washington from the east, had it not been for a series of developments: the improvement of the road through Crawford Notch in 1803; the deterioration of the Pinkham Notch road; the subsequent increase in traffic through Crawford Notch; and finally the arrival there of the Crawford-Rosebrook family which saw an opportunity on the mountain and seized it.

THE COMING OF THE CRAWFORDS

Around 1791, when the notch road was open but still rough, a young woodsman named Abel Crawford took over a settler's cabin just north of the gateway of the notch. In the winter of 1792, his wife's father, Capt. Eleazar Rosebrook, moved from Vermont to join him in that homestead, soon after which Abel moved on through the notch to new land 12 miles south. Now there were two branches of the Rosebrook-Crawford family, one on either end of the notch: the elder Rosebrook on the original site about 6 miles north of the notch's narrowest point (the "Gateway"), and Abel and Hannah Crawford down in Hart's Location about 6 miles south of the Gateway.

Initially both branches of the family worked farms, but the land was not meant to afford agricultural prosperity. They soon realized that providing room and board to travelers coming through the notch was a more promising livelihood. They worked on improving the notch road, aided by state funds in 1803, and gradually built up their inn-keeping business as traffic between Portland and parts west came to use this key thoroughfare more and more. . . .

In 1828 the Crawfords built a third family house for the accommodation of the notch trade, this one halfway between the other two, right at the

Gateway of the Notch. Here they installed Ethan's younger brother, Thomas J. Crawford, sixth of Abel's eight sons. This house prospered because of its strategic location at the Gateway; eventually its nearby successor grew into a major resort, known as the Crawford House, operating there in opulent splendor until its close during the 1970s.

Most of the lodgers at the Crawfords' gave little thought to the mountain heights. From 1803 when the road became passable for wagons, the notch was an important avenue of commerce. All year long cargoes of commodities streamed back and forth between Portland and the other coastal cities, and northern Vermont and the upper Connecticut Valley. Smuggling was said to be part of the trade. Winter brought no interruption to traffic; during the early days, winter was almost an easier time to move goods through the mountain passes, with as many as 150 sleds passing through the notch in a single day. Thus much of the inn business came from teamsters and farmers transporting their goods to market and bringing back their supplies.

Little by little, however, a tourist trade based on the magnificent mountain scenery began to emerge. The Rosebrook-Crawford innkeepers detected the start of this new business and became the first to capitalize on it.

As mountaineers and guides, the Crawfords have suffered the fate of many a legend: that of uncritical adulation in the eyes of posterity. Nearly every writer of White Mountain lore for the past century and a half has painted two-dimensional images in sunny pastels of Ethan as the genial mountain giant, performing Herculean feats of strength; Abel as the noble old patriarch of the hills; and their patient, hardy, pioneer-stock wives, Lucy and Hannah. . . .

Legend is nonetheless fundamentally correct in assigning to the Crawfords a major place in the history of Northeastern climbing. The first substantial wave of White Mountain tourists were guided up Mount Washington by this unique family: first by Captain Rosebrook, then Abel and Ethan, later Thomas, and still later Abel's son-in-law Nathaniel Davis, as well as by various others employed by the family at their several inns. The first mountain trails to receive regular and frequent use were the two cut by the Crawfords. The first personalities to receive major attention as figures associated with Northeastern mountains were Abel and Ethan. Both of these men, but especially Ethan, recognized the value of their colorful reputations as mountain "characters" and overlooked no opportunity to add to their own legends.

THE CRAWFORD PATHS

Soon after the road was made passable for wagons and stages in 1803, Captain Rosebrook began occasionally guiding curiosity-seekers through the woods and along the scrub of the long southwesterly ridge to the summit of

Washington. As early as 1808 he contemplated clearing a trail. By 1819 the tourist trade was sufficiently brisk to induce Abel and Ethan to cut the 8¼-mile trail that has survived to this day, though considerably relocated in places, as the oldest continuously used hiking trail in the Northeast.

The Crawford Path has always been a fine mountain trail. Its lower stretches cross a slope of lovely large spruce—much still virgin today—that gradually diminish in height and give way to birch and fir before the path suddenly curves into an open col between the peaks we now call Clinton and Eisenhower. The views from then on are such as to delight any lover of New England hill country. As the trail winds along and up the long ridge, it climbs over the graceful dome of Eisenhower, the open plateau of Franklin, and the fortresslike double-peaked Monroe, from which it drops down to the two little mountain tarns known originally as Blue Ponds (now Lakes of the Clouds). All the while, sweeping views to the distant horizons, with the endless waves of mountain ridges, compete with the dominant view ahead: the massive pyramid of the Northeast's largest mountain, Washington. From the lakes on, the trail winds slowly back and forth up the huge cone, as if reluctant to approach too directly into such an august presence.

The Crawford Path was at first but a slight improvement over the old bushwhack routes. One of the first parties to hike it described it as "obscure, often determined only by marked trees, some of which 'old Crawford' alone could discover." In the scrub above treeline, in dense fog, even Abel was "perplexed" at one point for almost an hour before picking up his trail. By 1820, however, when Alden Partridge walked up, he found that "the logs and underbrush are all cut out of the way and it is good walking."

In 1829 the opening of the inn at the Gateway brought more pedestrian traffic, and the path started to become worn enough to be followed readily. In 1840 the Crawfords widened and leveled the path so as to make it suitable for horses. This was the first of many mountain bridle paths built before the Civil War. Old Abel, then seventy-four, was the first man to ride horseback all the way to the top of Mount Washington.

Like the family, the Crawford Path has acquired some misinformation as part of its legend. It was not, for example, the first trail built up Washington; that was Gibbs's path. Nor was it the route used by Ethan Crawford for most of his widely celebrated guided ascents.

Two years after building the Crawford Path with his father, Ethan cut a different trail, this time with Charles Jesse Stuart of Lancaster, New Hampshire. Ethan's second "Crawford Path" ran along the valley parallel to the southwest ridge until it reached the base of Ammonoosuc Ravine, then climbed the due west spur to the summit. This trail received more use than the Crawford Path during the 1820s, as Ethan used it almost exclusively and left the original path to his father. Like its predecessor, the new path was rough: an 1824 climber described it as "a narrow footpath . . . impeded by rocks, stumps, fallen trees, bogs, morasses, and frequently by streams of water across which had fallen some neighboring tree that served as a bridge." Ethan had plans to make it passable for horses as early as 1827 but never finished the upper parts. In 1837 it still was full of "deep mud holes, the tangled roots, and the projecting stones and timber." After Horace Fabyan took over the business at the north end of the notch in the early 1840s, he improved the trail, making it a bridle path competitive with the newly improved Crawford Path. During the 1860s this route was taken by the Cog Railway and thereafter it ceased to be much used for foot or horse traffic.

From *Forest and Crag: A History of Hiking, Trail Blazing, and Adventure in the Northeast Mountains*, by Guy and Laura Waterman, Appalachian Mountain Club, 1989.

ROBERT MANNING

Nearly a half century before Benton MacKaye envisioned the Appalachian Trail, the Appalachian Mountain Club was actively developing trails in New England. Among the hardy enthusiasts were several indomitable women whose accomplishments are all the more amazing to contemporary hikers when the outfits they wore are taken into consideration. If Tuckerman Ravine, on the shoulder of Mt. Washington, is still considered today one of the most rugged and dangerous places in the White Mts. (rock slides, wild weather), what must it have been like in 1877 for Miss M. F. Whitman, in an ankle-length skirt and shoes we might wear for a cruise through a shopping mall? Whitman's detailed report to the AMC elicited the following commentary in a 1982 AMC publication.

Miss M. F. Whitman's Climb through Tuckerman Ravine

*I*N 1877, MISS M. F. WHITMAN STEPPED BOLDLY BEFORE THE GROUP GATHERED at the February AMC meeting and read a paper relating her adventure the previous summer in Tuckerman Ravine. Her paper was published later that year in Appalachia. The Club voted to admit women to membership at its second regular meeting, only a month after its formation, apparently without debating the issue. Whitman was the first of many vigorous women who were prominent in the Club, among them such mountaineering luminaries as Fanny Bullock Workman, Marjorie Hurd, Elizabeth Knowlton, and Miriam Underhill.

The accomplishments of early women climbers are remarkable given the extraordinary burdens placed (literally) upon them by the fashions of the day. Writing in *Appalachia* the year after Whitman, Mrs. W. G. Nowell describes the manner in which ladies' skirts would become so entangled in rocks, stumps, and undergrowth that jackknives would sometimes be required to cut their wearers loose. She cites a particular instance where a companion's skirt had been reduced to such a tangle of rags that it caught fast on a large jutting rock along the trail. The hiker's next step pitched her violently over a precipice where she dangled—caught by her skirt—over the rocks twenty-five feet below. Though she was dragged back from the abyss without harm, it was some time before the shaken lady could resume her journey. Nowell then suggests a mountain suit for women that would "be feminine and yet be adapted to exploring primeval forests." She describes the suit as ". . . made of stout gray flannel. The upper garment is a long gray sack, reaching to the knees. This is neatly buttoned and makes all the skirt that is needed. It is confined at the waist by a loose adjustable belt. The sleeves are full and are gathered into bands at the waist. The lower garments are loose, full, Turkish pants gathered into a band around the ankle. These are held up by being buttoned to the emancipation waist."

Whitman's adventure in Tuckerman Ravine began as a pleasant side trip but, due to the vagaries of White Mountain weather, developed into a harrowing and dangerous experience. Caught suddenly by a violent storm and then by darkness, she and her companion were forced into a desperate climb to reach the shelter of the Tip Top House on the summit of Mount Washington. Near the end of their journey, the climbers are reminded of Lizzie Bourne as an inducement to push on to the top. Bourne was the second of what are now scores of climbers to perish on Mount Washington. She began to climb the mountain with her uncle and cousin, September 13, 1855. A violent gale with freezing rain struck when the party was about three miles from the summit. After darkness, Lizzie became discouraged and could climb no further, so her uncle prepared a crude rock windbreak where the group spent an agonizing night during which Lizzie perished. At first light, the uncle and cousin tragically discovered that they were camped less than forty rods from the Tip Top House and safety.

From *Mountain Passages: An* Appalachia *Anthology,* edited by Robert Manning, Appalachian Mountain Club, 1982.

JOSEPH DODGE

Considered by some to be this century's best-known inhabitant of the White Mts., Joseph Brooks Dodge was Huts Manager for the Appalachian Mountain Club, based at Pinkham Notch, New Hampshire, smack on the Appalachian Trail. Dodge didn't just inspire others to perform Herculean tasks against tall odds (building the huts was a major engineering and muscle-testing endeavor over several decades): he was first in line with pick, shovel, pack, and materials. Dodge built awareness, too, passing along his own reverence for the environment through both words and deeds. Frederick Stott, describing Dodge, said he used the "moccasin telegraph" rather than the press release to educate visitors to the mountains. Dodge co-founded the weather observatory on Mt. Washington in 1932 and served as managing director there until his death in 1973. In 1955 Dartmouth College awarded Dodge an honorary Master of Arts with this commendation: "You have rescued so many of us from both the harshness of the mountain and the soft ways leading down to boredom that you yourself are now beyond rescue as a legend of all that is unafraid, friendly, rigorously good and ruggedly expressed in the out-of-doors."

An Old Hutman Reminisces

*I*T WAS ON JUNE 9TH, 1922, THAT I BID ADIEU TO MY FOLKS IN MANCHESTER-BY-the-Sea and climbed in the only piece of rolling stock the Club owned at the time, a model T Ford truck, with Red Mac, Johnnie White, and Ed Nelson. It was a real expedition to reach the White Hills in those days as there was no paved highway north of Rochester and we had the usual tire trouble that hot June day. We finally arrived late, just ahead of a thundershower, at Pinkham Notch Camp, where I was to be the hutmaster that summer.

The two log buildings were built at Pinkham Notch during the summer of 1920; Bill Loker was the first hutmaster and I was the second. When I looked over the interior that June day, it looked pretty bare, so I immediately started building various pieces of equipment, shelves, benches, and so on. Many small changes were made between daily cookery and the duty of killing the excessive numbers of porcupines that bothered us. Mac and I built new facilities for the men and women out in the woods and a much appreciated wooden canopy over the guests' washstand. Such jobs were sandwiched in between the preparation of meals for the registered and the unannounced guests. It always gave me a thrill to see how far I could stretch the soup and open a few more cans of this or that to expand a meal prepared for a dozen to serve sometimes three times that number. In those days we cooked entirely with wood at Pinkham, and it was another chore to work up wood ahead to be sure of good dry hardwood for the hot fires we needed. At Pinkham we got on nicely with the hardwoods, mainly beech, killed by the porcupines that girdled these trees three or four feet from the ground, working on winter snows.

The great numbers of porcupines caused Ed Nelson, the truck driver that summer, to call the place Porky Gulch, a name that has stuck through the years, replacing Pinkham Notch, even on incoming correspondence. Many a night we killed a dozen porkies. We clipped the noses for the 25¢ bounty, which was put in our meager kitty of those days. In the spring, we would collect the bounty from the town clerk in Gorham, buy strawberries and cream, then go home and make what we called a porcupine shortcake. Several years later, when I had been given ether for a leg injury, I was told that coming out of the effects I raved about porcupine shortcake and I had to make a complete explanation of what a porcupine shortcake was.

The next spring marked my arrival in the hills for good, as on May 7, 1926, I opened Pinkham Notch Camp, after bucking the snowbanks halfway up old Spruce Hill, where Tom Baker and I abandoned "Asma" my mountain-going Ford, and hiked into camp slumping deep in the thawing snows. We threw the key away that day, and Pinkham Notch Camp has been a year-round part of the Club activities in the White Hills ever since.

In October the Hut Committee called me to Boston. We had a very pleasant luncheon at the City Club, with light conversation, and I was awfully uneasy as I had misgivings that I was being hauled up on the carpet for something I had done that summer. Conversation ran on until George Rust asked me if I would be interested in keeping Pinkham Notch Camp open for the winter and make periodic trips to the other huts, Lakes-of-the-Clouds, Madison, and Carter Notch, to try to prevent the vandalism that had been rampant for several years when the huts were unmanned. I told the Committee that I would love the chance to keep Pinkham open for the winter. I could visualize the necessary work to make the camp livable for the winter and I determined that I would equip myself with some radio gear for communication.

Before Christmas we were snowed-up until the next May for wheel travel in any direction, and this gave a real feeling of isolation. But we made frequent trips to the Glen House for fresh milk and once every two weeks we skied into Gorham. Because of the fact that we could not anticipate our volume of business we had to backpack many heavy loads all the way from Gorham to camp, and eleven miles of uphill on skis is quite a chore with 100 pounds on your back. Owing largely to a very nice story in the old *Transcript* concerning the pioneering of the Club in Pinkham Notch, we had enough guests so that the camp lost only $119 that first winter of 1926-27.

The spring of '29 was all activity. The Committee had commissioned me to take over the log buildings at Lonesome Lake for a hut, build a hut of a new type of construction at Eagle Lake on Mount Lafayette, and add a kitchen, dining room, and hutmen's quarters at Madison. This indeed, in addition to the regular huts operations, was a large order for a young feller, but I was eager and willing and wanted to make good so that I took everything in stride.

The summer was certainly a very busy one, and many a night I lay in my bunk planning the morrow, but we completed, as far as possible, the scheduled jobs and closed in Greenleaf Hut on Mount Lafayette by October 12, just ahead of an early fall snowstorm. The next spring we completed this job, moved over to Carter Notch, and added a kitchen and hutmen's quarters to the stone hut.

Now we had a discontinuous hut chain, the four original huts in the Carter and Presidential range and Greenleaf and Lonesome Lake huts far to the west, with a gap of thirty-odd miles separating the Lakes-of-the-Clouds Hut from Greenleaf Hut on Mount Lafayette. What to do about it? The fall of 1930 was spent cruising much of the territory along the Twinway and Garfield Ridge trails, and two locations were chosen by the Committee, one at the head of Gale River and the second on the side of Whitewall Brook in Zealand Notch. To complete these two jobs in one year was a pretty big order, but we carried on. These were true pioneering jobs, back a long way from the usual forms of transportation and offering a real challenge.

Construction was quiet for the next few years until we launched into the big changes at Pinkham when we built the new Lodge in 1934 and in 1935 moved the log lodge and attached it to the former cookhouse making the Trading Post. These were home jobs and offered no great problems, but all the time we were increasing our demand for electrical power and after inventorying the Cutler River for over a year, we made an application to the Federal Power Commission for a permit to build a miniature Hoover Dam. Because we were on Federal land, the document issued the Club for a 15 HP plant on the Cutler River was the same as issued for the gigantic dam in Nevada. Isn't that something? This was a very interesting project and with additions and improvements served the Club nobly from 1939 to 1960, saving, over the years, many thousands of dollars. It wasn't the best regulated power but with reasonable care and attention served its purpose very well. This little plant was one of my crowning achievements and I was very fond and proud of its performance.

A major change was made and many conveniences were added to the kitchen at Pinkham in 1940. This was the year we took some of the drudgery from the hut boys and girls by installing a second-hand dishwasher and made the cooks happy with an upright baker and new cooking ranges. This year also marked the first catastrophe to the huts, the burning of Madison Hut on October 7. I was really sunk when I was called on the telephone and told of this fire. Fortunately for us no water was available to put on the fire, and consequently the masonry was not split but came through in good shape. We had old #2 hut to house a construction crew the next spring and we were able to get the hut functioning again that next summer.

The next major construction came in 1947, when we added a wing of two bunkrooms and additional toilet facilities to the Pinkham Lodge and practically made a complete face-lifting of the Lakes-of-the-Clouds Hut. The Pinkham job started early in May but was interrupted in early July to take advantage of the good summer weather to do a real big job at the exposed site of the Lakes hut. After a hectic summer but a fruitful one, we returned to complete the job left at Pinkham and connected up a new heating system to the rooms.

May of 1950, we had another unfortunate fire when Tuckerman Ravine Shelter, which we took over from the U.S. Forest Service in 1945 to run, burned completely. The skiers had to do without shelter the next winter, but, as the Forest Service had demolished a large building at their Bartlett depot, the usable materials were made available and in the winter of 1951-52, we toted most of the necessary lumber and other durable items over the snow on the Tuckerman Trail and during the summer the present structure was built.

This was the last big construction job I did for the Club, but over the years I often wonder how were we able to do so much with so little. But the spirit was there and until I was required to slow down in the late fifties I was always in with the gang pitching, swearing, but making the jobs percolate. I am very proud to have been a part of the work of developing a chain of huts in the White Mountains that the Club can feel is making it possible for thousands of persons to have a healthful and inexpensive vacation on the ridges of New England.

From *"An Old Hutman Reminisces,"* by Joseph Dodge (1963), in *Mountain Passages: An* Appalachia *Anthology,* edited by Robert Manning, Appalachian Mountain Club, 1982.

JOHN WHITE

Everyone who has enjoyed a stay at the Appalachian Mountain Club huts in the White Mts. owes a debt to the hardy hut crews, who not only cook and clean at the huts but pack in all the supplies and pack out the garbage. Some "packers" seem to have had the strength and endurance of Olympic athletes, though perhaps their daily ascents to the top of the Presidential Range seemed to them like mere strolls on Mt. Olympus, from whence they drew their strength. Robert Manning introduced the following piece in a now out-of-print collection; his comment precedes John White's reminiscence.

Packs and Packboards

OVER THE YEARS, PACKING HAS PROVIDED MANY EXCUSES AND OPPORTU-nities for mountain heroics, especially during periods of hut construction, when tons of additional materials must be hauled. The single-day record must be held by the anonymous packer who, in ten round trips, packed 1,000 pounds of cement in to Lakes-of-the-Clouds in 1927, traveling a combined total of thirty miles, while climbing and descending 13,000 feet. No wonder that in 1938 a number of Club members expressed their concern over adverse effects of packing in a petition to the Club president. The Hut Committee's subsequent investigation concluded that there was no inherent medical danger. Indeed, most former hutmen surveyed reported that the rugged physical condition they acquired during their years of packing was a valuable asset in later life.

White worked in the hut system from 1921 to 1924 and has returned to the White Mountains nearly every year since. . . .

The storehouse for the supplies for the Madison Spring Huts was in the Ravine House barn. You went in the side door on the lower level, through the stable room where the two big work horses were stalled, climbed up on a barrel to get the key and then unlocked the storeroom door. Here everything for the huts was piled up in a heap. Blankets back from the laundry were piled up on the shelf, clean and dry and good-smelling. A stack of new post cards, some shoe nails, a shiny new swill-pail, and several boxes of chocolate bars were lying about. But most everything else, the big bulk of the supplies, was in unbroken cartons. Soup and more soup. Klim and cocoa and canned fruits and all the vegetables, carton piled on carton, and more boxes of soup. One big box held a miscellaneous assortment of foodstuffs, salt and pepper and catsup and dates and breakfast foods and rice and macaroni and more such. Roughly there might be a ton of food and other articles locked up here in the Ravine House barn.

Through the back window of this little storage closet you could look out over the lush meadows to the single-line train tracks and the wooded hillsides of Adams and see the valley of the Snyder Brook winding upward to the shoulder of Madison. Up to the top of that valley this stuff had to go, up to where the shoulder of Madison broke the skyline, and then a few hundred feet more into the hollow of Madison Spring.

A case of soup weighed about fifty-five pounds. With a little urging it would go whole and unopened into the packsack. If you put it in first it would tend to be bottom heavy in the pack and bump you in the small of the back. Better to put in a blanket for softness and two big cans of Klim at the bottom, then the soup, and at the top something not too big or heavy, something perhaps that should not be crushed. Then if you stuffed in the woolly shirt that you needed for the down trip and tied up the throat strings you were all set and ready to go. You knew what it ought to weigh but you took a test heave to sample it: you set it on the barrel and got into the straps. You were off.

From *Mountain Passages: An* Appalachia *Anthology,* edited by Robert Manning, Appalachian Mountain Club, 1982.

ARTHUR HARRIS, JR.

We go to the mountains to escape worldly cares like politics, but the world follows close on our heels. During World War II, men who ordinarily would have looked after the Appalachian mountain trails were away, serving in the armed forces. Among those still on the home front were conscientious objectors like Arthur Harris, whose assignment was trail maintenance in the White Mts. From him we learn about the task of repairing mountain footpaths and about prejudice against pacifists in a time when the battlefront may have seemed more important than a hiking trail. Only a long view of history and of the environment can reconcile such views.

Wartime Maintenance in the Appalachian Mountains

I SUPPOSE THERE ARE FEW CLUB MEMBERS WHO DO NOT APPRECIATE THE WORK formerly done by the Civilian Conservation Corps in helping to maintain our forests. At one time there were CCC camps throughout the Appalachian Mountains. The men built and maintained trails and roads, constructed fire towers and shelters. One of their most important contributions was preventing and fighting forest fires.

Now that the CCC has been abandoned, some of their work has been taken over by the war objectors, of which I am one. We are occupying some of the vacated CCC facilities throughout the country, using their old equipment and working in the areas where their work was most vital. At the time I was inducted into Civilian Public Service at West Campton, New Hampshire, there were three such camps in the state, two of which served the White Mountain National Forest. These units repaired in a manner similar to Carrigain's, and some new lines were installed in the Swift River area. Though this camp continued until late fall, I went to cook for another unit operating out of Wild River Guard Station. After several weeks here, we moved to the abandoned CCC Camp at Gale River, near Bethlehem, where we worked until winter set in.

Meanwhile, during the summer, there had been other side camps at Waterville and Lincoln valleys, besides camps operating out of the smaller Gorham Camp.

In November, the entire personnel of the camps at Gorham and Campton moved south. Half of the men went to Lauray, Virginia, near the Skyline Drive. The rest of us came to Gatlinburg, Tennessee. This camp, formerly used by the CCC, is located at the northern entrance to the Smoky Mountain National Park. Gatlinburg, itself, is a sort of North Conway of the South, a tourist resort on the Park boundary. While we are no longer working for the Forest Service (Department of Agriculture), but for the Park Service (Department of Interior), the work is practically the same: maintaining trails, towers, and roads, and preventing and fighting forest fires. Here, too, we have side camps: at Big Creek and Smokemont on the North Carolina side of the Park, and at Cades Cove on the Tennessee side.

To one who has spent most of his time in the White Mountains, the Smokies appear much less attractive. While it is true that some of them are higher (though not much higher than Mt. Washington), none of them is at all spectacular. The mountains seem like large hills, for practically all of them are wooded to the tops. They lack the grandeur, the magnificence of the White Mountains. And though most of the mountains directly surrounding the camp itself are far higher than Chocorua Mountain, they lack the proudness of that peak. After working on trails such as Adams Slide, the Smoky Mountain horse trails (never more than 15% grade) are most uninteresting. My own dissatisfaction with the Smoky Mountains is shared by most of the men who had spent a year or two in the New Hampshire camps. Our Park Service foremen, many of whom have lived in the Smokies all their lives, cannot understand our attitude, and continually point out that their mountains are higher than ours. And when we say, "Yes, that's true, but they are all like overgrown hills down here," they look at us as though we don't know what we're talking about.

Almost without exception, these government men (employees of the Park Service and the Forest Service) treat us well despite our views regarding war. In New Hampshire, particularly, where they lived with us at side camps, a fairly close association between the men and the Forest Service employees sprang up. I had known several of the foresters before, and I found all these men still friendly to me. While we occasionally encountered some ill feeling among residents of areas in which we worked, none of the government men held any resentment toward us because of our belief. Perhaps in an off moment, one of our foremen confessed, "You fellows have something; you're just about a hundred years too soon, that's all." Here in Tennessee and North Carolina, our relations are much less good among the residents. But the Park Service employees for whom we work are friendly and helpful.

Defined, the job we are doing is called work of "national importance." However, many of the men who have no interest in mountains think it unimportant; the physical labor involved in clearing a mountain trail of windfalls seems useless to them, especially since all of us are working fifty-two hours a week for nothing, with merely an allowance of $2.50 a month. But to me, it seems really vital not to neglect our parks and forests during wartime, for if abandoned to the elements for even a few years, they would be so crippled that by the end of the war it might take several years to restore them.

I shall always and forever feel humble toward my many friends who are away fighting for these mountains we have climbed together. But meanwhile, I am glad that I can serve at the same time both my conscience and the mountains.

From *"Wartime Maintenance in the Appalachian Mountains,"* by Arthur Harris, Jr., *Appalachia,* Vol. X, 1944.

WILLIAM LOWELL PUTNAM

Even a midsummer day can bring hurricane-force winds and blinding snow to the top of Mt. Washington, the Appalachian Trail's highest point in New England (6,288 feet). To imagine the scene in winter, picture this: You and four other hardy meteorologist souls have battened down the hatches at the weather observatory on the peak infamous for suffering the wildest weather on the planet. It's spring in the valley but definitely winter up here, and a storm is raging that promises to test everyone's mettle. The building is anchored to the peak by chains . . . and faith. Outside, ice encrusts everything. The darkness is palpable. The wind screeches and moans. Your mission is to keep accurate records—or is it merely to survive to tell the tale? W. L. Putnam, lifelong alpinist, is a trustee of the observatory and chronicled its history, with due emphasis on the most amazing night in the record book: April 12, 1934.

Will They Believe It? 231 MPH!

*A*T 4 A.M., MAC SHOOK STEVE AWAKE AND THEN TURNED IN. THE BUILDING was shaking, but it was firmly chained to the rocks and the inhabitants did not fear, as some had in the past, that their lives might be in danger. Steve, too, soon noted that there seemed to be less velocity being recorded, only 110 mph, than the building sounds indicated likely, but the heat volume was already up to its maximum. Knowing his duty, for it was established routine, he carefully dressed in all the appropriate garments including a double skirted parka, and taking one of the Observatory's handy sticks, always in demand for knocking rime off the instrument mountings, he made for the doorway. The door was on the northerly side of the building, away from this wind, and opening it inward, against the enormous wind-induced vacuum, required a tremendous effort. Since the prevailing wind had always hit the observers on their left as they went out, Stephenson started to lean the usual way and was promptly bowled over by the blast which hit him from the right. Regaining his footing, some yards from the door, he struggled around the corner to the ladder, where, fortunately, the wind was at his back. It tore his parka skirt over his head, temporarily blinding him and making the ascent difficult, but when he tried again he found that he couldn't fall off, in fact he could barely move. After climbing up, he delivered a few blows on the anemometer mounting and it was clear again, rapidly picking up speed. Stephenson then threw down the club, which was never seen again, backed off the ladder and regained the shelter of the Observatory. According to Stephenson, uncorrected readings were by then peak-ing over 160 mph. When questioned later about his courage in facing this awesome blast, he responded, "If I'd known how strong the wind was, I'd never have gone out there. "

With morning light on April 12 came the usual round of radio contacts. Nothing more eventful had happened at the Cog Base Station, Joe's report from Porky Gulch was not much different, but Blue Hill was reporting east winds reaching Force 9 on Admiral Beaufort's scale, with zero visibility and a temperature of 43°F. It was a general storm, not just a local event around Mount Washington. Joe Dodge wanted to know more details of what was happening on the Summit, so Mac plugged the output from the anemometer's 1/30 of a mile contacts into the thousand-cycle tone generator that most radio transmitter installations have, and that output in turn into the 5 meter (60.5 MHz) transmitter. Dodge could then hear the "beeps" for himself. Counting 16 clicks in 10 seconds, Joe asked for a corrected reading. Pagluica thought a moment, moved the cursor on his slide rule, and came up with 146 mph, as corrected in the wind tunnel calibration chart.

While preparing lunch, Stephenson was amazed to see that the window near his cookstove was bulging in and out measurably with the impact of the gusts outside. Fortunately, everyone knew that the building, windows and all, was now protected with many inches of heavy ice, adding greatly to its inertia and somewhat to its strength. Yet, when he looked up, Stephenson was certain that the entire east wall of the building was bending perceptibly under the strain. Gusts were now much stronger than during the midnight watch.

After the noon radio contact, Dr. Brooks remained in touch from Blue Hill. It had been windy in Boston the previous day, he reported, with a lot of rain. But the weather was even more interesting up north and Mac now connected the tone generator into the 53 MHz transmitter, as he had done for Joe Dodge earlier. Corrected readings for some of the gusts were now over 200 mph!

All five persons on the summit were now listening to the rapid clicking of a telegraph sounder connected to the anemometer and the tone generator which continued to be broadcast on the 53 MHz transmitter for the benefit of any interested amateurs. The stopwatch was in constant use, and gusts were coming in at corrected readings of 220, then 225, even 229 mph. Three clicks in 1.17 seconds—a lull; then it came on again, three more in the same time—308 mph, uncorrected. From the calibration chart it meant two gusts of 231 miles an hour. It was 1:21 P.M. No greater wind had ever been recorded in the history of meteorology. Observer Pagliuca was concerned, "Will they believe it?" Everyone present knew the facts, more gusts were coming by—though with slightly diminished intensity—they had even transmitted the anemometer timings. Their building was still growling in awesome tones; but still, were all their instruments in good order?

The stopwatch, a critical item, was checked against the Nardin chro-

nometer, which was in turn routinely checked by almost daily synchroniza-
tion with the signals from the United States Naval Observatory. Stephenson
had timed several gusts corrected to 229 and Pagliuca had two at 231. The
anemometer had been calibrated by the National Bureau of Standards only
five months earlier. Then a radio ham near Portland was calling; he, too,
had heard the signals, and sensed the eventfulness of the weather. How
many others had been out there, too?

Later, when Pagliuca filled out the log book, he wrote:

> . . . At the 7:45 report we gave an average velocity of 149 mph with a max of 168
> mph. We had broken last winter's record by 4 miles, but indications were that
> we would go higher, much higher. How much, we did not know, did not even
> suspect. The synoptic map did not tell us, did not tell to our elect body of
> meteorologist friends at MIT, did not tell anybody. We found it out as the day
> went on. . . . The instruments were watched continuously so that they might
> give a continuous and accurate record of the various meteorological elements
> at work. The anemometer was particularly watched. . . . Mac hooked up the 1/
> 30-mile relay permanently so the gusts could be timed frequently to ascertain
> the max wind velocity.
>
> It was my impression that our heavy type anemometer would not be suit-
> able for measuring the peak value of gusts. . . . However, I decided to take
> short interval readings with a stopwatch, and selected timing three 1/30-mile
> clicks. Although theoretically unsound, this practice gave immediate results.
> After several test readings to gain experience, actual values began to show that
> as the average wind was increasing, the intensity of the gusts was also increas-
> ing to very high, almost unbelievable, values. As our calibration curve had
> been loaned to Mr. S. P. Fergusson of Blue Hill, I plotted another curve in a
> large scale and began extrapolating a few miles at a time. My God! While a five
> minute average between 12:25 and 12:30 gave us a velocity of 188 mph, values
> above 200 mph were being obtained for the three 1/30-mile clicks. Mac, Steve
> and I had been taking turns knocking ice from the anemometer post. Art and
> George, our guests, made themselves useful in many ways but particularly in
> attending to the fire, helping Steve in the kitchen and cleaning the front doors
> of snow while we were going in and out. . . . Between 12 noon and 1 P.M. the
> wind movement was 173 miles. Shortly after one, I set out to clean the ice from
> the anemometer post, followed by Art and George with a movie camera. We
> had made careful arrangements that we would go thru a certain sequence of
> motions to assure a good movie. But I disappeared in the fog up on the roof
> and as I turned towards them to see if they were operating, I felt the full blast
> of the 200 mph SE wind on my face. It was the warning that I had better pro-
> ceed for the anemometer, which I did. Kneeling on the platform I pounded the
> foot thick ice accumulation with all my strength. But alas! I was not making
> much impression on the rough frost. Perhaps a sledge hammer would have
> done a better job but I doubt if the strength of Polyphemus could move a sledge
> hammer in a 200 mph breeze. And I thought of mighty Polyphemus as the

wind was furiously blowing my parka out of my storm pants, the hood was on my face, almost blinding me. I could not waste much more time on the roof, besides my friends could be taking movies of a poor human prey of the wind without accomplishing what he had set out for. I reclined for a few seconds against the ice column, then I must have yelled something muffled by the leather mask, the hood, and the roar of the wind, as I jumped up and pounded the ice again. Hurrah! Big chunks of ice were now flying northwestward and disappearing in the dense fog without even having a chance of bouncing on the roof.

Down below, in the shack, Steve was timing gusts of 220 mph and occasionally of 229 mph. As I returned inside I could not believe what Steve told me, so I took the stop watch from him and started timing gusts myself—Yes, 229 mph—once—twice—Then a lull—I did not count. Then another gust—The barograph pens dropped in a vertical line for about .2 inch, the doors shook vigorously, the clicks increased in their rhythm. I snapped the stopwatch and timed three clicks: 1.17 seconds-—I knew it was a record—did not know how much—I felt as if the wind was decreasing, and hesitated a while, but as I heard the rhythm go up again I snapped the watch again and timed three more clicks: 1. 17 seconds.

Twice I yelled the time so that Art could put it down on paper. Then I grabbed the slide rule and with a single setting I read 308 mph uncorrected—Extrapolated my calibration curve again and read *231 mph*. 'Will they believe it?' was our first thought. I felt then the full responsibility of that startling measurement. Was my timing correct! Was the method O.K.—Was the calibration curve right—Was the stop watch accurate? Slowly, I began collecting the evidence. Mac checked the stop watch against the Nardin chronometer and found it O. K. Everyone in the house had been asked to make readings and repeatedly values above 200 mph were obtained. Steve and I took the greatest number of observations. Both of us had obtained several 229 mph readings. My two 231 mph readings were only a small fraction higher—they were true within the approximation of the particular method of measurement. My personal equation was not so bad in my ten months of snapping stopwatches in the laboratory of the General Electric Co. in Lynn, Mass. for the purpose of testing watt-hour meters.

Then again Dr. C. F. Brooks had timed our gusts from Blue Hill Observatory in Milton, Mass., 42 miles south of Mt Washington by radio! From 12:35 to 1:00 P.M. Dr. Brooks was snapping his stopwatch from the tower at Blue Hill timing our wind. Another success of our be-whiskered Mac. Well, in his own words, the Professor took five samplings of one or two minutes each, showing true velocities by five second intervals of 108 to 216 mph. The fastest 40 contacts, representing a true mile, came in only 17 seconds or at a rate of 3½ miles a minute (210 mph).

There was enthusiasm on the summit, almost a touch of excitement. We had measured by means of an anemometer the highest natural wind velocity ever recorded officially anywhere in the world.

From *The Worst Weather on Earth: A History of the Mount Washington Observatory*, by William Lowell Putnam, American Alpine Club, 1991.

EUGENE DANIELL

Taking to the trail in winter is an irresistible challenge for a small segment of the hiking population. Most winter hikers carry sufficient clothing, food and common sense to enjoy their treks without endangering themselves. Yet every year, on the Appalachian Trail or on linking trails in the Presidential Range, several people get into serious trouble, requiring heroic and costly rescue efforts by dedicated teams of mountaineers. Gene Daniell is secretary of the Appalachian Mountain Club's Four-Thousand-Footer Committee, and he knows that sometimes winter hikers leave their essential common sense at home. In correspondence he told us, "In such an atmosphere people who are addicted to the thrill of excessive risk-taking are often encouraged by the admiration they receive when they are lucky enough to escape the jaws of death unharmed." At 5,712 feet, the uppermost ridges of Mt. Jefferson (north of Mt. Washington) are above tree line and are exposed to the worst that winter can bring.

Hypothermia on Mt. Jefferson

O N FRIDAY, JANUARY 15, 1994, TWO UNIVERSITY OF NEW HAMPSHIRE STU-
dents, Jeremy Haas, 20, of Ithaca, NY, and Derek Tinkham, 20, of Saunderstown, RI, were dropped off by friends at the Appalachia trailhead. They planned a complete, several-day traverse of the Presidentials during their holiday break. Haas had some winter experience but it was of a questionable quality: He had been suspended from leading trips for the UNH Outing Club after numerous complaints about his devotion to pushing ahead at all costs, no matter what the abilities of his companions, including an incident two years earlier in which a participant on one of the hikes he led lost all ten toes to frostbite. Tinkham's winter experience was quite limited, not even close to the level required for such a demanding and perilous undertaking as this. The pair had chosen not to bring a tent, and their camping equipment and general gear was minimally adequate for average winter conditions on the Presidential Range. And the conditions they were about to face were far from average, as forecasts had made them well aware; indeed, there is some reason to believe that the severity of the predicted weather added to their fascination with the enterprise, promising added challenge and perhaps added glory.

That afternoon the two hikers ascended the Air Line to a point just below treeline (at the junction with the Upper Bruin Trail), and made a bivouac. The next morning the temperature was about -20° F and falling steadily, with winds of 80-100 mph and blowing snow and fog, but Haas and Tinkham apparently gave no thought to backing off. They climbed Mt. Madison, then continued over Mt. Adams to Edmands Col. On the way up Mt. Jefferson, Tinkham started to show signs of fatigue. Apparently he was "post holing"—breaking through the wind-blown crust into the softer drifts beneath, an extremely exhausting predicament—much more than Haas. Haas questioned Tinkham but received the response that Tinkham was sure he'd do better after crossing the summit of Jefferson.

Just past the summit, however, Tinkham was blown off a ledge and began to show the telltale signs of severe hypothermia—loss of motor coordination and incoherence—and as Haas described it, they descended the slope by "tumble and roll." At about the 5,000-foot level, Tinkham asked to get into his sleeping bag and Haas helped him accomplish this task. In the process Haas's hands became cold and stiff—which usually takes less than a minute in such conditions—and he was unable to get his gloves back on and had to continue wearing only thin liner gloves.

After leaving Tinkham at about 4:00 P.M., Haas struggled up Mt. Washington on hands and knees, reaching the observatory on the summit at about 8:00 P.M. The next day rescuers battled temperatures below -40° F and winds of more than 100 mph in a heroic effort that left nearly all of them—all highly experienced mountaineers with the best of equipment—with some degree of frostbite. They retrieved Tinkham's body, which was found halfway out of the sleeping bag in which Haas had placed him. Ironically, Tinkham's collapse probably saved Haas's life, since it is unlikely that Haas would have survived under the prevailing conditions with his grossly inadequate provisions for shelter if they had been able to carry out their intention of spending the night at Sphinx Col.

Analysis: There is no question that Haas and Tinkham were extremely foolhardy to persist in their objectives despite the inadequacy of their equipment and the severity of the weather. Their lack of good judgment has received ample condemnation elsewhere. And Haas added fuel to this fire of criticism when, instead of expressing appropriate contrition for one in his circumstances, he gave an interview to the *Boston Globe* in which he attempted to defend his actions and justify the undertaking as a whole. He stated that he and (as far as he knew) Tinkham were the kind of people who "need to focus into that void, get near the edge of life and death." He felt he had made the risks of the trip clear to his less experienced companion. "I told him it was going to be the most difficult, the most painful thing he'd ever experienced. . . . I told Derek before we left that this is a life-or-death situation, that being up here in this kind of weather is such an individual effort that this is essentially a solo. . . . Derek said this is something he very much wanted to experience." Though Haas later toned down his public statements, such unveiled arrogance made him an easy target for criticism.

Much of that criticism seems to this writer to have missed the mark, however. While Tinkham may well have undertaken his final journey in part from a fear of appearing less daring and valiant than his friend, by all accounts he went on it willingly and knowingly, even enthusiastically. And while Haas also received criticism for not noticing his companion's failing strength sooner and taking appropriate action, it is by no means certain that he could have done much more for Tinkham than he did. Tinkham's hypothermia appears to have progressed fairly quickly, and it is not clear that, even if Haas had taken action immediately upon observing his companion's growing fatigue during the ascent of Jefferson, he could have evacuated Tinkham successfully by any of the fairly difficult exit routes that lead from the Edmands Col area. As has been pointed out in these pages several times in the past, there is no easy route out of Edmands Col in severe weather. Therefore, it is likely that Tinkham's fate was sealed when the two hikers continued on from the summit of Adams, passing up the opportunity to descend the Lowe's Path to Gray Knob Cabin. As one of the rescuers commented, it was the kind of day when a stuck zipper might cost one's life.

More importantly, neither Haas nor Tinkham ever represented their enterprise as a sensible, well-considered mountaineering feat. Risk in mountaineering and the consequent loss of life are often defended as a necessary price for the personal growth that comes from accepting and overcoming difficult challenges, and for the enlargement of human spirit that comes from pushing at the limits that contain and restrict us. But it seems clear that in fact this particular challenge was a variation on the traditional penchant of many young men for undertaking some activity that brings them close to the jaws of death, and it is inevitable that some will miscalculate and see those jaws close on them irrevocably. It might be more appropriate to regard such risk in mountaineering—a risk that is basically undergone for its own sake and for the unique thrill of putting one's life on the line—as a partially disguised equivalent to such less-admired pastimes of this age and gender group as drag-racing, cliff and quarry diving, or such exotic activities as "elevator surfing"—jumping from the top of one high-rise elevator to one next to it that is moving in the opposite direction—a stunt that cost one University of Massachusetts student his life a few years ago. The present glorification of "extreme," high-risk activities is seductive for a significant number of young men and a not insignificant number of young women.

Perhaps the most important issue for the mountaineering community is whether we encourage senseless risk by glorifying the achievements of those who undertake unacceptable risks and succeed. (Of course defining unacceptable risk is the stickiest point of all.) We live in a world where a skilled technical climber can make an incredibly difficult ascent, and then be one-upped by someone who dares to do the same climb unroped. In such an atmosphere people who are addicted to the thrill of risk taking are often encouraged by the admiration they receive when they succeed. Clearly Haas and Tinkham expected to succeed, or at least survive, and presumably they expected to be admired for their nerve and fortitude. Perhaps they saw themselves as followers of the limit-extending tradition of Whymper, of Mallory and Irvine, and of countless others, a proposition that most expert mountaineers would probably reject derisively.

The question then remains: How can we render proper praise to mountaineering feats based on skill, resourcefulness, and true courage without honoring feats that are merely the product of a brash foolhardiness? As any student of mountaineering must conclude, you cannot make such a judgment merely by ascertaining whether the result was success or failure, survival or death.

From *"College Student Dies of Hypothermia on Mt. Jefferson,"* by Eugene Daniell, in *"*Notes: Accidents," *Appalachia,* December 1994.

PAUL HEMPHILL

Hanover, New Hampshire. The Occam Inn, a hostel frequented by Appalachian Trail hikers. What is jazz critic Paul Hemphill doing here, nursing sore knees? He wonders that himself, but his fine book about hiking long sections of the AT with his son provides a compelling answer. They covered many miles together and did a lot of family healing work en route, work that might never have been done back home.

Your Knees Aren't Your Problem

THE NEXT MORNING, A STEAMING SATURDAY SMACK-DAB IN THE MIDDLE OF July, I rolled out of my cot in the basement bunk room of the old tourists' home and went about my business like a condemned man whose only hope was that maybe there had been a last-minute pardon or a power shortage. David snored softly. Lurch was gone somewhere. I numbly showered and, for whatever odd reason, spent ten minutes trimming my salt-and-pepper beard. I didn't bother to massage or bandage the knees, nor even to take up the crutches, on the grounds that they might as well see the wreckage plain and unadorned. I slipped into my blue hiking shorts and my cleanest dirty T-shirt and my sandals and walked the block and a half to the Hitchcock Clinic.

At ten o'clock, having signed a bunch of forms at the front desk, I found myself idly swinging my legs as I sat on an examination table to await the doctor. I tried not to look at myself in the full-length mirror across from the table. Within a few minutes the doctor came in. It was a woman, about my age, and she pulled up a stool in front of me and began to probe the knees with her fingers while I babbled. *It's me and my boy, see, Georgia-to-Maine. . . . Seems like every time I tried a fifteen-miler the knees went out. . . . Trying to keep up with a bunch of teenagers was foolish. . . . I thought maybe there were some knee braces y'all know about just so we can do Katahdin. . . . I used to play baseball. . . .* She nodded pleasantly through all of that, fending off a few spasmic kicks toward her when she found the spots she was looking for, and I finally shut up when it occurred to me that this woman had probably seen every hiker's knee there was to be seen. She was yet to say a word.

"Maybe there's a knee brace I don't know about," I said. "I mean, Joe Namath and Kenny Stabler, those quarterbacks, they got these knees like robots. Every play some elephant comes in on 'em and knocks the shit out of 'em and they get up smiling. Isn't there something like that? I mean, I should've come in here a week ago, but, you know."

"Your knees aren't your problem," she said.

"Ma'am?"

"It's your knees that *hurt*."

"Tell me. 'Hurt' won't cover it."

"The problem is with your thighs," she said.

"The thighs."

"You lack bulk in your thighs."

"Bulk. In my thighs." I thought for a second. "I'm skinny."

"You're skinny," she said.

"Sonofabitch."

She had a lot of patients waiting—kids with poison ivy, mean-eyed old curmudgeons in town for their weekly placebos, alcoholics wanting just one more I-promise-it's-the-last extension on their Librium prescription, ruddy-cheeked Dartmouth lads with "tennis elbow"—but she had enough time to explain and to console. "I've got a fourteen-year-old son and he loves to backpack," she said. "The same thing kept happening to him. He's a frail kid, or at least he used to be. What I did was put him on a Nautilus program. You know Nautilus. The exercise machines. Athletes use them these days. We put him to work on one that was designed for that one thing, to build up his thighs, and I tell you that after about six months that kid could almost *run* up and over Mount Washington. You've got the same problem he had. You're asking too much of your knees."

"But I gotta walk the rest of the trail," I said.

"You'll never make it."

"Come on. They got drugs and things these days."

"You're making me beg you not to go," she said.

"This Cherokee told me about mind over matter."

"I'm not going to touch that. I'm just telling you that you'd get up there in the Whites above tree line and the winds would get up to seventy miles an hour and you wouldn't even be able to crawl for water and there's no way in the world that anybody could come and get you. Not in a helicopter, nothing. And what if it snows? And your son gets sick? And you run out of food? That would make a wonderful heroic story but I don't want to read it. Look. Go home, do Nautilus, try it again and call me about this time next year. My boy would love to walk the rest of the way to Katahdin with you."

David, awake and pacing when I shuffled back to the Occom Inn with the news, was nonplussed. It was over. I called Susan and made airline reservations and turned in my crutches and we bought respectable light-weight sweaters for an airplane ride and gobbled some pizza and tossed what grub we had left over into a box in the bunkroom for future hikers and squared the bill at the Occom and crammed everything into our packs. On the neat little twin-engine puddle-jumping commuter plane from Norwich, Vermont, to the Logan airport in Boston we chose seats on the left side so we could look at the White Mountains we might have walked to the end of the AT at Katahdin in Maine. On the mammoth Delta jet from Boston to Atlanta we chose seats on the right windows so we could see the Shenandoahs and the Smokies where we *had* walked. We were home before dark.

From *Me and the Boy: A Journey of Discovery—Father and Son on the Appalachian Trail,* by Paul Hemphill, Macmillan, 1986.

MAINE

The end and the beginning: atop foggy, mile-high Katahdin, Baxter State Park, Maine.

Trail miles: 281.4

Trail maintenance: Appalachian Mountain Club, Maine AT Club

Highest point: Mt. Katahdin, 5,267 ft. (Baxter Peak)

Broadest river: Kennebec, dangerous to ford, crossable by ferry (provided in season by Appalachian Trail Conference and Maine AT Club)

Features: Northern terminus of AT, 2,150+ miles from Springer Mt., Georgia. Western section begins with the Mahoosucs, known as the toughest, bedeviling narrow, rocky climb on the AT, then continues with several steep 4,000-ft. mountains, including Saddleback (4,116 ft.), which the AT climbs, and Sugarloaf (4,237 ft.), which the trail skirts. Northernmost section, from Monson to Mt. Katahdin, offers 100+ miles of isolated, roadless travel.

Parks, forests, and nature preserves: Grafton Notch State Park, Bigelow Preserve, Baxter State Park

Most intriguing name on the trail: Mooselookmeguntic Lake

Trail towns: Bethel, Andover, Rangeley, Caratunk, Stratton, Monson, Millinocket

V. COLLINS CHEW

In the Abenaki language, Katahdin means "preeminent mountain." English can do no better. Whether one starts or finishes an Appalachian Trail thru-hike here, or climbs Katahdin as a separate adventure, the experience is indelible. Much of the respect engendered by Katahdin (to the native people it was as much fear as respect, for they believed certain not-too-friendly gods lived up there) is rooted in the mountain's rugged geology. Rock expert V. Collins Chew tells us what's underfoot on massive Katahdin.

The Final Climb of the AT

THE FINAL CLIMB OF THE A.T. IS MORE THAN 4,000 FEET UP KATAHDIN, "GREATest mountain" in the language of the Indians inhabiting the area when European settlers arrived. Its 5,267-foot elevation indicates that its granite bedrock is erosion-resistant. Some suggest the bedrock hardened as minerals such as silica were deposited by rainwater seeping down from the former rock surface above the granite. Dr. Rodgers speculates the resistance of granite is related to the stress that has been placed on it. The Katahdin granite was intruded into position relatively late and may not have been stressed heavily. Older granites may have undergone considerable stress while at high temperatures.

Katahdin was sculpted by both continental and alpine glaciers. The continental glaciers smoothed the flat, high tableland as they scraped across the mountain. Alpine or valley glaciers sculptured bowl-shaped cirques around Katahdin's sides. The cirques on the east side are perhaps the most spectacular.

Southeast of the summit, the Knife Edge crosses the only arete near the A.T. Alpine glaciers on opposite sides of the ridge steepened their valleys until they eliminated the summit area between them, except for a narrow ridge resembling a hollow-ground knife blade. "Arete" translates literally as "fish bone."

Katahdin's summit is very different from the lower granite mountaintops, such as the smooth top of Moxie Bald. It more closely resembles the high peaks of New Hampshire's White Mountains — a jumble of angular boulders (felsenmeer, or rock sea). This jumble resulted from the long, cold winters that have occurred on these mountaintops since the end of the ice ages. Freeze-thaw cycles are thought to be the main cause of this broken rock, but recent research has shown that prolonged periods somewhat below freezing are most efficient at breaking up the rock. Continental glaciers would have carried away broken rock, so these angular boulders probably have formed since the continental glaciers melted.

Katahdin's resistant rock gives it imposing height, 1,700 vertical feet, and many acres above timberline. In this extremely cold place, only the hardiest plants live—highly adapted perennial wildflowers, some grasses, sedges, and lichens.

The views south and east from Katahdin are across the lake-dotted, once glacier-covered lowland. From the Baxter Peak summit, the lower South Peak of Katahdin rises above the line of the horizon, appearing higher than the true summit. The curvature of the Earth makes the distant horizon appear low, the South Peak high. Rarely in the mountains is the surrounding area flat enough to create this illusion.

For the northbound hiker, Katahdin is the spectacular end of the Appalachian Trail.

From *Underfoot: A Geologic Guide to the Appalachian Trail,* by V. Collins Chew, Appalachian Trail Conference, 1988.

MYRON AVERY

As much the father of the Appalachian Trail as his on-again, off-again compatriot Benton MacKaye, Myron Avery was determined to be the first person to walk the entire length of the trail. He took sixteen years to do it, from 1920 to 1936. Avery was an inveterate documentarian, keeping detailed notes on every outing, amassing an extensive collection of annotated maps. He was a native of tiny North Lubec, Maine, yet his ambition lifted him from Bowdoin College to Harvard Law School to the chairmanship of the Appalachian Trail Conference (1931–1952). A perfectionist and go-getter, Avery sometimes alienated those who moved more slowly, but he was after all an evangelist for a good cause and had the grace to patch up bruised friendships. We follow him on a trek through deep backwoods Maine, which today remains probably the most remote section of the entire Appalachian Trail. Avery's notes, dated 1937, are a composite of observations from years of hiking experience.

Afoot along the Two-Thousand Mile Appalachian Trail

KATAHDIN IN MAINE IS THE BEGINNING OF OUR JOURNEY. ONLY THIRTEEN feet under a mile in height, this mountain is a transplanted bit of the High Sierra, rising abruptly from a forest-mantled wilderness, broken only by the sheen of myriad lakes which seem to heliograph to the summit. The master architect so skillfully sculpturing this massive monolith was the glacier which stood down over New England and overrode its highest summits. Long after the continental ice sheet had receded, local glaciers persisted on the slopes of Katahdin, and the freshness of the cirques scoured out by them tell us they departed but recently; if we say they were still active only 15,000 years ago, no one can quarrel overmuch with us. . . .

It has been a day's journey to reach Katahdin from the railroad. We may have followed the historic route taken by Marcus R. Keep, a wandering missionary whose devotion to this region led him, in 1848, single-handed to blaze the first trail, "The Keep Path", to Katahdin. The church influence was then strong in mountaineering, for one of the first parties to be guided over the new trail was composed of ministers. Sunday, on the mountain, was devoted to preaching. The Bangor Democrat (August 18, 1849) faithfully reprints the very lengthy sermon which details the story of the creation and ascribes the creation of Katahdin to the sixth day.

Katahdin can lay claim to a literature scarcely equalled in extent by any other mountain in the United States. However, an exploded myth is that Katahdin is the first point in the eastern United States to greet the rising sun.

The northern half of Maine is an utter wilderness where travel is by canoe and "tote-roads". Not until it reaches Monson, 114 miles west of Katahdin, does the Trail approach a settlement. Were we to stray from the route, it would be many days and entail crossing large lakes and rivers, before we should—with good fortune—reach the towns to the south. So it might be expected we would leave Katahdin with heavy packs. But instead we plunge into the Maine wilderness along the Appalachian Trail with only a toothbrush and a handkerchief. This seeming incongruity of finding accommodations each night on a twenty-four day journey in the wilderness is explained by the existence of sporting camps, a form of hostelry peculiar to Maine, which add much to the pleasure of travel along the Appalachian Trail in that state.

We leave Katahdin between two stone monoliths, termed the "Gateway", and descend to Daicey Pond, on which is the first sporting camp we encounter. The route is distinctly indicated by Appalachian Trail markers. These are either diamond-shaped galvanized iron or square copper markers, which carry the "AT" monogram and the legend, "Appalachian Trail—Maine to Georgia". The main reliance in trail marking, we soon discover, is a series of white paint blazes, facing the direction of travel. The titanium oxide paint used not only assures an existence of four to six years for the marking but its luminous quality aids travel at night. A further reassurance is the "double-blaze", which prevents—through inattention—failure to notice a turn. Cairns built so as to be obviously artificial, and paint on rocks indicate the route where other marking is not possible.

The Trail leads from Daicey Pond along Nesowadnehunk Stream to the West Branch of the Penobscot River, a dark, rushing river, 200 yards in width, gathering momentum for its leap over Nesowadnehunk Falls with the ominous roar which, some distance back, warned of its proximity. The river is filled with "pulp", a mass of four-foot spruce and fir logs. It seems as if our journey along an unbroken trail for 2,050 miles might here reach an abrupt ending. By resort to the Guidebook detailing the trail route in Maine, we find, however, that here a cable bridge, built by the CCC, solves this problem.

The crossing of the West Branch has brought us into close contact—almost too much so—with the lumber industry, which in the Maine woods has passed through three stages: the primitive old pine times, the long spruce logs, and now the pulpwood.

Cut in the deep snows of winter, the logs were "yarded" on the ice and banks of streams, whose swollen torrents in spring carried them to the mills. The hardships of the men who broke the jams, ran the logs, "sacked" the rear, and stood waist deep in the ice-cold water from daylight to dark, and "camped" beside the rivers in the melting snows, developed a distinct type—at his best in white water and where danger threatened. The story of the river driver, with all his fortitude, courage, and even his shortcomings, has been graphically told by Mrs. Fannie Hardy Eckstorm in *The Penobscot Man*. . . .

Regretfully we leave the West Branch with its vivid past, cross several low ridges and descend to the long irregularly shaped Rainbow Lake. Its shores have been burned and the resulting desolation impresses in an unforgettable fashion the need for care in the forest. The Rainbow Lake Camps, however, are in a wooded oasis in the burned lands.

The third day is an effortless journey to Nahmakanta, most remote in the Maine wilderness. If anywhere there is peace and isolation, it is at Nahmakanta, encircled by high hills. Even the loggers have been gone from here for a decade. Nahmakanta is Indian for "Lake of the largest fish", but its piscatorial qualities—which we do not test—fade beside its other allurements.

The trail next day leads along Nesuntabunt (three-headed) Mountain and down the age-old Nahmakanta Tote-road. From the White House Camps, at the head of Pemadumcook Lake, we look over the enormous lower lakes on the Penobscot West Branch, here a veritable inland sea.

Next morning the way is over Potaywadjo Ridge, descending to the picturesque Joe Mary Lakes. Forty miles away, the massive bulk of Katahdin still dominates the landscape. But to the south a perfectly-shaped dome—Joe Mary Mountain—enhanced by its abrupt rise from the level setting of the Lower Lakes, intrigues our interest. A five-mile blue-blazed side trail leads to its summit—and the entire route of the past five days' travel lies before us.

Beyond the twin Yoke Ponds Camps, White Cap, towering over the surrounding country, is the loadstone toward which our next day's journey is directed. From the camps at West Branch Ponds is made the long traverse over it. Here is an enclosed lookout tower of the Maine Forest Service, one of some seventy-five towers from which an unceasing vigil is maintained. The panoramic view from White Cap (3,707 ft.) is superb—it challenges that from Katahdin. Nestled high on its slope are ponds which also are relics of the glacier.

The long descent from White Cap leads to one of the most spectacular parts of the Trail in Maine—the Gulf of the West Branch of Pleasant River. Here the stream is deeply intrenched in a slate canyon. Waterfalls, sheer walls, and fantastic shapes and formations succeed each other. So completely had this region been forgotten that the builder of these side trails had to find, in 1934, the points of interest through descriptions in the fifty-year old Hubbard and Farrar Guidebooks of Northern Maine.

From York's Long Pond Camps a tremendous barrier looms across the route. It is the Chairback-Barren Range, a densely forested group of five peaks. The difficulty of carrying the Trail through this region proved an almost insuperable obstacle to the completion of the Maine link. Often we wonder how such an extensive trail was developed, far distant from any outdoor organizations. The explanation is Walter D. Greene, Broadway actor and Maine guide. For years Greene had made solo trips along what is now the Appalachian Trail. Attracted to this project, he developed a feasible route for 120 miles of a high scenic order. We spend two days in the virgin forest on the Chairback-Barren Range with its delightful trail and high-lying ponds, the second day bringing us to Bodfish Intervale, entirely surrounded by mountains. As we travel these cathedral groves of spruce and fir, we term Greene's accomplishment one of the great feats in the annals of trail building. . . .

Resuming our journey down the Trail, from the Chairback-Barren Range we travel for a day through the Little Wilson region, a forested plain. In crossing this stream we notice a pile of slate, built up like an abutment. This was a support of the bridge on the old stage road and is the sole remains of the once flourishing village of Savage's Mills, settled in 1824 and abandoned in 1858. The forest has obliterated all traces of the settlement; from the forest to the village and back again to the forest, the cycle is complete.

Beyond is the village of Monson and the once flourishing community of Blanchard in the Piscataquis Valley. From Blanchard an easy day's journey brings us to the fire warden's camp on Moxie Bald Mountain, a long bare crest whose rocks are often shattered by lightning. The next day's travel leads to Troutdale Cabins on Moxie Pond, the center of an interesting mountain and fishing region. A canoe ferry is made at the Narrows. Crossing an abandoned division of the Maine Central Railway, another example of reversion to the wilderness, the Kennebec River is reached. Here occurs the second ferrying on the Maine section. We are now on a historic path—the

Arnold Trail across the Great Bend of Dead River. The gallantry and hardship of this daring march by Benedict Arnold through the Maine wilderness to attack Quebec in the dead of winter is graphically described by Kenneth Roberts in *Arundel*. Had this expedition succeeded, Arnold might have been the hero of the American Revolution instead of its despised Judas.

From Blanchard to Mt. Bigelow (4,150 ft.) the route of the Trail was developed by Supervisor Robert G. Stubbs of the Maine Forest Service. From Mt. Bigelow to Sugarloaf, whose symmetrical bare cone (4,237 ft.) is Maine's second highest mountain, we follow 15 miles of trail constructed by Game Warden Helen N. Taylor. Continuing through the wilderness, the Trail traverses Mts. Abraham and Saddleback, from both of which Forest Service towers afford splendid views.

At Grafton Notch, our de luxe traveling ends. Until we reach the Appalachian Mountain Club Huts in New Hampshire, we carry a complete camping outfit.

There has recently grown up in New England a school advocating lightweight camping equipment. Its leader was Arthur C. Comey, past Chairman of the New England Trail Conference. Formerly the camping-out hiker resembled a human packhorse. Now we are equipped for ten days in the woods, yet our packs weigh only thirty pounds. Our pack is the Bergans Meis, developed for use in the Norwegian Army. We use a three-pound down sleeping bag. The tent, which will accommodate two people, weighs four pounds. The cooking utensils are two light-weight aluminum pails, a fry pan, fork, and spoon. For longer trips, a six ounce reflecting baker is added for making bread or even such a luxury as cake. A one pound Hudson's Bay axe, a first aid outfit, compass, matches, inspirator, Meta tablets, maps, and Guidebook, woolen underwear, and socks complete the outfit. The food is surprisingly light in weight. Of late, palatable precooked and dehydrated vegetables have appeared. Flour, rice, dried fruits, Canada bacon, chocolate, raisins, and other concentrated foods offer sufficient variety for ten days. The canned food is beef and chicken, from which we prepare with rice the evening piece de resistance, after having filled the aching void with quarts of soup made from the so-called dynamite soup tubes.

From Grafton Notch, 11 miles from the Maine–New Hampshire line, steep climb leads to the fire lookout on Old Speck (4,200 ft. app.), as this peak is affectionately termed. Here begin the splendid trails of the Appalachian Mountain Club. The Club, founded in 1876, is the oldest and largest mountaineering organization in the country. Its membership numbers over five thousand and it maintains an extensive hut, shelter, and trail system. From Old Speck for some 28 miles, in a two-day trip, we follow the Appalachian Mountain Club's Trail along the Mahoosuc Range through an unbroken wilderness with names such as Goose-Eye, Fulling Mill, Dream Lake,

Full Goose, Mount Success, and Popsy Spring, to Gorham on the Androscoggin River. At Gorham we divest ourselves of the camping equipment, to travel with only a toothbrush and a Guidebook.

From *Afoot along the Two-Thousand Mile Appalachian Trail*, by Myron Avery, unpublished manuscript, 1937, Appalachian Trail Conference.

KATHRYN FULKERSON

High spirits and high times: They start for the hiking crowd even before the trip begins. It's only through the spirit of play that one can lose oneself for hours in the serious game of packing one's pack. Kathryn Fulkerson, of Washington, D.C., recounted her pleasure in preparing for a hiking holiday on Maine's Appalachian Trail in 1939. Her comrades were members of the Potomac Appalachian Trail Club.

Trail Diary, 1939

*I*S THERE ANYTHING SO INTERESTING TO A HIKER AS A PACK AND ITS CONTENTS? Instructions had been given for the great endurance test—the hike of the A.T. after the Conference—the packs could not exceed 12 lbs in weight. This pack was to carry change of clothing and personal essentials for the 12 days on the Trail. The criterion by which we were going was the 1935 pioneer trip which 14 hardy members of the Club took one August, and when the weather was icy and the rain poured most of the time. Based on this uncheerful prospect most of us went in heavily for woolies and rain equipment with sweaters, parka etc. However the weight must be kept within the limit, so many enlightening and interesting weights were taken and statistics made of packs and contents. Margaret and I took ours to the Sanitary and had lots of fun weighing boots, socks, shirts, undies, bathing suits, etc. I believe I have a list of the weights of all hiking equipment and clothing from my 3 lb. frame pack to my 11 oz. tennis shoes. . . .

At one of the meetings Myron had showed just what he carried in his pack, and we also had the invaluable List of Minimum Equipment for light travelling, but you can't believe how hard it is to keep a pack to 12 lbs. The Gerber (best of all light weight frame packs) weighs 3 lbs with the shoulder pads attached, and mine has a few zippers added a la Bergans. In the top flap per instructions goes hanky (a bandanna) oiled silk bag for valuables, another of moleskin etc. for feet; a tiny box of bandades, a tinier tin box with needle and thread, and my small and most convenient flashlight. In an outside pocket the P.A.T.C. drinking Cup, my knife, and Watson Match Box filled with matches and a spare flash bulb. Also my tiny can of boot grease from Beans which was never used and came back home at the half way mark. An oiled silk tobacco pouch made a fine case for the half lb of emergency rations we had to take—dried apricots and raisins—and Oh how glad those two half starved boys were on Katahdin when I met them on the Knife Edge and turned over my emergency rations into their hat, and disposed of some of the packs of lifesavers I was carrying—a pack of gum and a life-saver pack is each an ounce in weight and I had three of each till then.

Inside the pack I had a series of 4 or 5 or more oiled silk bags—the kind you buy for vegetables in an icebox. They are the very best things for camping, or packing in any form—have been using them all summer. One good sized bag would take the extra pair of wool breeches which I had to carry for change of clothing and in case we got in cold and drenched (which thank goodness we never did). I would have been better off with a light pair of cotton slacks, but how could we know it would be warm in Aug, in 1939, when in Aug. 1935 it was cold and wet—very wet. Thank goodness on this trip we had but one rain and were in it only a short time. However the new rain suits were necessary as part of the equipment of our packs. Marian and I got ours at Sport Center—the golf rain suits which have a nice zipper jacket and a wrap around skirt and weigh about 11 oz. The featherweight Bean oiled silk rainshirt weighs 6 oz but is not so nice as this kind. I got one and sold it to someone before I left. Also got the Bean rain hat as this type of rain suit does not have the sewed on hood of the old Bean Rainshirt—the whole thing is far lighter than the old rain shirt was. I did not take mine along. That useful garment has served its time, and saved many of us from wet and cold—but it is absolutely no good in summer as you get far wetter with it on than without—it condenses moisture—and so do the oiled solid rainshirts I find. Marian's is a nice light blue and mine is brown—the old rainshirts were olive green, and we all looked like pixies in them. Besides the rain suit another useful garment which I got for 4 of us earlier in the summer was the cotton poplin parka with hood for warmth over our flannel shirts in the evening. I found it was really useful and wore it some. That and my very fine light flannel shirt—bright red Greenbrier, which I have had for years—was all and more the warmth needed on this trip.

Another of the transparent silk zipper bags was used for extra shirt and hankies, and the very thinnest undies I could find to keep light weight. Had, however, to take a zipper of wool snuggies in case of cold—and it didn't get cold so sent them back at half way stop, as I did most of the socks I had taken. We needed plenty of socks, as I found that my new boots were easier when padded with 2 prs. wool and a silk. I was really a little short on socks at the end. I took all my old silk ones along to wear under the wool to avoid blisters, and I had no blister during the trip.

A silk bag of pajamas (my nice old blue satin ones which go along on most Shelter trips and are so light and worn out that they weigh scarcely anything, but are handy like slacks to wear about the cabins). And then the most essential toilet articles. I got us all the army mirrors—polished steel at Sport Center for 25¢. I got my tooth paste in small tubes—3 of them: one for Conference, one for trip down trail and one to send in at Yokes. Same with Ponds Cold Cream. Took a couple folding toothbrushes, and what a hunt I had for them before the trip—it seems they don't make those nice ones that shut like a knife anymore, and I don't like the kind I got. Also hunted long before I found the last folding nail file in town like the two I had and lost. I ordered from Bean before I left the good old Bean's fly dope and did I use it at the Conference! Put some in a tiny tin powder box and carried in my pocket. Did the same with sun cream, and both were in constant demand. Also had my pocket 3 ply pencil compact which holds a little dab of cold cream, sun cream, and chapped lip cream—it did for the trip with a little augmenting. Had Kleanex tucked everywhere, and a pocket full of Kleanex is a lifesaver when perspiration drips in ones eyes as one dashes down the trail. There I guess you have the whole story of the pack which broke the camels back—a very innocent pack and a very poor sort of a camel.

From *Report of the Maine Trip, August 18–September 4, 1939,* by Kathryn Fulkerson, unpublished manuscript, 1939, Appalachian Trail Conference.

PERCIVAL BAXTER

Mt. Katahdin is the crown jewel of Maine's Baxter State Park, one of the largest wilderness areas in the United States (over 200,000 acres). The park is the namesake of Governor Percival Baxter, who had a vision of the role the Katahdin region could play, not only in his state's recreation industry but also in wildlife preservation and in helping the human spirit to re-create itself in wild places. Over three decades and against daunting odds (an unwilling legislature, a resistant logging industry), Baxter lobbied for and sometimes personally purchased tens of thousands of acres for the park. Practically shamed into following his philanthropic lead, Maine eventually adopted Baxter's plan with admirable enthusiasm and stewardship. Here are a few of the governor's eloquent comments on the park that so rightly bears his name.

Greatest Mountain

To Maine Sportsmen's Fish and Game Association, January 1921

To most people Mount Katahdin is but a name. To those who have both seen and climbed the Mountain, it is a wonderful reality, and the memories of a trip to its summit remain vivid through the years. At present the great Mountain, weather-beaten by time and scarred by the avalanche, is almost inaccessible, the journey entailing expense, hardship and discomfort. The grandeur of the Mountain, its precipitous slopes, its massive cliffs, unusual formation and wonderful coloring cannot be surpassed or even equalled by any mountain east of the Mississippi river. Katahdin rises abruptly from the plain to the height of 5,273 feet, and, without foothills to detract from its solitary dignity, stands alone, a grim gray tower overlooking the surrounding country for hundreds of miles. It is small wonder that the aboriginal Indians believed it to be the home of the spirits of wind, storm and thunder.

The history of these lands is fascinating. It is a story of violent speculation in which fortunes were lost and men's reputations ruined, and in which fortunes were won and great timber-owning families were established, and made wealthy for generations to come. It is a story of intrigue and corruption, where powerful and selfish men often took that to which they had no right, from those too weak to defend themselves and their property. It is a story in which the rights of the people in a princely inheritance were given away or bartered for a song, for the folly of which future generations forever will pay.

To Governor H. A. Hildreth and the Legislature, January 1945

I want pleasant foot-trails built and attractive campsites laid out in the valleys, by the brooks and on the shores of the waters. Sites where simple forest lean-tos and small log cabins are available for those who love nature and are willing to walk and make an effort to get close to nature.

Everything in connection with the Park must be left simple and natural, and must remain as nearly as possible as it was when only the Indians and the animals roamed at will through these areas. I want it made available to persons of moderate means who, with their boys and girls, with their packs of bedding and food, can tramp through the woods, cook a steak and make flapjacks by the lakes and brooks. Every section of this area is beautiful, each in its own way. I do not want it locked up and made inaccessible; I want it used to the fullest extent but in the right, unspoiled way.

From *Greatest Mountain: Katahdin's Wilderness*, by Percival Baxter, Scrimshaw Press, 1972.

DAVID HORTON

Calling himself an "ultra-runner," David Horton set out in 1991 to break the record for the fastest thru-hike on the AT. With no apparent sense of irony, his report to the Appalachian Trail Conference begins with a quote from Thoreau, a saunterer whose own deliberately slow pace—the better to see things—calls into question the motives behind a trail-race against time. Are Horton and the other AT speed demons heroes or lunatics? Most would no doubt find the accomplishment amazing and yet hard to admire. Perhaps its meaning for the rest of us, if it has one, is that on the Appalachian Trail expressions of unbridled individuality can run free in a way they cannot in ordinary society. Judge for yourself.

Running for the Record

F OR YEARS, I HAD DREAMED OF RUNNING THE APPALACHIAN TRAIL (A.T.). The summer of 1991 allowed me the opportunity to fulfill that dream. . . .

From time to time, individuals have attempted to set a speed record for hiking the entire A.T. However, the Appalachian Trail Conference (A.T.C.) does not officially recognize any type of records on the A.T. On the other hand, The Appalachian Long Distance Hikers Association (A.L.D.H.A.) does recognize and certify the speed record for the A.T. The unofficial record was set in 1990 by Ward Leonard of Salt Lake City, Utah. Mr. Leonard's time was 60 and one-half days. His time was not ratified by A.L.D.H.A. because there was some question about the "completeness" of his hike.

Not wanting to be away from my family any more than possible, but being a competitive ultra-runner, and wanting to set a record, I determined (with my wife's somewhat permission) that I would try to complete the A.T. in less than 60 days. Actually, my pre-determined goal was 56 days, thus allowing for a few rest days if needed.

My initial plan was to use a very light-weight backpack (approx. 16 lbs or less) and mail food and supplies to various post offices along the way (as most thru-hikers do) . However, through a plea in *Ultrarunning*, and friends hearing about my endeavor, I was able to enlist various people who graciously gave of their time and resources to crew me through the A.T. This allowed me to do the A.T. as you would a typical ultra (handlers meeting you at road crossings with supplies and encouragement!). Because of this, all I had to carry was a fanny pack and a water bottle. Sometimes, depending on the degree of help I had available, I only carried a water bottle.

On May 9, at 6:45 a.m., I started from Springer Mountain, GA. Two days earlier, Scott Grierson, of Bass Harbor, ME, had started with the same goal as I . . . 56 days on the A.T. Scott, who used the trail name "Maineak" was an experienced hiker, who only walked the trail. A typical day for him was some 16-17 hours walking. My trail name was to be "The Runner".

It rained continuously for nine of the first 12 days on the trail and was very foggy for the most part. This was good in that it kept the temperatures down, yet, it kept me from enjoying the views along the trail. My last day out of the Smokies, I developed shin splints (tendonitis) in my right leg. It progressively worsened and a few days later, it began in my left leg as well. Both shins were swollen, red, very painful to the touch, which produced excruciating pains while running/walking downhills. On the advice of Dr. Gary Buffington, I started taking anti-inflammatory medication and would ice down my shins 2-3 hours every night.

These problems abated somewhat, but still persisted into and through most of Virginia. I spent two weeks in Virginia, as one-fourth of the A.T.'s mileage lies in the state in which I reside. During all this time (just under 1,000 miles from GA to Harper's Ferry, WV) I had stayed two days behind the "Maineak". I was able to keep track of his progress by checking the registers at the shelters on the trail.

Even with the shin problems and other minor aches and pains, I was able to stay exactly on schedule averaging 38.3 miles a day. My shins began feeling better as I approached West Virginia and Maryland. As a result of getting rid of these shin problems, finally getting in shape, cooler weather, and easier terrain, I was able to pick up the pace, and for the next 18 days (days 26-43) I averaged 44.4 miles per day. On two successive days in Pennsylvania, I increased my mileage to 52 and 51 miles. Part of this was due to the terrain and the fact that I was feeling good! However, the biggest factor was that I had heard that Maineak went 50 miles in one day in the same area.

With the increased mileage, I started gaining on the Maineak. On the 39th day (just inside the southern border of Vermont), I caught up with Maineak—1,574.6 miles from the start in Georgia. I had only four miles left for the day, so I walked and talked with him the rest of the way.

For the next four days, we played leap-frog. He would hike until 10:00 or 11:00 P.M. and as a result, would go beyond where I had stopped at 4:00 or 5:00 P.M. The following days I would again pass him at earlier and earlier points. The last time I saw Maineak was about 15 miles east of Hanover, NH. on my 43rd day out. We had become good friends and it was somewhat disappointing not seeing him each day. He was very helpful in telling me a great deal about what lay ahead for me on the trail. However, when I asked him about Maine, he would only say "It's all a warm-up for Maine". When I asked him what he meant, he would only say, "you'll see!"

A typical day during the early stages of the run started a little after 6:00 A.M. and run/walk for 10-11 hours per day. Later on, I started around 5:30 A.M. and eventually in the last three weeks, began the day at 4:45 A.M.

I would eat a good breakfast (if available) and usually eat a turkey and cheese sandwich around 12:30 or 1:00 P.M. During the day, I would drink about 1 and 1/2 gallons of the replacement drink, Conquest, and eat 5-6 Skor candy bars and occasionally a Power Bar. As long as I had Conquest available, I never bonked or had any trouble, and miraculously, I never got tired of it. In the evening, I would try to find a food bar or a buffet. This was possible until I reached the Northeast states. Nearly all of the people who helped me were ultra-runners who understood my physical, mental and nutritional needs to such a degree that I really didn't have to worry about those things.

As I was making great progress in this section (44.4 miles per day) from Maryland to the White Mountains in New Hampshire, I was starting to get a little self-confident and thought I had it in the bag and the worst was behind me. I was sadly mistaken!

The White Mountains of New Hampshire were the prettiest place on the A.T., but also the most difficult. I thought I knew what a rocky trail was, having run the Massanutten Mountain Massacre. I was wrong. I thought I knew what steep hills were, having done the Barkley Marathon twice. I was wrong. The White Mountains were extremely rocky and steep. They don't seem to know what a switchback is in New Hampshire. Most of the trails go straight up and straight down the mountains. It was just as slow going down as it was going up.

To this point, my overall average time I spent on the trail was 11 hours and 25 minutes. In the last ten days (New Hampshire and Maine), I averaged 13 hours and 37 minutes on the trail. It was very difficult to run any at all. Walking, rather than running, was the basic mode of transportation in this area. Access for my crew was also very limited because there were so few road crossings. As a result of this, several times in the last one and one-half weeks, I developed low blood sugar. The amount of sleep I was getting each night also went down.

After spending three unbelievably difficult days in the White Mountains, I finally made it into Maine. I thought I could just cruise easily the rest of the way to Mt. Katahdin (northern terminus of the A.T.). I was again proven wrong!

The Maineak had warned me about Maine, but I had no idea what was in store in this last state. The mountains were not as big, but the climbs were just as steep. Much of the trail in Maine is new. Therefore, it was rocky, full of roots, swampy, and just generally very unrunable. Also, my progress in Maine was just as slow as it was in the White Mountains.

The last week in Maine found me to be a mental and emotional wreck. I would break down over the least little problem or set back. Every time I thought about my family, home, a normal life; I would completely break down and cry. I was also getting physically exhausted and would fall 5-6 times or more each day. My toes were so sore and swollen. I kept stubbing them on rocks and roots. However, the thought of quitting or taking a day off, never entered my mind. Even though I was getting so close to finishing in Maine, it wasn't until Saturday (the day before I would finish) that I realized that I was actually going to finish. For so long it had felt like I was on a perpetual treadmill and I would never get off. I was jealous of other people who were living a normal life.

One of the things that really helped me through these difficult times were all the letters, cards and packages of "goodies" that I would receive at the post office drops along the way. It meant so much to read how people were praying for me, encouraging me, and counting on me finishing in record time. This exerted a certain amount of pressure on me that it was very important, not only to me, but to countless others, to finish what I had started. Especially important to all of those who came out and crewed me through this endeavor. They were sharing in a very real part of this accomplishment as well.

Many times when I would be climbing those vertical ascents in the White Mountains, I would claim God's promise in Phil. 4:13 "I can do all things through Christ who strengthens me" and Phil. 4:19 "My God shall supply all your needs according to his riches in glory by Christ Jesus." He never failed me!

At 2:00 P.M. on June 30, 1991, I reached the Katahdin Stream Campground; 5.2 miles from the summit of the last mountain I would have to climb. After getting some Conquest, food and warmer clothing, I began the 4,000 ft. ascent (the single biggest climb on the A.T.) at 2:10 P.M.

I had thought every day for the past 52 days about this moment. And I was not to share this moment alone — My 17 year old son, Brandon, and crew members/friends, Nancy Hamilton, Doug Young, Jack McGiffin and Glenn Streeter accompanied me to the top of Mt. Katahdin, as my wife, Nancy, drove around to the other side of the mountain to wait on us.

The temperature at the base of the mountain was about 70 degrees. At the top it was 50 degrees with wind gusts of 40-50 MPH. The climb up was fun, yet very difficult. About 1500 ft. of the climb was technical as evidenced by the pitons in the rocks for handholds. Getting to the top of the last mountain at 4:35 p.m. was a tremendous feeling of "relief". I knew then that I could finally stop, I didn't have to climb another mountain, I was free to resume a "normal" life once again.

A few months later:

Recovery is coming very slowly. I ran 2 miles today and felt horrible. I still can't sleep at night for dreaming I'm still on the trail and have to cover a few more miles. I wake in the mornings wet with sweat. Nancy says I keep her awake by tossing and turning and talking continually in my sleep. I'm not sure what to expect in the future.

From *"A Summer to Remember: 2,144 Miles on the Appalachian Trail,"* a *2,000-Miler Report to the Appalachian Trail Conference,* by David Horton, Appalachian Trail Conference, 1991.

RAYMOND BAKER

Back in the 1960s, crossing the Kennebec River deep in the interior of Maine was a hair-raising experience for any Appalachian Trail hiker. Some have drowned there, trying to ford the river; others have waited days for a canoeist to appear. Nowadays, in season, canoes are kept available for hikers, but when Raymond Baker thru-hiked in 1964 he was on his own, facing an insurmountable barrier. That is, until some Québecois lumberjacks materialized out of the forest, and on that hangs a tale.

Crossing the Kennebec

AFTER DETOURING A BUNCH OF BAD BLOWDOWNS, I MADE THE KENNEBEC River before dark. Now I was in for a real surprise. I knew there was a spot one needed help, but didn't realize this was it. I found a rowboat chained and locked on my side; on the other, about a hundred yards across, a canoe was pulled up on the bank. With no one in sight on either side, they didn't do me a bit of good.

Deciding to camp at a long-abandoned old farm house, I left my pack and returned to the river for water. Heading back I met three French-Canadian lumberjacks. They had come back, after supper at the camp, to haul out one more load of pulp before dark. Only one could speak a little English. I asked how far to the nearest bridge, and he replied twenty-four miles downstream. We all returned to the river and checked again, with the same results. The rowboat securely fastened and the canoe on the far bank, with no one in sight.

They suggested I accompany them back to the lumber camp, as soon as they got this one load of pulp out.

The way these young fellows worked, I knew they weren't being paid by the hour, but by the number of cords they hauled out and stacked. They seemed to work in pairs or small groups, this group being real ambitious, getting a load out after supper.

Returning three or four miles to camp, they pointed out the cookhouse and bunkhouse, then left me on my own. Entering the dining room I found the cook and his helper talking with a friend. I tried to convey the message that I would like some supper but got nowhere. The "cookie" took me to the bunkhouse with the same results. Another building where a light showed, turned out to be an office, where a man seemed to be having a hard time making out income tax reports. He spoke some English and said he would be with me in a moment. Meanwhile, the cook's helper had contacted the only English-speaking person in the camp. We went back to the cookhouse and he talked to the cook in French. In almost less time than it takes to tell it, he had things rolling. Homemade bread, with all kinds of meat and bologna, instant coffee, plenty of cookies; I never had it so good.

My English-speaking friend questioned me about the trip. He would then translate in French for the rest, and we had a real jolly time of it. The lumberjack who spoke some English told me a truck was leaving at 4:00 A.M. to cross at the bridge 22 miles downstream and I could go along. When I spoke to my friend, who seemed to be pretty much in charge here, about it, he said he thought it best to go back to the river crossing where I was last night. He is in charge of maintenance and had to go back to repair a caterpillar tractor which had broken down. I could go on back with him.

The cookie took me to the bunkhouse and showed me an empty upper bunk. Playing his light straight down so as not to disturb anyone, he led me directly to an empty bunk, about the very center of the building. Such an assortment of snorts, snores, grunts, and groans, one seldom has a chance to hear. They didn't keep me awake long, however, I may have even joined the chorus, for the next thing I knew the first bell was ringing.

Two bells would ring early in the morning, the first to dress and wash up, the second means, "Come and get it." The cook is boss in his own domain, so I waited till he found me an empty place. The men wasted little time on conversation and were soon done eating and out. The room was spotless and the food excellent. We were soon back at the river, they to repair the large "cat," and I to wait for the man with the canoe to cross over. His small crawler and cart were here but no one to use them. I found out he hadn't crossed yesterday, didn't look like he would today. Tomorrow was Saturday, so I didn't think much of my chances. Deciding the repairs on the cat was too big a job to do in the field, they returned to the lumber camp. They told me I might walk up along the river and try to attract attention from a gas station, with cabins, a half mile up. The only life I saw was a pair of young 'coons. I called and blew my whistle, but it was quite far across and I didn't make contact.

I decided to use a stick as a staff to steady myself and try to wade it. I couldn't tell how deep it was in the center, but the current was quite strong.

Just as I started back to the crossing, a station wagon, containing two women, pulled out on a sandbar. One yelled over, asking if I was the hiker who wanted to cross. I replied in the affirmative and they said a man with a canoe was waiting.

Returning to the crossing, the canoe was still on the far bank and no one in sight. I waited a bit and soon a pickup truck came down the road blowing its horn. This proved to be my man; he soon had the canoe in the water and on his way across. An expert with a canoe, he negotiated the swift current without mishap. I bought supplies at Caratunk, a small town along the Kennebec River. I was told that the man in charge of maintenance at the lumber camp had gotten in touch with his wife, who lives across the river, by some sort of radio-telephone hookup. She in turn called the village store, a sort of community center, and the mission was accomplished in short order. Why he hadn't thought to call his wife earlier, I'll never know.

From *Campfires Along the Appalachian Trail*, by Raymond Baker, Carlton Press, 1971.

BILL IRWIN

No matter how you slice it, Bill Irwin deserves applause. Other handicapped people have hiked the Appalachian Trail, including those with muscular dystrophy, but Irwin is the only blind person to have walked all 2,150 miles. He could not have done it without his trusty guide dog, aptly named Orient, or without the generous help of many friends along the route. Nor could he have done it without a wellspring of courage and resilience within himself. That wellspring was his religious faith; yet after sorting out the meaning of the adventure, Irwin remains refreshingly realistic in his advice to other hikers who might think a thru-hike in itself will unknot a tangled mind.

Trail Diary, 1990

ONE THING THRU-HIKERS TOLD ME AT THE BEGINNING WAS THAT I'D BECOME so adapted to the Trail's conditions that my adjustment in the other world—the real world, the world where they run thermostats, lights, switches and telephones—would be difficult. I didn't believe them then.

I do now.

Most thru-hikers look back on their Trail days as one of the most significant times in their lives. They make scrapbooks of pictures, poems, and journal entries, and tell their stories proudly to anyone willing to listen. Children and grandchildren will fall asleep to vivid descriptions of adventures on the A.T.

In every thru-hiker's memory, an investment of time, energy, and money that a lot of folks consider insane occupies a shelf labeled Commitment/Freedom. These two stand together as inseparable elements of a great enterprise.

That's the way it was for me. On a two thousand-mile canvas, God had painted a stunning picture for me of the freedom that comes from the commitment to walk His way. I was still new at the business of following the Lord and hoped I'd never forget the lessons and the people of the Appalachian Trail.

I think I'm now more tolerant of people than I used to be. After the wide variety of experiences I had on the A.T., I don't think I'm as bothered by the little things as I used to be. They seem so insignificant in the overall scheme of things. Living with so many different kinds of people in such close quarters in all kinds of environments has helped me overlook and tolerate a wider variety of behavior than before.

I also came to several reconciliations and understandings along the way. Some were things I didn't know I needed to know.

I realize I could have done it another way, another trail, another route, or maybe something entirely different. It could have been anywhere, doing anything. The A.T. was only a vehicle. It was there to facilitate events that would never otherwise have happened. A lot of things were within me, internal things. It took some of the events along the way, some of the hardships, some of the solitude, to bring about new ways of thinking and believing. The Trail forced me to deal with things I'd never bothered to deal with before. That had been my way. And I have a lot more confidence now, not only in myself, but in Orient as well.

The months on the Trail also increased my faith. Or maybe it renewed my faith. During the drive back, it dawned on me how much faith I had regained in people. There had been times in my life when I'd become very cynical about people. But for the months I'd been on the A.T., the people experience was very, very positive, warm and reassuring. I met wonderful people the whole way.

I don't miss the pain, the loneliness, the hardships, the cold, the heat of the A.T. I never enjoyed the hiking part. It was something I felt compelled to do. It wasn't my choice.

But there are nights when I'm on the Trail again. I'm in a sleeping bag and I take a breath of that cool, invigorating air, hear Orient snuffling around in the woods, smell that forest smell, and I'm there again!

Then I awaken out of the semi-sleep state and discover I'm not out there—I was only sleeping, dreaming about the Appalachian Trail. And, in that moment, a sadness washes over me again.

Maybe I miss it more than I know.

Does Orient miss it? When we go back hiking, even for a short while, Orient is so obviously elated when he sees the Trail head that he just has a fit. He's beside himself. The first couple of hours on the Trail, he can't stand it, he wants to push, push, push. To me, he's obviously fallen in love with backpacking.

A lot of days my activity is confined to talking on the telephone all day and Orient gets bored with that. Orient has the need to get out and run, to go in the woods and—I think—to relive some of the things we did on the Trail. He'd go back on the Trail right now. Immediately. He hasn't forgotten the Appalachian Trail.

It was a growing experience for Orient. He didn't like it at first, then he eventually learned to love it. But unlike most people, he made the transition from Seeing Eye dog in the city to dog guide on the Trail and back again easily.

Would I recommend it to someone else? I don't know. The A.T. is very risky. There is an awful lot of risk in setting aside six months of your life and living a new lifestyle. But the biggest risk is the return. Since I've returned to Burlington, I've seen people I came to care about have trouble with the transition back into this world. Once you've been out there, a lot of people have difficulty returning. I have even heard of people who have committed suicide because they couldn't make that return. Others tell me they've got to keep hiking, keep trying to recover that "Trail magic." I tell them that retreating back to the Trail isn't going to solve their problems.

I just spent a weekend with the Appalachian Long Distance Hikers' Association convention in Pipe Stem, West Virginia. A lot of the people I talked to there are still looking for the same things they hoped to resolve before they started on the Trail. And when they didn't discover them, they instead decided to go to another trail, or spend six months discovering the bottom of the Grand Canyon.

I can see how other people fall into this trap, especially people who didn't find the Trail as physically difficult as I did. The Trail is a good escape from reality, and there's the whole social experience of the thru-hiker "family" and "Trail magic." But it is unrealistic to expect the wilderness to resolve a lot of issues for you, issues you've never resolved anywhere else. Sometimes it is easier to be a part of a community moving nearly two thousand miles than it is to confront and resolve deep personal problems and questions right there at home.

As a counselor, I know they're just buying time to resolve the issues they want to resolve, but don't know how.

My advice to such people is, "The answer is not on the Trail. It's in *you*. You can't get away from *you* atop Mount Katahdin. You're still there. I don't have all of the answers and I never will. But I know this: You don't need the Appalachian Trail to find yourself. You struggle with your problems in the reality of the world you left behind."

I think it is clear from this book where I found my Answer.

From *Blind Courage*, by Bill Irwin, WRS Publishing, 1992.

HENRY DAVID THOREAU

Surely one facet of genius is the ability to distill meaning from the fog of uncertainty. When Thoreau climbed Mt. Katahdin in 1847, he never made it to the summit (fog), got lost (more fog and clouds), sprained an ankle (fell out of a tree?), and confronted a brutish nature unlike anything he'd seen at placid Walden Pond. The result? A remarkable book, Ktaadn *(later published as part of* The Maine Woods, *1864), with keen observations on geology and plant life, backwoodsmen and their ways, and the spiritual energies, some benign and some not, swirling around the summit of the Katahdin he never really saw. Thoreau took seriously, as metaphor, what contemporary hikers confront as well: the Abenaki god Pomola, who presides atop Katahdin and rarely welcomes visitors. Ascending and descending the mountain, Thoreau's route included trails nowadays incorporated in the AT. So as we climb Katahdin, it's easy to imagine that Henry David climbs there with us, still hoping for a break in the clouds.*

Of Chaos and Old Night

IN THE MORNING, AFTER WHETTING OUR APPETITE ON SOME RAW PORK, A wafer of hard-bread, and a dipper of condensed cloud or waterspout, we all together began to make our way up the falls, which I have described; this time choosing the right hand, or highest peak, which was not the one I had approached before. But soon my companions were lost to my sight behind the mountain ridge in my rear, which still seemed ever retreating before me, and I climbed alone over huge rocks, loosely poised, a mile or more, still edging toward the clouds; for though the day was clear elsewhere, the summit was concealed by mist. The mountain seemed a vast aggregation of loose rocks, as if some time it had rained rocks, and they lay as they fell on the mountain sides, nowhere fairly at rest, but leaning on each other, all rocking stones, with cavities between, but scarcely any soil or smoother shelf. They were the raw materials of a planet dropped from an unseen quarry, which the vast chemistry of nature would anon work up, or work down, into the smiling and verdant plains and valleys of earth. This was an undone extremity of the globe; as in lignite we see coal in the process of formation.

At length I entered within the skirts of the cloud which seemed forever drifting over the summit, and yet would never be gone, but was generated out of that pure air as fast as it flowed away; and when, a quarter of a mile farther, I reached the summit of the ridge, which those who have seen in clearer weather say is about five miles long, and contains a thousand acres of table-land, I was deep within the hostile ranks of clouds, and all objects were obscured by them. Now the wind would blow me out a yard of clear sunlight, wherein I stood; then a gray, dawning light was all it could accomplish, the cloud-line ever rising and falling with the wind's intensity. Sometimes it seemed as if the summit would be cleared in a few moments, and smile in sunshine; but what was gained on one side was lost on another. It was like sitting in a chimney and waiting for the smoke to blow away. It was, in fact, a cloud-factory, —these were the cloud-works, and the wind turned them off done from the cool, bare rocks. Occasionally, when the windy columns broke in to me, I caught sight of a dark, damp crag to the right or left; the mist driving ceaselessly between it and me. It reminded me of the creations of the old epic and dramatic poets, of Atlas, Vulcan, the Cyclops, and Prometheus. Such was Caucasus and the rock where Prometheus was bound. Æschylus had no doubt visited such scenery as this. It was vast, Titanic, and such as man never inhabits. Some part of the beholder, even some vital part, seems to escape through the loose grating of his ribs as he ascends. He is more lone than you can imagine. There is less of substantial thought and fair understanding in him than in the plains where men inhabit. His reason is dispersed and shadowy, more thin and subtile, like the air. Vast, Titanic, inhuman Nature has got him at disadvantage, caught him alone, and pilfers him of some of his divine faculty. She does not smile on him as in the plains. She seems to say sternly, Why came ye here before your time. This ground is not prepared for you. Is it not enough that I smile in the valleys? I have never made this soil for thy feet, this air for thy breathing, these rocks for thy neighbors. I cannot pity nor fondle thee here, but forever relentlessly drive thee hence to where I *am* kind. Why seek me where I have not called thee, and then complain because you find me but a stepmother? Shouldst thou freeze or starve, or shudder thy life away, here is no shrine, nor altar, nor any access to my ear.

> "Chaos and ancient Night, I come no spy
> With purpose to explore or to disturb
> The secrets of your realm, but   .   .   .
> .   .   .   .   .   .   as my way
> Lies through your spacious empire up to light."

The tops of mountains are among the unfinished parts of the globe, whither it is a slight insult to the gods to climb and pry into their secrets, and try their effect on our humanity. Only daring and insolent men, perchance, go there. Simple races, as savages, do not climb mountains, —their tops are sacred and mysterious tracts never visited by them. Pomola is always angry with those who climb to the summit of Ktaadn.

According to Jackson, who, in his capacity of geological surveyor of the State, has accurately measured it, the altitude of Ktaadn is 5300 feet, or a little more than one mile above the level of the sea, and he adds, "It is then evidently the highest point in the State of Maine, and is the most abrupt granite mountain in New England." The peculiarities of that spacious table-land on which I was standing, as well as the remarkable semicircular precipice or basin on the eastern side, were all concealed by the mist. I had brought my whole pack to the top, not knowing but I should have to make my descent to the river, and possibly to the settled portion of the State alone, and by some other route, and wishing to have a complete outfit with me. But at length fearing that my companions would be anxious to reach the river before night, and knowing that the clouds might rest on the mountain for days, I was compelled to descend. Occasionally, as I came down, the wind would blow me a vista open, through which I could see the country eastward, boundless forests, and lakes, and streams, gleaming in the sun, some of them emptying into the East Branch. There were also new mountains in sight in that direction. Now and then some small bird of the sparrow family would flit away before me, unable to command its course, like a fragment of the gray rock blown off by the wind.

I found my companions where I had left them, on the side of the peak, gathering the mountain cranberries, which filled every crevice between the rocks, together with blueberries, which had a spicier flavor the higher up they grew, but were not the less agreeable to our palates. When the country is settled, and roads are made, these cranberries will perhaps become an article of commerce. From this elevation, just on the skirts of the clouds, we could overlook the country, west and south, for a hundred miles. There it was, the State of Maine, which we had seen on the map, but not much like that, —immeasurable forest for the sun to shine on, that eastern *stuff* we hear of in Massachusetts. No clearing, no house. It did not look as if a solitary traveler had cut so much as a walking-stick there. Countless lakes, — Moosehead in the southwest, forty miles long by ten wide, like a gleaming silver platter at the end of the table; Chesuncook, eighteen long by three wide, without an island; Millinocket, on the south, with its hundred islands; and a hundred others without a name; and mountains, also, whose names, for the most part, are known only to the Indians. The forest looked like a firm grass sward, and the effect of these lakes in its midst has been well compared, by one who has since visited this same spot, to that of a "mirror broken into a thousand fragments, and wildly scattered over the grass, reflecting the full blaze of the sun." It was a large farm for somebody, when cleared. According to the Gazetteer, which was printed before the boundary question was settled, this single Penobscot County, in which we were, was larger than the whole State of Vermont, with its fourteen counties; and this was only a part of the wild lands of Maine. We are concerned now, however, about natural, not political limits. We were about eighty miles, as the bird flies, from Bangor, or one hundred and fifteen, as we had ridden, and walked, and paddled. We had to console ourselves with the reflection that this view was probably as good as that from the peak, as far as it went; and what were a mountain without its attendant clouds and mists? Like ourselves, neither Bailey nor Jackson had obtained a clear view from the summit. . . .

Nature was here something savage and awful, though beautiful. I looked with awe at the ground I trod on, to see what the Powers had made there, the form and fashion and material of their work. This was that Earth of which we have heard, made out of Chaos and Old Night. Here was no man's garden, but the unhandseled globe. It was not lawn, nor pasture, nor mead, nor woodland, nor lea, nor arable, nor waste land. It was the fresh and natural surface of the planet Earth, as it was made forever and ever, —to be the dwelling of man, we say, —so Nature made it, and man may use it if he can. Man was not to be associated with it. It was Matter, vast, terrific, —not his Mother Earth that we have heard of, not for him to tread on, or be buried in, —no, it were being too familiar even to let his bones lie there, —the home, this, of Necessity and Fate. There was clearly felt the presence of a force not bound to be kind to man. It was a place for heathenism and superstitious rites, —to be inhabited by men nearer of kin to the rocks and to wild animals than we. We walked over it with a certain awe, stopping, from time to time, to pick the blueberries which grew there, and had a smart and spicy taste. Perchance where *our* wild pines stand, and leaves lie on their forest floor, in Concord, there were once reapers, and husbandmen planted grain; but here not even the surface had been scarred by man, but it was a specimen of what God saw fit to make this world. What is it to be admitted to a museum, to see a myriad of particular things, compared with being shown some star's surface, some hard matter in its home! I stand in awe of my body, this matter to which I am bound has become so strange to me. I fear not spirits, ghosts, of which I am one, —*that* my body might, —but I fear bodies, I tremble to meet them. What is this Titan that has possession of me? Talk of mysteries! Think of our life in nature, —daily to be shown matter, to come in contact with it, —rocks, trees, wind on our cheeks! the *solid* earth! the *actual* world! the *common sense! Contact! Contact! Who* are we? *where* are we?

From *Ktaadn*, by Henry David Thoreau, 1848, revised for *The Maine Woods*, 1864; reissued by Crown, 1981.

STEVE SHERMAN & JULIA OLDER

Though the passage of time might render slightly out-of-date a few of the following answers to the most frequently asked questions thru-hikers have to face from their friends and admirers, there's a remarkable timelessness to these facts: Thru-hiking women tend to gain body mass and weight; men lose weight. There are crowds in New England's wilderness and few people to be seen on Georgia's AT, though it is closer to Atlanta than the White Mts. are to Boston. Blackflies terrorize everyone; sweet Connecticut is a breeze. While each hiker and each hike taken may be different, there is a comfort in the common wisdom of those who have walked this way. Especially in the final question and its unequivocal answer.

Answers

Preparation and conditioning time: *two months.*

| Expenses for two: | *per diem* | $ 7.71 |
| | *total (142 days on the trail)* | $1,095.00 |

Body weight:

		BEFORE	AFTER
	Julia	*106*	*112*
	Steve	*160*	*154*

Pack weight: *Julia 23-28 lbs.*
Steve 32-38 lbs.

Boots to walk 2,000 miles: *one pair each.*

Average mileage: *15 miles per day*
Fastest—22 miles a day in Shenandoah National Park

Slowest—8 miles per day in Stekoah, N.C.; White Mts., N.H.; Mahoosuc, Me. (or about 1 mile per hour).

Began: *April 11*
Finished: *September 7 (150 days)*
Extreme verified temperatures: *18 degrees, Big Stamp Gap, Georgia.*
                               101 degrees, Woodstock, N.H.

State easiest to walk: *Connecticut*
Most tedious: *Pennsylvania*
Most deer sighted: *Virginia and New York*
No deer sighted: *Maine and New Hampshire*
Most people: *White Mountains, N.H.*
Least people: *Georgia*
What we should have taken but didn't: *blackfly hoods*
What we did take but shouldn't have: *pocket signal mirror*
                                      complicated compass
                                      waterproof match holder
State with most Trail mileage: *Virginia (452 miles)*
State with least mileage: *West Virginia (10 miles)*
Serious injuries: *none*
Amount of money found on Trail: *$1.84*
Would we hike it again?: *Yes*

From *Appalachian Odyssey,* by Steve Sherman and Julia Older, Stephen Greene Press, 1977.

Mt. Katahdin Trail Register Notes

The sublime, the ridiculous, the practical, and the poetic: The inspiration people draw from a mountaintop will be as variable as the weather they encounter at the peak. On Katahdin, Springer, and a hundred peaks in between, Appalachian Trail hikers leave both footprints and spirit-prints, small fragments of themselves from rarefied moments of determination, exasperation, or joy.

8/27/48 Frederick Larson, Mansfield, MA
   3:25 A.M., Left campsite at 10:30 P.M. Cool climb with gas lantern.

9/16/60 Phyllis Roach Lees, Newington, CT
   James W. Lees climbed this rock pile for the umpteenth time this date; and his blind foolish wife followed. "—whither thou goest . . . !"

9/16/60 no name   tiny scrap of paper with love poem
   High on the top of Katahdin, / Someday I'll stand close by you. / We'll open this tiny love letter, / and read it up there in the blue. / The misty clouds whirling below us, / We stand there / our love at last firm, / You'll kiss me and tell me you love me, / Then lead me to our happy home.

From "Trail Registers—Mt. Katahdin," Appalachian Trail Conference.

JUSTIN ASKINS, WENDELL BERRY

A long hike, such as an Appalachian Trail thru-hike, or a long life given frequently to walking in the hills, assumes a sense of purpose. The purpose may be as lightweight as fun with friends or as weighty as searching for God in nature. At the end of the trail there is the chance at least for meaningful closure, though as with a hike itself, this too requires effort and time. Two poets take us now to closure in this volume. Justin Askins won the Appalachia *poetry prize in 1980 with his untitled poem about interior walking on decidedly unblazed trails. Wendell Berry, also an environmentalist-philosopher, reminds us that though a troubled world stumbles forward unrepentantly, we can find solace in nature, if we will but go out quietly to look.*

It was the American patron saint of walkers, Henry David Thoreau, who said, "I went to the woods because I wished to live deliberately, to front only the essential facts of life, and see if I could not learn what it had to teach, and not, when I came to die, discover that I had not lived." Those who first dreamed the Appalachian Trail, those who built it for us, and those who use it wisely today have the same chance to front those essential facts and to find in the mountains the stirring questions, the peace, and the freedom that resonate in Askins' and Berry's eloquent verse.

JUSTIN ASKINS

When You Come to Where the Trail Ends

When you come to where
the trail ends
and stones begin
to be placed one upon the other
crowding into a wall
that splits the land,
and stumps break
the elegant curve of birch
angling to the emptiness,
when a light mist
turns to cold
drenching rain
and you crawl
into your own
sense of outside:

do you walk into the cleared field
expecting no worse than a gentle admonishing
that your muddy tracks have disturbed
the rows of seed waiting to join
the inevitable harvest,
do you draw back and fold
those earlier steps into a neat deck
of snapshots certain to please
the vicarious roamer
emptying your blood on the path
even as you struggle to alert him
of your intimate presence,
or do you draw open your hood
to the icy rain,
laugh at believing in anything
other than the cold
wet soft murmur of rills
threading the shadowy edge of forest,
and turn again to the darkening trail
as a child to the wind of night.

From *"When You Come to Where the Trail Ends,"* by Justin Askins, in *Mountain Passages: An* Appalachia *Anthology,* edited by Robert Manning, Appalachian Mountain Club, 1982.

WENDELL BERRY

The Peace of Wild Things

When despair for the world grows in me
and I wake in the night at the least sound
in fear of what my life and my children's lives may be,
I go and lie down where the wood drake
rests in his beauty on the water, and the great heron feeds.
I come into the peace of wild things
who do not tax their lives with forethought
of grief. I come into the presence of still water.
And I feel above me the day-blind stars
waiting with their light. For a time
I rest in the grace of the world, and am free.

From "The Peace of Wild Things," in *Openings,* by Wendell Berry, Harcourt Brace, 1968.

Credits and Sources

Henry David Thoreau: Walking
From "Walking," *Atlantic Monthly,* June 1862.

Donald Culross Peattie: The Joy of Walking
From "The Joy of Walking," *The New York Times Magazine,* April 5, 1942.

Thomas Connelley: The Explorers: From DeSoto to Kephart
From *Discovering the Appalachians,* Stackpole, 1968.

Ferdinand Lane: The Appalachians: Their Rise and Fall
From *The Story of Mountains* by Ferdinand Lane. © 1950 by Ferdinand Lane. Used by permission of Doubleday, a division of Bantam Doubleday Dell Publishing Group, Inc.

Ann & Myron Sutton: A Special Dignity in Naming; The Adventurers; Gregory Bald; Like Walking on a Carpet
From *The Appalachian Trail: Wilderness on the Doorstep,* © 1967 by Ann and Myron Sutton. Reprinted by permission of HarperCollins Publishers, Inc.

Gerald Lowrey, Jr.: American Ideas of Wilderness
From *Benton MacKaye's Appalachian Trail as a Cultural Symbol,* unpublished doctoral dissertation, Graduate Institute of the Liberal Arts, Emory University, 1981.

Wallace Stegner: Wilderness and the Geography of Hope
From "Wilderness and the Geography of Hope," *Voices for the Earth: A Treasury of the Sierra Club Bulletin,* Sierra Club Books, 1979.

Aldo Leopold: The Ethical Sequence
From *A Sand County Almanac: And Sketches Here and There* by Aldo Leopold, pages 202–203, 223. © 1949, 1977 by Oxford University Press. Reprinted by permission.

Benton MacKaye: An Appalachian Trail: A Project in Regional Planning
From "An Appalachian Trail: A Project in Regional Planning," *Journal of the American Institute of Architects,* 1921, as reprinted in *The Appalachian Trail Conference Member Handbook,* 11th edition, Appalachian Trail Conference, 1978.

Nathaniel Goodrich: The Attractions and Rewards of Trail Making
From *Mountain Passages: An Appalachian Anthology,* Robert Manning, editor, Appalachian Mountain Club, 1982.

Michael Frome: The Evolution of Trails
From *Uncommon Places,* by David Muench, Introduction by Michael Frome, Appalachian Trail Conference, 1991.

Guy & Laura Waterman: On the Trail's Founding Fathers; The Crawfords of Crawford Notch
From *Forest and Crag: A History of Hiking, Trail Blazing, and Adventure in the Northeast Mountains,* Appalachian Mountain Club, 1989.

Miles Jebb: Backpackers
From *Walkers,* Constable, 1986.

Michael Lanza: A Breed Apart: Appalachian Trail Thru-Hikers
From *Backpacker,* December 1993.

James Dickey: Springer Mountain
From *Poems 1957–1967,* © 1978 by James Dickey, Wesleyan University Press by permission of University Press of New England.

Colin Fletcher: Weight; How Far Can I Expect to Walk in a Day?
From *The Complete Walker: The Joys and Techniques of Hiking and Backpacking,* Knopf, 1968.

Earl Shaffer: Trail Diary, 1948
From "Report of Hiking Trip via Appalachian Trail, From Mt. Oglethorpe, Georgia (April 4, 1948) to Mt. Katahdin, Maine (August 5, 1948)," *Appalachian Trail Conference Report,* 1948.

Bruce Otto: Trail Diary, 1974
From "Stepping Into Joy: 142 Hiking Days, Spring to Fall, Georgia to Maine Along the Appalachian Trail," *Appalachian Trail Conference Report,* 1974.

Eliot Wiggenton: Forecasting Weather
From *The Foxfire Book,* by Eliot Wiggenton. © 1968, 1969, 1970, 1971, 1972 by The Foxfire Fund, Inc. Used by permission of Doubleday, a division of Bantam Doubleday Dell Publishing Group, Inc.

Larry Luxenberg: Difficulties and Dangers along the Trail
   From *Walking the Appalachian Trail,* Stackpole, 1994.
Steve Sherman & Julia Older: Georgia—78 Miles; It's Too Damned Hot; Answers
   From *Appalachian Odyssey,* Stephen Greene, 1977.
David Brill: Fear
   From *As Far as the Eye Can See: Reflections of an Appalachian Trail Hiker,* Rutledge Hill, 1990.
Springer Mountain: Trail Register Notes
   From "Trail Registers—Springer Mountain," Appalachian Trail Conference.
Michael Frome: Genius of the Species
   From *Strangers in High Places: The Story of the Great Smoky Mountains,* University of Tennessee Press, 1980.
Randy Russell & Janet Barnett: The Wicked Witch of Nantahala
   From *Mountain Ghost Stories and Curious Tales of Western North Carolina,* John Blair, 1988.
Charles Konopa: The Botanical Garden
   From *Hiking the Appalachian Trail,* vol. 2, James Hare, editor, Rodale Press, 1975.
William Bartram: Most Gay and Brilliant Flowering Shrub
   From *Travels of William Bartram,* Yale University Press, 1958.
Benton MacKaye: Letter to Smoky Mountains Hiking Club
   From a Smoky Mountains Hiking Club handbook, 1933.
Linda Tatsapaugh: Trail Diary, 1990
   From *Hunger Hiker Hits the Trail—Appalachian Trail Conference Report,* 1991.
Suzie Rosenblith: Trail Diary, 1993
   From Thru-Hiker Report to Appalachian Trail Conference, 1993.
Catherine Eich: Trail Diary, 1984
   From Thru-Hiker Report to Appalachian Trail Conference, 1984.
Claude Leineke: Trail Diary, 1976
   From *"Your Feet Must Be Stronger Than Your Head!"; or Memories of an Appalachian Trail Summer,* Thru-Hiker Report to Appalachian Trail Conference, 1976.
William O. Douglas: One Leg in Carolina, The Other in Tennessee
   From *My Wilderness: East to Katahdin, Adventures in the American Wilderness from Arizona to Maine,* Doubleday, 1961.
Mic Lowther: Walking North
   From *Walking North* by Mic Lowther, self-published trail narrative, 1990.

Ray Hicks: A Haint
   From *Mountain Voices,* Warren Moore, editor, Globe Pequot, 1988.
Jerome Doolittle: Zenith's Tulip Tree
   From *The American Wilderness: The Southern Appalachians,* By Jerome Doolittle and the Editors of Time-Life Books © 1975 Time-Life Books, Inc.
Edwin Way Teale: It Rises Again
   From *Dune Boy: The Early Years of a Naturalist,* Dodd, 1943.
Thomas Jefferson: A Notice of Its Mountains and The Natural Bridge
   From *Notes on the State of Virginia,* 1787, University of North Carolina Press, 1955.
David Bates: The Potomac Appalachian Trail Club and the Issue of a Skyline Drive
   From *Breaking Trail in the Central Appalachians,* Potomac Appalachian Trail Club, 1987.
Charles & Nancy Perdue: Shenandoah Removals
   From "Appalachian Fables and Fact: A Case Study of the Shenandoah National Park Removals," in *Appalachian Journal,* Vol. 7, No. 1–2, Autumn/Winter 1979–80. © 1980 by Appalachian State University/Appalachian Journal. Used with permission.
Karen Berger: Trail Days in Damascus
   From *An American Pilgrimage,* manuscript in progress.
Roderick Peattie: The Doctrine of Signatures; The 'Sang Diggers
   From *The Great Smokies and the Blue Ridge: The Story of the Appalachians,* Roderick Peattie, editor, Vanguard, 1943.
Frederick Cotton, M.D., & Ralph Larrabee, M.D.: First Aid in the Woods
   From *Guide to Paths in the Blue Ridge,* Potomac Appalachian Trail Club, 1934.
Bob Barker: Trail Diary, 1984
   From Thru-Hiker report to the Appalachian Trail Conference, 1984.
Cindy Ross: Trail Diary, 1981
   From *A Woman's Journey on the Appalachian Trail,* East Woods, 1982.
Scott Huler: Bringing the Trail's Lessons Back to Life
   "Bringing the Trail's Lessons Back to Life," *The News & Observer,* Raleigh, North Carolina, May 22, 1995. Used by permission.

Congress of the United States: An Act to Establish a National Trails System

From *National Trails System Act*, as amended, November 10, 1978, United States Congress.

Christopher Whalen: Maildrops

From *The Appalachian Trail Workbook for Planning Thru-Hikes*, Appalachian Trail Conference, 1993.

James Hare: Grandma Gatewood: A Legend Along the Appalachian Trail

From *Hiking the Appalachian Trail*, James Hare, editor, Vol. 1, Rodale Press, 1975.

Jeff Walker: Trail Diary, 1990

From "High Adventure in Schuyler, VA.," a Thru-Hiker Report to the Appalachian Trail Conference, 1990.

Harry Caudill: O, Appalachia!

From "O, Appalachia!" *Intellectual Digest*, April 1973.

Paula Strain: The Potomac, The Shenandoah, and Jefferson Rock

From *The Blue Hills of Maryland: History Along the Appalachian Trail on South Mountain and the Catoctins*, Potomac Appalachian Trail Club, 1993.

Scott Weidensaul: Castanea: A Ghost Flowering in the Woods

From *Mountains of the Heart: A Natural History of the Appalachians*, Fulcrum, 1994.

J. Peter Wilshusen: Geology of the Delaware Water Gap

From *Geology of the Appalachian Trail in Pennsylvania*, Pennsylvania Geological Survey, 1983.

Richard Turner & Robert Turner: 2,000-Miler Report

From *2,000-Miler Report to the Appalachian Trail Conference*, 1990.

Herbert Durand: Why Everyone Should Know the Ferns

From *Field Book of Common Ferns*, G. P. Putnam's Sons, 1928.

Walt Whitman: Song of the Open Road

From "Song of the Open Road," collected in *Leaves of Grass*, 1855.

Margaret Keating: The Bear Mountain Bridge

From *In the Hudson Highlands*, Appalachian Mountain Club, New York Chapter, 1945.

Jesse Benedix: Mountain Laurel

From *In the Hudson Highlands*, Appalachian Mountain Club, New York Chapter, 1945.

New York–New Jersey Trail Conference: Barring of Harriman Section Threatened

From *Guide to the Appalachian Trail, From the Housatonic River in Connecticut to the Susquehanna River in Pennsylvania, Via the Hudson River at Bear Mountain, Delaware Water Gap and Lehigh Gap*, New York–New Jersey Trail Conference, 1934.

Barton Brown: 2,000-Miler Report, 1977

From *2,000-Miler Report to the Appalachian Trail Conference*, 1977.

Ellen Coletti: 2,000-Miler Report, 1984

From *2,000-Miler Report to the Appalachian Trail Conference*, 1977.

Richard Satterlie: 2,000-Miler Report, 1978

From *2,000-Miler Report to the Appalachian Trail Conference*, 1978.

Ronald Fisher: An Appalachian Trail Wedding; On Genevieve Hutchinson

From *The Appalachian Trail*, National Geographic Society, 1972.

Hal Borland: The Bog

From *Hill Country Harvest*, by Hal Borland, Lippincott, 1967.

Odell Shepard: Mother Earth

From *The Harvest of a Quiet Eye*. © 1927, © renewed 1955 by Odell Shepard. Reprinted by permission of Houghton Mifflin Co. All rights reserved.

Walter Pritchard Eaton: Letter to Benton MacKaye, June 23, 1922

From correspondence of Walter Pritchard Eaton, Appalachian Trail Conference.

Benton MacKaye: Outdoor Culture

From "Outdoor Culture—The Philosophy of Through Trails," address to the New England Trail Conference, January 1927, in *From Geography to Geotechnics*, University of Illinois, 1968.

James MacGregor Burns: Shays's Rebellion

From *Vineyard of Liberty*, Knopf, 1982.

Berkshire County: Trail Register Notes

From Appalachian Trail Registers, Berkshire Section, Appalachian Mountain Club, 1993–1995.

David Emblidge: Hiking beside an Eerie Presence

From "Hiking beside an Eerie Presence," *Berkshires Week, Berkshire Eagle*, June 25, 1993.

Richard Wilbur: "A Wall in the Woods: Cummington"

From "A Wall in the Woods: Cummington," © Richard Wilbur and *The New Yorker*.

Herman Melville: To Greylock's Most Excellent Majesty
From *Pierre*, 1852.

Henry David Thoreau: Alone on Greylock's Summit
From *A Week on the Concord and Merrimack Rivers*, 1849.

William Haviland & Marjory Power: Corn Legend
From *The Original Vermonters* © 1994 by the Trustees of the University of Vermont, p. 192, by permission of the University Press of New England.

Robert Frost: The Bear
From *The Poetry of Robert Frost*, edited by Edward Connery Lathem. © 1956 by Robert Frost. © 1928, © 1969 by Henry Holt and Co., Inc. Reprinted by permission of Henry Holt and Co., Inc.

Michael Frome: The Tree and the Forest
From *Whose Woods These Are: The Story of the National Forests*, Westview, 1962, 1984.

David Appell: What I *Really* Saw
From "What I *Really* Saw," *Appalachian Trailway News*, Nov./Dec. 1994.

Maurice Brooks: Alpine Summits
From *The Appalachians*. © 1965 by Maurice Brooks. Reprinted by permission of Houghton Mifflin Co. All rights reserved.

Jean Langenheim: Lichens and Mosses
From *Mountain Flowers of New England*, Appalachian Mountain Club, 1964.

Robert Manning: Miss M. F. Whitman's Climb Through Tuckerman Ravine
From *Mountain Passages: An* Appalachia *Anthology*, Robert Manning, editor, Appalachian Mountain Club, 1982.

Joseph Dodge: An Old Hutman Reminisces
From "An Old Hutman Reminisces," in *Mountain Passages: An* Appalachia *Anthology*, edited by Robert Manning, Appalachian Mountain Club, 1982.

John White: Packs and Packboards
From *Mountain Passages: An* Appalachia *Anthology*, edited by Robert Manning, Appalachian Mountain Club, 1982.

Arthur Harris, Jr.: Wartime Maintenance in the Appalachian Mountains
From "Wartime Maintenance in the Appalachian Mountains," *Appalachia*, Vol. X, 1944.

William Lowell Putnam: Will They Believe It? 231 MPH!
From *The Worst Weather on Earth: A History of the Mount Washington Observatory*, American Alpine Club, 1991.

Eugene Daniell: Hypothermia on Mt. Jefferson
From "College Student Dies of Hypothermia on Mt. Jefferson," in "Notes: Accidents," *Appalachia*, December 1994.

Paul Hemphill: Your Knees Aren't Your Problem
From *Me and the Boy: A Journey of Discovery, Father and Son on the Appalachian Trail*, Macmillan, 1986.

V. Collins Chew: The Final Climb of the AT
From *Underfoot: A Geologic Guide to the Appalachian Trail*, Appalachian Trail Conference, 1988.

Myron Avery: Afoot along the Two-Thousand Mile Appalachian Trail
From *Afoot along the Two-Thousand Mile Appalachian Trail*, unpublished manuscript, 1937, Appalachian Trail Conference.

Kathryn Fulkerson: Trail Diary, 1939
From "*Report of the Maine Trip, August 18–September 4, 1939*," unpublished manuscript, 1939, Appalachian Trail Conference.

Percival Baxter: Greatest Mountain
From *Greatest Mountain: Katahdin's Wilderness*, Scrimshaw Press, 1972.

David Horton: Running for the Record
From "*A Summer to Remember: 2,144 Miles on the Appalachian Trail*," a 2,000-Miler Report to the Appalachian Trail Conference, 1991.

Raymond Baker: Crossing the Kennebec
From *Campfires Along the Appalachian Trail*, Carlton Press, 1971.

Bill Irwin: Trail Diary, 1990
From *Blind Courage*, by Bill Irwin with David McCasland. © 1992, WRS Publishing, Waco, Texas. Reprinted by permission.

Henry David Thoreau: Of Chaos and Old Night
From *Ktaadn*, 1848, revised for *The Maine Woods*, 1864; reissued by Crown, 1981.

Mt. Katahdin: Trail Register Notes
From "Trail Registers—Mt. Katahdin," Appalachian Trail Conference.

Justin Askins: When You Come to Where the Trail Ends
From *Mountain Passages: An* Appalachia *Anthology*, edited by Robert Manning, Appalachian Mountain Club, 1982.

Wendell Berry: The Peace of Wild Things
From *Openings*, © 1968 by Wendell Berry, reprinted by permission of Harcourt Brace & Company.